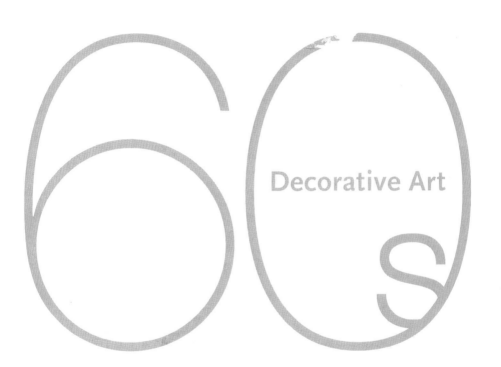

60s Decorative Art

To stay informed about upcoming TASCHEN titles,
please request our magazine at www.taschen.com/
magazine or write to TASCHEN, Hohenzollernring 53,
D–50672 Cologne, Germany, contact@taschen.com,
Fax: +49-221-254919. We will be happy to send you a free
copy of our magazine which is filled with information
about all of our books.

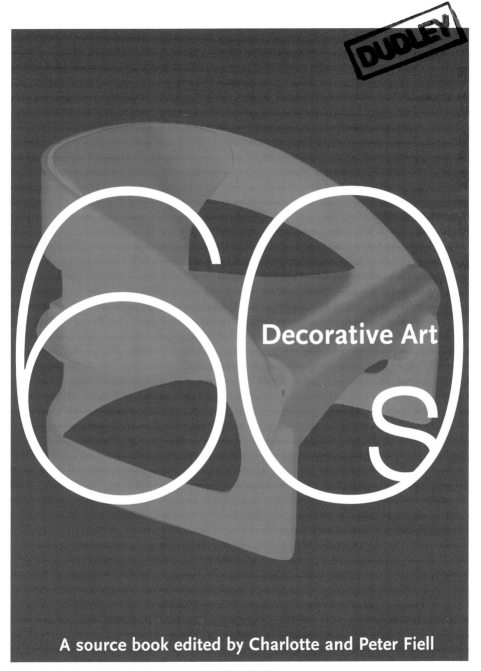

DUDLEY

60s

Decorative Art

A source book edited by Charlotte and Peter Fiell

TASCHEN

KÖLN LONDON LOS ANGELES MADRID PARIS TOKYO

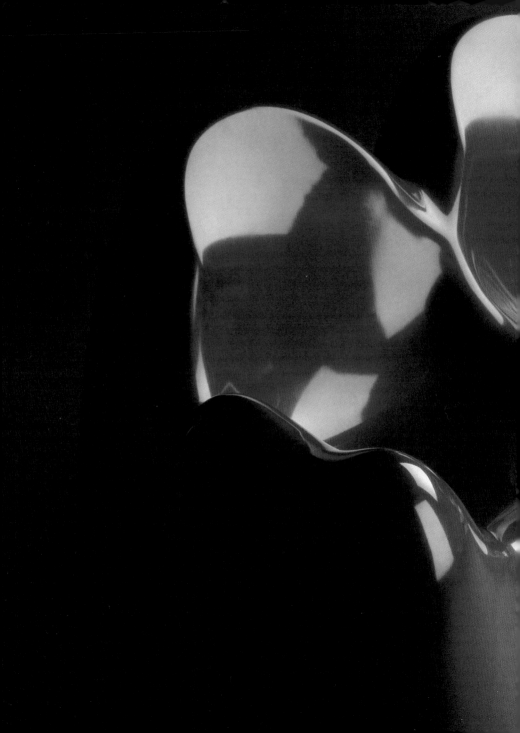

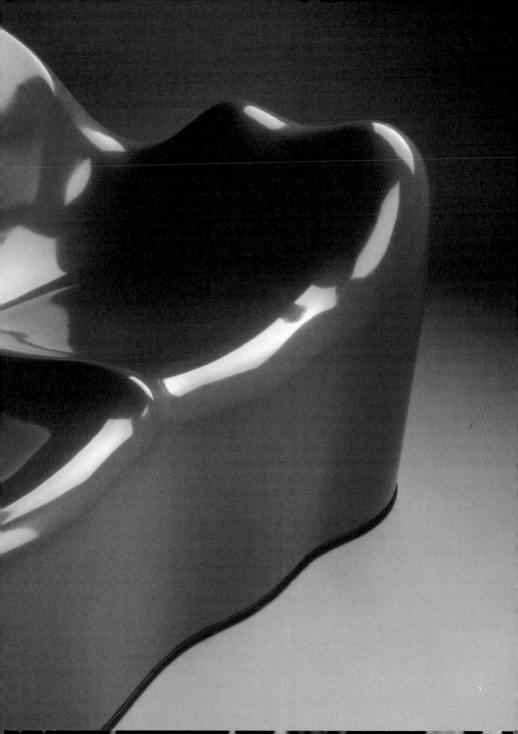

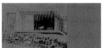
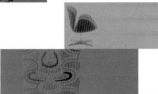

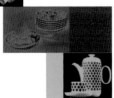

CONTENTS
INHALT
SOMMAIRE

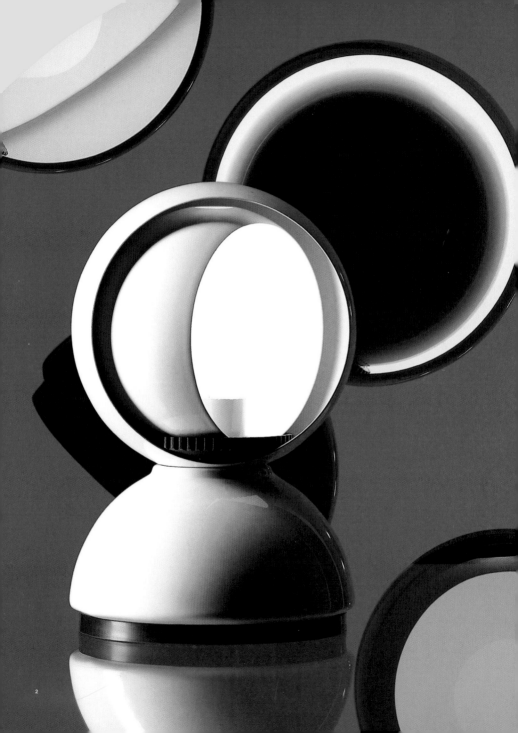

1. Wendell Castle, *Molar* sofa for Beylerian, 1969
2. Vico Magistretti, *Eclisse* lamp for Artemide, 1965
3. Enzo Mari, Selection of vases for Danese, 1968–1969

The "Decorative Art" Yearbooks

The Studio Magazine was founded in Britain in 1893 and featured both the fine and the decorative arts. It initially promoted the work of progressive designers such as Charles Rennie Mackintosh and Charles Voysey to a wide audience both at home and abroad, and was especially influential in Continental Europe. Later, in 1906, *The Studio* began publishing the *Decorative Art* yearbook to "meet the needs of that ever-increasing section of the public who take interest in the application of art to the decoration and general equipment of their homes". This annual survey, which became increasingly international in its outlook, was dedicated to the latest currents in architecture, interiors, furniture, lighting, glassware, textiles, metalware and ceramics. From its outset, *Decorative Art* advanced the "New Art" that had been pioneered by William Morris and his followers, and attempted to exclude designs which showed any "excess in ornamentation and extreme eccentricities of form".

In the 1920s, *Decorative Art* began promoting Modernism and was in later years a prominent champion of "Good Design". Published from the 1950s onwards by Studio Vista, the yearbooks continued to provide a remarkable overview of each decade, featuring avant-garde and often experimental designs alongside more mainstream pro-

ducts. Increasing prominence was also lent to architecture and interior design, and in the mid-1960s the title of the series was changed to *Decorative Art in Modern Interiors* to reflect this shift in emphasis. Eventually, in 1980, Studio Vista ceased publication of these unique annuals, and over the succeeding years volumes from the series became highly prized by collectors and dealers as excellent period reference sources.

The fascinating history of design traced by *Decorative Art* can now be accessed once again in this new series reprinted, in somewhat revised form, from the original yearbooks. In line with the layout of *Decorative Art*, the various disciplines are grouped separately, whereby great care has been taken in selecting the best and most interesting pages while ensuring that the corresponding dates have been given due prominence for ease of reference. It is hoped that these volumes of highlights from *Decorative Art* will at long last bring the yearbooks to a wider audience, who will find in them well-known favourites as well as fascinating and previously unknown designs.

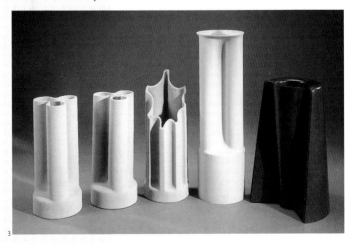

3

4. Alan Fletcher, *Clam* ashtrays, late 1960s
5. Livio Castiglioni & Gianfranco Frattini, *Boalum* lamp for Artemide, 1969

Die »Decorative Art« Jahrbücher

Die Zeitschrift *The Studio Magazine* wurde 1893 in England gegründet und war sowohl der Kunst als auch dem Kunsthandwerk gewidmet. In den Anfängen stellte sie einer breiten Öffentlichkeit in England und in Übersee die Arbeiten progressiver Designer wie Charles Rennie Mackintosh und Charles Voysey vor. Ihr Einfluss war groß und nahm auch auf dem europäischen Festland zu. 1906 begann *The Studio* zusätzlich mit der Herausgabe des *Decorative Art Yearbook*, um »den Bedürfnissen einer ständig wachsenden Öffentlichkeit gerecht zu werden, die sich zunehmend dafür interessierte, Kunst in die Dekoration und Ausstattung ihrer Wohnungen einzubeziehen.« Diese jährlichen Überblicke unterrichteten über die neuesten internationalen Tendenzen in der Architektur und Innenraumgestaltung, bei Möbeln, Lampen, Glas und Keramik, Metall und Textilien. Von Anfang an förderte *Decorative Art* die von William Morris und seinen Anhängern entwickelte »Neue Kunst« und versuchte, Entwürfe auszuschließen, die »in Mustern und Formen zu überladen und exzentrisch waren.«

In den zwanziger Jahren hatte sich *Decorative Art* für modernistische Strömungen eingesetzt und wurde in der Folgezeit zu einer prominenten Befürworterin des »guten Designs«. Die seit 1950 von englischen Verlag Studio Vista veröffentlichten Jahrbücher stellten für jedes Jahrzehnt ausgezeichnete Überblicke der vorherrschenden

avangardistischen und experimentellen Trends im Design einerseits und des bereits in der breiteren Öffentlichkeit etablierten Alltagsdesigns andererseits zusammen. Als Architektur und Interior Design Mitte der sechziger Jahre ständig an Bedeutung gewannen, wurde die Serie in *Decorative Art in Modern Interiors* umbenannt, um diesem Bedeutungswandel gerecht zu werden. Im Jahre 1981 stellte Studio Vista die Veröffentlichung dieser einzigartigen Jahrbücher ein. Sie wurden in den folgenden Jahren als wertvolle Sammelobjekte und hervorragende Nachschlagewerke hochgeschätzt.

Die faszinierende Geschichte des Designs, die *Decorative Art* dokumentierte, erscheint jetzt als leicht veränderter Nachdruck der originalen Jahrbücher. Dem ursprünglichen Layout von *Decorative Art* folgend, werden die einzelnen Disziplinen getrennt vorgestellt. Mit großer Sorgfalt wurden die besten und interessantesten Seiten ausgewählt. Die entsprechenden Jahreszahlen sind jeweils angegeben, um die zeitliche Einordnung zu ermöglichen. Mit diesen Bänden soll einer breiten Leserschaft der Zugang zu den *Decorative Art* Jahrbüchern und seinen international berühmt gewordenen, aber auch den weniger bekannten und dennoch faszinierenden Entwürfen ermöglicht werden.

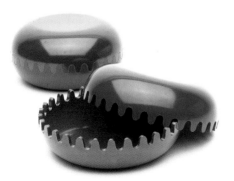

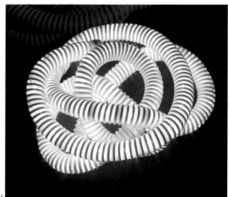

4

5

PRÉFACE

Les annuaires « Decorative Art »

Fondé en 1893 en Grande-Bretagne, *The Studio Magazine* traitait à la fois des beaux-arts et des arts décoratifs. Sa vocation première était de promouvoir le travail de créateurs qui innovaient, tels que Charles Rennie Mackintosh ou Charles Voysey, auprès d'un vaste public d'amateurs tant en Grande-Bretagne qu'à l'étranger, notamment en Europe où son influence était particulièrement forte. En 1906, *The Studio* lança *The Decorative Art Yearbook*, un annuaire destiné à répondre à « la demande de cette part toujours croissante du public qui s'intéresse à l'application de l'art à la décoration et à l'aménagement général de la maison ». Ce rapport annuel, qui prit une ampleur de plus en plus internationale, était consacré aux dernières tendances en matière d'architecture, de décoration d'intérieur, de mobilier, de luminaires, de verrerie, de textiles, d'orfèvrerie et de céramique. D'emblée, *Decorative Art* mit en avant « l'Art nouveau » dont William Morris et ses disciples avaient posé les jalons, et tenta d'exclure tout style marqué par « une ornementation surchargée et des formes d'une excentricité excessive ».

Dès les années 20, *Decorative Art* commença à promouvoir le modernisme, avant de se faire le chantre du « bon design ». Publiés à partir des années 50 par Studio Vista, les annuaires continuèrent à présenter un remarquable panorama de chaque décennie, faisant se côtoyer les créations avant-gardistes et souvent expérimentales et les produits plus « grand public ». Ses pages accordèrent également une part de plus en plus grande à l'architecture et à la décoration d'intérieur. Ce changement de politique éditoriale se refléta dans le nouveau titre adopté vers le milieu des années 60 : *Decorative Art in Modern Interiors*. En 1980, Studio Vista arrêta la parution de ces volumes uniques en leur genre qui, au fil des années qui suivirent, devinrent très recherchés par les collectionneurs et les marchands car ils constituaient d'excellents ouvrages de référence pour les objets d'époque.

Grâce à cette réédition sous une forme légèrement modifiée, la fascinante histoire du design retracée par *Decorative Art* est de nouveau disponible. Conformément à la maquette originale des annuaires, les différentes disciplines sont présentées séparément, classées par date afin de faciliter les recherches. Les pages les plus belles et les plus intéressantes ont été sélectionnées avec un soin méticuleux et on ne peut qu'espérer que ces volumes feront connaître *Decorative Art* à un plus vaste public, qui y retrouvera des pièces de design devenues célèbres et en découvrira d'autres inconnues auparavant et tout aussi fascinantes.

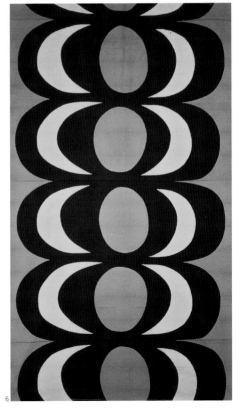

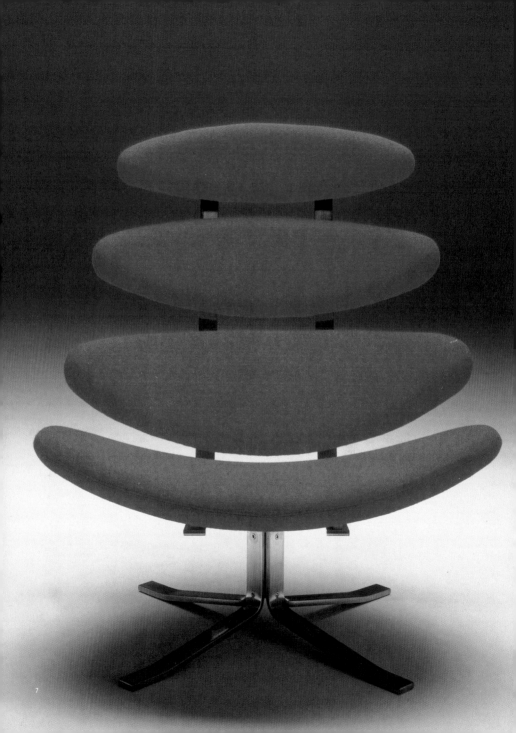

Youth Culture and Lifestyle Fashion

The 1960s were a decade of unprecedented social change. Characterised by emancipation and permissiveness, they saw the suburban dream of the 1950s renounced in favour of a utopian vision of alternative lifestyles. Cognisant of the failings of the previous generation, young people in particular agitated for a better world in the face of the rapid urbanisation of the West. Their collective social conscience and pursuit of sex, drugs and rock'n'roll were key uniting features that led the youth movement to become a powerful force in sixties' society. Cities such as London, Paris and New York became cultural epicentres of this phenomenon, while advances in mass communications made possible the true globalisation of youth culture. The decorative arts acted as a social barometer of these changes and reflected the hopes and aspirations of this new generation.

In the early 1960s, as in previous decades, the decorative arts were divided into two distinct categories – the crafted object and the industrially manufactured product. During this period, the notion of "Good Design" remained influential and Finnish products in particular were widely celebrated for their high quality and design integrity. In Italy, the Neo-Liberty style continued to flourish, while German design was characterised by the logical planning and geometric purity that was largely responsible for bringing about its "economic miracle". Japanese design continued to exert a strong influence upon Western artists, who drew potent inspiration from its traditional aesthetic, as well as from its mass-produced industrial products. America, which had the most competitive market-place, on the one hand promoted design excellence through, for example, the furniture and exhibition designs of Charles and Ray Eames, while on the other produced some of the worst quality and badly designed products of any industrialised nation.

Design was promoted not only by the plethora of lifestyle journals that emerged during the decade, but also by the establishment of institutions such as the Design Centre in London, which acted as a showcase for high-quality progressive products. What the principles of "Good Design" actually were, however, was a question which much of the public would have been hard pressed to answer. The glossy magazines and colour supplements which packed their pages with the latest trends in interiors and furnishings were ultimately spotlighting changes in taste rather than

fundamental innovations in design. Similarly, cautious retailers preferred to stick with tried-and-tested products, or "knock-offs" of previously successful designs, rather than risk the introduction of more progressive manufactured goods.

Even though design was now a truly international phenomenon, consumers were thus largely fashion conscious rather than design conscious. Manufacturers felt compelled to bring out new cars, furniture, glassware, metalware etc. annually to sate this seemingly never-ending appetite for the grooviest, coolest and hippest products. This search for the "new" also brought the increasing introduction of ethnic objects into interior design. As air travel became more accessible, so did trinkets from the Far East, India and Mexico. Such objects were regarded as offering an outlet for personal expression within interior design, as too did experimental Pop designs. Although the Design Council and publications such as *Decorative Art* advocated well-designed and good-value products that were impervious to the evanescence of fashion, the youth generation required short-lived, fun and gimmicky solutions that were cheap and expendable.

Visions of the Future

In the 1960s the idea of "living units" rather than homes reflected the influence of Modernist architects such as Le Corbusier and Ludwig Mies van der Rohe as well as the changing demographics of Western populations – the new generation did not aspire to its parents' ideal of suburban security. Instead, youth culture fought for liberation from traditional domestic bonds and expectations – the wide availability of the contraceptive pill and the ensuing culture of sexual liberation meant that "settling down" was no longer necessarily desirable nor a requirement. The 1960s also saw the proliferation of concrete modular tower blocks on city skylines, although these sad homages to Le Corbusier's utopian dreams were often shoddy and over-hasty in their construction. Futuristic visions were also reflected in Moshe Safdie's Habitat project for Expo '67, which was made up of cell-like units that were adaptable to differing sizes of family.

The Space Age also did much to fuel the imaginations of designers and consumers and led to futuristic and modular design becoming increasingly popular. The earth tones of the 1950s gave way to bold black and white patterns inspired by Op Art, while textiles and wallpapers took on dynamic designs and vibrant, "synthetic" colours. As class structures became less fixed, the prejudices that had in the past favoured antiques over modern furnishings slowly ebbed. Reissued tubular metal furniture by Le Corbusier, Marcel Breuer and Ludwig Mies van der Rohe in particular was increasingly used in domestic interiors, as well as in prestigious contract environments. Classic designs such as these rapidly assumed a social cachet and accelerated the acceptance of more progressive design in general. During this period, too, great emphasis was placed on the importance of light in interiors, which in turn led to more windows, brighter lighting, white walls and even white floors. There was also a sudden realisation of the benefits of "knock-down" furniture, which could be collapsed and easily transported by an increasingly nomadic populace.

Expression and Experimentation

As the decade progressed, design became ever more stylistically diverse, allowing greater personal choice and greater freedom of expression. Bold new concepts were explored within the sphere of interior design – from the sunken seating pit to the self-contained living unit that comprised everything needed for daily life: kitchen, bathroom, bedroom and so on. Furniture design also became an arena for experimentation, leading to inflatable PVC seating and the ubiquitous beanbag. These new designs and the fashion for cheap yet comfortable, brightly-coloured floor cushions reflected the more casual lifestyle of the 1960s. This new informality was also reflected in the preference for heavy rustic glassware over cut crystal or delicate glassware. By the mid to late 1960s, youth culture was irreverently challenging the status of the Modern designer by advancing the notion of democratic design through the do-it-yourself, anything-goes school of practice.

During this time, too, the divisions between art and design became increasingly blurred, with established artists such as Victor Pasmore and Eduardo Paolozzi dabbling in design, and designers such as Ettore Sottsass executing symbolic "art-like" furniture. Performance art also influ-

enced design – De Pas, D'Urbino and Lomazzi's *Blow* chair and Gaetano Pesce's *Up* Series produced the same spontaneous quality as an art "happening". Interiors by designers such as Verner Panton became spatial experiences, while futuristic habitations, mega-structures and self-regulating environments were projected by radical design groups such as Superstudio and Archizoom.

The 1960s were essentially a kaleidoscope-like decade in which colour and form changed rapidly and interacted unexpectedly to produce sensory stimulation. The utopian dreams of the Bauhaus were somehow strangely reflected and at the same time subverted in the Pop designs of the 1960s. The invisible chair famously predicted by Marcel Breuer was realized by Quasar Khanh and De Pas, D'Urbino and Lomazzi with their inflatables, while Josef Albers' paper and cardboard experiments were the antecedents of Peter Murdoch's expendable throwaway fibreboard furniture. Socialism had been replaced by capitalism, community by individualism, collective responsibility by personal freedoms. For better or for worse, momentous and irreversible cultural change had taken place.

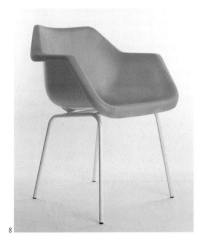

8

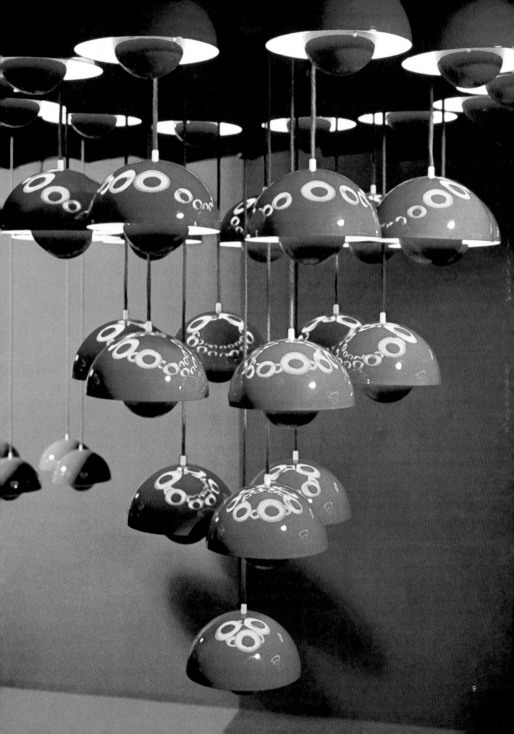

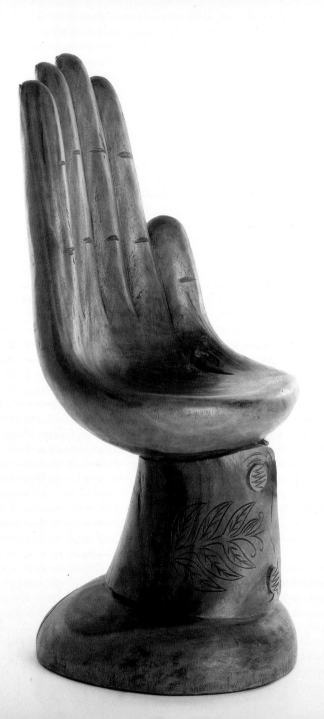

EINLEITUNG
DIE SECHZIGER JAHRE

10. Pedro Friedeberg (attributed), *Hand* chair, c. 1968
11. Kaj Franck, *Nuutajarvi Notsjo* chalice vase for Orrefors, c. 1965

Jugendkultur und Lifestyle Mode

Die sechziger Jahre waren ein Jahrzehnt der sozialen Veränderungen. Emanzipation und Freizügigkeit waren die erklärten großen Ziele, und die utopische Vision alternativer Lebensstile löste den Traum der fünfziger Jahre – ein Leben im eigenen Haus in den sicheren Vororten der Städte – ab. In den westlichen Ländern schritt die Urbanisierung rapide voran. Im Bewusstsein des Scheiterns der Generation ihrer Eltern agitierte die Jugend für den Aufbau einer besseren Welt. Ein kollektives soziales Bewusstsein und das Ausleben von Sex, Drogen und Rock'n'Roll waren Ideale, welche die Jugend vereinten und zu einer maßgebenden Kraft in der Gesellschaft der sechziger Jahre werden ließ. London, Paris und New York waren die kulturellen Epizentren dieses Phänomens, und die ungeheuren Fortschritte in der Entwicklung der Massenmedien bahnten den Weg zu einer umfassenden Globalisierung der Jugendkultur. Die angewandte Kunst reagierte als soziales Barometer auf diese Veränderungen und reflektierte die Hoffnungen und Wunschvorstellungen dieser neuen Generation.

In der angewandten Kunst wurden in den frühen sechziger Jahren wie in vorangegangenen Jahrzehnten noch immer zwei verschiedene Kategorien unterschieden – kunsthandwerkliche Objekte und seriengefertigte Industriegüter. In den sechziger Jahren bestimmten die Maßstäbe des »guten Designs« die Richtung. Finnische Produkte wurden zum Inbegriff harmonischen zeitgenössischen

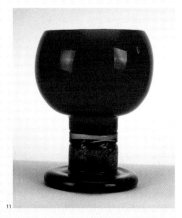

11

Formempfindens und hoher Qualität. In Italien hielt sich der Neo-Liberty Stil. In Deutschland war Formgebung durch logische Planung und geometrische Klarheit charakterisiert und hat wesentlich zum »Wirtschaftswunder« beigetragen. Japanisches Design übte einen unverändert starken Einfluss auf die westlichen Künstler aus, die sich von der Ästhetik traditionellen japanischen Handwerks einerseits und industriell gefertigten Massenprodukten andererseits inspirieren ließen. Die USA, das Land mit den schärfsten Wettbewerbsbedingungen der westlichen Welt, förderten hochmodernes Design wie die Möbel- und Ausstellungsentwürfe von Charles und Ray Eames, produzierten aber gleichzeitig Industriegüter mit der schlechtesten Formgebung und minderwertigsten Qualität aller Industrienationen.

Design gewann immer mehr an Bedeutung, was durch das wachsende Angebot von Lifestyle Journalen und die Einrichtung von Institutionen wie das Design Centre in London, das als Schaufenster für zukunftsorientierte Formgebung auftrat, zum Ausdruck kam. Was nun eigentlich unter »gutem Design« verstanden wurde, konnten die meisten Verbraucher nicht konkret nennen. Illustrierte Zeitschriften und Farbbeilagen, deren Seiten mit den neuesten Trends für Interieurs und Möbel gefüllt waren, forcierten letztendlich nur Veränderungen des Geschmacks, nicht aber richtungsweisende Innovationen in der Formgebung. Auch vorsichtige Möbelhäuser orientierten sich vorzugsweise an gängigen Produkten oder Kopien erfolgreicher Entwürfe, statt formschöne zeitgenössische Industriemöbel anzubieten.

Obwohl Design sich inzwischen zu einem wahrhaft internationalen Phänomen entwickelt hatte, war das Gros der Verbraucher eher mode- als designbewusst. Die Industrie stand unter dem Druck, jährlich neue Prototypen von Autos, Möbeln, Glas- und Metallwaren zu entwerfen, um den scheinbar unersättlichen Hunger nach den verrücktesten, coolsten und modischsten Novitäten zu stillen. Auf der Suche nach diesem »Neuen« wurden nun auch ethnische Objekte in die Innendekoration einbezogen. Die Ausweitung des internationalen Flugverkehrs erleichterte den Import von Dekorationsobjekten aus dem Fernen Osten, Indien und Mexiko, die ebenso wie experimentelles Pop-Design geeignet waren, einen persönlichen Stil bei der Gestaltung von Interieurs zu verwirklichen. Obwohl sich das Design

Council und Publikationen wie *Decorative Art* für ausgewogenes und preiswertes Gebrauchsdesign jenseits der modischen Trends engagierten, bevorzugte die Jugend modische und witzige Designlösungen, die Spaß machten, preiswert und leicht austauschbar waren.

Zukunftsvisionen

Das die sechziger Jahre bestimmende Konzept – »Wohneinheiten« statt Häuser – reflektierte einerseits den Einfluss der Architekten der Moderne wie Le Corbusier und Ludwig Mies van der Rohe und andererseits die demographischen Veränderungen in den Ländern der westlichen Welt. Die junge Generation lehnte das Ideal eines Lebens in sicheren Vorstädten, von dem ihre Eltern geträumt hatten, ab und kämpfte für die Befreiung ihres Lebens von traditionellen häuslichen Bindungen und Erwartungen. Im Zuge des erleichterten Zugangs zu Verhütungsmitteln und der damit einhergehenden sexuellen Freizügigkeit wurde ein »sesshaftes Leben« nicht mehr als wünschenswert oder notwendig erachtet. In diesen Jahren begannen sich modulare Wohntürme aus Zement in den Silhouetten der Großstädte durchzusetzen, obwohl diese traurigen Huldigungen an Le

Corbusiers utopische Träume oft schäbig und allzu hastig gebaut wurden. Futuristische Visionen spiegelten sich auch in Moshe Safdies Habitat Projekt für die Expo '67 wider: zellenähnliche Einheiten, die sich unterschiedlichen Familiengrößen anpassen ließen.

Das Weltraumzeitalter hatte dazu beigetragen, die Imagination von Designern und Konsumenten zu beflügeln und zukunftsweisenden modularen Entwürfen zu größerer Popularität zu verhelfen. Die Erdtöne der fünfziger Jahre wurden durch kräftige, von der Op-Art inspirierte Schwarzweißmuster abgelöst. Textilien und Tapeten wurden in dynamischen Mustern und leuchtenden »synthetischen« Farben hergestellt. Als Folge der durchlässiger werdenden Klassenstruktur der Gesellschaft nivellierten sich auch Wertvorstellungen, die antike Stilmöbel höher bewerteten als modernes Möbeldesign. Kopien moderner Stahlrohrmöbel von Le Corbusier, Marcel Breuer und Ludwig Mies van der Rohe wurden nicht nur in der Gestaltung repräsentativer Räume, sondern zunehmend auch in der Einrichtung privater Wohnungen verwendet. Solche klassischen Möbelentwürfe förderten das Sozialprestige und beschleunigten auch dadurch die Akzeptanz eines fortschrittlichen Stilempfindens in der Öffentlichkeit. In dieser Zeit wurde auch auf die Beleuchtung von Innenräumen mehr Wert gelegt und begünstigte Entwürfe mit mehr Fenstern, hellerer Beleuchtung, weißen Wänden und Böden. Man erkannte den Vorteil von Klappmöbeln, die zusammengefaltet und von einer ständig mobiler werdenden Bevölkerung leicht transportiert werden konnten.

Ausdruck und Experiment

Im Verlauf dieses Jahrzehnts wurde das Stilempfinden vielfältiger und bot dem Einzelnen eine größere persönliche Auswahl und Freiheit des Ausdrucks. Auf dem Gebiet des Interior Design wurden gewagte neue Konzepte ausgelotet – die nun versenkbaren Sitzen bis zu isolierten Wohnmodulen reichten, die alles Lebensnotwendige enthielten: Küche, Bad, Schlafzimmer und so weiter. Möbeldesign wurde zu einem Feld des Experimentierens, dessen Ergebnis aufblasbare PVC-Sitzmöbel und der allgegenwärtige »Sitzsack« waren. Derartige Entwürfe, gepaart mit einem Faible für preiswerte, aber bequeme leuchtend bunte Bodenkissen, waren Ausdruck des zwanglosen Lebensstils der sechziger

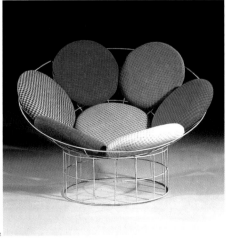

12

Jahre. Diese neue Informalität drückte sich auch in einer Vorliebe für schwere rustikale Gläser aus, die geschliffene Kristall- oder zarte Gläser verdrängten. Mitte bis gegen Ende der sechziger Jahre stellte die Jugendkultur den Status des modernen Designers schamlos infrage und setzte ihm das Konzept des demokratischen Design mit Do-It-Yourself- und Alles-ist-erlaubt-Praktiken entgegen.

In diesen Jahren verwischten sich auch die Grenzen zwischen Kunst und Design zunehmend. Etablierte Künstler wie Victor Pasmore und Eduardo Paolozzi begannen, auch als Designer kreativ zu werden, und Designer wie Ettore Sottsass entwarfen Möbelstücke, die zeitgenössischen Skulpturen nicht unähnlich waren. Auch Performance-Kunst beeinflusste das Design – De Pas, D'Urbino und Lomazzis »Blow Chair« und Gaetano Pesces »Up-Serie« hatten die gleiche Spontanität wie die Happening Kunst. Wohnlandschaften von Designern wie Verner Panton wurden zu einem wahren Raumerlebnis, während futuristische Bauentwürfe, Megastrukturen und autoregulatorische Environments von radikalen Designteams wie Superstudio und Archizoom projektiert wurden.

Die sechziger Jahre glichen im Grunde einem Kaleidoskop, in dem Farbe und Form sich laufend verändern und durch unerwartete Interaktionen die Sinne stimulieren. Utopische Ideen des Bauhauses wurden wieder aufgegriffen, aber gleichzeitig vom Pop-Design der sechziger Jahre unterwandert. Der unsichtbare Stuhl, den bereits Marcel Breuer schon vorausgesagt hatte, wurde von Quasar Khanh und De Pas, D'Urbino und Lomazzi in den Aufblasmöbeln realisiert. Josef Albers Papier- und Pappexperimente wurden zu Vorläufern von Peter Murdochs Wegwerfmöbeln aus Fiberkarton. Der Sozialismus wurde durch den Kapitalismus abgelöst, an die Stelle von Solidarität trat der Individualismus, und kollektive Verantwortung wurde durch persönliche Freiheit ersetzt. Veränderungen von großer Tragweite hatten stattgefunden und waren nicht mehr rückgängig zu machen.

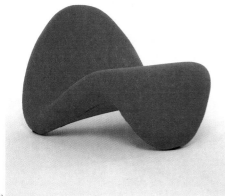

13

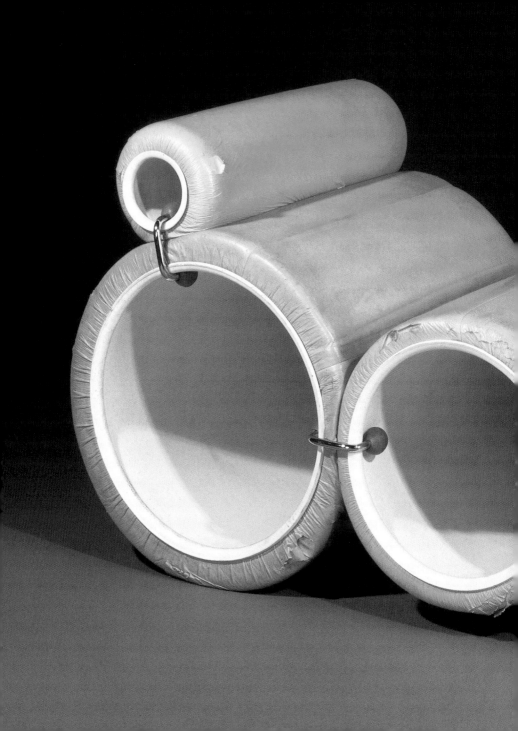

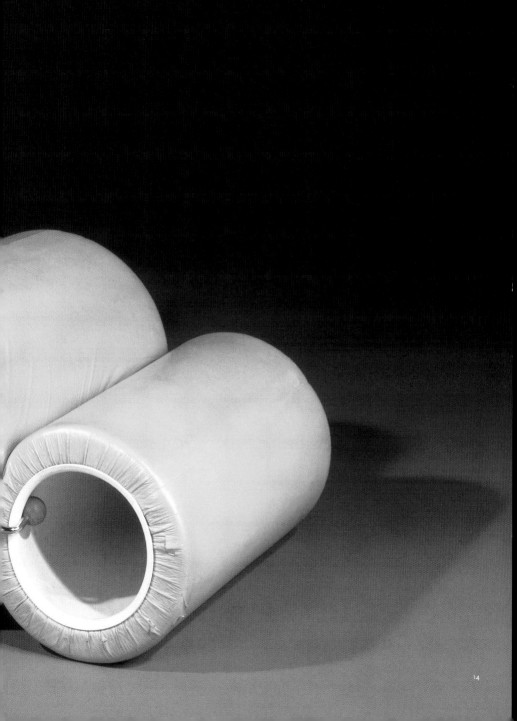

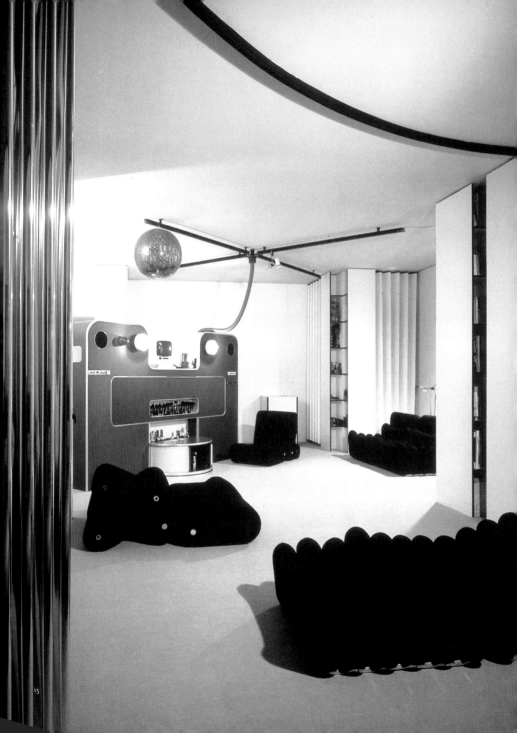

15. & 16. Joe Colombo, Views of an interior with a *Roto-Living Unit*, 1969;
Cabriolet bed, 1969; *Additional Living System* 1967–1968 and *Multi* chairs, 1970
17. Joe Colombo, *Combi-Centre* storage unit for Bernini, 1963–1964

La culture de la jeunesse et la mode du style de vie

Les années 60 furent une décennie de bouleversements sociaux sans précédent. Caractérisées par l'émancipation et la permissivité, elles marquèrent le renoncement au rêve urbain des années 50 en faveur de l'adhésion à une vision utopique de styles de vie alternatifs. Conscients des échecs de la génération antérieure, les jeunes, notamment, manifestèrent leur volonté de vivre dans un monde meilleur et leur rejet de l'urbanisation rapide de l'Occident. Leur conscience sociale collective et la quête du « sex, drugs and rock'n'roll » furent des facteurs unificateurs qui firent de la jeunesse une force puissante de la société des années 60. Des villes comme Londres, Paris et New York devinrent les épicentres culturels de ce phénomène, tandis que les progrès dans le domaine de la communication de masse rendirent possible une vraie globalisation de la culture de la jeunesse. Les arts décoratifs jouèrent un rôle de baromètre social de ces bouleversements en reflétant les espoirs et les aspirations de cette nouvelle génération.

Au début des années 60, comme au cours des décennies précédentes, les arts décoratifs étaient divisés en deux catégories distinctes : les objets fabriqués à la main et ceux produits industriellement. Au cours de cette période, la notion du « bon design » continua à jouer un rôle important. Les produits finlandais, notamment, étaient très appréciés et reconnus pour leur grande qualité et l'intégrité de leur design. En Italie, le style « neo-liberty » continuait à fleurir. Le design allemand, lui, se caractérisait par une conception logique et une pureté géométrique qui étaient en grande partie à l'origine de son « miracle économique ». Le design japonais exerçait toujours une forte influence sur les artistes occidentaux, qui s'inspiraient de son esthétique traditionnelle ainsi que de ses produits de consommation de masse fabriqués industriellement. L'Amérique, qui possédait le marché intérieur le plus compétitif, offrait à la fois un design d'une excellente qualité au travers, par exemple, des meubles et des expositions de design de Charles et Ray Eames, et certains des produits les plus mal fabriqués qui soient et d'une qualité pire que dans toute autre nation industrialisée.

Le design était promu non seulement par la pléthore de magazines sur le style de vie qui fleurirent tout au long de la décennie mais également par des institutions nouvelle-

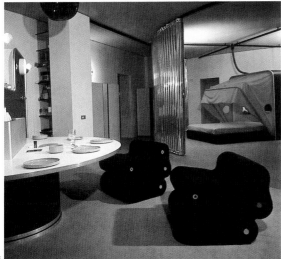

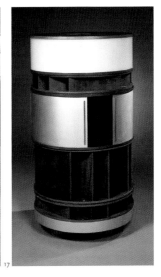

16   17

ment créées telles que le Design Center de Londres, qui servait de vitrine aux produits de qualité les plus innovants. Cependant, le public aurait été bien en peine de définir ce qu'étaient au juste les principes du « bon design ». Les revues sur papier glacé et leurs suppléments en couleurs qui présentaient les dernières tendances en matière de décoration d'intérieur et d'ameublement promouvaient plutôt des changements de mode que des innovations fondamentales en matière de design. De même, les détaillants prudents préféraient s'en tenir aux objets et meubles ayant déjà fait leur preuve ou aux ersatz d'anciens articles s'étant bien vendus plutôt que de se risquer à présenter des produits manufacturés plus progressistes.

Même si le design était devenu un phénomène véritablement international, les consommateurs s'attachaient plus à la mode qu'au design des objets. Chaque année, les fabricants se sentaient obligés de sortir de nouveaux modèles de voitures, de meubles, d'objets en verre et en métal pour satisfaire cet appétit apparemment insatiable pour les produits les plus dans le vent. Cette quête du « nouveau » se traduisit également par l'apparition de plus en plus marquée d'objets ethniques dans la décoration d'intérieur. Les voyages en avion devenant plus accessibles, on vit fleurir les babioles d'Extrême-Orient, d'Inde ou du Mexique. Ces dernières permettaient d'apporter une touche personnelle dans la décoration d'intérieur, tout comme les designs pop expérimentaux. Le Design Council et des publications comme *Decorative Art* défendaient des produits intelligemment conçus et d'un bon rapport qualité-prix qui étaient à

l'abri de l'évanescence de la mode, mais la jeune génération voulait des solutions éphémères et amusantes qui étaient aussi bon marché.

Visions du futur

Dans les années 60, on se mit à penser davantage en termes « d'espaces de vie » plutôt que de maisons, reflétant l'influence d'architectes modernistes tels que Le Corbusier et Ludwig Mies van der Rohe, ainsi que les changements démographiques des populations occidentales. Contrairement à leurs parents, les jeunes n'aspiraient pas à l'idéal de sécurité de la banlieue résidentielle. Au contraire, la nouvelle génération luttait pour se libérer des aspirations et des liens domestiques traditionnels. L'avènement de la pilule contraceptive et la libération sexuelle qui s'ensuivit signifiaient que « s'établir » n'était ni nécessairement souhaitable ni requis. Les années 60 virent également la prolifération des tours d'habitation en béton dans les villes, bien que ces tristes hommages aux rêves utopiques de Le Corbusier aient été souvent de mauvaise qualité et construits à la hâte. Le projet Habitat de Moshe Safdie, réalisé pour l'Expo 67, reflétait également des visions futuristes, avec des unités cellulaires s'adaptant à la taille de la famille qui les habitait.

L'ère spatiale nourrit également beaucoup l'imagination des designers et des consommateurs et entraîna la grande popularité du design futuriste et modulaire. Les tons terreux des années 50 cédèrent la place aux motifs contrastés noirs et blancs inspirés de l'op art, tandis que les textiles et les papiers peints se paraient de motifs dynamiques et de vibrantes couleurs « synthétiques ». Les structures de classes devenant moins figées, les préjugés qui, par le passé, avaient fait la part belle aux meubles anciens par rapport aux modernes, s'estompèrent peu à peu. Les rééditions de meubles tubulaires en métal de Le Corbusier, Marcel Breuer et Ludwig Mies van der Rohe, notamment, étaient de plus en plus utilisées dans les intérieurs privés comme dans les lieux officiels prestigieux. Ces classiques furent rapidement investis d'un cachet social et accélérèrent l'acceptation par le plus grand nombre d'un design plus progressiste. Au cours de cette période, on mit également l'accent sur l'importance de la lumière dans les intérieurs, ce qui se traduisit par davantage de fenêtres, des éclairages plus lumineux, des murs et même parfois des

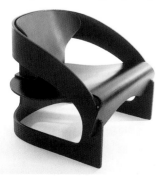

18

sols blancs. On prit aussi conscience soudain de l'intérêt des meubles «démontables», qui pouvaient se plier et être facilement transportés par une population de plus en plus nomade.

Expression et expérimentation

Au cours de la décennie, le design se diversifia de plus en plus, permettant un plus grand choix personnel et une plus grande liberté d'expression. Dans le domaine de la décoration d'intérieur, on explorait sans cesse de nouveaux concepts audacieux, comme les banquettes installées dans des fosses au milieu du salon ou les «espaces de vie autosuffisants» qui comportaient tout ce dont on avait besoin pour la vie quotidienne: cuisine, chambre à coucher, salle de bains, etc. La conception des meubles devint également un domaine d'expérimentation, aboutissant au siège gonflable en PVC ou à l'incontournable fauteuil poire. Ce nouveau design, associé à la mode des poufs colorés bon marché mais néanmoins confortables, reflétait le style de vie plus nonchalant des années 60. Cette même décontraction se retrouvait dans la prédominance du verre épais et rustique par rapport au cristal ciselé et au verre délicat. Entre le milieu et la fin des années 60, la culture de la jeunesse défiait même le statut du créateur moderne en promouvant la notion du design démocratique à travers le «do-it-yourself» et l'école du bric-à-brac.

Durant cette même époque, les divisions entre l'art et le design devinrent de plus en plus floues. Des artistes établis

tels que Victor Pasmore et Eduardo Paolozzi s'essayaient au design tandis que des designers comme Ettore Sottsass réalisaient des meubles symboliques «artistiques». L'art de la performance influença également le design: le fauteuil gonflable de De Pas, D'Urbino et Lomazzi et la série de sièges de Gaetano Pesce offraient la même spontanéité qu'un «happening» artistique. Les intérieurs réalisés par des décorateurs tels que Verner Panton devinrent des expériences spatiales, tandis que des groupes de designers radicaux tels que Superstudio et Archizoom concevaient des habitations futuristes, des méga-structures ou des environnements autorégulateurs.

Les années 60 furent essentiellement une décennie kaléidoscopique où couleurs et formes évoluèrent rapidement et s'influencèrent mutuellement de manière inattendue pour produire des stimulations sensorielles. Le design pop fit réapparaître les rêves utopiques du Bauhaus de manière étrangement pervertie. La chaise invisible prédite par Marcel Breuer trouva sa réalisation dans les meubles gonflables de Quasar Khanh, De Pas, D'Urbino et Lomazzi. Les expériences en papier et en carton de Josef Albers préfiguraient les meubles en fibre de bois jetables de Peter Murdoch. Le socialisme avait été remplacé par le capitalisme, la communauté par l'individualisme, la responsabilité collective par les libertés individuelles. Pour le meilleur et pour le pire, des bouleversements culturels immenses et irréversibles avaient eu lieu.

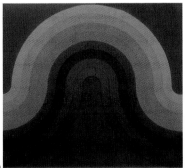

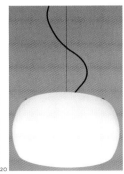

19

20

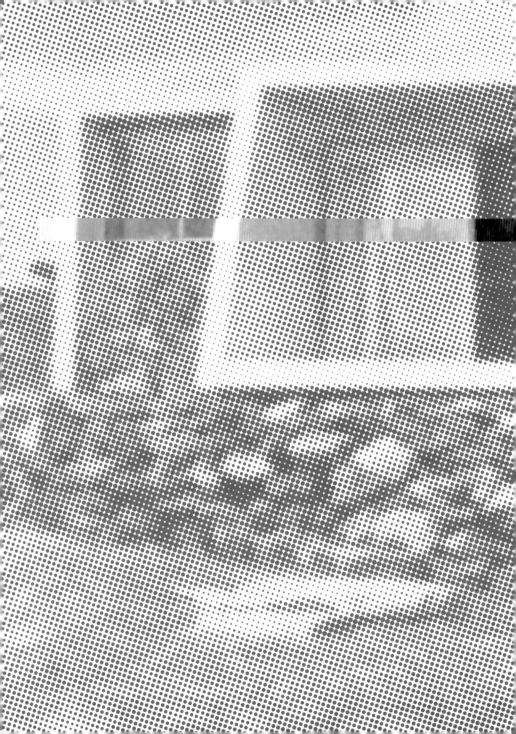

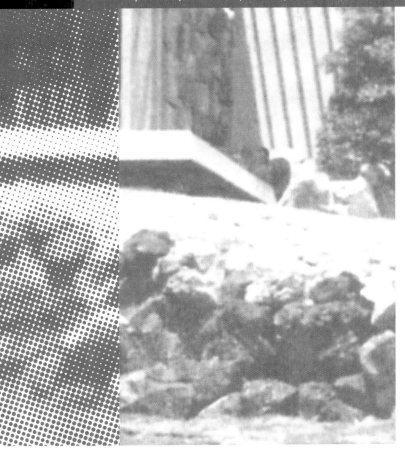

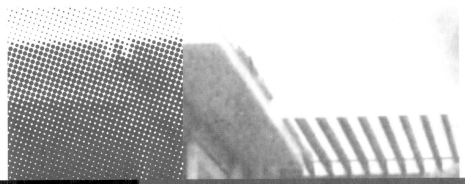

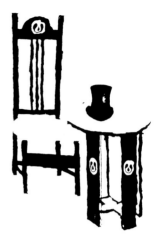

IN 1906, HOUSES were rich, dark and exceedingly comfortable. Today's houses are products of functionalism and 'fitness for purpose'. They are neither rich nor dark, a shade inhuman and often lacking the visual and physical comfort for which no amount of light and colour will compensate. Design is all-important and here to stay. Comfort goes by the board and may return tomorrow. The bleak difference between Edwardian and modern furniture is the richness of decoration of the former and the preoccupation with undecorated expanses of the latter. A splendid example of Ernest Gimson's work was shown at the 1952 exhibition of Victorian and Edwardian Decorative Arts at the Victoria and Albert Museum: a cabinet of 1910 in brown ebony inlaid with mother-of-pearl and gleaming with bright iron handles. What would be its modern equivalent? One refuses to believe that the days of well-*decorated* furniture have gone forever. And, if there is no demand for decorated furniture, why should top designers of exhibition rooms persuade manufacturers to let them doll up their dull chests-of-drawers – or resort to using antique pieces to enliven their schemes?

But the late 'fifties have certainly shown signs of greater subtlety and delight in form. Some of the moulded fibre glass chairs express the real elegance of a proper and original use of a new material. Even more to the point is the fact that many manufacturers of mass-produced furniture have realised that the present generation is no longer interested in travesties of former styles. They want the best they can afford from the designers of their age.

MAISONS APPARTEMENTS MOBILIER

En 1906 la plupart des maisons étaient somptueuses, sombres et confortables à l'excès. Aujourd'hui, les maisons sont créées en fonction du rôle utile à remplir. Elles ne sont plus somptueuses ou sombres, mais un soupçon inhumaine, manquant souvent de confort visuel et physique que ni la lumière ou la couleur, aussi abondantes soient-elles, ne compenseront. Ce qui compte c'est la forme qui dure. Le confort est sacrifié, mais peut revenir demain.

La triste différence entre les meubles du début du 20e siècle et les meubles modernes, c'est la richesse de l'ornementation chez les premiers et l'importance donnée aux grandes surfaces nues chez les seconds. On se refuse à croire que l'époque du mobilier très orné est à jamais révolue. Et si la demande en ce qui concerne le meuble orné est inexistante, pourquoi les décorateurs les plus fameux des Salles d'Exposition ne persuaderaient pas les fabricants de leur permettre de recourir à des objets antiques pour donner plus d'animation à l'ensemble de leurs projets?

Mais la fin des années cinquante a certainement permis de constater une plus grande subtilité et joie dans le modèle créé. Certaines des chaises en fibre de verre moulée expriment une réelle élégance qui vient de l'emploi judicieux et original de la matière nouvelle. Ce qui ressort encore davantage, c'est le fait que de nombreux fabricants de meubles en série ont constaté que les travestis d'anciens styles n'intéressent plus la génération actuelle. Des dessinateurs de son époque, ce qu'elle désire obtenir ce sont les styles les plus intéressants que lui permettent ses moyens.

CASAS APARTAMENTOS MOBILIARIO

En 1906, la mayoría de las casas eran lujosas, oscuras y sumamente cómodas. Hoy día, las casas son producto de un diseño práctico, 'apropiado para su cometido'. No son ni lujosas ni oscuras, un tanto inhumanas y a menudo carentes de la comodidad visual y física que ni la luz ni el color pueden compensar. El diseño es lo más importante y se ha inculcado firmemente en la costumbre. Se ha sacrificado la comodidad, que tal vez vuelva en el futuro.

La principal diferencia entre el mobiliario de la época eduardina y el moderno radica en la lujosidad decorativa del primero y la preocupación de dar un aspecto de vastedad desierta al segundo.

Mas durante los últimos años se han observado indicios de mayor belleza de forma. Algunas de las sillas de fibra de vidrio moldeada expresan la verdadera elegancia que corresponde al uso debido y original de un nuevo material. Todavía más importante es el hecho de que much os fabricantes de muebles producidos en serie se han percatado de que la presente generación ha dejado de interesarse en las parodias de los antiguos estilos. Busca lo mejor, que s e medios le permite, de los diseñadores de su propia edad.

HÄUSER WOHNUNGEN MÖBEL

Im Jahre 1906 waren die meisten Häuser prunkvoll, dunkel und gemütlich. Unsere modernen Häuser sind das Ergebnis von Funktionalismus und 'Zweckentsprechung'. Sie sind nicht mehr prunkvoll und dunkel, aber dafür ein klein wenig unmenschlich, und es fehlt ihnen oft an jenem visuellen und physischen Wohlbehagen, für das kein noch so grosser Aufwand an Licht und Farbe jemals ein Entschädigung sein kann. Künstlerische Formgebung ist von grösster Wichtigkeit und aus unserem Leben nicht mehr wegzudenken. Die Bequemlichkeit ist nicht mehr da, aber sie wird morgen vielleicht wieder da sein.

Die Möbel aus der Zeit Eduards VII. unterscheiden sich von unseren heutigen Möbeln in einem Hauptpunkt: Sie waren prunkvoll verziert, während grosse schmucklose Flächen unsere Möbel charakterisieren.

Zu Ende der Fünfziger Jahre waren sicher Zeichen dafür vorhanden, dass sich der Geschmack änderte und die Freude an schönen Formen wieder auftauchte. In einig er der gegossenen Fiberglas-Stühle zeigt sich die Eleganz, mit der ein neues Material richtig und seiner Eigenart entsprechend behandelt wird. Weiterhin haben eine Anzahl von Fabrikanten, die Möbel serienmässig herstellen, endlich eingesehen, dass die gegenwärtige Generation nicht mehr an Travestien vergangener Möbelstile interessiert ist und dass sie das Beste im Rahmen der zur Verfügung stehenden Mitteln haben will, das Formgeber ihrer eigenen Zeit entworfen haben.

Town house with Library in New York City

designed by Felix Augenfeld, A I A : associate architect Jan Hird Pokorny

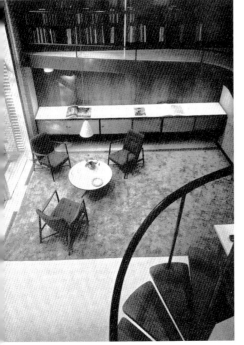

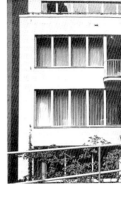

Back view from second-floor roof garden

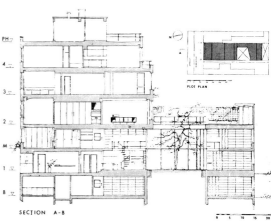

SECTION A-B

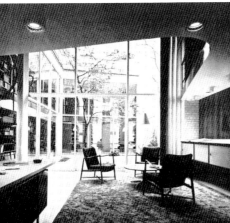

A LIBRARY of some 50,000 volumes, chiefly on political history and social science, is the nucleus around which this four-storey steel frame house is planned. The owner, an author and book collector, wished to arrange it in such a way that it would also be accessible to fellow scholars and students. At the same time, he wished to use the building as a private residence for himself and his wife, and to have a separate apartment for a caretaker-librarian. To avoid unnecessary interference the different functions of the building were to be kept independent from one another, but all had to be contained within a narrow site 25 feet 4 inches × 100 feet in a built-up residential area. The sectional drawing shows the solution, with the library arranged on three levels, wrapped around a glass-walled central garden patio.

◀ Views from mezzanine balcony down to first-floor library and from first-floor library into patio-garden

photos: Alexandre Georges

Town house with library in New York City

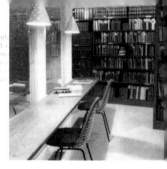

Library detail ▶

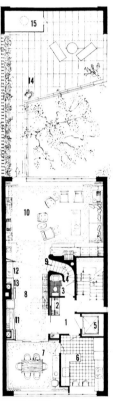

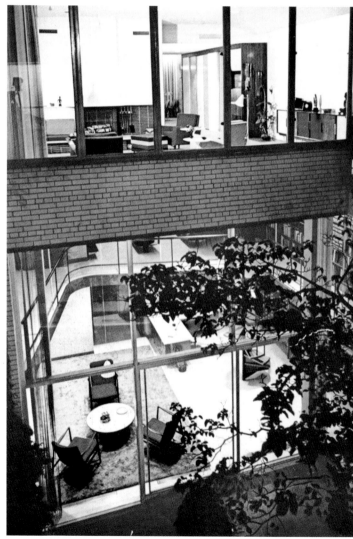

Good daylight for the core of the building and almost complete transparency of the space is achieved. On the first floor a feeling of height is created by the introduction of an intermediate mezzanine level cut out in the shape of a balcony. The owner's study is also on this level, affording him easy access to the whole library. On the second and third floors, connected by a private staircase, is his four-bedroom maisonette flat.

The librarian's flat, which has two bedrooms, is on the fourth floor. Illustrated below is the owner's living-room—colourful and spacious—with an interesting bench seat built into the fireplace wall. It opens onto a roof-garden at the rear, and a short passage connects it with the dining-room at the front of the building.

The street front is faced in travertine and Venetian glass mosaic, other exteriors in glazed brick. Interiors designed by the architect.

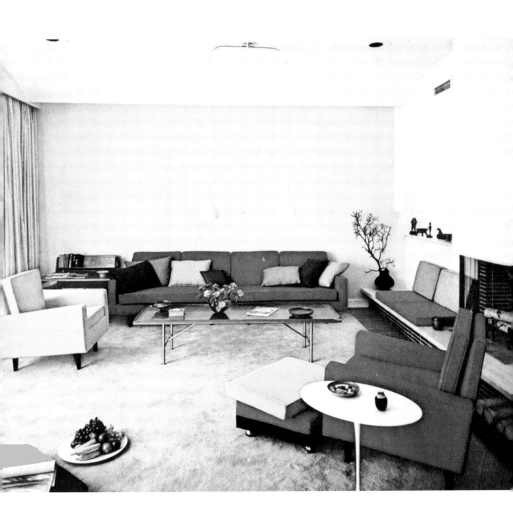

w into first, mezzanine and second floors

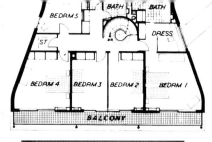

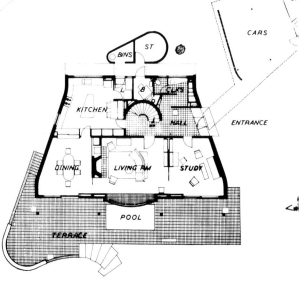

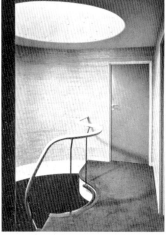

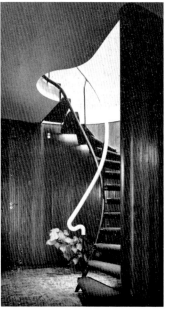

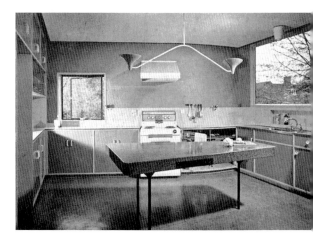

The architect was asked to plan this house with the living-room and main bedrooms all facing south, which meant a layout wider at the front than at the back. This posed some problems successfully overcome in a design with splayed and curving-in side walls which, blinker-like direct the outlook towards the main garden and provide privacy from the road.

With the exception of the window-pierced south wall faced in grey-black Mineralite, the exterior is in grey facing bricks with a white mosaic tiled fascia. Slender black concrete columns carrying the roof overhang are an important factor in the proportion of the design.

The hall is panelled in afrormosia with grey-green Japanese grass cloth above, and the open stairway treads and upper landing are carpeted in dark green, the wall lit at each step level.

An open-plan living/dining room and study open off the hall, separated, if desired, by concealed sliding doors. Against a quiet background of pale grey walls and polished Missander wood-block flooring, interest is focused on the fireplace wall in Napoleon marble with an inset illuminated display slot; just below this and to the right of the fireplace, is a hidden panel which opens to reveal a television set. A built-in radiator system runs beneath the wide black-tiled window-sill.

In the kitchen the fittings include a fixed terrazzo-top 'island table', the drawers fitted with chopping and pastry boards, rolling pin, etc. The colour scheme is in two shades of grey.

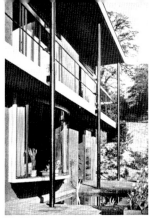
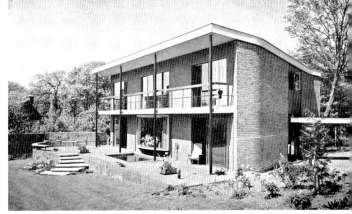

House at Hampstead, London *designed by Patrick Gwynne,* LRIBA

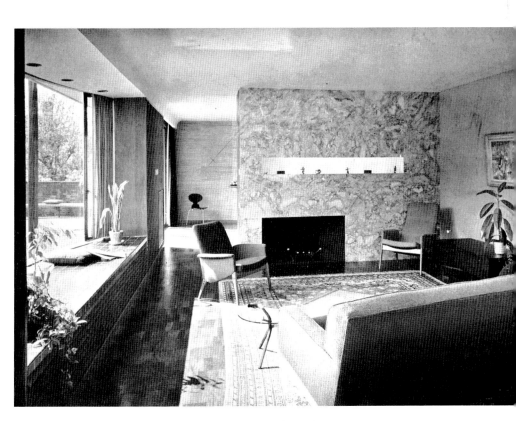

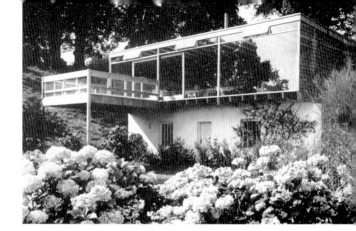

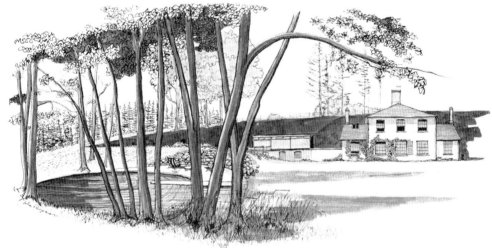

Flat near Maidstone, England

Architects: Spencer and Gore

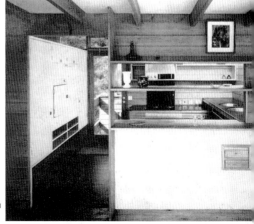

Designed as an annexe to an existing Regency house sited within a fold of the Kentish hills, this two-bedroom cedar-board flat built over the garage commands an extensive view through a glazed wall of 12-foot bays extending the whole length of the south side. One of the bays is a sliding door giving access to a sun deck projecting from the living-room and increasing the living space. The interior is lined in Pacific coast hemlock and the ceiling in Stramit boarding is painted white on the underside.

Interior fittings include a built-in oven and a double-sided display and storage unit between the living-room and kitchen where the stainless steel sink unit and electric rings are set into asbestos work tops.

Photos by Mann Bros., courtesy 'Architectural Design'

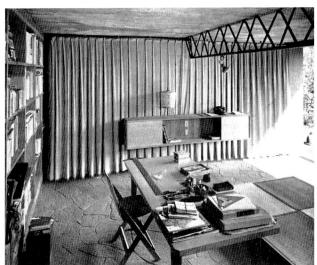

House in Ohtaku-Tokio, Japan

Architect: Kiyosi Seike

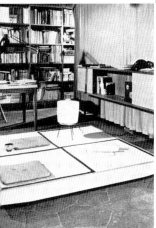

Constructed on the open-plan system, this is a small reinforced concrete house built by the architect for his own use. The interior shown is a combined study and living-room with a 'window wall' on the south side, part of which can be slid downwards into the basement thus opening up the interior to the garden.

The ceiling in rough concrete is supported on a welded steel bar painted red. Built-in bookshelves and a suspended wall cabinet keep the floor space clear. The heating system is inlaid under the floor. This is paved in green flagstones, with the paving continuing out into the garden and establishing a harmonious relationship between exterior and interior. The wood framed platform of traditional *tatami* rush mats mounted on casters is also designed to be used indoors or out with equal felicity.

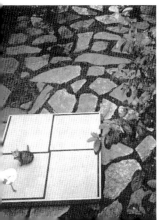

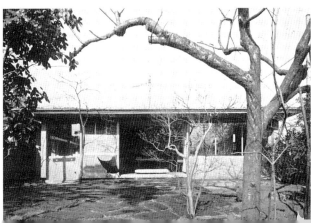

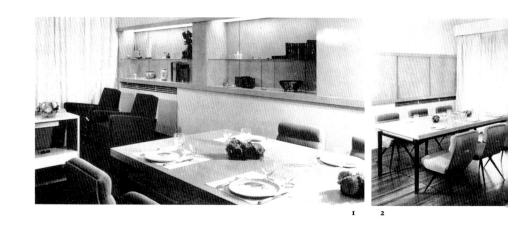

1   2

Apartment in Paris *designed by Jacques Dumond*

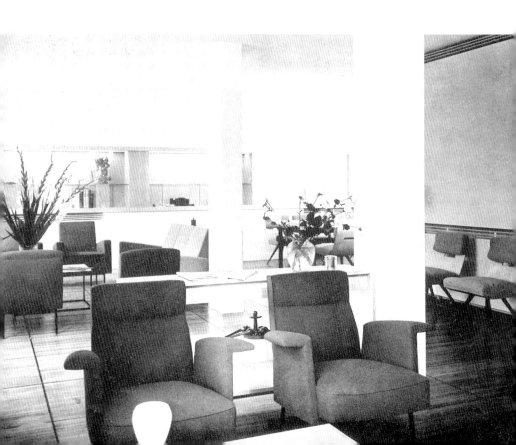

Situated on the seventh and eighth floors of a new building, this apartment was designed for a family of five with young grown-up daughters and a son. To enable the young people to entertain their friends independently the lower floor is designed as a separate unit with a private staircase to the upper floor containing the main living/dining room, kitchen, laundry, and parents' bedroom and dressing room.

1-3 The air-conditioned living-room with white walls, windows curtained in white silk and a walnut parquet floor; the furniture is in polished ash and black lacquer with upholstery in grey, blue and ochre. At one end is a full-length display cabinet and opposite, beneath the bookshelves, is a hung bar-cabinet (**4-5**) with slide-out glassware shelves. A built-in radiator central heating system lines the walls.

6 The son's study/bedroom with adjustable wall shelves faced in black and white Formica, metal frame chair and desk with grey Formica top, surround lacquered blue. **7** The bathroom with black tile floor, green fittings, bath niche in faience tiles decorated with motifs in grey and pale green. The shaving table and small shelves are in acajou with bright green Formica tops. **8** Girl's bedroom with pale grey walls, dark grey carpeting, and window curtains in a black print on white. The chair and table are in white-lacquered metal with light grey Formica top and dark grey surround. The bedcover is a vivid blue and the armchair is upholstered in tobacco brown.

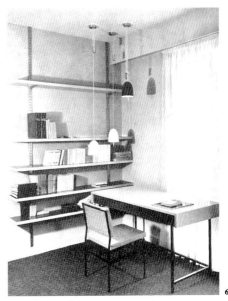

6

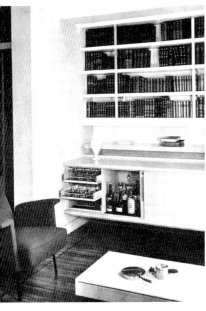

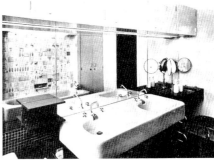

7

4
5

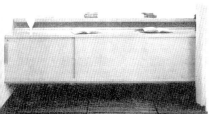

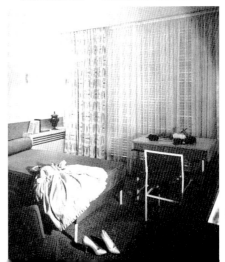

8

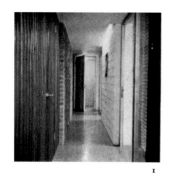
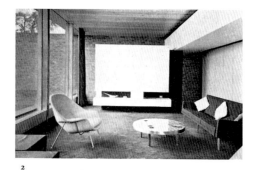

I   2

House at Hampstead, London

Architects: Higgins & Ney & Partners AARIBA

Built on a quite small steeply sloping site overlooking north-west London, this house has succeeded in being completely integrated—in its site, in its function and architecturally. The levels allowed a well-defined separation of main entrance, and service entrance, the latter to a first-floor kitchen and dining room with, on the same floor, the living room and master bedroom suite. Children's rooms are situated on the ground floor, visible in **4**; this achieves an effective separation of child and adult activities and permits their easy use as bed-sitting rooms in later teenage years.

Also, by raising the main rooms, it has been possible to achieve a larger, more spacious living area than the site suggests and to exploit fully the magnificent view to the south. At the rear, **5**, on the same level, the dining room in summer opens right into the shaded copse. Waxed, grooved Canadian pine supplies surfaces of ceilings, and all doors are in mahogany panels. Interior brickwork is left unsurfaced where it forms the logical continuation of an exterior wall, for example, on the first floor landing, seen in detail **9**. The only remaining large interior wall surface, in the living room, right, is panelled in soft harmonising tan coach-hide-finish Arlinghide. In this room against the natural finish colours and against the charcoal carpet and black settee, colour accents are introduced mainly in the chairs. The writing desk is teak on a cast iron base with built-in lighting and its own separate filing unit. At the other end of the room, **2**, the part-wall forms a screen to the stairway and, in the room, a surface on which home film shows can be conveniently projected

1 View through children's corridor on ground floor
3 Rocking chair in steel rod with foam padded pancake cushions

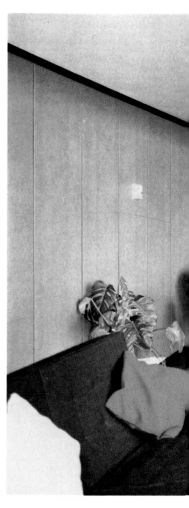

4   5

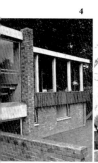
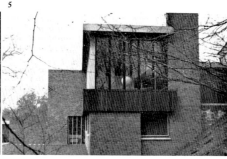

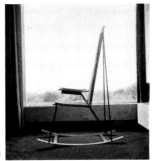

3

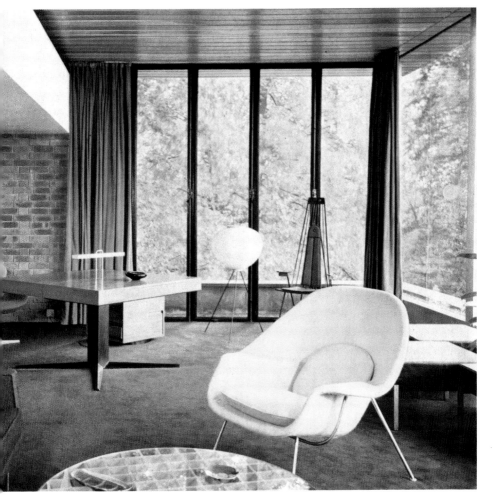

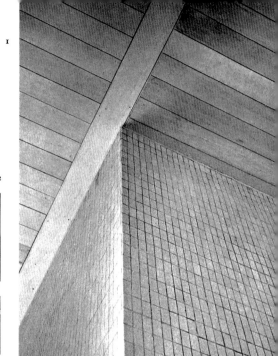

1

2

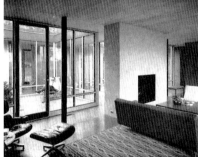

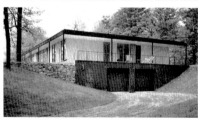

House at Belleville, Ontario

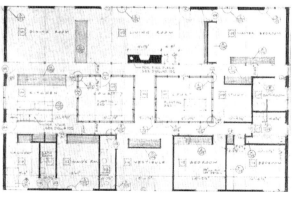

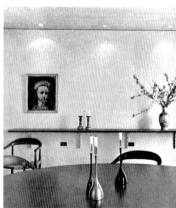

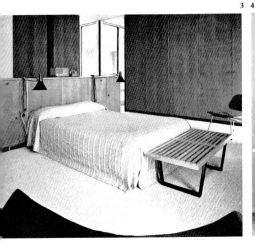
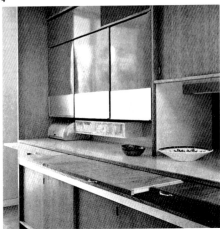

rchitects: Grierson & Walker, MMRAIC, ARIBA

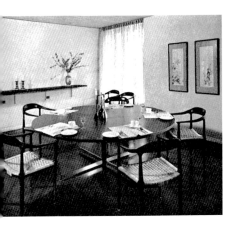

Located on a plateau at the north end of a 200-acre open site adjacent to the Moira River, which forms the western boundary, this house is a simple rectangle sitting on a podium, consisting of three structural bays in width and five in length.

Planned on a steel grid 18½ feet square, the rooms are grouped around two open courtyards, the walls of which are completely glazed and views into these courts are obtained from all parts of the house. Spaces flow freely into each other. This feeling of continuity is heightened by the boarded (basswood) ceiling used throughout the interior and extended over the external colonnade, and the uniform grey-green slate and concrete floor.

Against a neutral background of off-white plaster walls and curtains in open-weave yellow linen sheer, colour is introduced in upholstery, throw cushions and carpets. Interior illumination is by flush mounted ceiling pot lights, recessed incandescent strip lights and free standing floor lamps. Flood lighting mounted in adjacent trees creates pools of light filtering through trees and branches to the interior courts.

1, 2 Detail of living room: free-standing fireplace faced with small white speckled mosaic tile, matching the exterior walls. **3, 4** The master bedroom and kitchen, with large areas of simply arranged built-in fittings in white oak stained to a fumed oak finish.

5, 6 Dining room with 7-foot mahogany table, rush-seated chairs, and neat display shelf.

Interior designers: Kenneth G. Warren Associates

1961–62 · houses and apartments · 41

A four-bedroom apartment designed by the architect for his own family, and devised as a continuous system of interconnecting rooms divided by three successive sliding Modernfold partitions. This plan gives a feeling of unity and greater space than the area would seem to offer, emphasised by the continuous diagonal-stripe pattern of floor tiles and ceiling and a colour scheme common to the whole area: white with yellow in tones shading from light to mustard to burnt sienna. Continuity is also expressed in the arrangement of shelves and fittings along the full length of the window facade.

BELOW: through views from end to end
RIGHT: entrance and dining end of the living area illustrated on the facing page. The settee and armchair are upholstered in white and yellow with reddish brown/white/black cowskin rug and tabourets.
All furniture and fittings are custom-made to the designs of the architect.

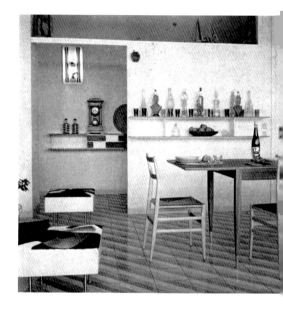

Apartment in Milan

Architect: Gio Ponti

courtesy Domus

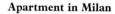

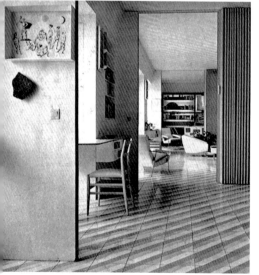

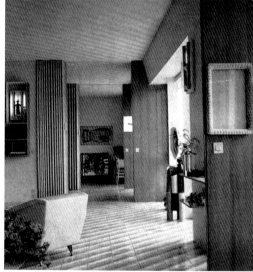

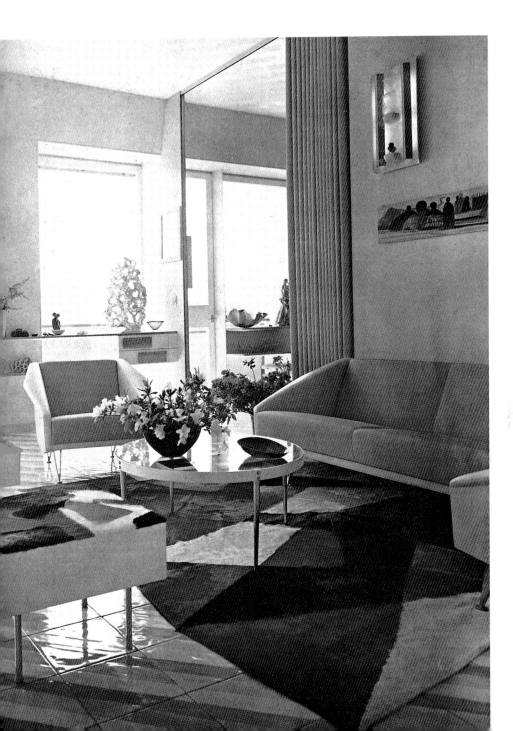

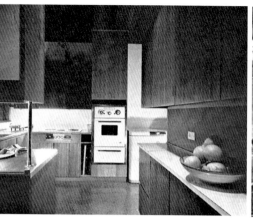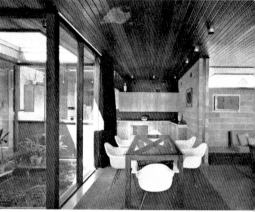

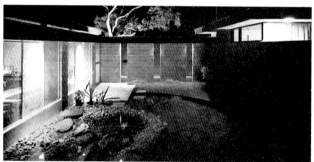

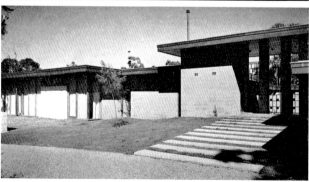

House at St. I

Architect: Ross Thorne

The architect, in sharing this home with his parents, wanted separate studio facilities for his work. The plan therefore has a central garden court with living rooms on one side and the studio, connected by a covered way, on the other. This in-turned arrangement is suited to the site—two-and-a-half acres of flat, stunted native bush bordering on a main road, with virtually no view. The house, built of grey concrete blocks, has a long ground-hugging appearance, with a variation of three roof levels, the highest being at the porch to the main court entered through high wrought iron gates. The whole of the living space, comprising verandah, living/dining area and fitted kitchen, is planned as a single unit

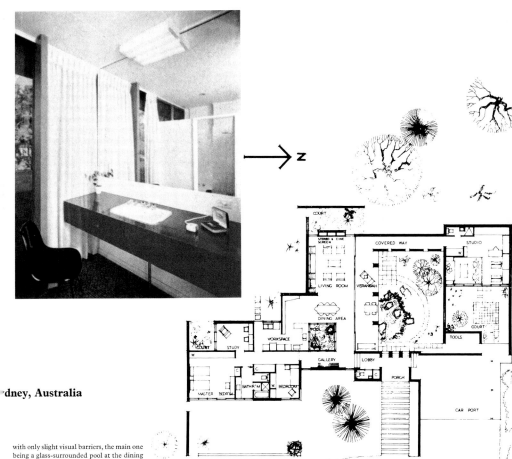

Z →

dney, Australia

with only slight visual barriers, the main one being a glass-surrounded pool at the dining end dividing the way to the two principal wings. Frameless glass sliding panels open the whole living space to the verandah and central court.

The illustrations on this page show the vivid colourings of interior furnishings against a neutral background. The living room ceiling is in varnished boards, the floor terrazzo, using multi-colour river pebbles. On the right is a ciné screen of white finely perforated plastic with loud-speakers behind.

In the kitchen, the built-in fittings are in Queensland maple with stainless steel and white plastic bench tops.

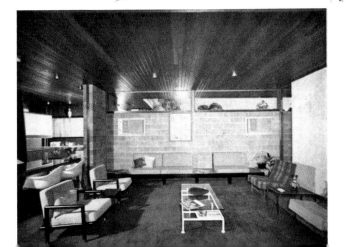

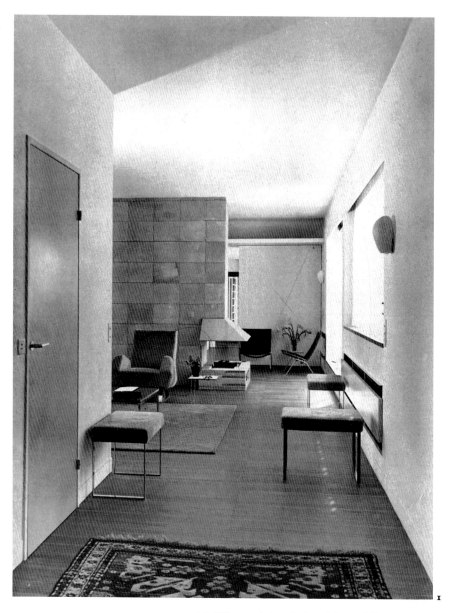

1

1, 2 Living room: An interesting feature is the central chimney piece of pink
refractory tiles with aluminium-hooded open hearth at one end opposite the
window wall. Aluminium is also used for the built-in storage fitment with doors
faced in Formica in white and three greys, and for the framework of the fabric-
panelled sliding screen to the right of it. Flooring is parquet with a deep pile
ochre rug defining the sitting area and contrasting with the light grey 'surnyl'
upholstery of the stainless steel armchairs and small stools.
Interior designed and executed by Jacques Dumond FRANCE

3, 4 In this interior a dramatic effect is created by the white dining group which, together with sheer white wool window draperies and linen-panelled white end wall, highlight a monochromatic colour scheme in citrus tones. The dining table seats six; the 78-inch long oval top is available in white plastic laminate, walnut veneer or marble finishes, the aluminium base in white, charcoal or grey finishes. Together with the fibreglass-reinforced-polyester moulded chairs, it forms part of the single pedestal collection designed by Eero Saarinen for Knoll Associates, Inc. Interior by the Knoll Planning Unit under the direction of Florence Knoll USA

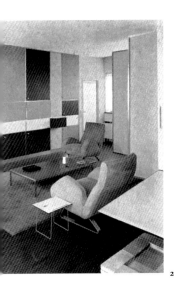

2

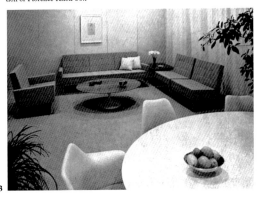

3

4

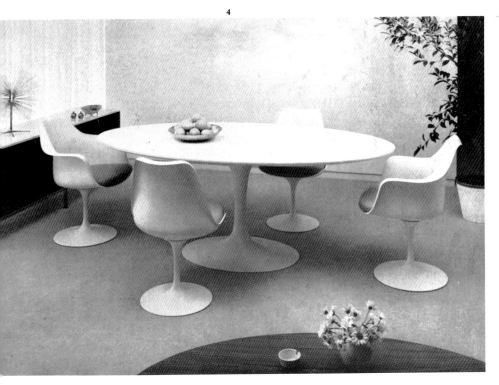

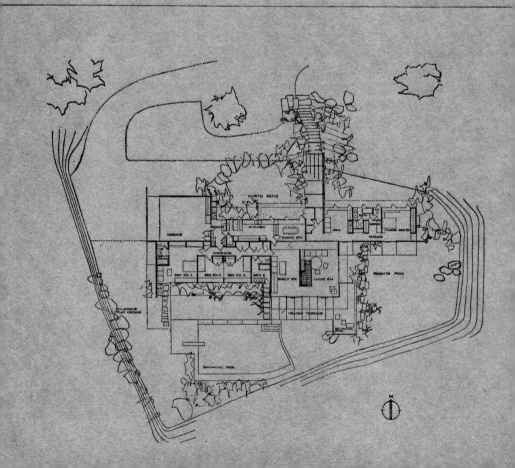

GARAGE

NORTH PATIO

KITCHEN

DINING RM

BATH

DEN

MASTER BED RM

BED RM 3

BED RM 1 BED RM 2 BED RM 3 BATH 2

FAMILY RM

LIVING RM

FRIGHTS PATIO

HEATED TERRACE

CHILDRENS PLAY GROUND

SWIMMING POOL

House at Beverly Hills, California

for Dr and Mrs Henry E. Singleton: Architect Richard J. Neutra, FAIA

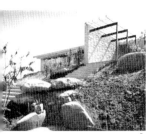

'Where exactly does a tree stop to be beautiful and begin to be utilitarian?' So has Richard Neutra defined the difficulty of separating the utilitarian from the aesthetic. He does not question the possibility of the architect achieving harmony between the two.

On a particular area on the top of a mountain a form will grow which will be found to be a family home, ideal for all its requirements. The form retains the space, without disturbing the contour of the land by being large and low-roofed. To bring into the living area the commanding views towards the Pacific and over the plains, the San Fernando Valley and a mountain lake, visual barriers are reduced to a minimum: steel cased frames support the overhanging roof; the glass walls slide back to extend the area on to a radiant-heated terrace with reflection pool.

In the family room 2 floor-level seating permits relaxation 'close to the mountain' (the chair in the right foreground with an elastic metal backrest was

The house is reached from the north by an ascending drive terminating at a parking area, from where an interesting stairway, 1, leads up to the entrance

pergola and the north patio (again in 3 through the kitchen). The driveway also continues westward to the garage. *Photos: Julius Shulman*

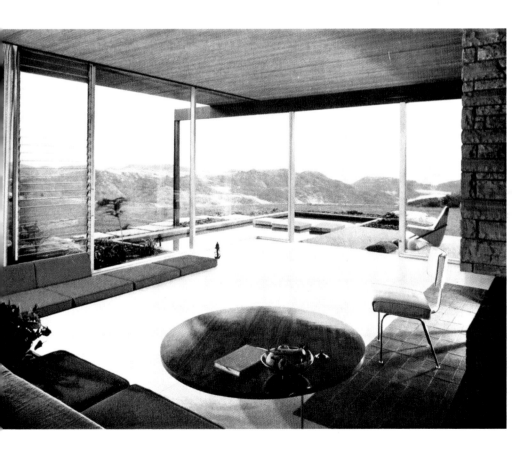

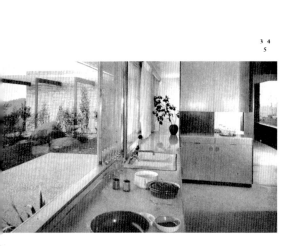

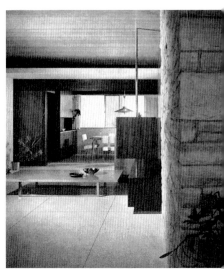

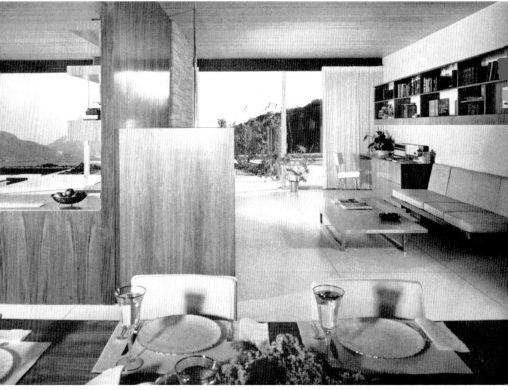

House at Beverly Hills, California

Architect, Richard J. Neutra, FAIA

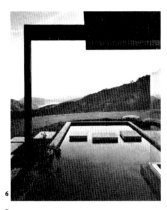

6

7

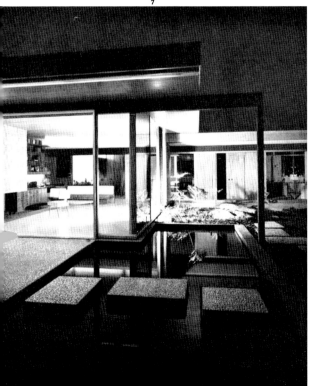

designed by Richard Neutra for dining or desk work). At the right, too, is the natural stone fireplace which divides this room from the living room. These areas connect directly, without break in floor or ceiling levels, with the dining room seen, from the family room, in **4**, and in the foreground **5**.

This latter illustration looks back into the family room at right and living room at left. From the kitchen **3** sliding doors open onto the shady north patio where the family often dines informally. A hatch leads through into the dining room.

On this page, **6**, outward again over the reflecting pool to the southeast, which seems to continue and bring the distant lake close to the house: and, **7**, back from the pool into the living room with the parents' wing to the right.

The children's wing lies to the west with convenient access to the swimming pool area.

Like the form, colours are the result of thinking of the house, its material, its needs, as a whole.

Associate designers:

Benno Fischer
Serge Koschin
John Blanton
Thaddeus Longstreth

Photos: Julius Shulman

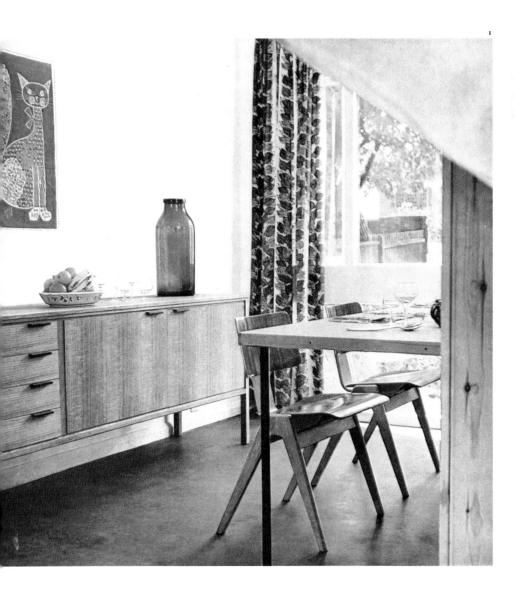

'Menelaus' a house at Wimbledon, near London
Architect, Norman Plastow, ARIBA, LSIA

2

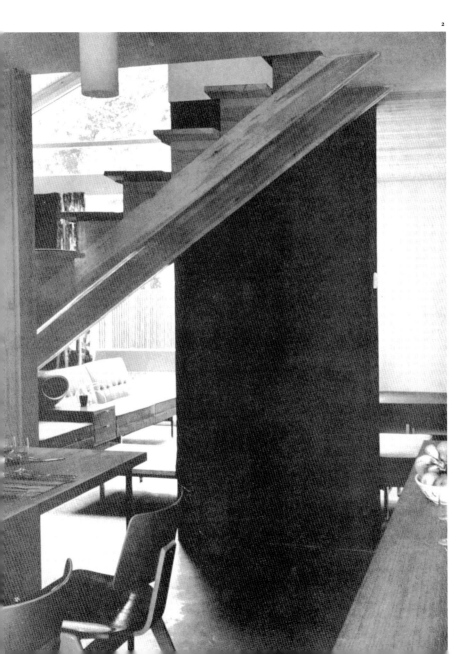

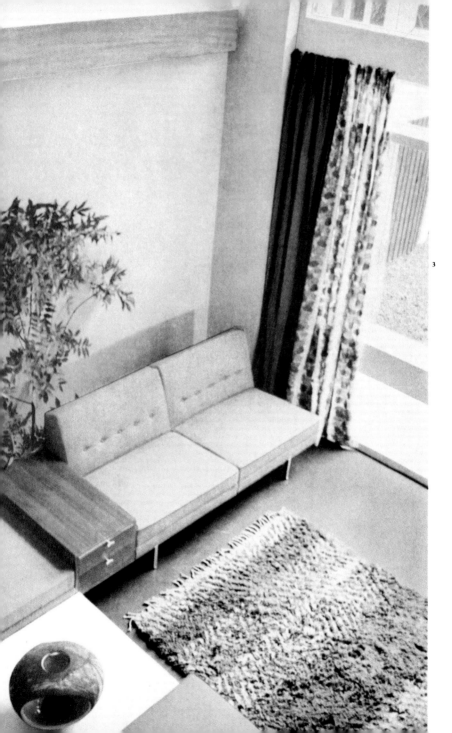

3

Menelaus' a house at Wimbledon
Architect, Norman Plastow, ARIBA, LSIA

The architect built this open-plan house on a small site in the midst of an older developed area. Partly screened from the roadway by its garage and by a tree growing fortuitously on the site, maximum seclusion has been achieved, yet a spacious living area provides for varied arrangements. The main floor area totals but 637 square feet and the space is broken into only by the working kitchen, the hallway and the open stairway flanked by the load-bearing central pillar seen 2 on page 21.

Spaciousness is increased by the double height of part of the living-area achieved by reducing the bedroom sizes to desirable minimums. The lighting of the high main wall is seen opposite. The facing high wall provides display for a large mural. The lower-ceilinged, more intimate end of the living room 4, with interchangeable teak-veneered wall fitments Danish 'Royal', designed by Poul Cadovius, from Streatvales (Sales) Ltd; white Indian-type rug *Tangier* made by Rivington Carpets, and a hand-woven rug by Peter Colling-wood. The occasional chair in the background is

designed by the architect; the unit furniture is from the 30-inch *Modular Seating* range designed by Herman Miller and made by S. Hille & Co. Ltd. The stoneware pot is by Ruth Duckworth at the Crafts Centre of Great Britain. The whole area is warmed by under-floor, thermostatically con-trolled heating.

In 1, the dining space is seen from the open stair-case looking towards the front of the house. On the 7-foot aformosia sideboard *Pendennis* by Archie Shine Ltd, is a large Finnish jar in green glass from Danasco. The tea-towel-cum-wall hanging *Pussi* is made by Almedahls of Sweden. The curtains—*Skogsryd* designed by Gisela Hertz for Borås Wäfveri—in one colourway are repeated in a second colourway of brown, olive and yellow on the main windows at the rear (again page 22), there linked with Danasco Plain in olive-green.

Apart from the Atlas display fitting seen in 4 the light fittings are designed and made by Plus Lighting Ltd.

Photos: Carl Sutton

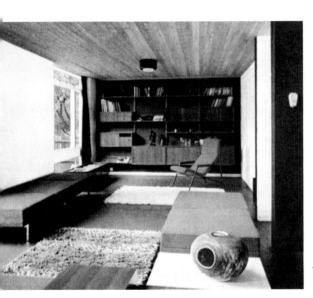

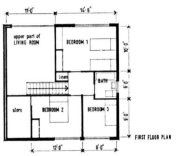

upper part of LIVING ROOM · BEDROOM 1 · liner · BATH · store · BEDROOM 2 · BEDROOM 3

FIRST FLOOR PLAN

11'·0" · 14'·6" · 10'·0" · 6'·0" · 12'·0" · 6'·0"

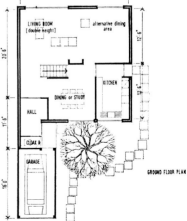

LIVING ROOM [double height] · alternative dining area · KITCHEN · DINING or STUDY · HALL · CLOAK R · GARAGE

GROUND FLOOR PLAN

25'·6" · 20'·6" · 12'·6" · 11'·6" · 16'·0"

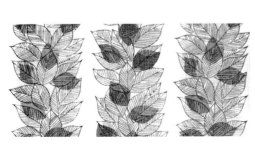

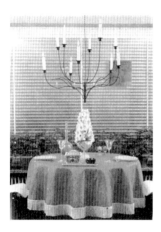

Apartment in Stockholm

Designer, Astrid Sampe

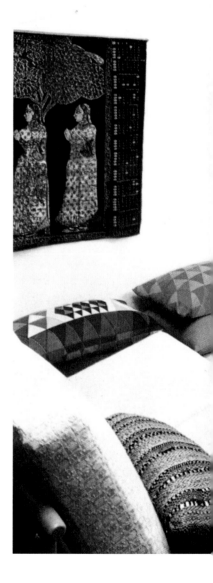

Winter in Northern Europe means long hours of cold and darkness. Set in this darkness, sheltered from it, in the centre of Stockholm, is the flat of Astrid Sampe, glowing with colourful, beautiful objects, warmed by the traditional porcelain stove, and proof that colour plus cosiness can equal good design. Many of the furnishings are of Mrs Sampe's own inspiration. As head of the textile workshop of AB Nordiska Kampaniet (NK), she is among Sweden's (and the world's) leading designers. She is an adviser on schemes as diverse as prison interiors and ambassadorial suites.

In her living room is one of the famous Marieberg stoves of eighteenth century design, with brass doors and tiles decorated with sepia brown flowers. It is the focal point of the room, exuding friendliness and warmth, with cushions piled along a low fireside seat. In front of it is a deep textured handwoven rug by Viola Gråsten, a glass-topped coffee table by Florence Knoll and a Charles Eames moulded plastic chair; in the background, a *Triva* display shelf. The settee is upholstered in a linen hand-print by Sven Markelius.

A light pinoleum blind separates the living from the dining end where, against a geranium-filled window, a table can be set up. It is laid with Orrefors crystal and plates in light blue on a deep crimson Thai silk fringed tablecloth.

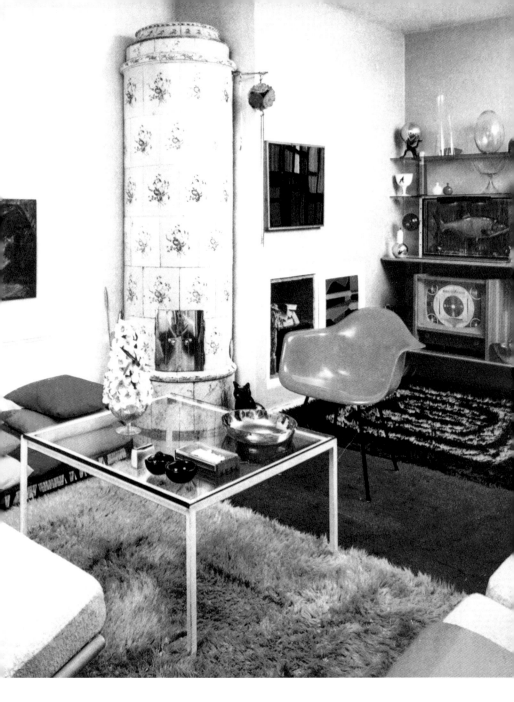

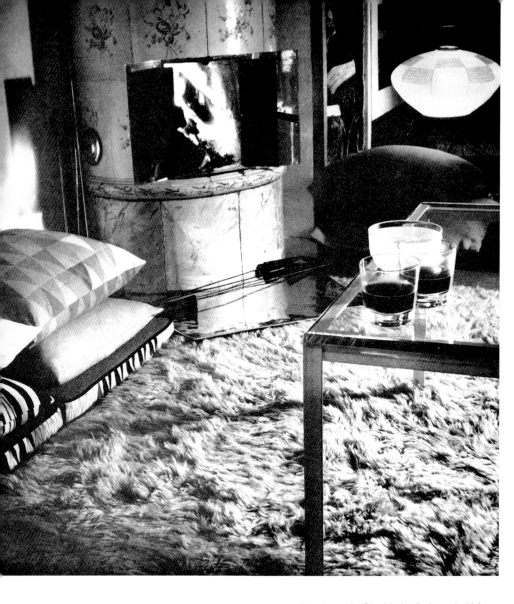

Apartment in Stockholm *Designer, Astrid Sampe*

The special atmosphere of the fireside can perhaps
be better appreciated in close-up.

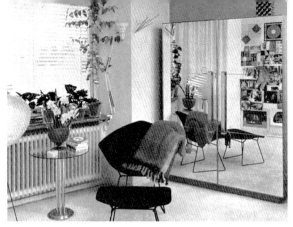

TOP: A corner of Mrs Sampe's bedroom. Reflected in the mirrored doors is the *Active wall* on which are pinned personal photographs of family and friends along with current posters, invitations or even menus from favourite restaurants. In the foreground a Harry Bertoia chair and stool upholstered in purplish-black with a handloomed rug by Viola Gråsten in pinky-orange colourings.

CENTRE: Library wall in Mrs Sampe's study, with doorway leading to the bedroom. On the display shelves folk art is side by side with modern ceramics and glass from many countries.

BOTTOM: Drawing table in teak with black glass top. This was specially designed for Mrs Sampe by Hans Harald Mølander. The spacial sculpture is by Carl Fredrik Lunding, crystal bowl by Tapio Wirkkala. On the wood block floor are handwoven cow-hair runners from the NK Textile Workshop.

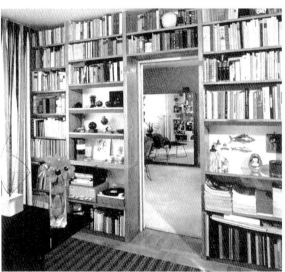

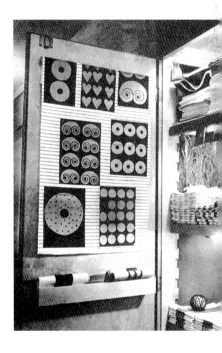

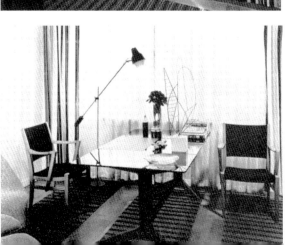

The linen cupboard where, ranged on well lit shelves are many of the household linens designed by Mrs Sampe for Almedahl and Dalsjöfors.

Photos: Studio Conard

House at Dragon Rock, New York State
Architect, Russel Wright

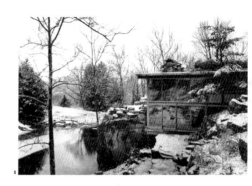

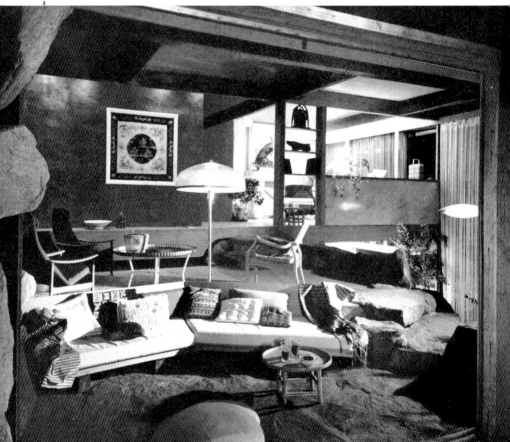

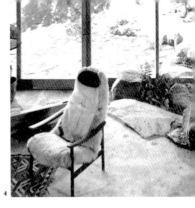

ussel Wright, architect and owner, built this house
a Dragon Rock in two distinct parts, designing it
fit both the site by the waterfall and rock-pool
ad also the habits of the occupants. Built of local
aterials, it is almost chameleon-like, so well does
blend with its surroundings. In fact to *blend* with
ature and to *contrast* with nature are basic to its
onception: man-made and organic materials co-
xist: lighting, as on the stage, is used to create
fluid pattern of solid and translucent, advancing
d receding surfaces, changing hourly and with
e seasons

terrace, running along the edge of the pool, and a
lf-covered patio up the slope link the main house
th the studio-living wing 1. Inside the main block
ere are several levels. Stairs lead down from the

entrance to the den (illuminated from above
through vinyl ceiling) which is built above the
kitchen 9 and has a high balcony onto the dining
area below

The main feature of the two-level living room 2, 3
is the great stone fireplace (rising above the roof
line) and the angled sofa (winter cover, tan wool;
summer white vinyl), built against the upper floor
level, which faces both fire and windows onto the
terrace over the pool, with distant views of the
gorge of the Hudson River. Steps cut out of the
rock lead down to the dining area, 10 feet below

The wall holding a Chinese embroidery panel is of
heavily textured dark green plaster embedded with
hemlock needles. In winter, the flagstones of the
living room floor are covered by a Caucasian

4

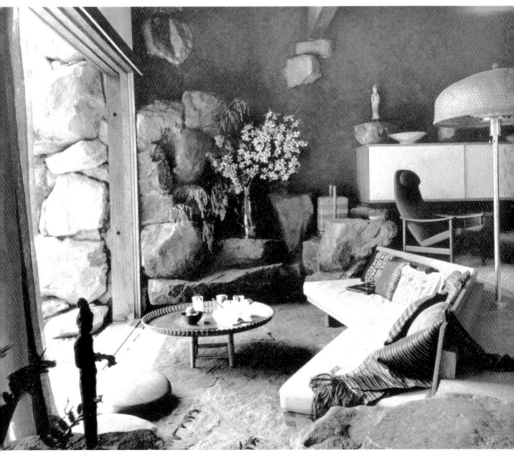

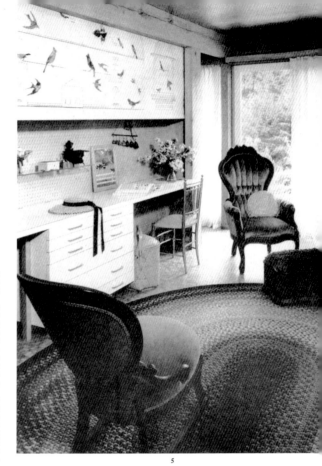

House at Dragon Rock
Architect, Russel Wright

Khilim rug: in summer, a tatami mat. The Danish teak chair **4** also changes from Italian sheepskin cover to blue fabric. The lamp shade is a far eastern basket, the trays are Indian brass

His daughter's bedroom **5** leads out to a terrace 22 feet above the pool. The walls and ceiling are covered in pink metallic foil paper and the window curtains are of pink ninon net over white Swiss eyelet linen. On the one-inch-square mosaic oak floor laid by Miller Brothers is a Hummel Maid multicolour braided rug. The Victorian armchair is upholstered in olive green velour, the rocker in pale blue. Stratopanel drawers and cupboards in white Formica are built-in here, as throughout the house

This room, together with the housekeeper's room adjoining, constitute the 'harem wing' with private bathroom **6**. This has a sunken tub into which water flows from the rocks like a waterfall (temperature controls by the Swiss Simix Company). The floor, in Murano glass tile in five shades of blue set in vivid blue mortar, is floodlit through a Filon luminous ceiling. Exotic butterflies mounted between plastic decorate the sliding door

The studio **7**, **8** also has alternating winter and summer furnishings. In winter white screens carry formalised patterns of local flora; the natural-coloured Japanese sofa fabric becomes bronze-coloured and light cushion covers become earth-coloured; the Harry Gitlin counter-balanced light loses its white linen accordion cover; an Icelandic sheep rug replaces the Siamese willow matting on the pegged oak plank floor. The desk is faced in white Formica with Stratopanel drawers. The chrome-based round rotating table was designed by Russel Wright, using laminated plastic

The kitchen **9**, blasted out of solid rock, is in a neutral scheme of natural white oak, white enamel appliances, white Formica, and Armstrong bleached cork floor, with a luminous ceiling lit through panels of Dow's Styrofoam. Beyond the sink is a fine view of the waterfall. The built-in gate-leg table is designed by Russel Wright; to the left a pass-through to the dining room through a 14-foot counter-balanced cabinet which can be pushed up to a pocket in the ceiling

Photos Louis Reens (2, 7, 8, 9) & Alexander Georges

5

6

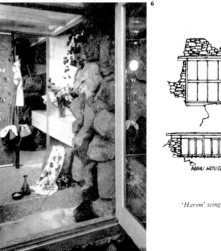

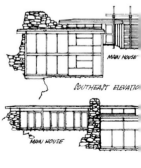

SOUTHEAST ELEVATION

MAIN HOUSE

MAIN HOUSE

'Harem' wing   Living-dini

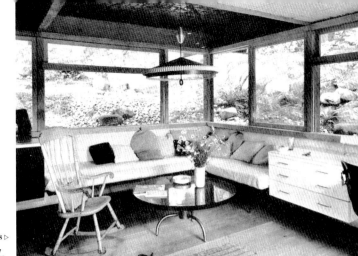

8 ▷

7

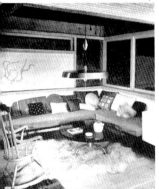

9 ▷

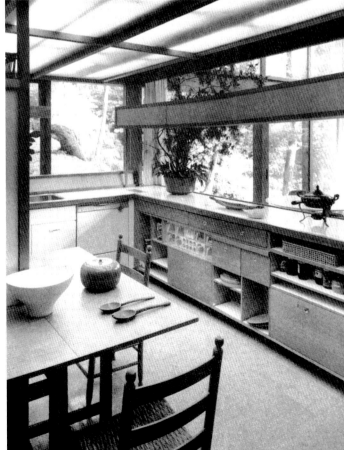

WEST ELEVATION

STUDIO

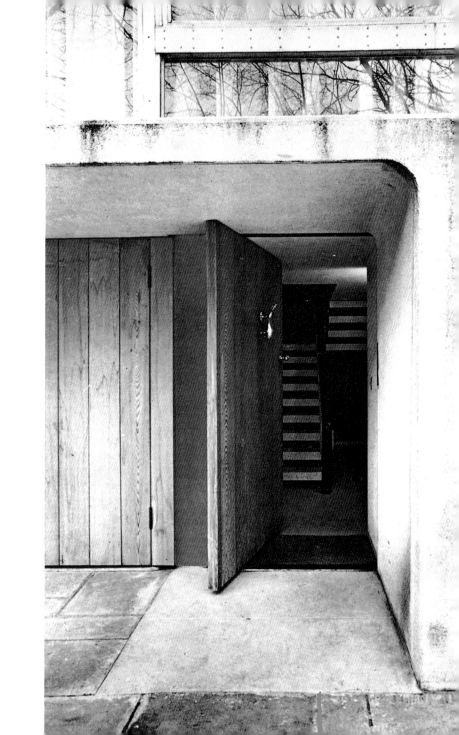

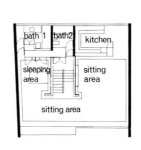

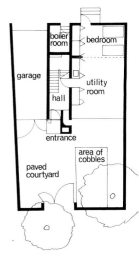

use in Kensington, London for Mr and Mrs de Trafford

itect Timothy Rendle ARIBA
e I in association with Sir Hugh Casson,
lle Conder and Partners

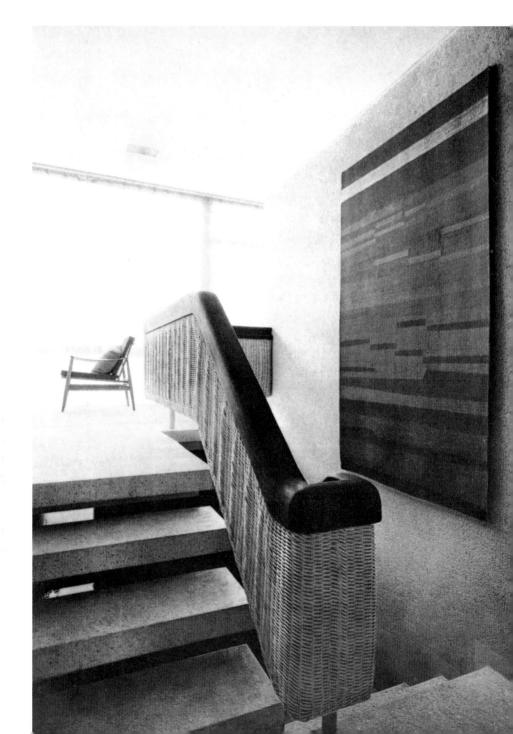

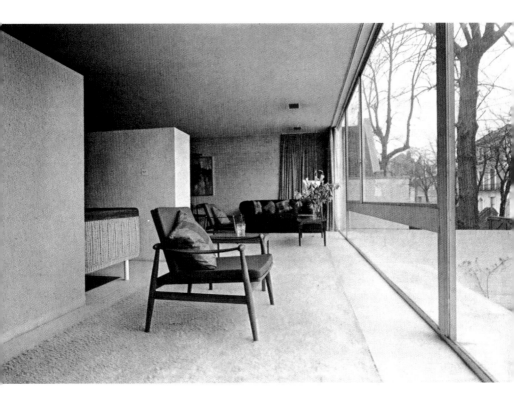

House in Kensington, London for Mr and Mrs de Trafford

Architect Timothy Rendle ARIBA

The front door swings inward, pivoting at a point some three-quarters across its extreme width. Closed, it fits back against the concrete face and into the frame formed by the structure to present, with the doors of the garage, a continuous solid panelling of 6·5 cm natural cedar.

It gives the key to this large *pied-à-terre* built in a quiet residential street of the city to serve the needs of a family often living in the country, but entertaining a good deal in Town.

The architect was given a free hand to design a house combining elements of luxury, with ease of maintenance. With this freedom he has used two materials, wood and concrete, which dominate both the structure and the internal surfaces and shapes. On the exterior the surface of the concrete is soon weathered: in the interior the walls reappear with white hammered rendering. End walls of the main living area are plaster-finished, with grass paper keeping the general tone. Floors are of white terrazzo with natural long-haired carpeting set into a shallow well through the living areas. Stair treads are of precast terrazzo. Precast terrazzo, too, forms the bathroom

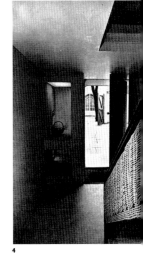

The house is maintained without resident help: often it is unoccupied, but tradesmen's deliveries can be made through the ingenious niche in the hallway.

4

House in Kensington, London

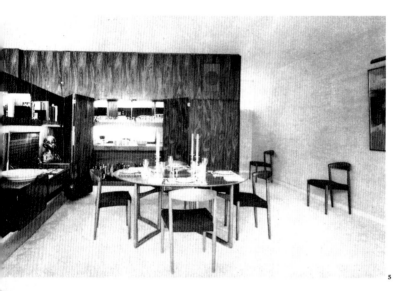

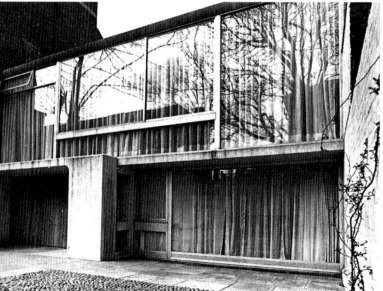

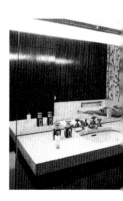

components—the hand basin and the form into which the bath is set, 7.

As can be seen from the plan, the house is more than usually 'open': sitting, dining, bedroom and kitchen areas are divided by timber cupboard units which spread from the central staircase wall. The dark, rich tones of the rosewood impart necessary warmth and intimacy. Curtains are of Indian raw silk. There are well-placed accents of colour and texture; the tapestry on the staircase wall 2 was custom woven by Ruth Harris, the balustrade was created by a cane designer, Kennet Taylor, ARCA, working on the spot weaving directly into the metal frame lining the rosewood handrail. The chair in the foreground 3 is from France & Son A/S, as is also the dining table 5; the dining chairs are from Finmar. The bed 8 is orange-covered. A few modern paintings add focal interest.

The kitchen 9 is screened, not shut off from the dining-end and is doubly accessible through the hatchway in the cupboard fitment.

Some of the seven young children of the family often accompany their parents and are accommodated in the flexible room 10, which covers that part of the ground-level not taken up by garage, entrance hall and utility room. An all-white effect is carried through the vinyl flooring and the Marley room-divider, which enables the space to be broken up into bedrooms, used for extra entertaining or turned into a separate flatlet with its own toilet unit and a 'kitchen' unit both completely shut into folding doors on each side of the room door. Heating throughout the house is by ducted air from a gas-filled boiler.

5

6

PHOTOS: CRISPIN EURICH

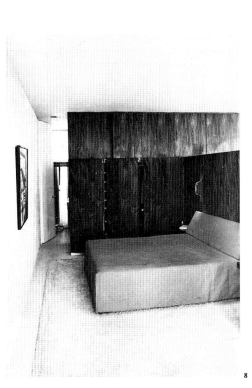

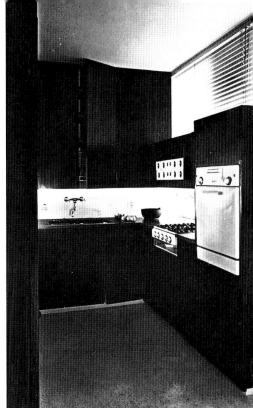

8

9

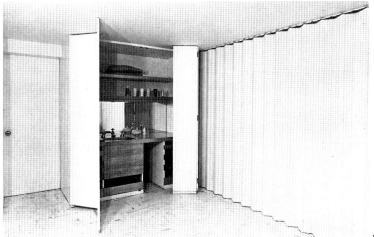

10

Villa near Tokyo for Mr Matsuura

Designed by Ichigaya Office, Rengo Sekkeisha

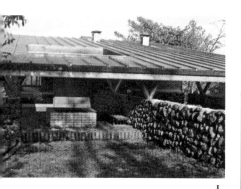

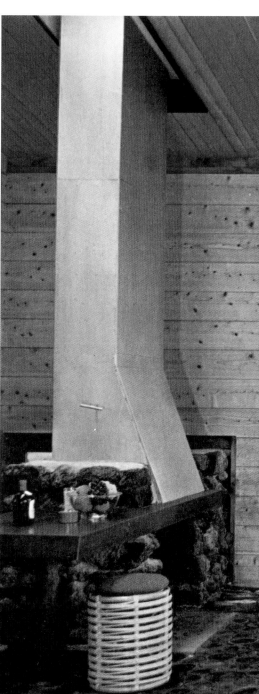

1

2

Escape from a shell in the city is not retreat to another shell in the Japanese countryside. It means living with Nature with the minimum of 'break' between earth and floor, between air and interior space. So that this house has continuity with the hills in its floor levels, in the lines of its wide sloping roof: the large eaves are stretched lower over the sloping ground, and under them a car can drive in. Where the ground falls away to the south-east on the opposite side of the house the floor is extended to a sundeck above the larch trees growing on the wide hill-side 6.

Space and proportions have been fixed as factors common to a number of

PHOTOS: F. MURASAWA
COURTESY *Kenchiku Bunka*

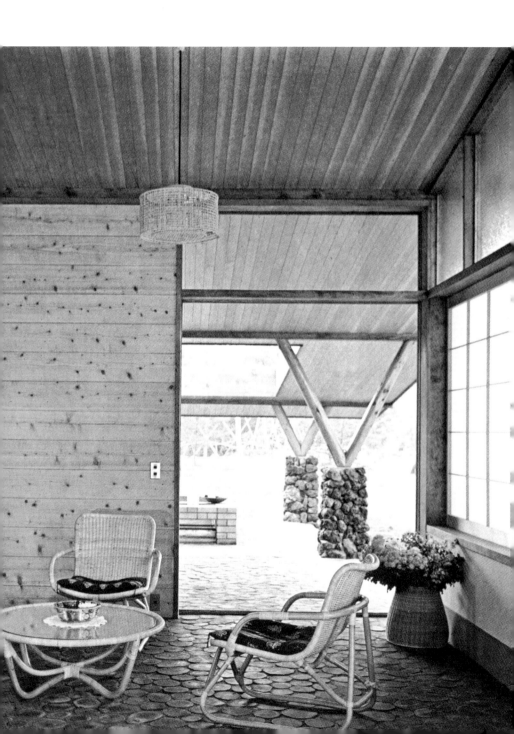

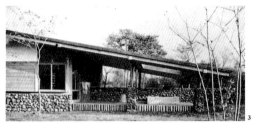

3

**Villa near Tokyo
for Mr Matsuura**

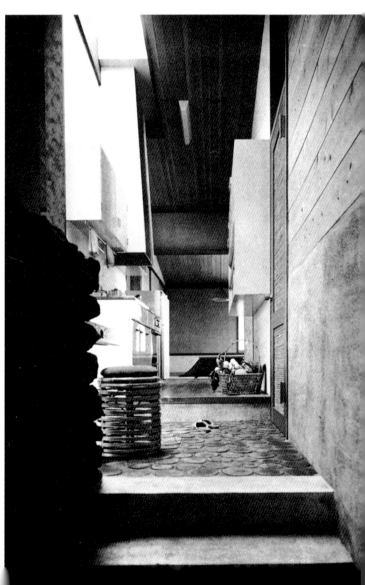

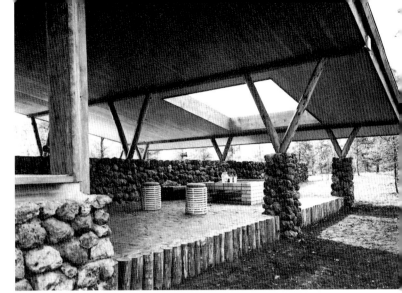

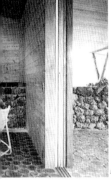

5

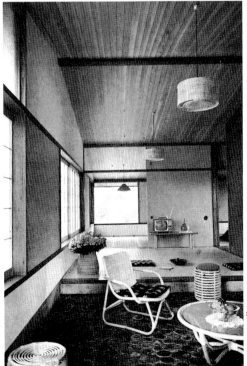

6

8

villas built by the Ichigaya Office. But individual arrangement is demanded to achieve advantageous siting and to suit the desires of the owners. In Mr Matsuura's house the wall of Assam hot stones screens the car from the terrace 7, where barbecues can be held on hot evenings. This wall continues into the interior to a stove built of the same stone: the chimney is supported on a lintel which continues to form a dining table.

According to mood and weather the wall at this end can be partially 'removed' and the room and terrace are continuous in the floor of un-squared nutwood blocks. There is then an uninterrupted view from the guest room, a raised sleeping area spread with wisteria-vine *tatami*, background 8.

The ceilings are lined with Japanese cedar plywood and surfaces of walls and fitments are generally of Lauan flooring with clear lacquer finish. 4 shows a view through that half of the villa behind the line of the wall to other sleeping rooms, food storage and necessary utility space.

PHOTOS: F. MURASAWA
COURTESY *Kenchiki Bunka*

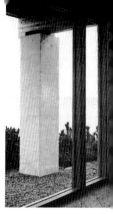

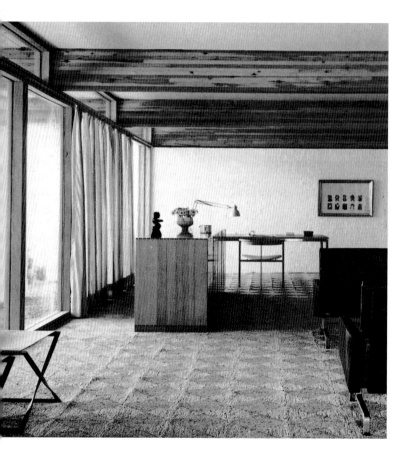

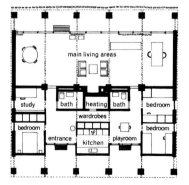

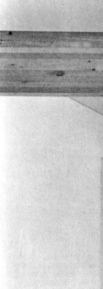

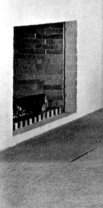

study

bath   heating   bath   bedroom

main living areas

wardrobes

bedroom

entrance   kitchen   playroom   bedroom

Family house near Copenhagen

Architects Hanna and Poul Kjærholm

On a small site overlooking the Sound north of the city, the architects built this single-storey house for themselves and their two young children.

The structure is a series of white-washed brick pillars which carry six large cross-beams of laminated wood on which rests the flat built-up roof. Extending the length of the house, the large living/dining/work-room faces the Sound: the bedrooms and kitchen are around and behind a central walled unit containing two bathrooms and the furnace room which provides controlled floor heating throughout the house.

Interior walls are either of the same white-washed brick as the pillars or of untreated pinewood which merges with the doors and cupboards of the same wood. From every room there is direct access to the garden through the window-walls. The floor of the main room is completely covered with natural-colour Spanish matting with curtains of natural-colour pure silk.

All the furniture has been designed by Mr Kjærholm except for the book-shelves-cupboard unit which was designed by Mogens Koch.

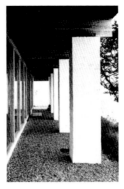

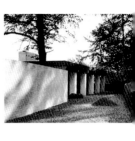

PHOTOS: K. HELMER-PETERSEN

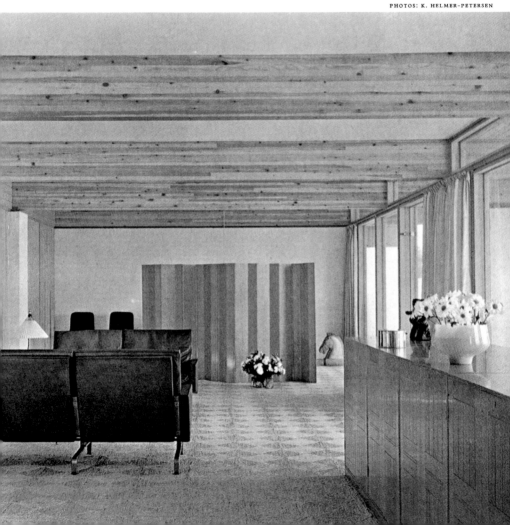

Paris apartments

Designer Jean Royère

2, 3
Bedroom-in-a-corridor, the bed co
cealed by two sliding doors in o
Desk, bookshelves, white-painted c
boards are ranged on the left. Wind
curtains and bedcover in a red/bl
on white diabolo print by l'Impress
des Dauphins. The pouffe is cove
in white fur velvet.

4
Student's bedroom with built-in b
book-shelves and hanging desk in c
the desk front pulls down and out
form a small table. Dark brown vel
covers the bed: the light-blue ceil
creates space, a feeling augmented
the curtains—a bird print on satin,
l'Impression des Dauphins.

5
Fireplace in dark brown brick w
marble surround: it incorporates
storage space and cupboards with
sliding doors.

1
Living-room with curved sofa and armchair in pearl-grey velvet on a violet
carpet: on the white walls is a tapestry
by Picart le Doux—green, mauve and
pink on a black ground. Cabinets are
of sycamore with panels of yellow
fabric: on the white sheepskin rug a
black Formica-topped table.

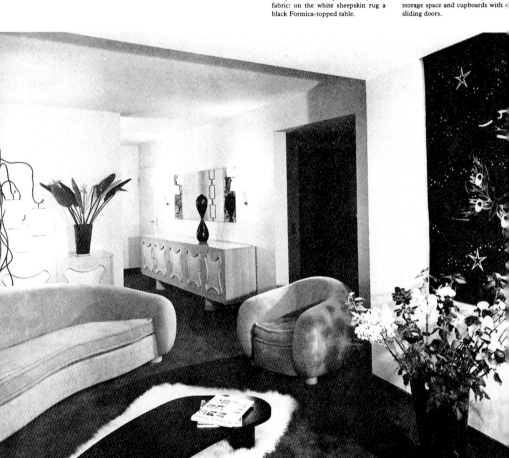

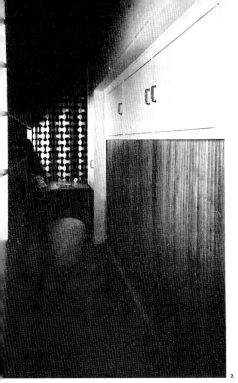

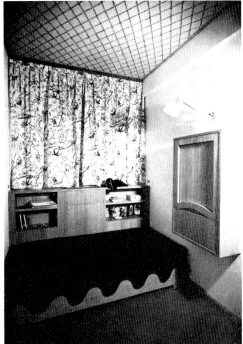

2

4

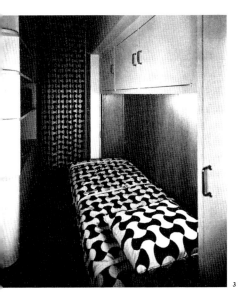

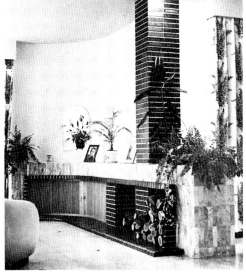

3

5

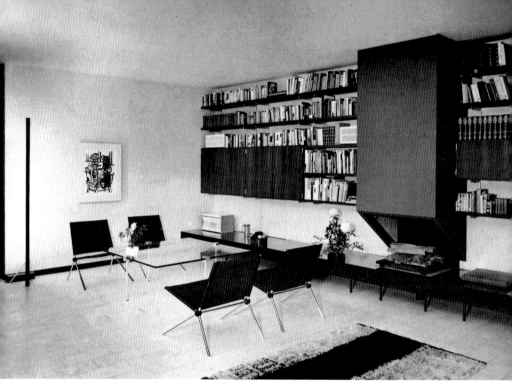

PHOTO: INGE GOERTZ-BAUER

Living-room of a house at Düsseldorf

Designer Professor Paul Schneider-Esleben

The sharp, simple use of black and white is broken only by the teak book-shelving on either side of the chimney, itself formed from black sheet steel lined with firebrick. Interest is added through texture—on the white marble floor is a grey-to-black Rya rug, de-signed and made by Kirsti Ilvessalo of Finland: on the walls raw white silk meets the white plaster ceiling: on fine chromium-plated steel frames, the chairs have black leather seats and backs. The chairs are made by Hans Kaufeld to the design of Paul Schneider-Esleben, who also designed the glass table.

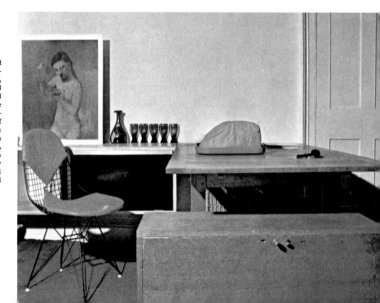

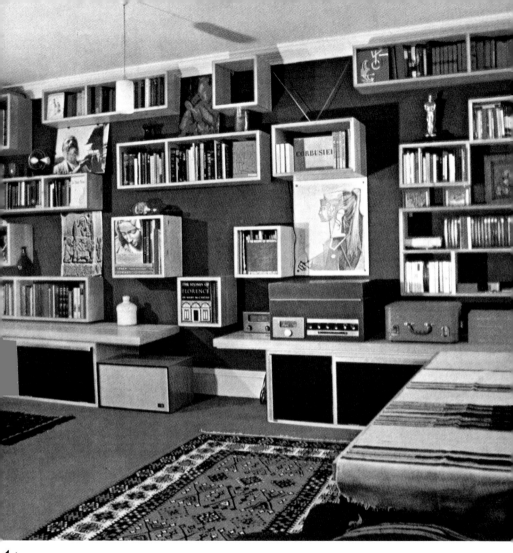

◀▲ An architectural-photographer
with wide interests, John Donat has
in consequence a varied collection of
books, documents, records and un-
classified trivia. To accommodate it,
one wall of his apartment has been
given an exciting pattern of storage
units planned on a module, deter-
mined by the overall size of groups of
books. Cut from pine, the units are
attached directly and simply to the
brick walls.

A Turkish *Khilim* rug echoes the warm
colours and textures of covers and
woods.

Apartment in Camden Town, London *Designer* John Donat ARIBA

Holiday Home at Hald Beach, Kattegat

Architect Ole Hagen MAA

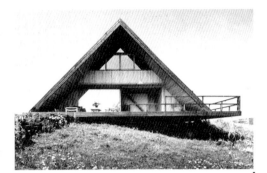

1

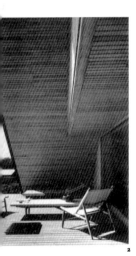

2

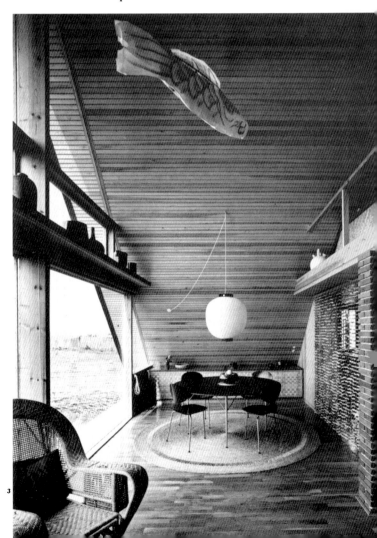

3

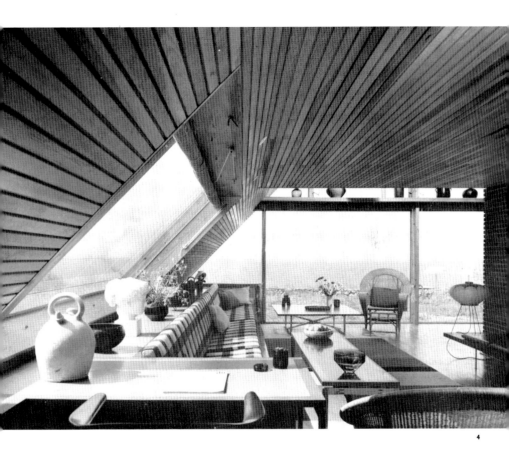

4

t the top of high cliffs on Zealand's ʒrthern coast this tent-like house has ʒen sited so that its 'open ends' face ʒt over the sea at one end and into the ʒuntryside at the other.

is the holiday home of the architect, ʒs wife and their children.

ʒhe roof extends to the balcony as walls ʒeltering a deep, wide terrace on ʒe south, from where large sliding ʒors lead into the living-room. ʒminating this room is the fireplace ʒ dark brick with hearth and exten- ʒns to each side formed from a slab ʒ dark soapstone.

ʒhe architect himself designed the ʒg, bench-like sofa with its black/ ʒite/grey check cushions, the work- ʒ desk, the sideboard and sofa tables.

At the other, northern, end 3, the room opens up to a double height dining area having a magnificent view over the Kattegat through the glass gable— in fine weather from the open balcony. The kitchen, separated from the dining area by a light bead curtain, has walls tessellated in light blue and cupboard doors finished in similar tones.

Walls and ceilings of the house are finished with pine strip and the par- quet floor is of oak, the wood providing a fitting background for fine hand- woven Danish rugs, and for the archi- tect's collection of ceramics and chairs by various Danish designers.

All window areas are double glazed and hot-air central heating is controlled from a boiler room in the cellar.

PHOTOS STRUWING

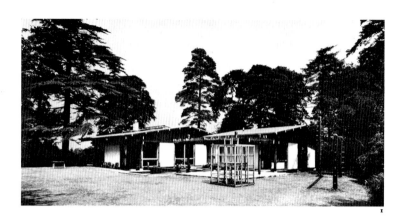

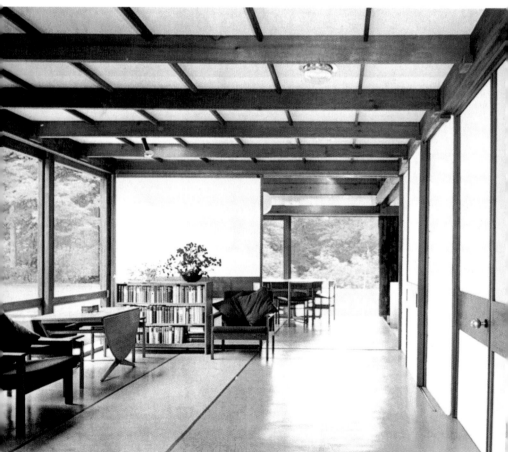

ouse in **Keston, Kent**

chitects Howell, Killick, Partridge & Amis

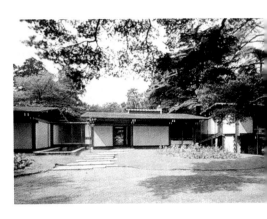

gether with a site made beautiful by well-placed cedars and pines the hitects were given great freedom to ign this family house on the edge of Kentish Weald. The only require-nt was that living, parents' and ldren's areas should be clearly ined: as the site was not suitable for atrium construction, the architects ated a central living area with the ldren's wing to the left, and the ents' wing to the right, strung out oss its width, 3. Visual interest and cticality are served by raising the ents' wing and its balcony over the port, right. The house is completely identified with the landscape and with the wild-life which gambols between the edge of the wood and the house. Construction throughout is of cedar with the structural details providing the main decorative element of the interior. Timber-framed sliding doors, finished with white P.V.C. panels create areas of privacy or a more intimate atmosphere.

The entrance opens into the large hall-lounge area, 2 leading into the dining area beyond, and from the dining area a cosy sitting-room opens to the right. The chairs, dining chairs and tables are from France & Co. Other fittings

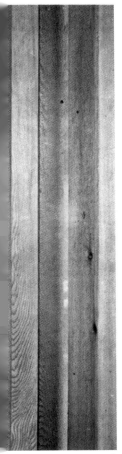

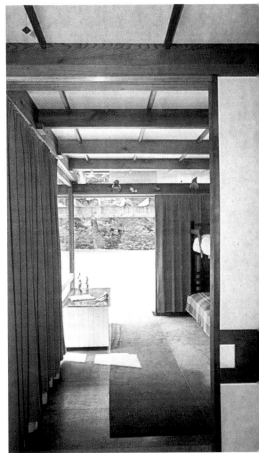

2

4

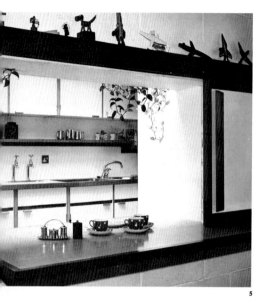

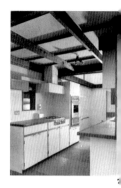

House in Keston, Kent

5

are generally planned for the house by the architects or made by the owner. Kitchen fitments, include the broad through-surface to the playroom, which allows quick meals to be served to the boys, and provides space for more elaborate cooking preparations. **6**, parents' room: **8**, the north-east corner of the house with the sitting room: **9**, the dining-room from the lawn and woods at rear, **1**.

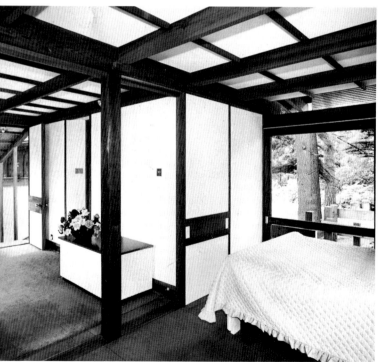

6

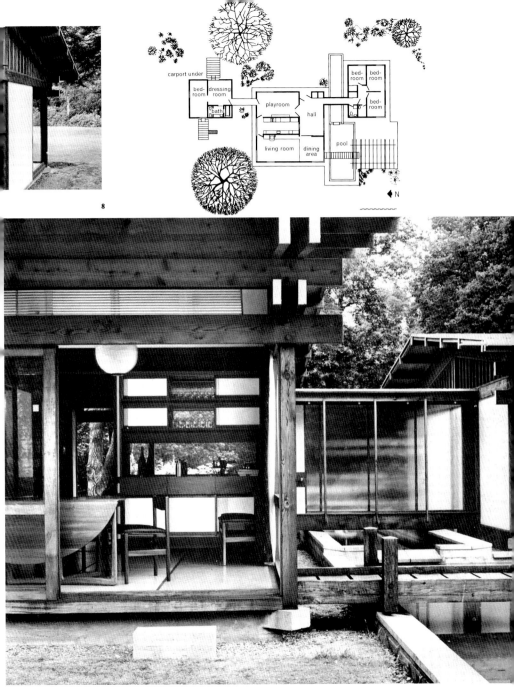

carport under

bed-
room | dressing
room

bath

playroom

living room | dining
area

hall

bed-
room | bed-
room

bed-
room

pool

N

8

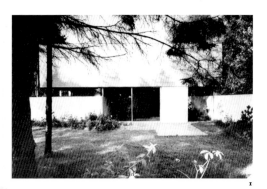

1

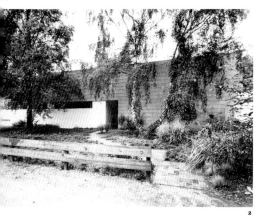

2

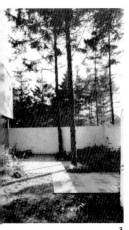

3

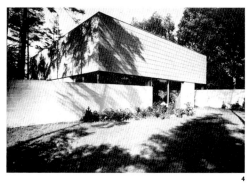

4

**House plus Studio
near Hamburg**
Architect Timm Ohrt

5

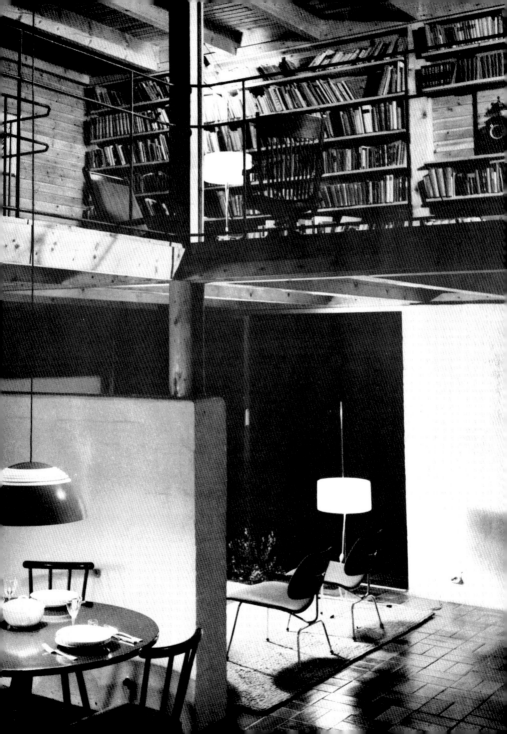

House and atelier near Zürich
architect Helmut Rauber

The stony path seems to lead from the road only to a sunny meadow above the Lake of Zürich. The impression is hardly disturbed by the small doorway to the passage between garage and main building. On to this passageway open entrances to the atelier of one of Switzerland's most successful and individual advertising agents and to the private house of Mr and Mrs Halpern and their children.
Most frequented rooms of both atelier and house are situated on the ground floor: 'service' rooms are beneath in the space created by the slope of the hillside, although here too is the main conference room and director's office 5 opening direct to the terrace and pool through the sliding glass wall. The pool and terrace link, visually and physically, the otherwise quite separate parts of the building and

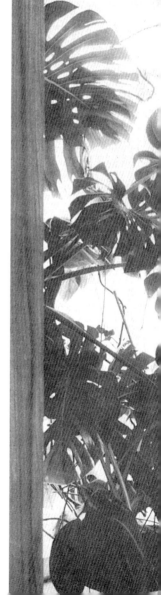

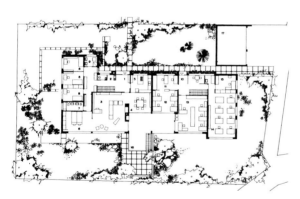

GROUND FLOOR PLAN

1, entrance private house.
2, wardrobe.
3, living-room.
4, dining-room.
5, kitchen.
6, bedroom.
7, bath.
8, children's rooms.
9, children's washroom and laundry.
10, entrance advertising agency.
11, reception.
12, office media department.
13, account executives.
14, atelier.
15, treasurer.
16, terrace.
17, garage.

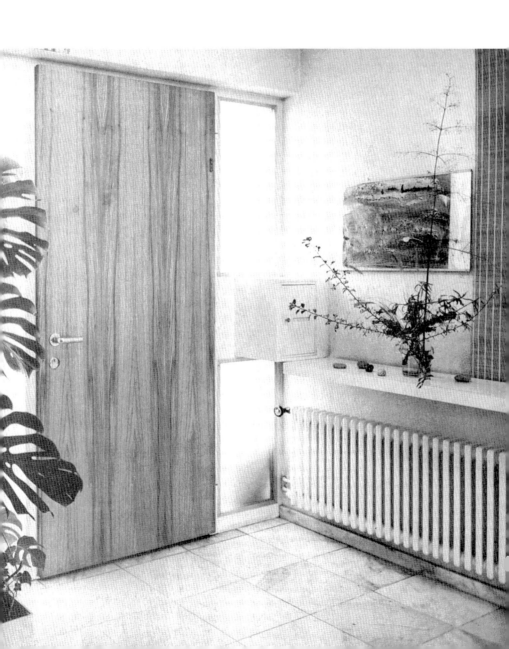

House and atelier near Zürich

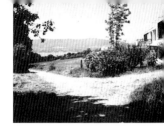

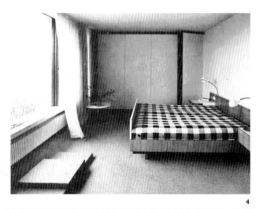

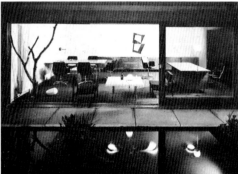

4

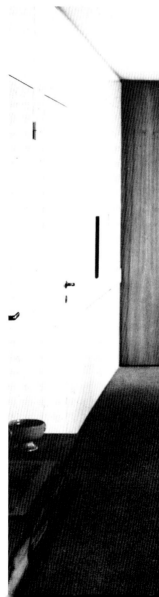

5

the whole structure of the building is orientated towards this, the southern aspect with views to the lake and city **2, 3.**

The exterior walls are of white-painted concrete, the flat roof, also of concrete successfully harmonising the mass of the building in the hillside.

All finishes and fittings were conceived as an integral part of the building—thus room depths and heights were planned to accommodate standard units: wardrobes, kitchen cupboards and living-room fitments are all in the Wohngebau range with matt white finishes. The doors too are painted white. The entrance hall of the house, pages 18/19, has a floor of light grey Swiss marble. A sliding door between living room and the main bedroom, with some other wood components, are of a pale oiled timber which warms but does not darken the overall light, cool effect of the interior. From the hall open the three children's rooms and the remaining space is divided up, first by a sliding-screen between living area and parents' room **4** then by the fireplace wall between living and dining areas **6, 10** and by the all-embracing wall fitments of the kitchen **7, 8.** The result: in the house, the same directness and clarity which mark the campaigns to sell coffee, clothes and cooking-stoves, which are dreamed up in the business end of the building.

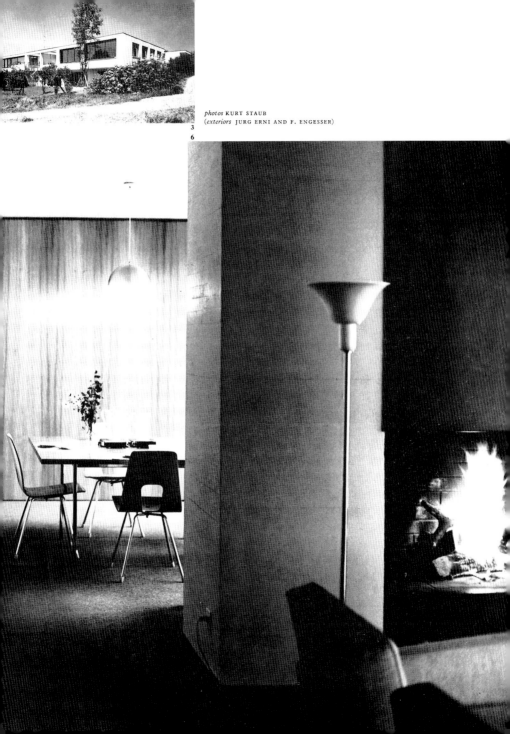

photos KURT STAUB
(*exteriors* JURG ERNI AND F. ENGESSER)

3
6

7, the serving hatch to the dining area.

8, the kitchen with Wohngebau fitments and Therma electrical appliances. The Therma cooking table includes hot-plates which swing up when not in use, to reveal stainless steel mixing basins dropped into appropriate cavities.

9, the fireplace wall is faced with black steel: furniture is by Knoll International with the exception of the long chair by le Corbusier, of chrome steel upholstered in cow-skin.

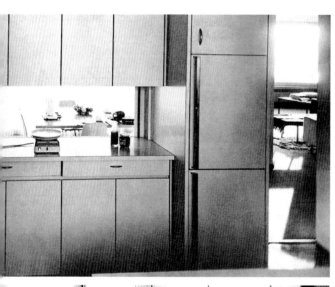

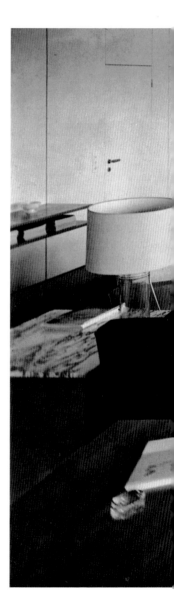

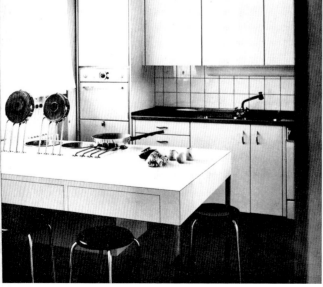

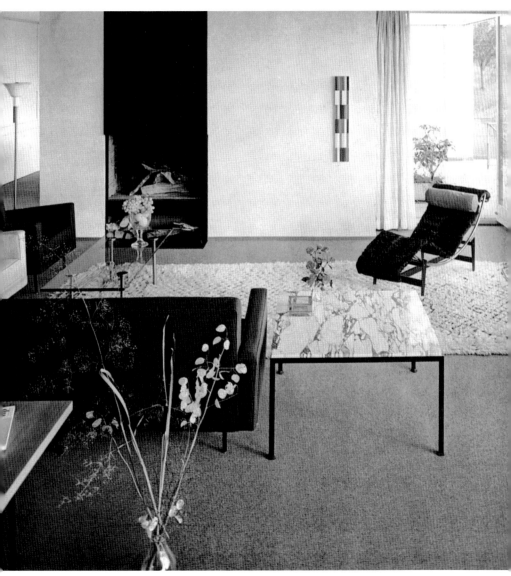

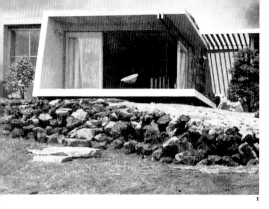

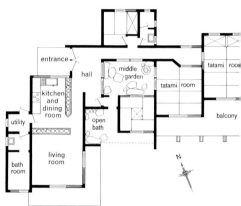

entrance

hall

middle garden

tatami room

tatami room

kitchen and dining room

utility

open bath

balcony

bath room

living room

N

1

2
3

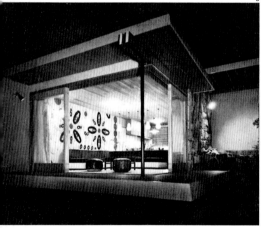

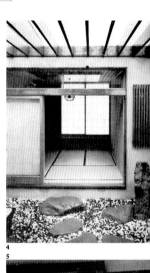

4
5

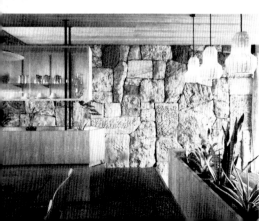

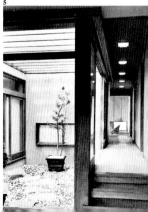

Ko Residence

Architects GAD and Associates

...ressing its horizontal lines the
...tects of this house have emphas-
...he sloping site and the changing
... levels—used partly to accom-
...ate the site, partly to give
...nism to the structural effect.
...truction is mainly of wood,
...ever possible using single, large-
...n timbers, where necessary iron
...es.
...e are two distinct areas of the
..., one influenced by Western
..., e.g. in its seating elements, and
...taining traditional characteristics,

...living-room from the south.
...chen.
...er garden and *tatami* room.
...trance hall and inner garden.
...th aspect from the east.
...ing-room.

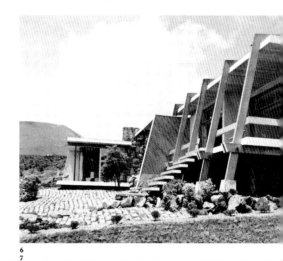

6
7

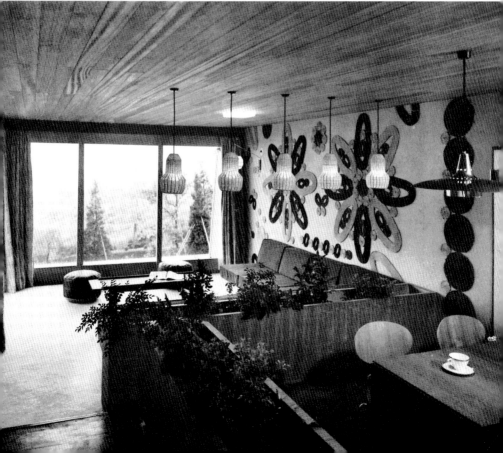

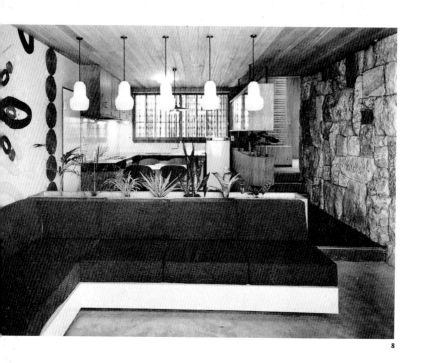

8

The Ko Residence

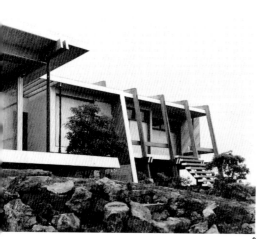

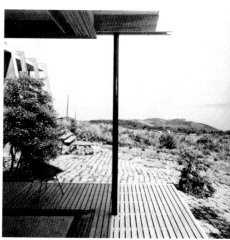

9 10

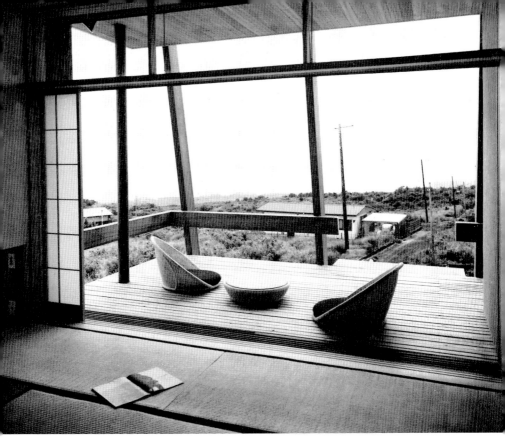

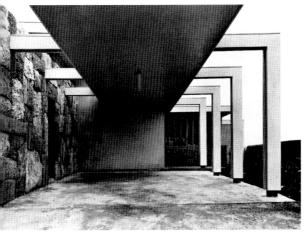

as in the *tatami* rooms **9–11**. These areas are unified by the inner garden **4, 5** which also serves as a passageway and gives light to the entrance hall. While features suited to modern life have been introduced in the main living areas **3, 7, 8** the house suggests continuing use of the materials which have served Japanese building so well for so long. The large-section timbers have become a definite element in the design: *igusa*, used in the making of *tatami* mats, is used too for the flower decorations designed by Teruko Yoshida **2, 7**: the *tatami*, all-purpose, rooms are divided from the other areas and from the exterior by light sliding-screens.

8, dining-room from living-room.
9, *tatami* rooms, south side.
11, balcony of *tatami* rooms.
12, carport.

photos FUMIO MURASAWA
courtesy Kenchiku Bunka

11
12

House for Mr Barz, near Stuttgart
architect Harry G. H. Lie

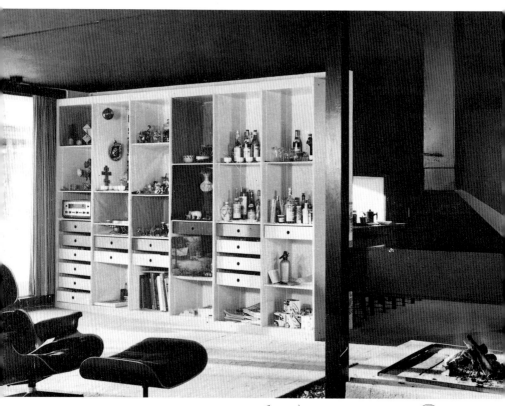

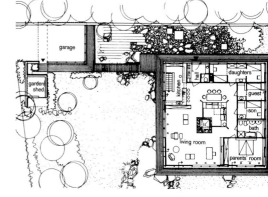

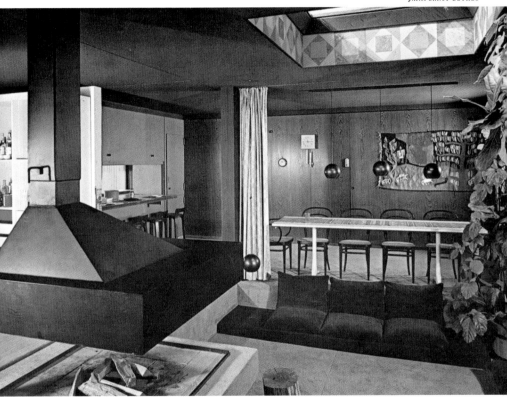

spacious and luxurious house has
ted from the essentially simple
on which it is built.

pine-timber construction (on
rete foundations and basement,
ce rooms) used a basic module of
metres which accommodated
dard units throughout. Steel
ns, concealed, support the roof and
nuous ceiling, the roof itself
isting of a layer each of boarding,
matting, pressure-compensating
t, roofing felt, cork tiles, plus three
phalt felt, topped with gravel.
dow-wall panels of double-glazed

or Linex-Glasal units also help to
stiffen the whole structure. They open
as doors to the surrounding terrace or
swing up as windows.
Dark brown painted panels form the
suspended ceilings: in children's
rooms and guest-room they conceal
the warm-air heating system—else-
where this is suspended in the basement ceilings.
The heart of the house is the sunken
fireplace, surrounded by fair-faced
concrete and fireclay tiles with a hood
of double-walled black iron sheeting.
The whole remaining area of the living

space is covered by sandy, long-
haired Perlon carpet.
Colour is used in the dining alcove in
a Lurçat tapestry and in the frieze of
tiles around the roof-light: it is used
in the wall fitment 1 in jewel colours
of emerald and ruby and purple and
yellow to line the alcoves or to paint
occasional drawer-fronts and in small
'islands' formed by chairs.
Curtains are used only for screening
certain alcoves, e.g. dressing-rooms:
the deep overhang of the roof and the
excellent siting of the house makes
them unnecessary. (And on pages 34/5)

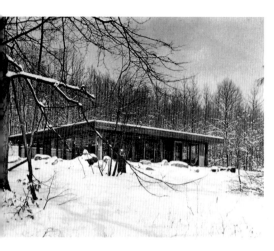

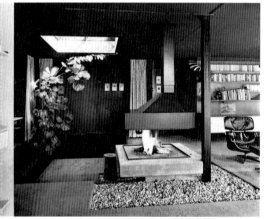

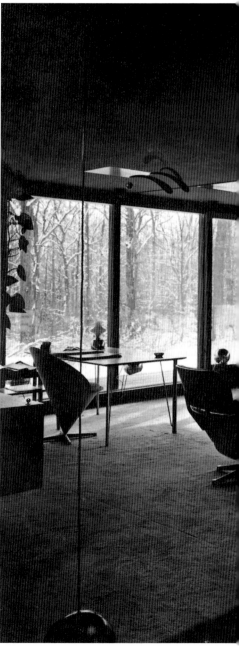

House for Mr Barz, near Stuttgart

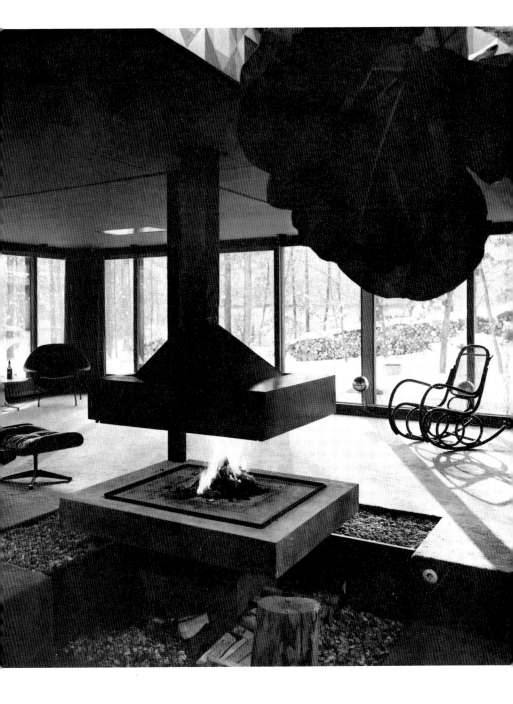

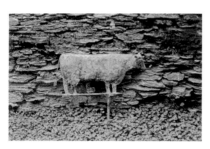

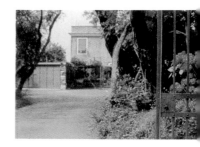

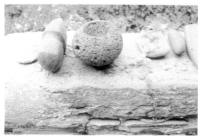

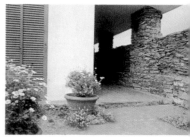

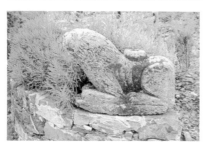

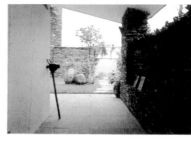

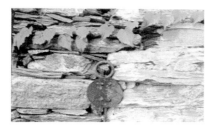

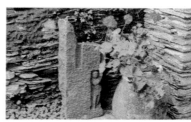

A home among the olive groves of Liguria
for Leo Lionni

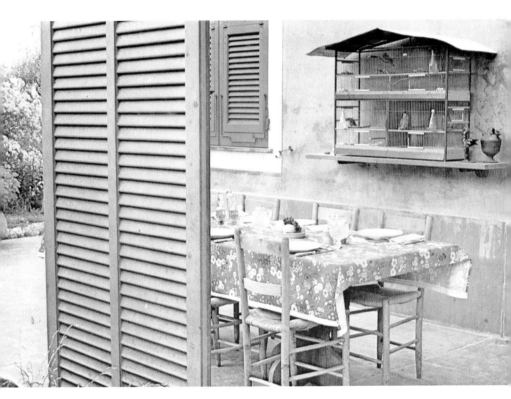

Like other beautiful stretches of coastline the area around the Gulf of Tigullio has lost much of its quiet and magic spell and only in the hinterland can they be recaptured.

Among the olive groves Leo Lionni found a typical Ligurian country house with pink fresco finish, green shutters and slate floors.

American editor, painter and *avant-garde* designer, Leo Lionni has an apartment in New York but he decided that here, in the midst of this countryside he would make his home and a home for the treasures which he has collected during years of travel. His son, Louis, an architect, collaborated and advised on necessary details of structure and design: the interior has been entirely rethought but local, or at least Italian, materials have been used so that while there is no false rusticity, neither has an alien feeling been created. The result is a setting in which the large collection of pieces are grouped with selective discipline: sometimes an important piece is placed in juxtaposition with a small, simple thing but the whole shows evidence of an informed and affectionate knowledge of the artist and his craft.

Not only inside the house but on paths, patio and garden walls, places have been found for some of the owner's treasures. Above, a spot for eating.

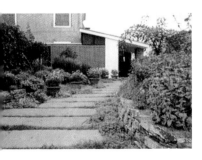

A home among the olive groves of Liguria

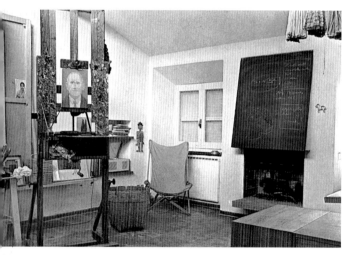

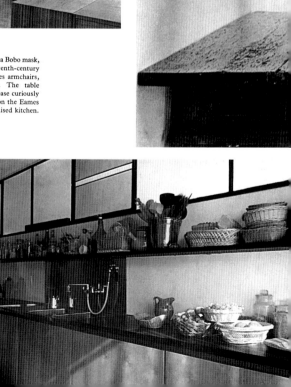

In the studio: the work-table, travel souvenirs, Indian marionettes, Aztec figure, all part of a traveller's collection. There is obvious pleasure from the 'islands' of controlled disorder in the midst of a highly ordered whole. In the living-room: a Calder mobile, a sculpture by Giacometti, a Bobo mask, Persian carpet, seventeenth-century German cupboard, Eames armchairs, Sarfatti-Arteluce lamps. The table rests on a wood brazier base curiously reminiscent of the base on the Eames chair. Below, the modernised kitchen.

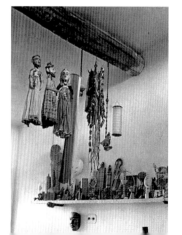

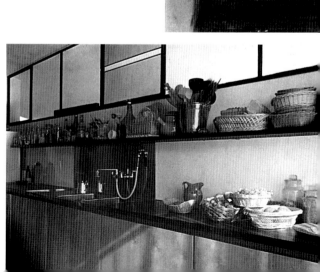

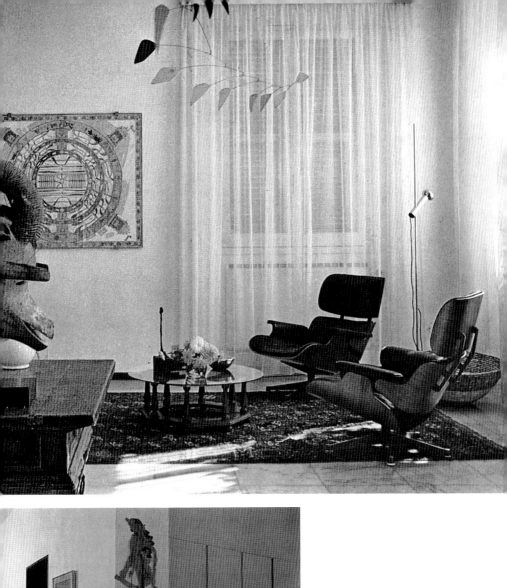
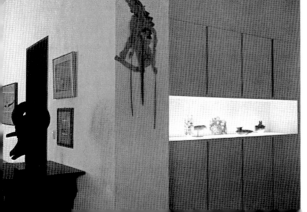

A home among the olive groves of Liguria

Again the living-room: le Corbusier chair, George Nelson sofas by Herman Miller, Mexican figurines on the shelf, in a sudden quickening which vivifies the rigorous rhythm of the decoration. On the walls works by Ben Shahn, Morandi, Klee, Boudin, a Dogon mask, Katchina dolls, a group of Coptic, Indian, Maya and Persian objects. The Bobo mask, penitentes sculptures from New Mexico. The floor is in white Carrara marble, the shelves in ash, the lamp is from Arteluce.

At right, the door to the studio and a mosaic in the studio: below it, a Calder mobile and two works by the American primitive Werner.

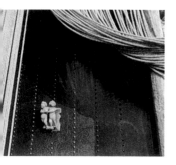

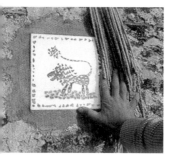

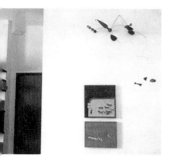

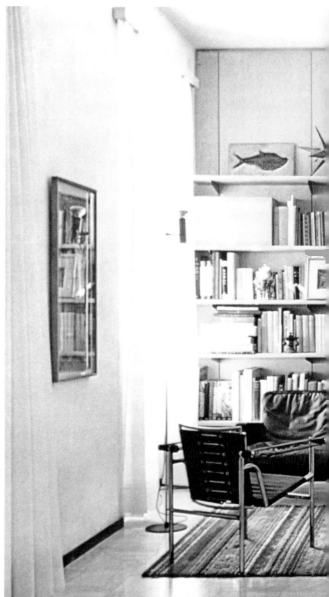

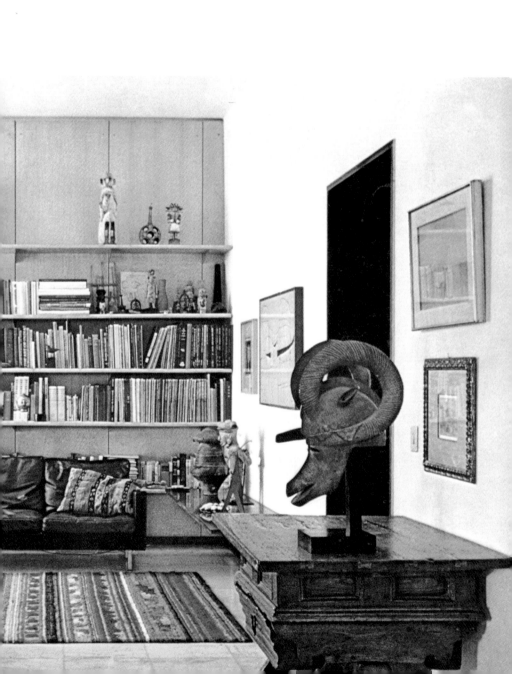

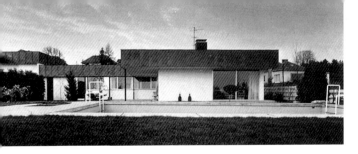

The Architect's Home near Vienna

architect Carl Aubö

photos JOWA PARASINI

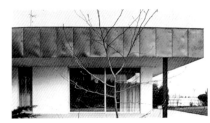

This is a large one-storey house on the hills slightly above Vienna and over looking the city.

The wide, overhanging copper roof supported by a steel frame construction filled by exposed concrete, painted white, or by sliding glass walls.

The interior is arranged for a large family so that sleeping areas are situated in one arm of the L-shaped building separate from living areas in the other. They are separated not only by the structure but, perhaps even more strongly, by furnishing.

The whole house has curtains

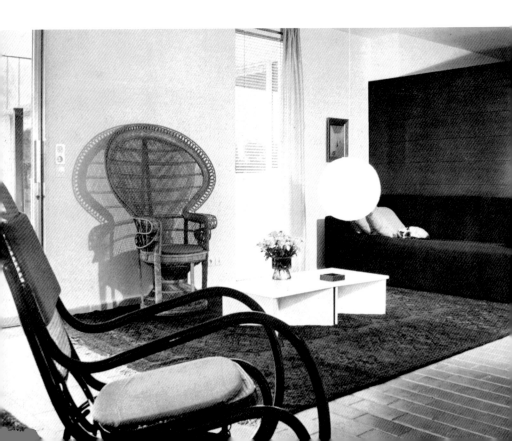

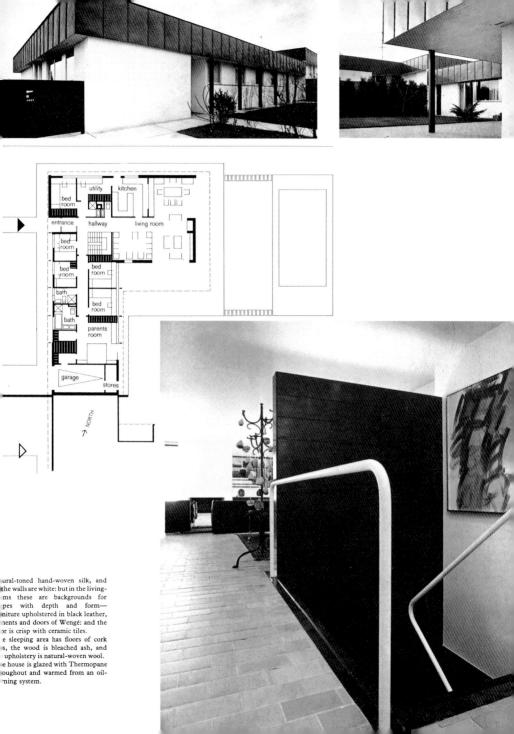

ural-toned hand-woven silk, and the walls are white: but in the living- ms these are backgrounds for pes with depth and form— niture upholstered in black leather, ents and doors of Wengé: and the r is crisp with ceramic tiles.

e sleeping area has floors of cork s, the wood is bleached ash, and upholstery is natural-woven wool.

e house is glazed with Thermopane oughout and warmed from an oil- ning system.

bed room
utility
kitchen
entrance
hallway
living room
bed room
bed room
bath
bed room
bath
parents room
garage
stores

NORTH

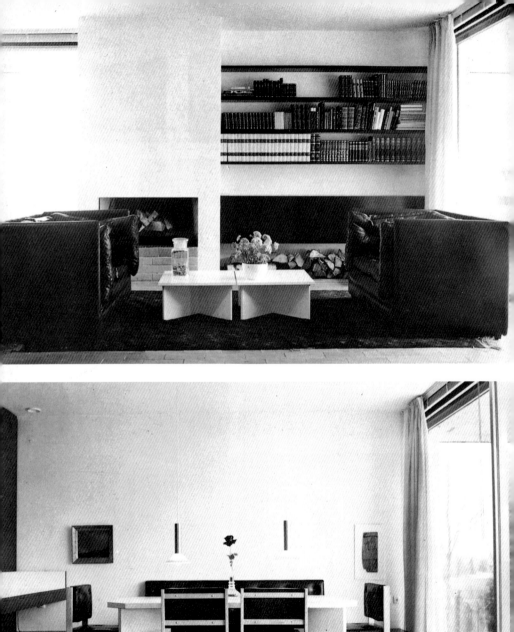

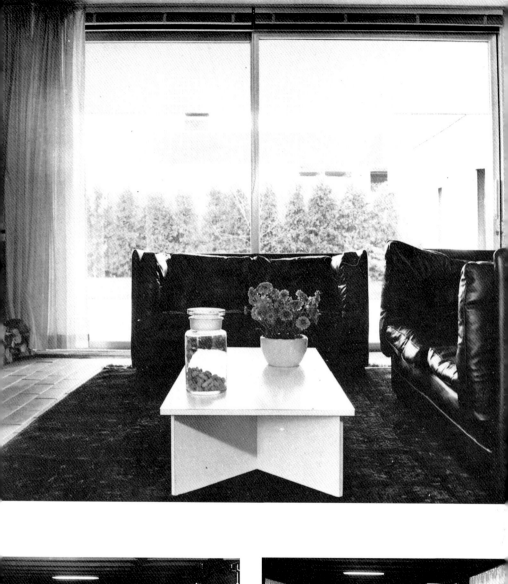
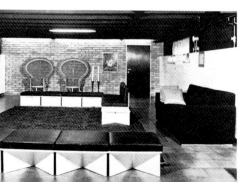
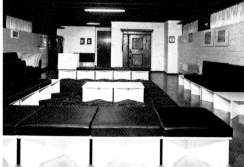

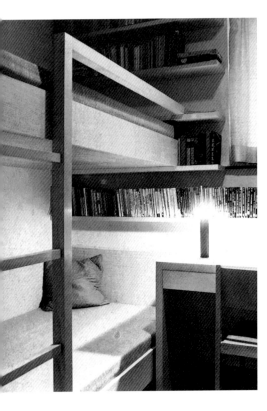
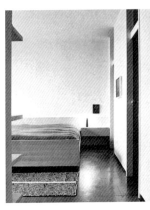
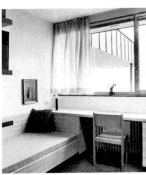
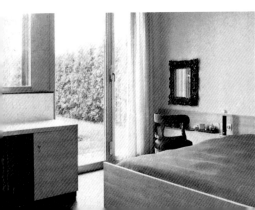
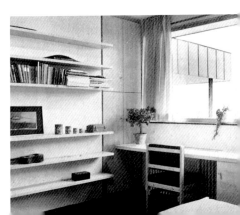

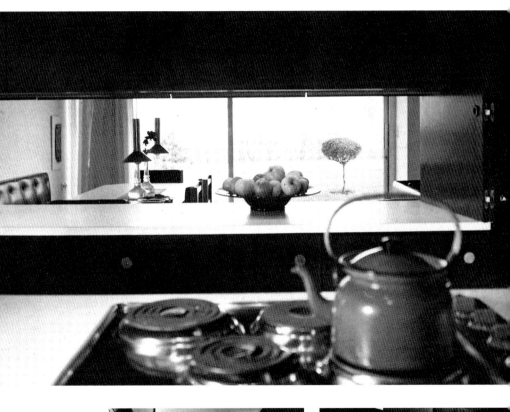

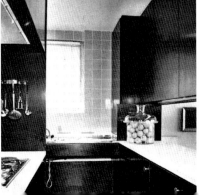

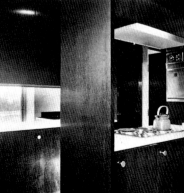

Rosewood combined with stainless
steel, and stainless steel with
upholstery in Ascot brown, all on a
cinnamon-toned rug over a white
tile floor
Upholstery is *Chamois*, a Win
Anderson Fabric by Jack Lenor
Larsen, Inc.
Room designed by Barbara D'Arcy
USA

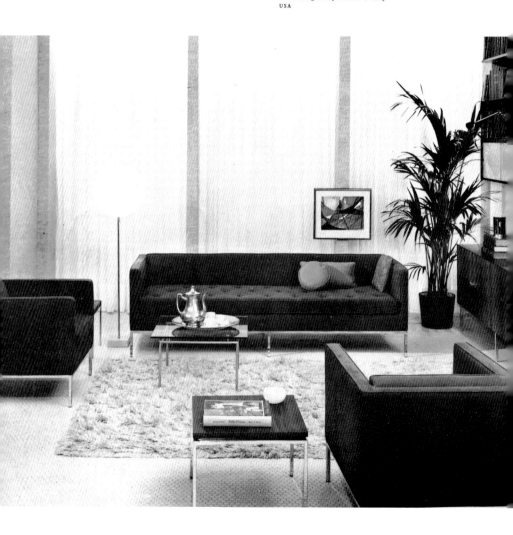

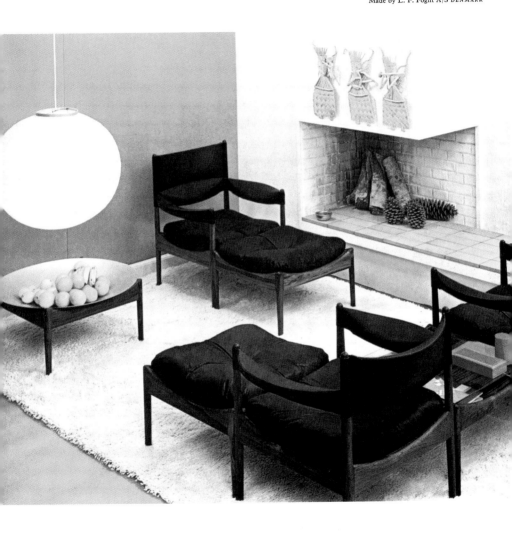

Chimney corner furnished with units
from the *Modus* range (the cushions
of black leather, feather filled)
designed by Kristian Vedel for
Søren Willadsens Møbelfabrik
DENMARK
Moskus carpet, a broadloom, 200 cm
wide, available also in olive green
and dark brown
Made by L. F. Foght A/S DENMARK

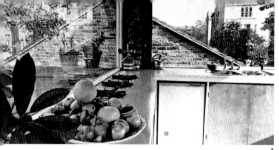

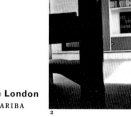

A 'tower-house' in London
architect John Winter ARIBA

1

2

3

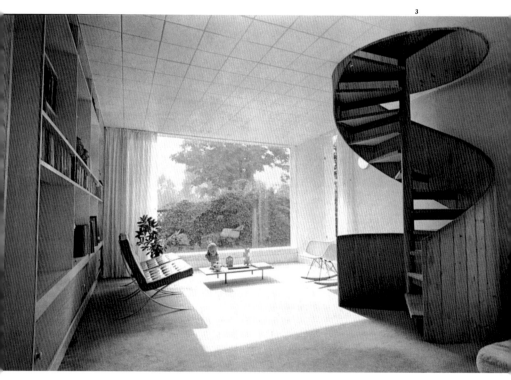

John Winter and his wife found a tiny coachhouse near the Zoo and the Park, which they demolished and rebuilt, necessarily on the former foundation. The work was accomplished by the Winters themselves—with help from piping and wiring specialists and from 'parties' where instead of cocktails, guests were offered beer and concrete-mixing. On the small rectangle (6·5 × 4·6 metres) rose a straight, tower-like little house for themselves and, now, for two small sons as well. The whole floor area is represented by the living-room on the first-floor, broken only by the shaft through which the spiral staircase rises from

the entrance hall below to kitchen and roof above 3, 5, 7. Rather like spending all on one glorious meal the Winters decided to have this room full of space and light and warmth. Warmth is from the sun in summer streaming through window-walls, and from Crane skirting heating in winter: space and light are effected by an uncluttered expanse of pale fawn carpet, and by plain white curtains against plain white paintwork. The only pattern is that which comes from books, pictures and other items in the wall fitment, from the chairs—Mies van der Rohe's *Barcelonas*, two others in moulded plywood by Charles Eames: and from

the black-iron rich pine wall of the stair.
In the space behind the camera is the fireplace and an unobtrusive sleeping area.
Downstairs, 5, are tiny rooms for children, bath and storage.
Life is lived most actively, however, on the roof 1, 4. Here is a working-dining area sandwiched between two useful balconies: a roof-garden where children play in the air, plus a roof-kitchen where the family eats. Double-glazed to be warm in winter, shaded in summer, its splendid tree-top atmosphere is rivalled by few other kitchens in town (or country).

photos CRISPIN EURICH

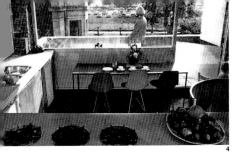

4

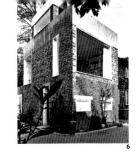

6

5

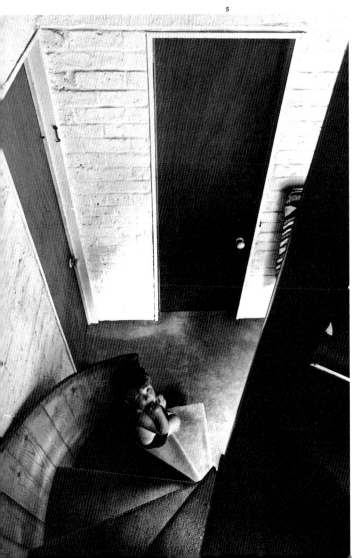

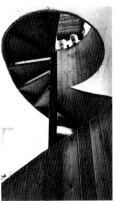

7

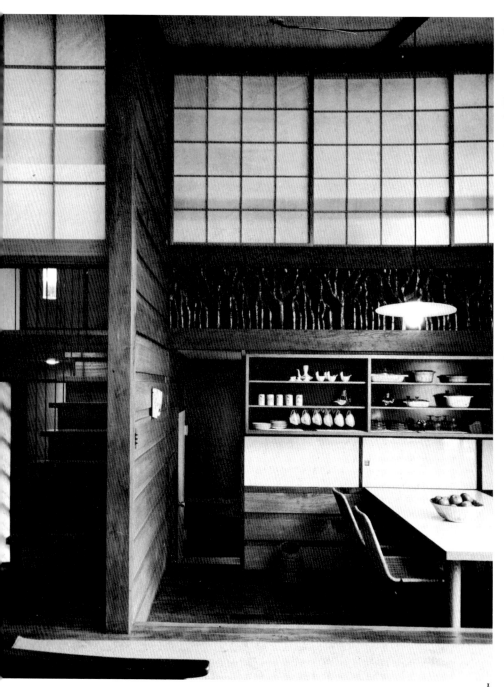

I

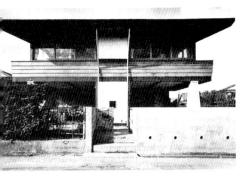

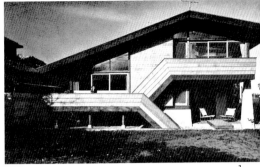

3

1 & 2 Tatami Room
3 Kitchen Area
4 Dining Area
5 Living Room

1 Residence, Japan

itects N. Nakajima and Associates

N ◄—

ographs Okamoto, courtesy Kenchiki Bunki

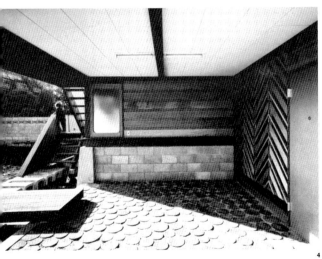

4

is is a family house in a
urban area. To cope with a
h humidity rate skipped floors
three levels were decided upon.
covered terrace, with kitchen,
ity and service areas on the
th and the maid's rooms on the
rth sides occupy the ground
r.

The central living room is on a
mezzanine floor with the
bedrooms above.
This arrangement provides close
relationships between several
spaces with different functions.
Quiet *tatami* rooms are placed on
the north side and more active
areas on the south with easy access

5

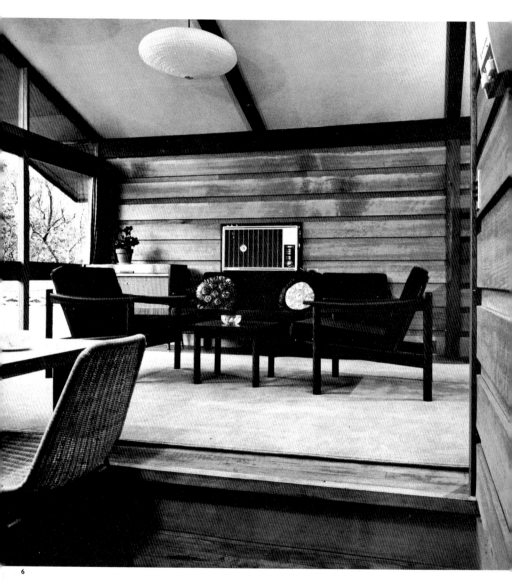

6

HM Residence, Japan

architects N. Nakajima and Associates

to the exterior. The dining room is on a lower level of the central 'deck' while the ceiling follows the roof slope and creates a free atmosphere for these spaces. The internal central staircase is supplemented by an exterior stairway.

1 dining room from living room
2 east side view
3 south side view
4 covered service yard
5 entrance hall
6 living room
7 exterior stairway
8 living room north side
9 bedroom
10 child's room

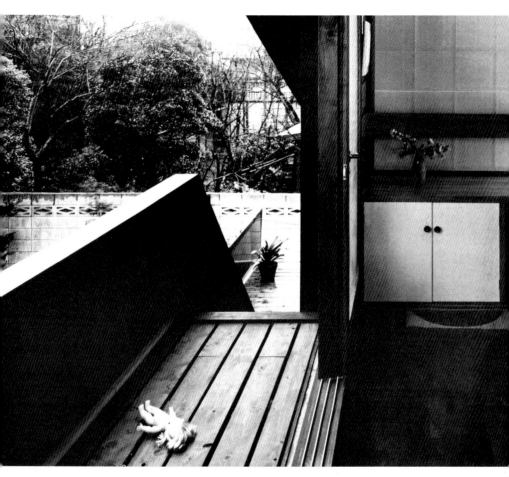

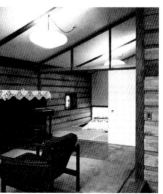
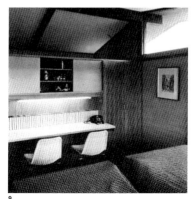
9

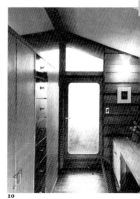
10

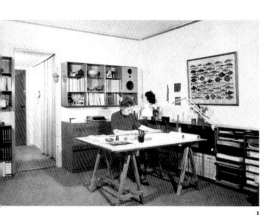

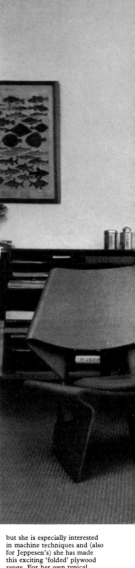

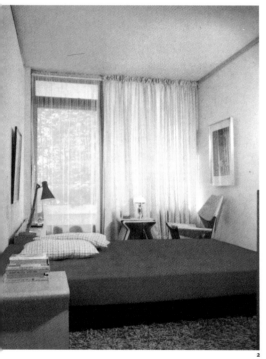

Modern apartment near Copenhagen
The home of Grete Jalk

This small apartment could be found almost anywhere in the world: here it is surrounded by pleasant woods and has a view to the coast. It is distinguished too by its warmth—a warmth which has little to do with centigrade. Grete Jalk is one of the most interesting of Denmark's designers today: for P. Jeppesen's Mobelfabrik she has designed many fine pieces of furniture for cabinet-making,

but she is especially interested in machine techniques and (also for Jeppesen's) she has made this exciting 'folded' plywood range. For her own typical, none-too-large, multi-purpose apartment, it seems exactly right: the non-bulk, the sharpish lines, the surprising springy resilience. Real wood complements real wool, sheep-hair rug from Yugoslavia and the glowing cocoa-fibre floor.

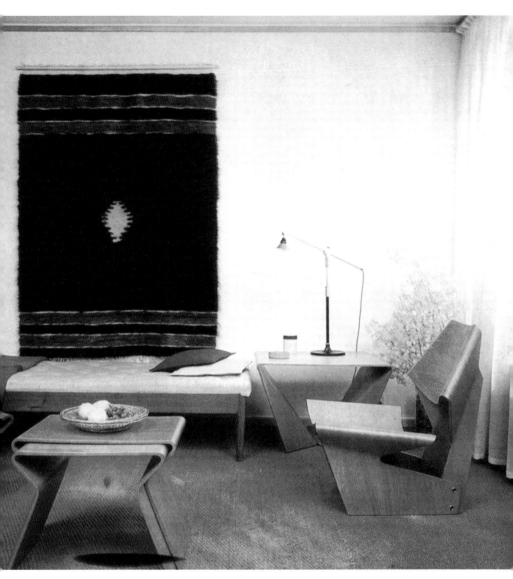

1, The designing-table is of an
early, proved and simple type,
for quick dismounting! Beyond it,
the bedroom **2,** bed covered in
its daytime dress of cherry wool:
for the night this is removed
and replaced by the single feather
bedding unit which serves the
Continent so simply in all seasons.

photographs Helmer-Petersen

House in Canonbury, London
interior by Max Clendinning ARIBA

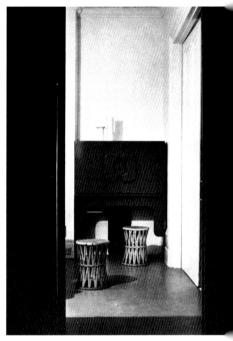

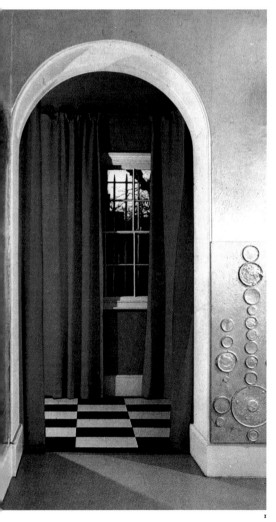

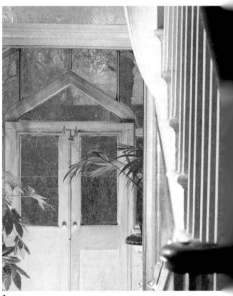

1   3

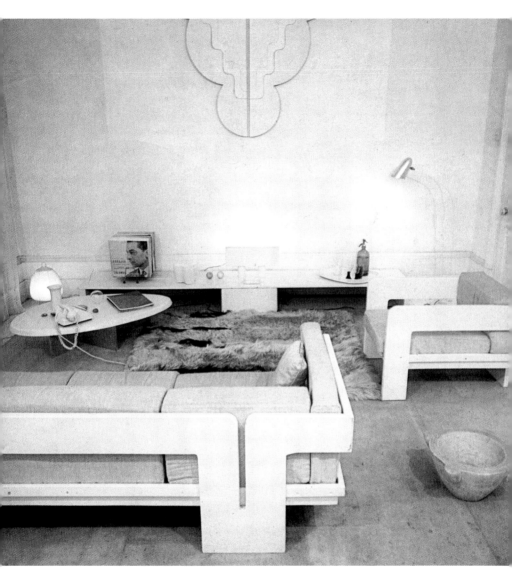

In the true tradition of young architects Max Clendinning has recently turned furniture designer. Without compunction he has also turned his Regency-style house into a setting for his ultra-modern designs.
In fact the clear lines of the furniture are not so incompatible with the character of the house as might seem probable. The structure is left unchanged:

white paint picks out original woodwork mouldings: but ceilings are treated without respect—painted in motifs which echo the furniture shapes. The result: cool Pop on a nineteenth-century backcloth. At the door a scarlet grotto greets the visitor: 1, looking back to the L-shaped entrance hall, scarlet painted walls meet floor-to-ceiling scarlet curtains and black/white vinyl tiling floor

and relief decoration on the silver wall is made from paint-tin lids—small metal waste is turned into art. A tiny conservatory manages to be green in winter time, 3. The sitting room, 4 is cool with whites and pale mushroom tones. The furniture is a prototype design, white-lacquered with oatmeal linen-covered cushions, curtains are off-white linen sheer by Primavera and the rugs are goatskins.

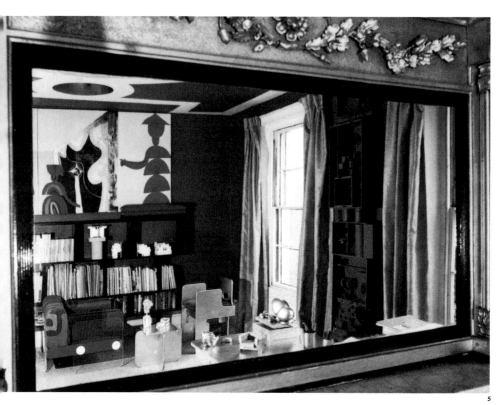

5

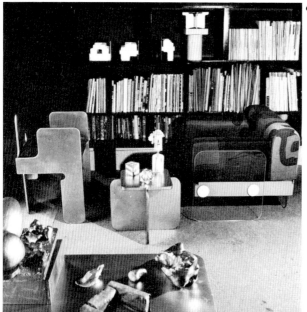

6

House in Canonbury, London
interior by Max Clendinning ARIBA

The white is sharper in the
kitchen/dining room 7, where the
only spots of colour are the red
lacquered cabinet and a painting
by Joe Tilson. The dining table
is of plate metal glass on a white-
lacquered plywood frame, the
chairs completing the suite
upholstered in oatmeal Irish tweed.

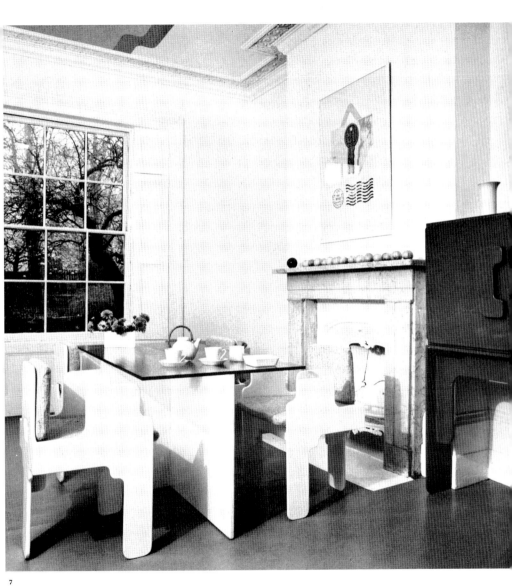

7

On the first floor is complete contrast: Mr Clendinning's den-cum-office is bright rather than light. Walls are a dark muddy ochre, the shelving is heavy timber planking, black-stained, with above them the large painting by Ralph Adron. The mirror in which the whole picture of the room is reflected is heavily gilt and 'silver' paint has been used liberally to unify the little pieces in the room. The large armchair with the early 30's look is a prototype with Perspex sides: a production model is available with solid plywood sides, lacquered in several colours, as are now some of the paper prototypes. Most of the furniture both upstairs and downstairs represents the development of the *Maxima* and other ranges now in production either by Race Furniture or by Clendinning Bros of Armagh, all based upon the minimum number of interchangeable components.

photographs John Donat

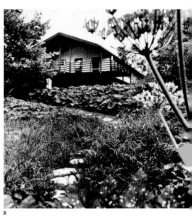

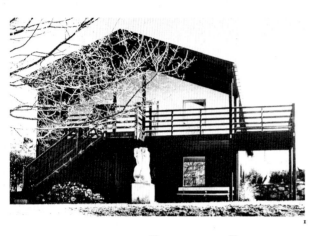

Borge Mogensen's House near Copenhagen
architect Erling Zeuthen Nielsen in collaboration with Borge Mogen

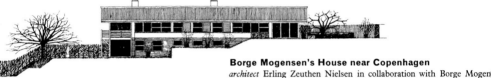

This long, simple building cons basically of two large rooms eac at one end of the house with bedrooms and bath between. It stands on a north slope with the sitting room looking over the Ermelunden valley, at the other end the dining room opening to sun room and in fine weather to atrium type garden.

The house has grown from a smaller base as its use became more defined and this, its completed form, was achieved with the co-operation of architects Arne Karlsen and Allan Jensen. Interior and furniture designer Borge Mogenson is noted for the strong lines of his furniture. In his own home all the furniture his own design, the fitted units lowing the module of the build Solidity and strength may be sa to be the motif of the house: scrubbed deal floors meet scrub walls where bricks are visible beneath the thin rendering.

The spruce board ceiling follow the roof line and the strong mullions of the window repeat the module of the building, as cupboards, bookcases and the fitted window tables, seen in 8 the window of the dining room Tables and chairs part of the serial production of Fredericia Stolefabrik.

1 The balcony looking over the valley is part of the recent addi to the house: dark stained timbe railing against sky and house. The outer walls are painted glossy black below and white above with window frames of bright, varnished deal.

3

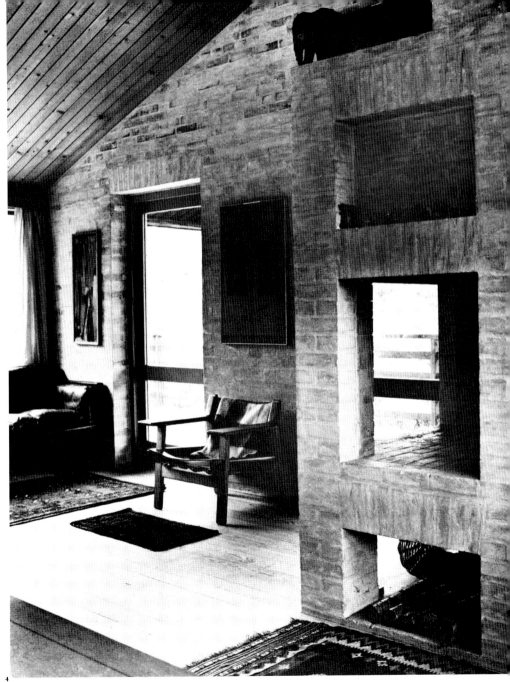

4
photographs Jesper Høm

Borge Mogensen's house near Copenhagen

3 The kitchen is separated from the dining room by a cupboard wall: it opens to a garden room for enjoying the sun behind glass walls (the atrium lies beyond). 4, and 8 Sitting room with access to the large balcony in 1. 5 Bedroom walls are panelled, the ceilings covered with recessed boards. 6, 7 The garden room is a light timber structure which can be opened on to the atrium—the flooring following a continuous pattern of clinker bricks to the same module as the house itself.

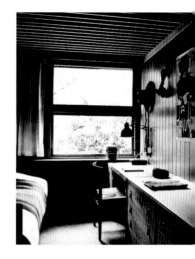

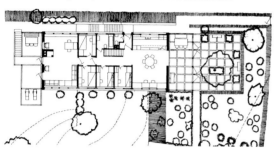

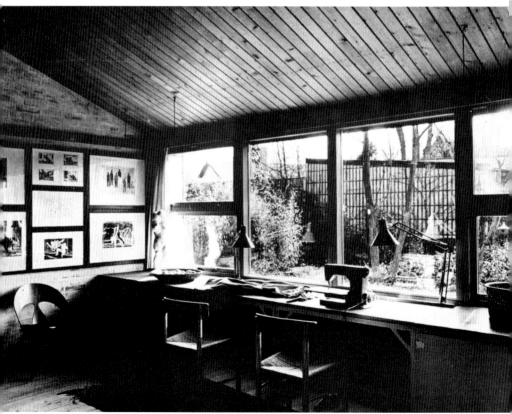

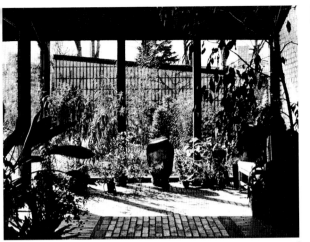
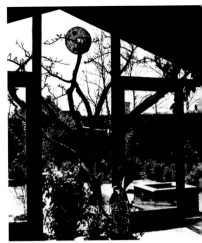

6   7

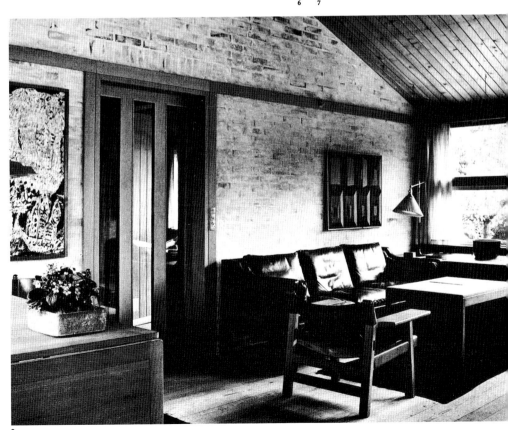

9

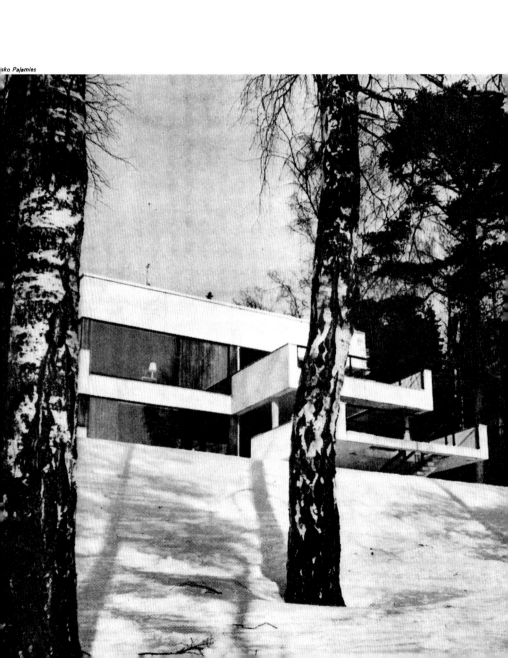

The Villa Aarnio,Kuusisaari near Helsinki
architect Toivo Korhonen
interior architect Esko Pajamies

1 the façade to the sea
2 traditional sauna pails
3 overleaf: lounge/hall on the ground
floor with concrete screen and mirror-
frame: a small bar is tucked behind them

photographs Eero Aarnio

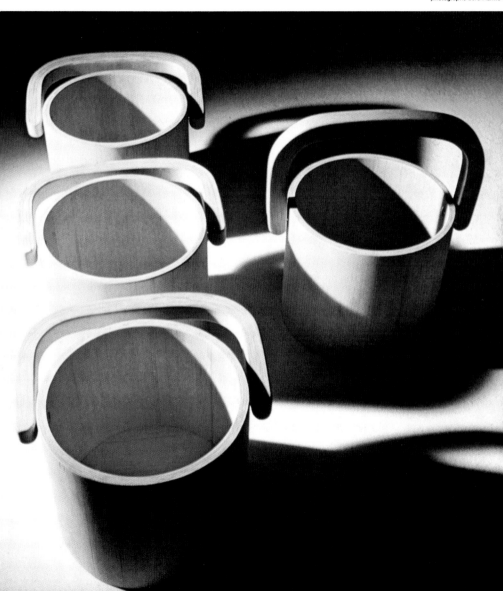

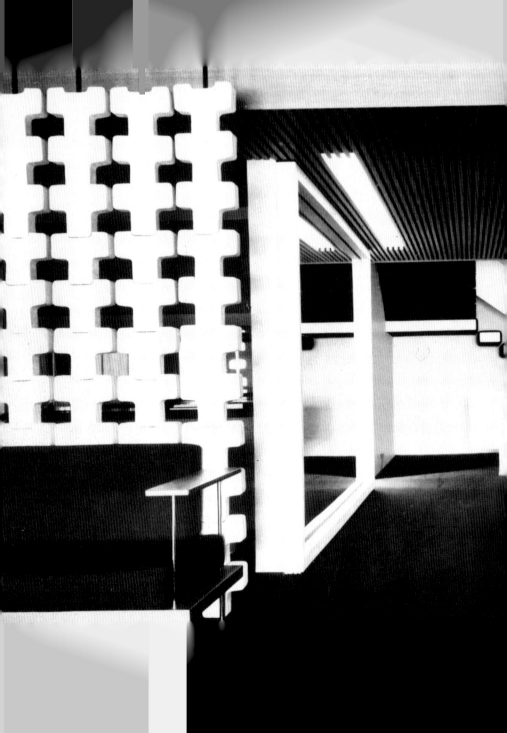

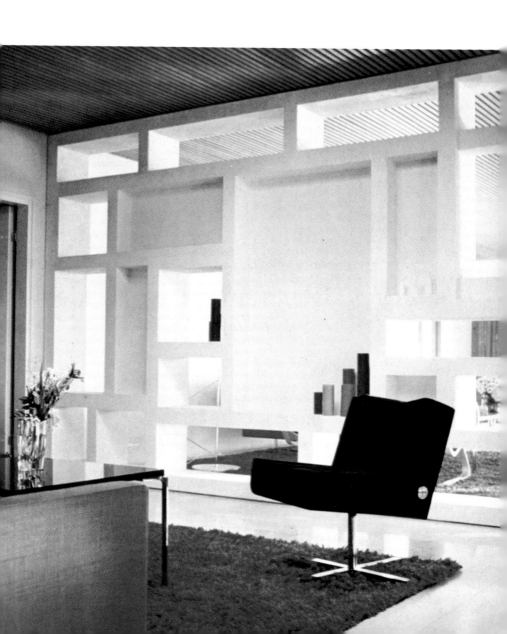

The Villa Aarnio, Kuusisaari near Helsi▮
architect Toivo Korhonen
interior architect Esko Pajamies

e spirit of this house has been
ned to that of a ship in which the
erior arrangement is dictated by the
erall form. Its form thrusting out as it
es towards an inlet from the sea has
haps sprung from the site itself.
e size and structure of the house also
ggest a modern castle fortified not by
wbridge and portcullis but by central
ating and intercommunications
stems, by deep-pile carpets and
ntrolled lighting.
e structure inside and out is of
nforced concrete; in the interior,
shed and painted matt white, it

forms balustrade, room partitions,
screens and floor-to-ceiling mirror
frames – placed to still further enhance
the interior spaces: faced with cobalt-
blue ceramic tiles it is the walls of
kitchen, toilet rooms and indoor
swimming pool.
Floors are partly covered by Carrera
marble, partly by firm woven carpets and
deep-pile hand-made carpets fitting
planned depressions in the marble.
The ground floor consists of the long,
central lounge/hall (pages 18–19)
running the depth of the house from
front to back, flanked on one side by

the indoor swimming pool, the sauna
and the lower balcony, on the other by
several service and storage rooms.
4 the living-room and 5 looking into
the entrance hall.
The main furnishings are architectural
details. Movable items have also been
specially designed: desk-lamps, floor-
lamps, sauna pails, chairs and tables.
Bangkok teak and Oregon pine make
the built-in furniture of kitchen, parents'
and children's rooms and the strip
ceilings are also of Oregon pine.

5

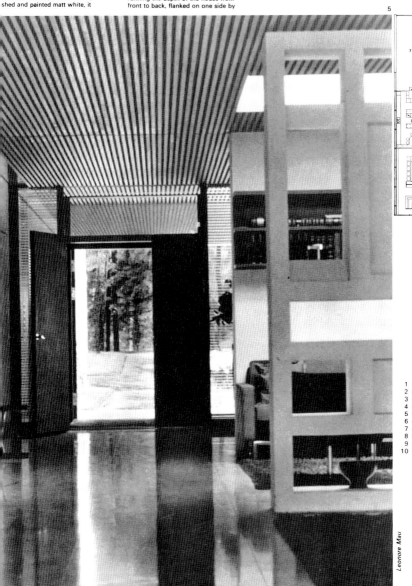

1 study
2 bedroom
3 bathroom
4 balcony
5 living-room
6 entrance hall
7 garage
8 kitchen
9 dining-room
10 library

Leonore Mau

The Villa Aarnio,
Kuusisaari near Helsinki

architect Toivo Korhonen

interior architect Esko Pajamies

photographs
Eero Aarnio
Esko Pajamies
Pietinen   6–8   9–11

Details of the swimming pool 9 the
sauna 6, and lamps and chairs designed
by Esko Pajamies especially for the
house.
The fireplace easy chair of rattan woven
on a chrome-plated steel frame with
Thai silk-covered cushion.
Table and floor lamps: the bases of cast
steel, supports and arms of chrome-
plated tube, the floor lamp with a shade
of opaque Perspex.

10, Lounge chair, bent laminated bee
upholstered with Thai silk over foam
rubber. Lower-backed, longer-legged
chairs with leather upholstery were m
for the dining room, both versions by
Boman Oy.
Opposite: Rooms on the first floor wh
has all the main living areas, includin
the kitchen, the bedrooms, bathroom
and, because of the rising ground bet
the house, the garage.

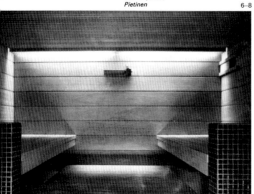

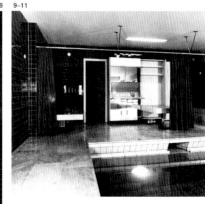

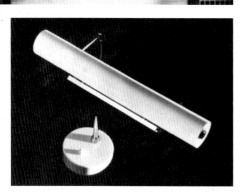

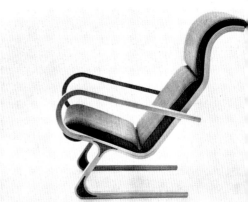

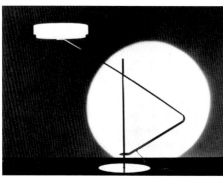

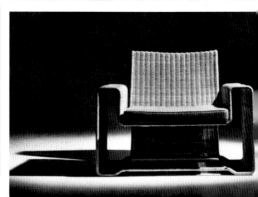

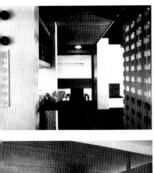

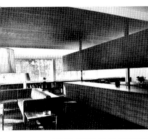

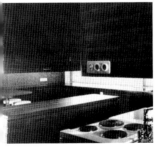

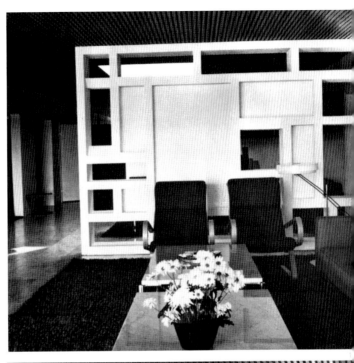

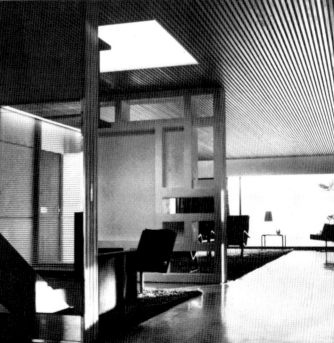

5
6

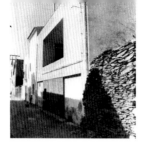

A Summer House at Cadequès, Spain
architect Lanfranco
Bombelli Tiravanti

1 | 3
2 |

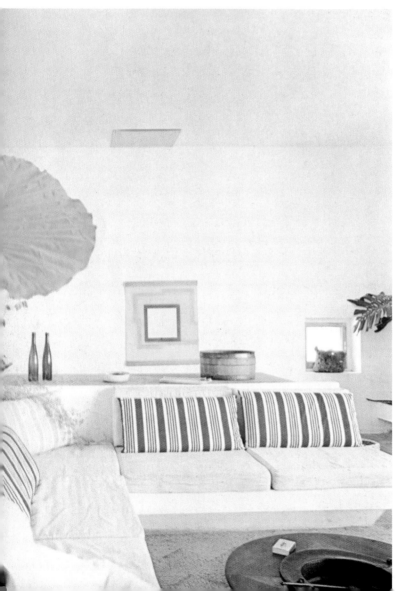

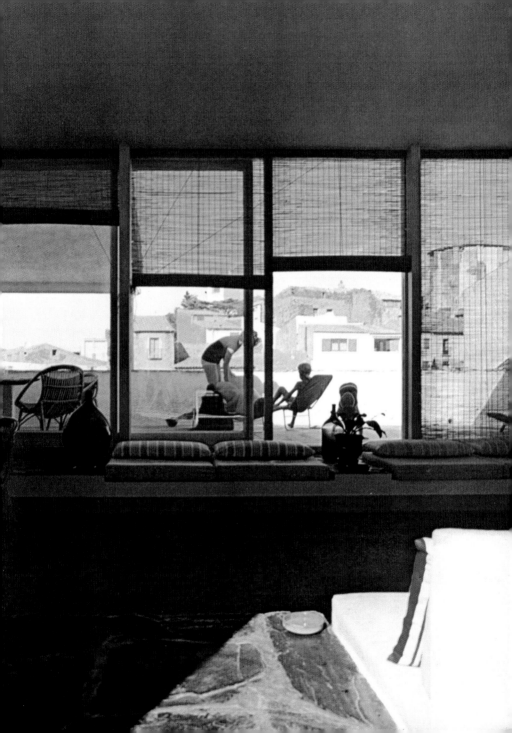

A Summer House at Cadequès, Spain
architect Lanfranco Bombelli Tiravanti

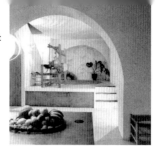

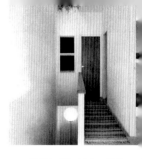

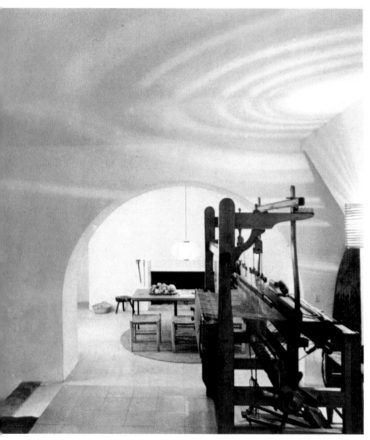

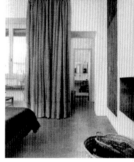

4	6
5	7

Lanfranco Bombelli Tiravanti is an Italian architect who works in Spain an for himself and his family he reconstructed an old house, abandoned by its peasant inhabitants and falling into dilapidation.
The entrance floor was a stable, the upper part an unpractical two-storey structure 10·50 × 10·50 metres.
Walls were repaired and extended, windows re-made, old natural stone walls lime-washed white.
Designed primarily for the summer, the house is open to the east and has only essential doors inside, with the sleeping area 'suspended' and isolated in space to increase ventilation, between the ground and top, living, floor.

1 the entrance to the house on street level: the sliding door gives on to the courtyard or patio, covered by the second-floor terrace but lit and aired by the window above. To each side are kitchen, dining room and part of the old building (see 4 and 5)
2, 3 in the living-room with the terrace and the village and sea beyond: walls and ceilings are white, the long divan built in in cement with cushions of beige rustic handweave and striped sailcloth. The floor is sunk to a depth of 30 cm to accommodate the feet and covered with Spanish woven straw matting. A concrete relief by Verena Lowensberg is on the further wall, 2
4, 5 the dining-room seen 5, from the entrance with the Swedish loom of the architect's wife. The arch is part of the original structure
6, 7, 8 details of the first floor corridor, parents' room with dressing-room and bath, the children's bunk-bed built in of cement, covered with Majorcan handweaves in vivid colours.
10 the living-room chimney and staircase to the lower floors

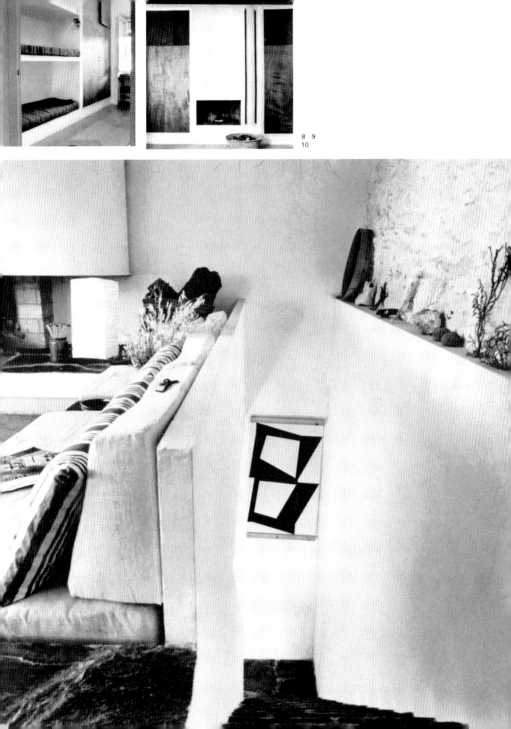

8 9
10

A Summer House at Cadequès, Spain

architect Lanfranco Bombelli Tiravanti

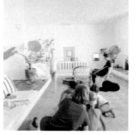

11 the living-room seen 12 from the terrace. The table is a local stone slab on a base of lime-washed concrete. The straw blinds are those typical of the Mediterranean region
13 the living-room chimney with the divans and 'paddling pool' – the sunk area for the feet. Along the window wall which opens to the terrace are the flagstones of local grey stone. The rattan chairs are Spanish-made

11
12 13

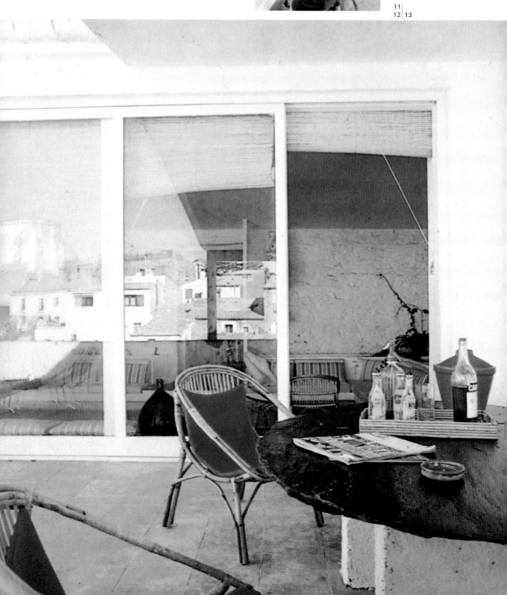

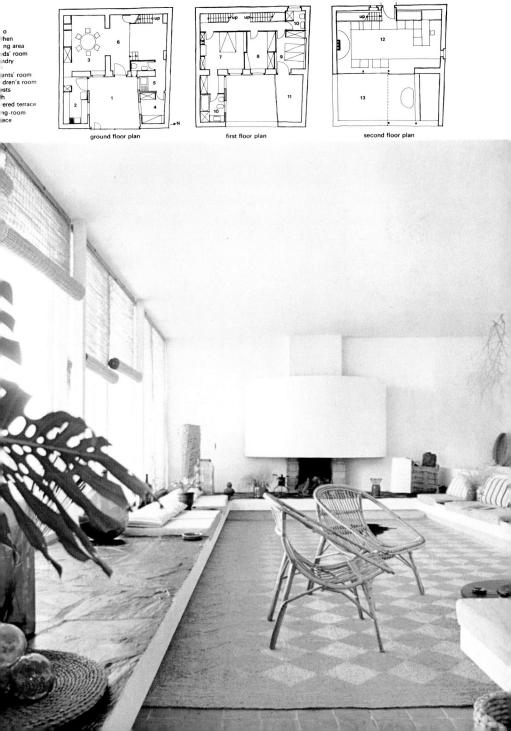

o
hen
ng area
ds' room
dry

ents' room
dren's room
sts
h
ered terrace
g-room
ace

ground floor plan   first floor plan   second floor plan

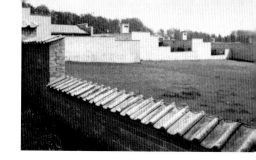

A House in The Terraces, Fredensborg, Denmark
architect Jørn Utzon
interior design Rolf Middelboe

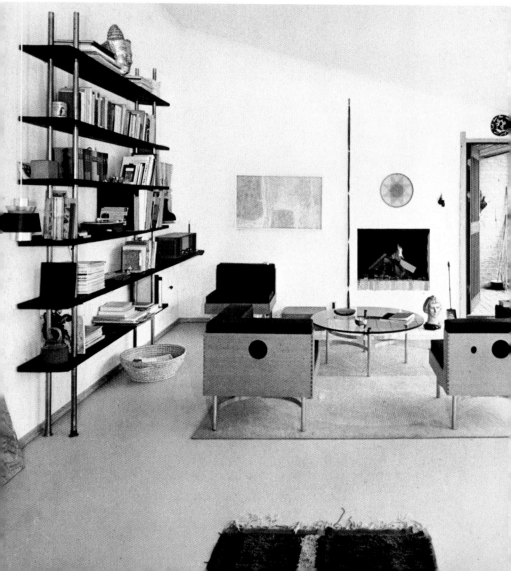

The Terraces is a development set in the North Zeeland landscape: from the surrounding gentle slopes it suggests a small fortified town of yellow brick and red tiles, and was designed to provide some qualities of the medieval city-state, in particular its protection from the outer world.

The single-storied houses attract tenants of wide-ranging interests: the completely undomesticated can dine in the restaurant and/or hire other facilities provided to give freedom from care. But Rolf Middelboe and his wife with one of the best-situated houses having a view of fields and woods, have created a very personal milieu.

The large central living-room has furniture designed by Finn Juhl and Rolf Middelboe himself, against white walls and on white linoleum-covered floors. The low square armchairs are of golden Oregon pine with heavy soft cushions of feather-filled black leather. These, the table in front of the fireplace, the bookcase were all designed by Middelboe as well as the rugs and curtains in festival stripes of red, yellow, gold and orange – colours used again and again, sometimes with a strong clear blue.

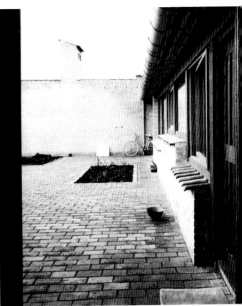

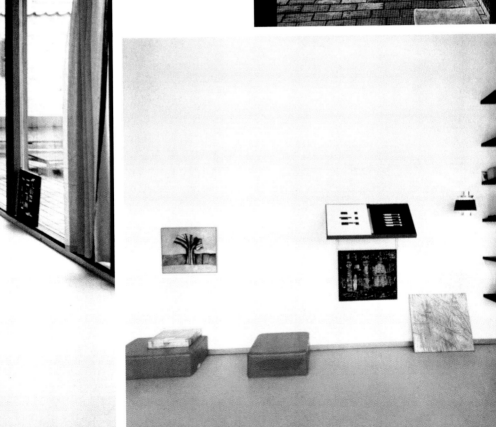

A House in The Terraces, Fredensborg, Denmark
architect Jørn Utzon
interior design Rolf Middelboe

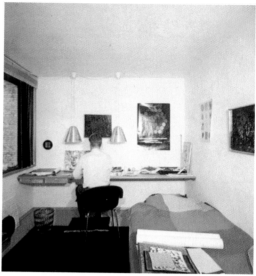

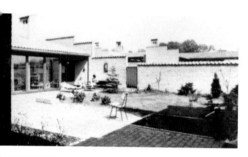

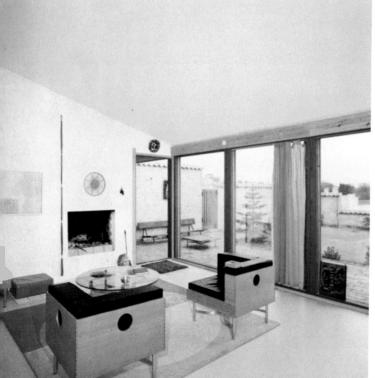

Husband and wife each have a room furnished according to their respective needs.

Mrs Middelboe's room has a big sleigh bed designed by her husband and a toilet table-cum-writing desk designed by Finn Juhl.

Middelboe's own room is taken up by a large work table and a bed covered like every other available surface with scraps of material, samples, drawings, etc for he works in wool and leather and paper as well as glass and metal and constantly experiments.

The sheltered patio/garden, above, is conveniently easy to reach and perfectly secluded by the walls which give the whole complex its unique effect. Here it can be seen in relation to each end of the living-room – at right, the area generally in use as a dining-room, towards the kitchen. The cupboards can be opened from the kitchen or from the living-room.

Above this view, one of the red-lead-painted, roughly finished doors, which help to give The Terraces its character. Rolf Middelboe keeps all the housekeys by the main entrance under the general care of an old family portrait.

photographs Gunvor Betting
copyright P.A.F. International Ltd

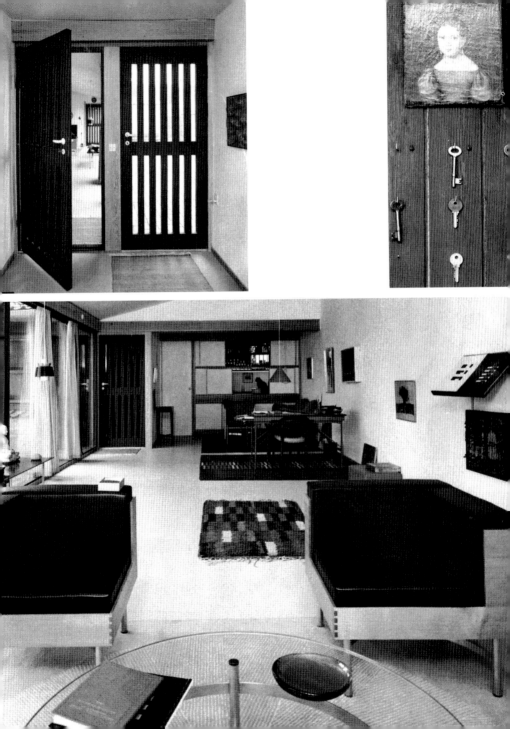

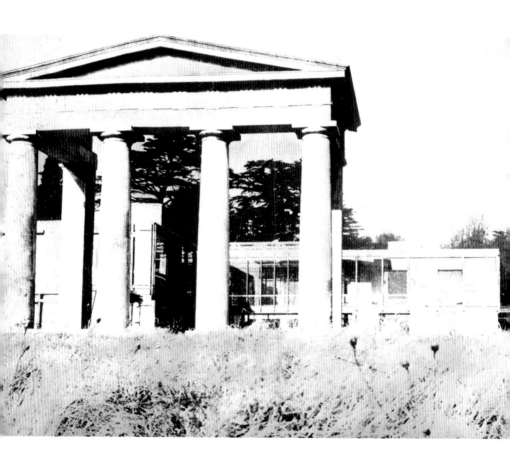

Stratton Park, Hampshire
architects Stephen Gardiner & Christopher Knight
decoration consultant William McCarty

Stratton Park is the estate of the Baring family and the house has been built on the site of an earlier 'big house' of which only the portico has been retained.

Although one feels an uncompromising modernity of outlook would have eschewed it the great stone portico is visually dramatic to a degree, dominating the view from all the main rooms. Contrary to photographic appearances it belongs to the interior rather than the exterior. It is not usual to approach the house from the south.

The normal approach from the opposite side is no less satisfying as the new structure comes into view rising behind the old stabling blocks, tied to them by the single storey structure of the entrance, hall and courtyard.

It is when one enters the hall, 5 that the portico makes its first impact, taking the eye back and along the lily pool, into the conservatory, until the whole plan of the house is comprehended.

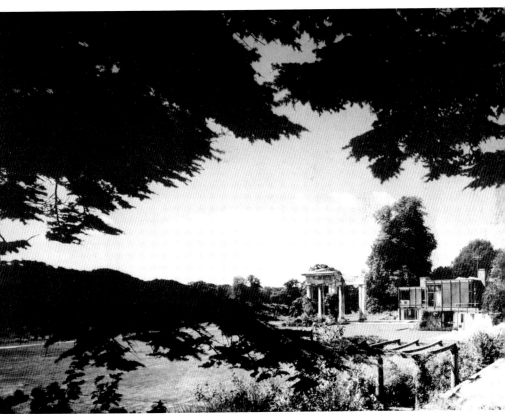

photograph Henk Snoek

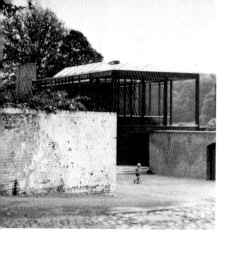
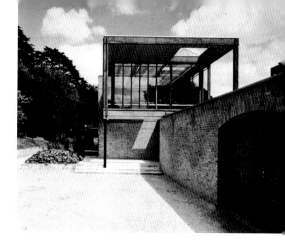

photograph Henk Sn

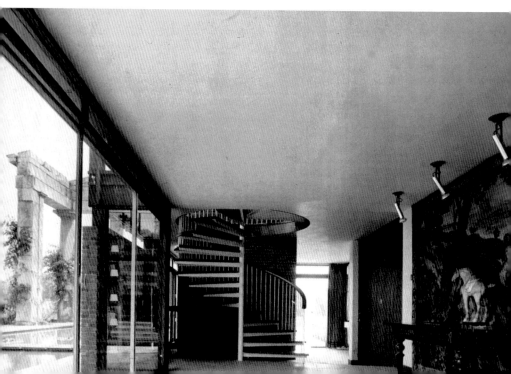

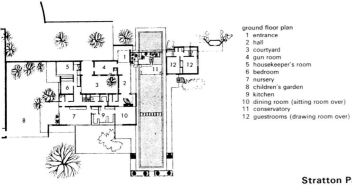

ground floor plan
1 entrance
2 hall
3 courtyard
4 gun room
5 housekeeper's room
6 bedroom
7 nursery
8 children's garden
9 kitchen
10 dining room (sitting room over)
11 conservatory
12 guestrooms (drawing room over)

Stratton Park, Hampshire
architects Stephen Gardiner & Christopher Knight
decoration consultant William McCarty

photographs Mike Busselle

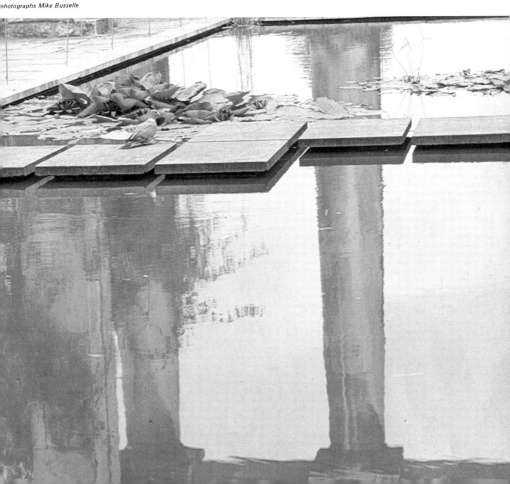

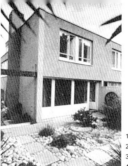

A home near Basle, Switzerland
with tapestries by Vera Isler

Suburbia, currently offering the handiest
available living space, shelter and comfort may
be shunned by the out-and-out individualist.
Even the fairly orthodox of the world's cities
prefer cleverly converted peasants' huts.
Not so, or not so often, in Switzerland.
There the national temperament tends to
improve upon rather than rebel against what is.
So have the Islers – journalist and artist – put their
stamp of individuality upon this one-of-a-series
house in the environs of Basle.
The approach for example: together they
turned every one of the small patches of garden

1
2 5 6
3
4

photographs Martin Hesse

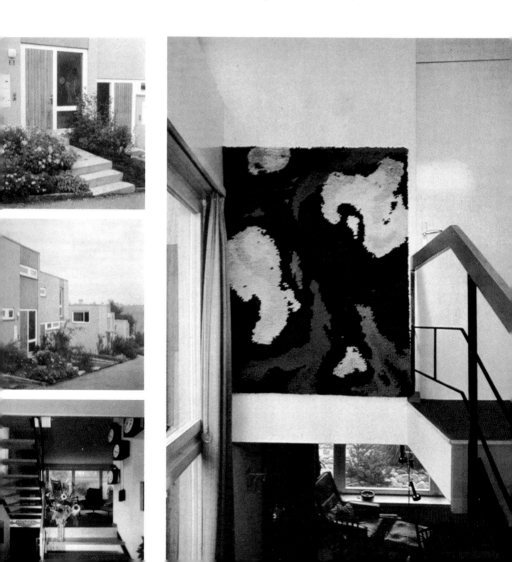

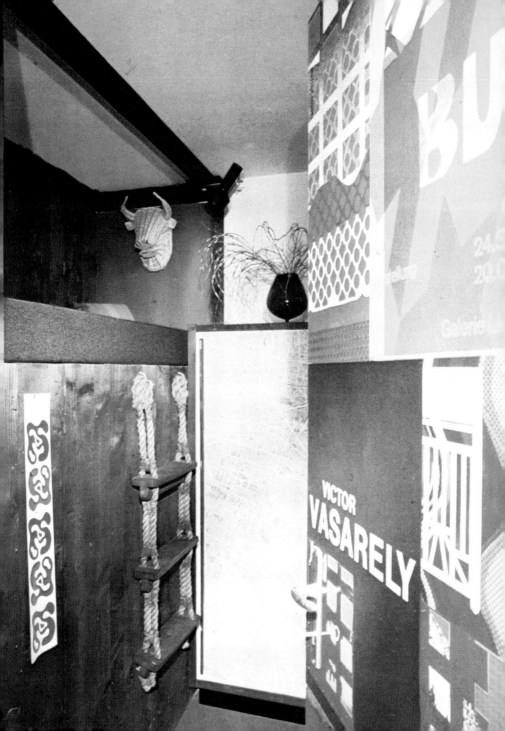

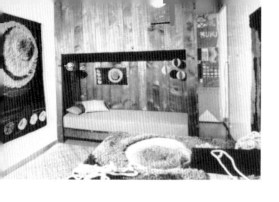

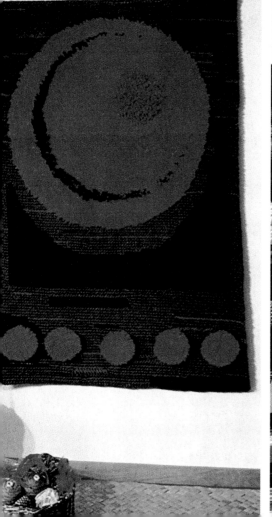

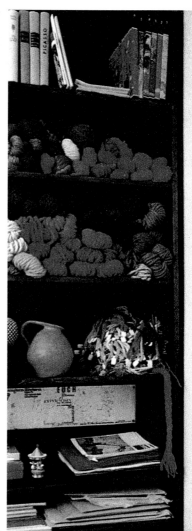

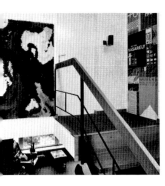
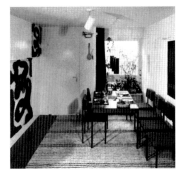
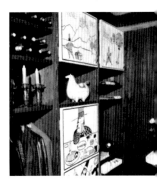

A home near Basle, Switzerland
with tapestries by Vera Isler

into a patch of riotous colour, or a focus of interest centred on a shrub set in Rhine flints. The interior, 4, 5 follows the levels of the site. Its arrangement, its plain walls and straightforward timbers proved entirely suitable as home, studio for Frau Isler and background for her three-dimensional tapestries.

From the dining room on the entrance floor to the living room on the next level, 4 the staircase arrives at the entrance to a guest room: at the top of the stairs *Summer 66* (on the guest-room door a collection of prints and posters).

On the wall of the dining room, 11 are two more tapestries *Happening* and *Imprisoned*. In the atelier itself, 7–9 is the riot of colour from the wool store and projects in hand: on the wall by the cabin bed *Fireball*.

The Islers' collection of old Provencal clocks are grouped on the staircase wall, 13.

7	10	11	12
8	9		13

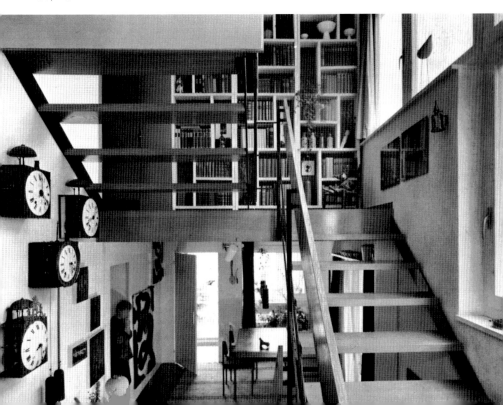

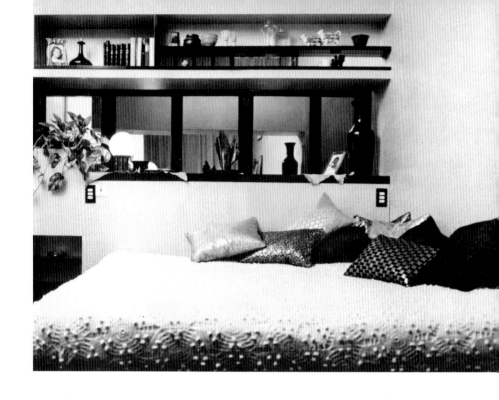

Apartment in Milan
designer Sergio Asti

| 1 | 4 |
| 2 3 | 5 6 |

As yet few apartment blocks are planned in such a way as to offer individual tenants the possibility of structural alteration.
Italian architect and designer Sergio Asti accepted the limitations of his new apartmen as a challenge.
He wished to give a feeling of continuity to rooms and to create a spatial arrangement which divided without separating. The first he achieved by using the same black carpeti throughout, carrying it up the walls to form 40 cm deep wainscot, and by finishing all w and partitions with the same silver and orang design: opposite and on pages 58-9.
Screen 'walls' of varying heights serve to cre separate areas and are at once functional an decorative. For example the partitions which separate the hall, 3 from the living room, 2, and the living room from the dining area, 4 deep enough for the installation of plant-hol as well as lighting equipment.
The wall of the living-room is filled by books shelving of a type designed for office files, olive-green-finished and perfect in this particular setting.
Divans are covered in putty-white velvet by Brunelli, and scattered with cushions covere Japanese silks in jewel colours of blue, gold and red. Similar cushions are found on the coverlet of white crocheted cotton in the bedroom, 1. Here the partition becomes a fitment holding books, glasses and other accessories.
With so much general stability it has been possible to integrate successfully Sergio Ast rich collection of modern Italian art (on the walls of the hall) the antique and modern gl silver and ceramics, and the pair of stainless-steel-framed armchairs, like the le Corbusier reclining chair, made in Italy by Cassina.

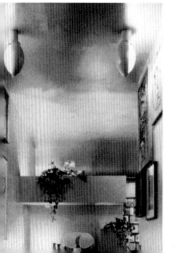

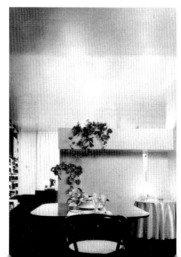

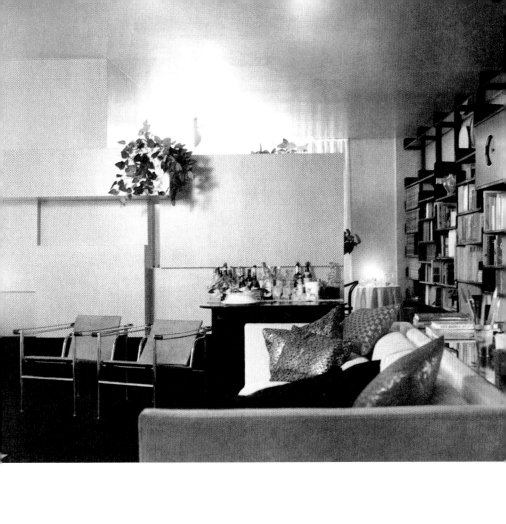

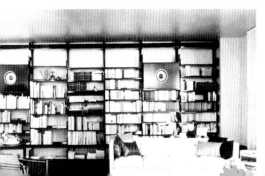

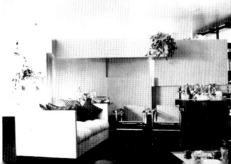

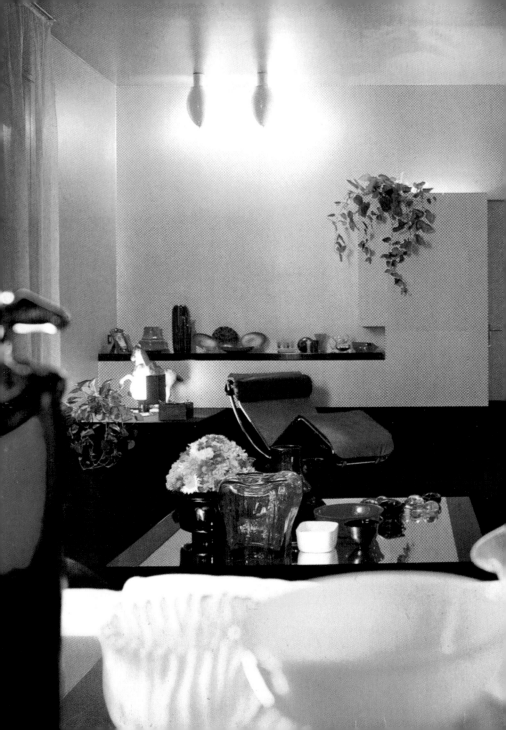

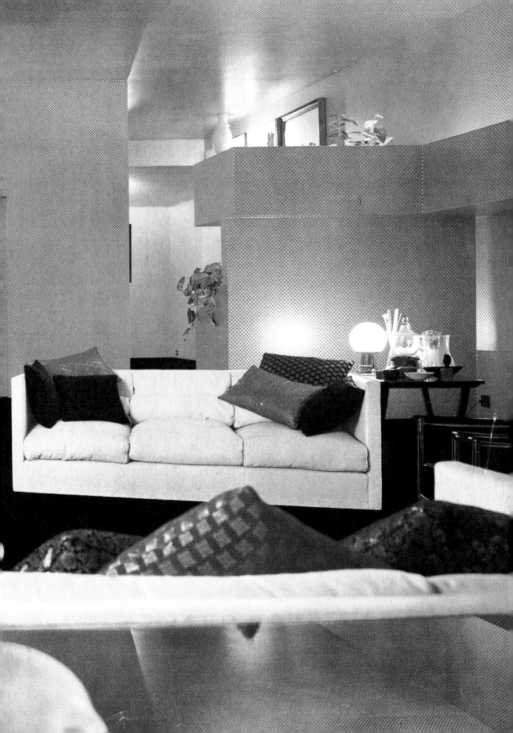

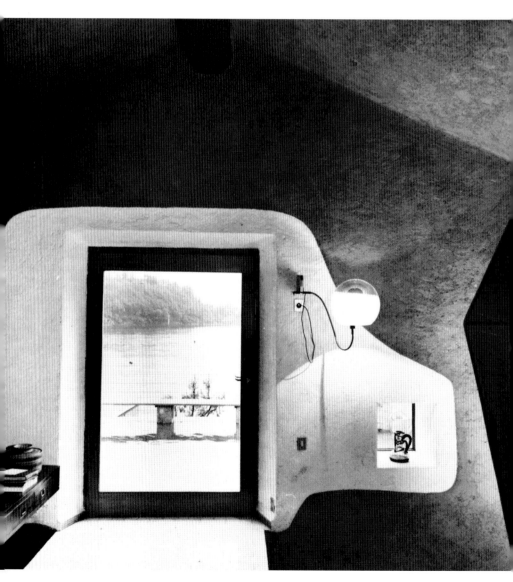

Lakeside house at Como
designers Ico and Luisa Parisi

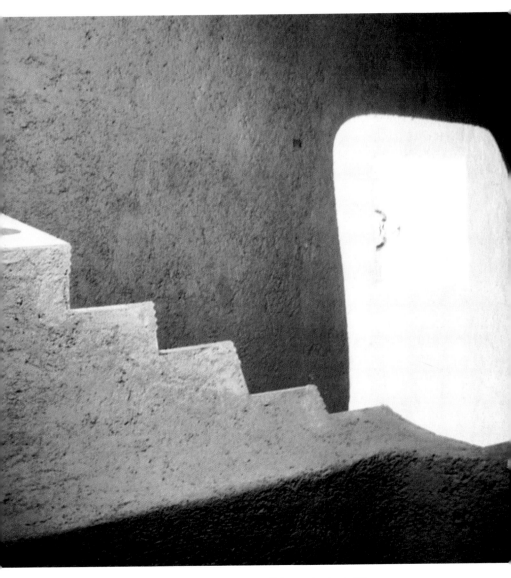

Lakeside house at Como
designers Ico and Luisa Parisi

A small house in the old village of Spurano on the shore of Lake Como was modernised and internally re-designed to provide this week-end house for two architects, Ico and Luisa Parisi Care was taken to integrate the appearance of necessary structural additions—bathroom, hallway, porch, terrace—with the surrounding buildings.
Sharp white ceramic floor tiles and risers with blue treads and roundels are on the stairs which lead from the porch to the floor above.
A collection of chopping boards was painted by artist friends of the architects: Fontana, Munari, Baj, Radice, Reggiani, Somaini, Rui, Galli etc.

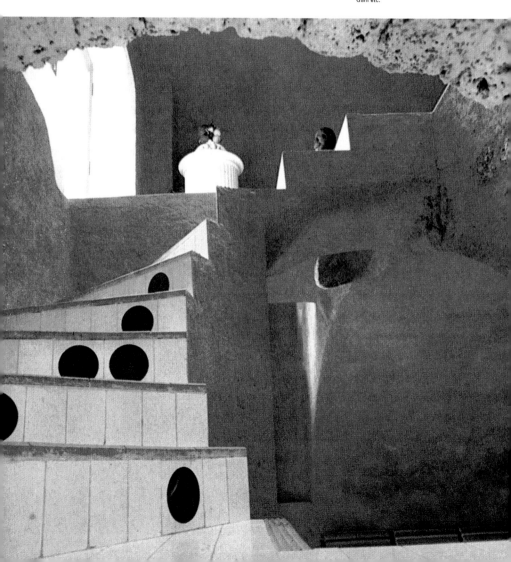

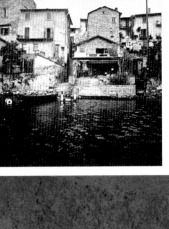
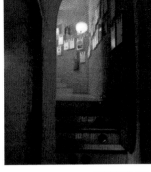
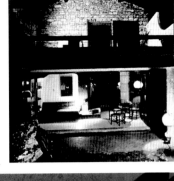
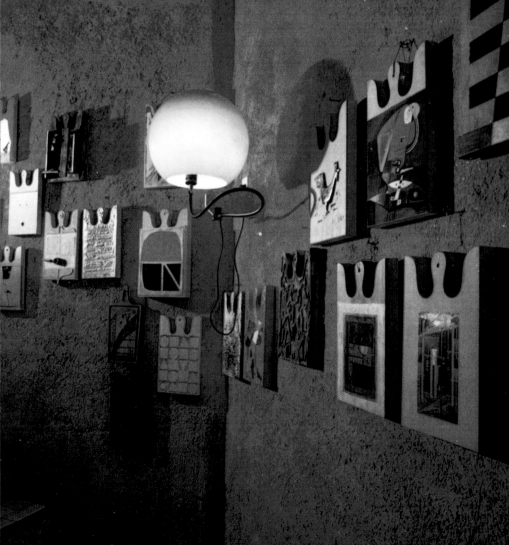

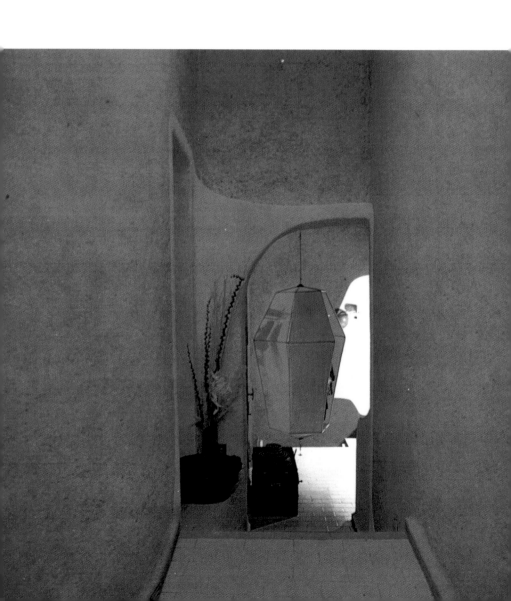

Lakeside house at Como
designers Ico and Luisa Parisi

The interior has been opened up to produce
a large space in which kitchen, bar and sitting
room are separated only by function.
The whole house is heated by the white
ceramic stove, especially made by Thun of
Bolzano, which reaches from the ground
to the floor above.
Walls and ceilings are painted continuously
bright red over rough-cast with window areas
broadly patterned in white to emphasize the
design of spaces and shapes.
The lantern in which the walls are reflected
so strongly was designed by the architects.
The other lamps are designed by Ico Parisi
for Arteluce.

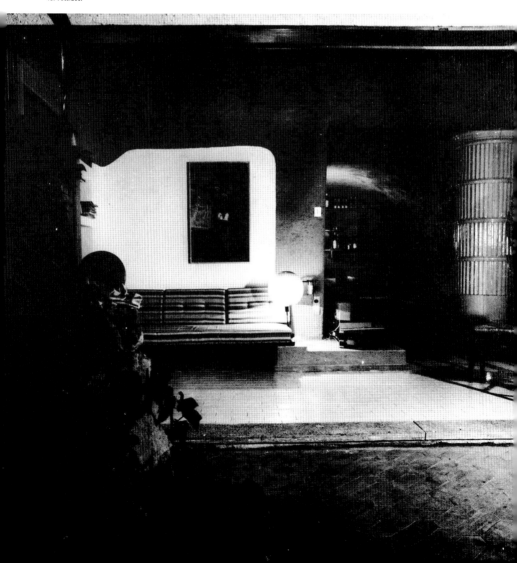

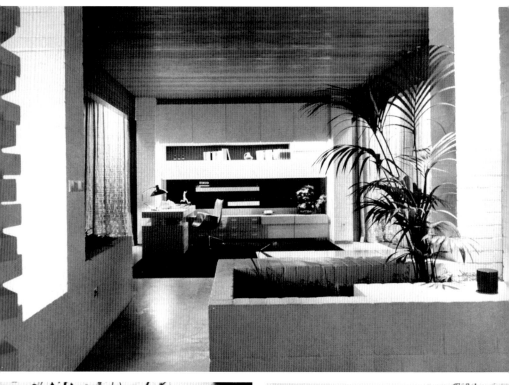

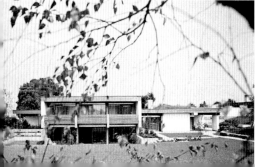

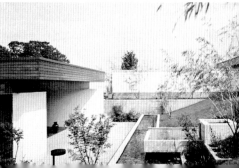

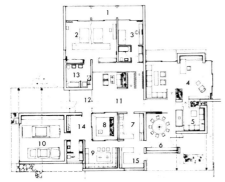

House at Pflaumloch, near the Bavarian border
architects Hans Kammerer and Walter Belz
in collaboration with Klaus Kucher

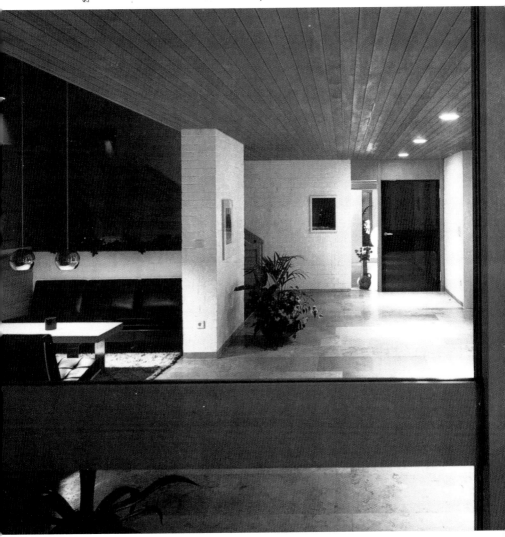

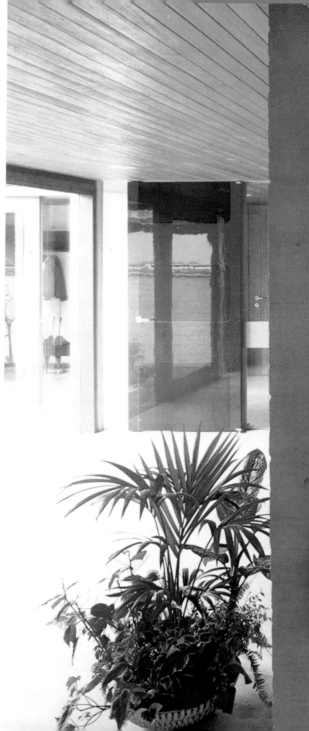

House at Pflaumloch,
near the Bavarian border
architects Hans Kammerer and Walter Belz
in collaboration with Klaus Kucher

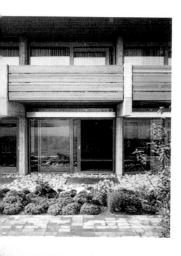

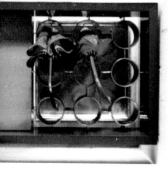

5
6 & 7

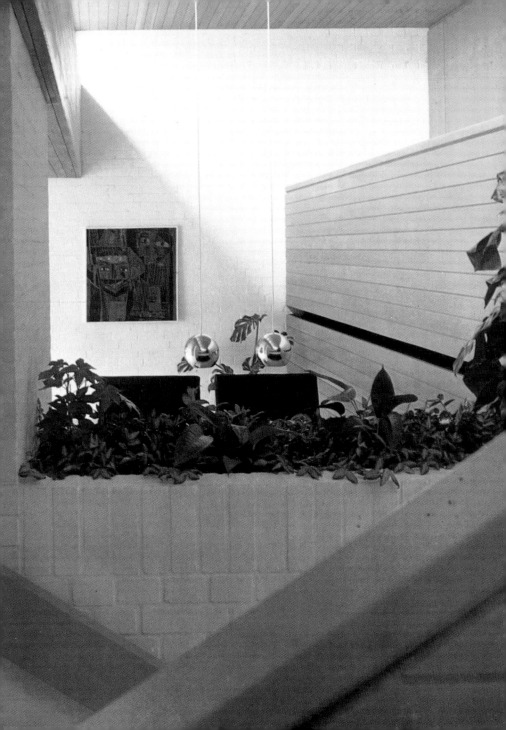

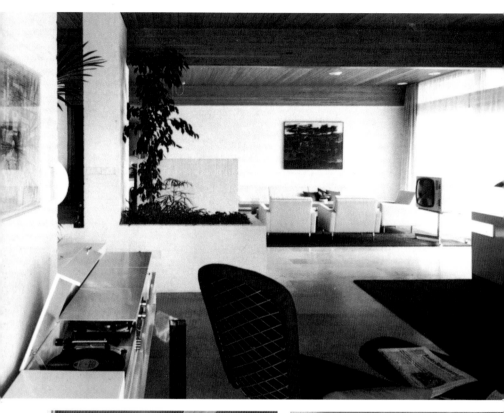

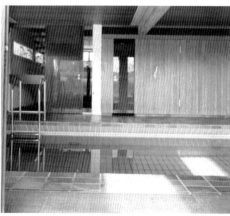

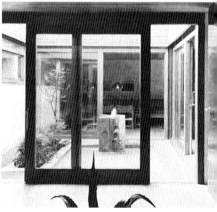

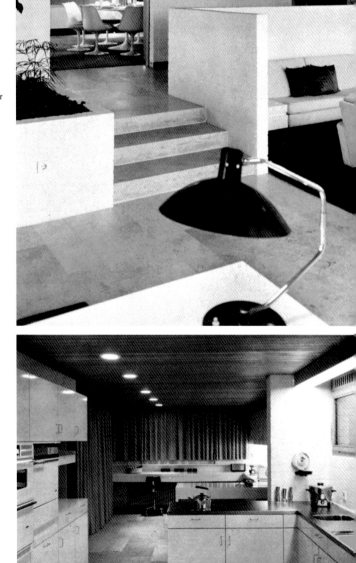

House at Pflaumloch, near the Bavarian border
architects Hans Kammerer
and Walter Belz
in collaboration with Klaus Kucher

On the outskirts of a newly built-up area
of smaller houses this site offered little natural
interest or variety; it was therefore landscaped
to create a fold of land into which the house
was integrated.
This handling of the site secured privacy for
those areas where it was most desired—a
sheltered approach, terrace and entrance hall
with access to sauna and swimming pool a
half-flight down on the lowered level.
The open plan living area levels are further
varied, the main sitting room 3 steps down
from the circulation area and a snuggery a
further 3 steps down.
Bedrooms are above the sauna and pool areas.
White-painted sandstone forms both exterior
and interior walls, including certain 'structural
furniture', e.g. the planting areas which soften,
screen and divide the living space.
Roof, ceiling and window-frames are all
of Oregon pine, the roof being insulated by
several layers of roofing felt and ballasted
with gravel.
Floors are of Jura marble with fitted carpets.

picture
  1 the study seen from the snuggery well
  2 south elevation of the house across the
     garden
  3 fountain court at the west side
  4 entrance hall with reception area to the
     left
  5 detail of south facade
  6 umbrella stand
  7 entrance hall from stairs leading to the
     bedrooms
  8 sitting area from the study/hi-fi corner
  9 detail of swimming pool
 10 interior fountain courtyard from the
     entrance hall
 11 view to the dining room with sitting area
     on the right
 12 general view of kitchen

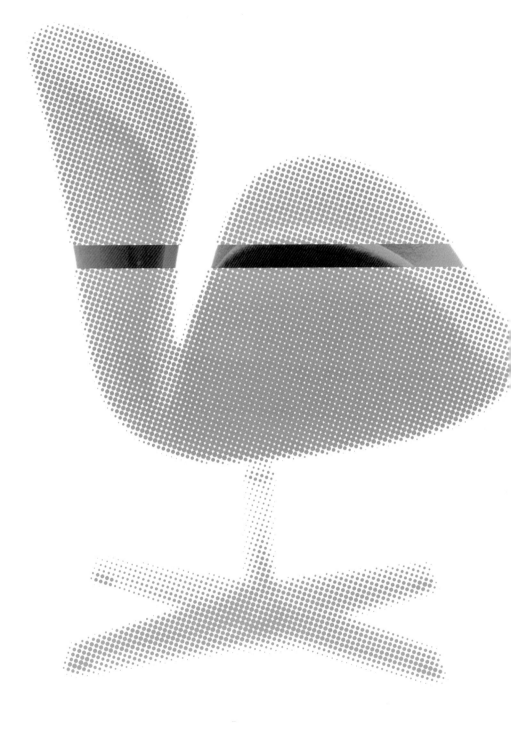

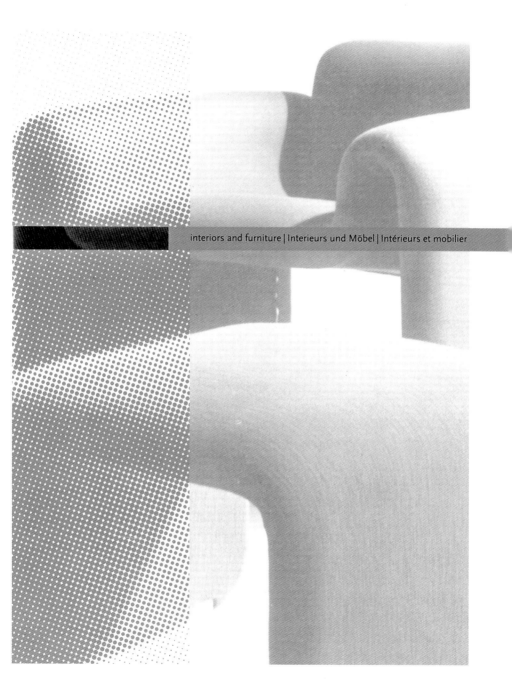

interiors and furniture | Interieurs und Möbel | Intérieurs et mobilier

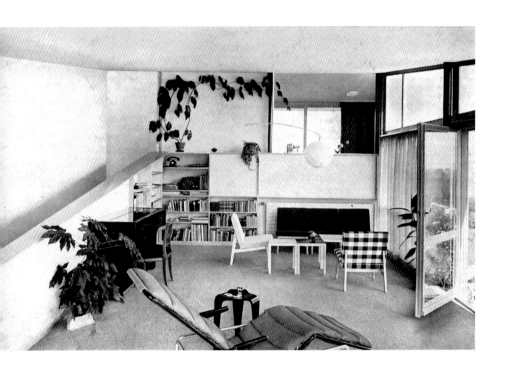

▲ This living room is part of a large studio/living/dining area which can be separated by sliding partitions. A ramp leads up to the studio (background) and bedrooms, its balustrade being integrated with the half-height bookshelf wall. Home of the architect Alfred Altherr, SWB Zürich SWITZERLAND

▼ Mahogany cabinet with birch top and framing, with one cupboard fitted as a bar. The table on sculptured legs has a Securit glass top. Interior designed by Max L. van Megen. Executed by NV Asscher HOLLAND

The G-Plan *Liang* sofabed converts to a full length double bed by lifting the front of the seat which releases a hinge, allowing both back and seat to lie flat. Interior sprung, with storage for bedding under the seat. Made by E. Gomme Ltd UK   ▼

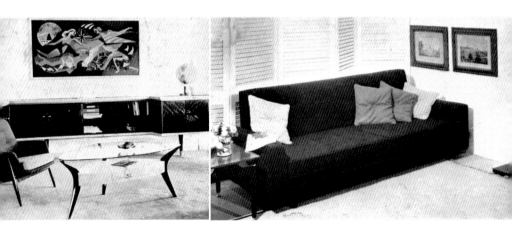

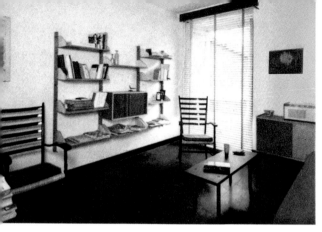

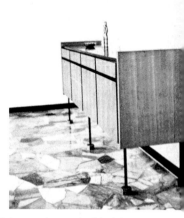

▼ Hi-Fi in a setting attuned to its golden tones. The Studio 1 Combination receiver/record player with separate speaker cabinet, designed by Max Braun GERMANY

▲ Study/reception room furnished for a painter with low-cost mahogany units, Chiavari chairs and small slate-topped olivewood table. The wall fitting is made up of demountable units permitting variable arrangement of shelves and cabinets. ▲ Cherrywood cabinet with black iron legs resting on cherrywood feet—detail from interior Designed by Prof. Marcello Parigi, executed by F. Sabbadini, Chiavari ITALY

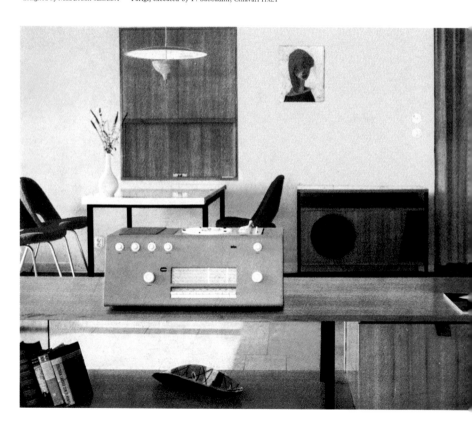

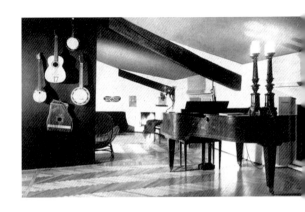

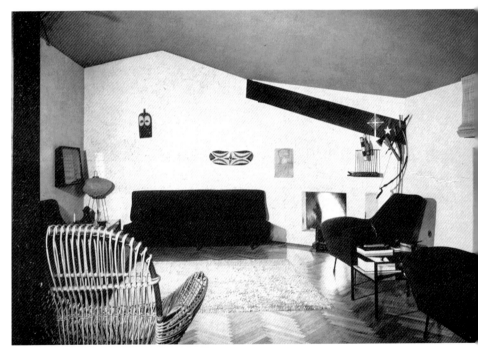

Living-room of an 'attic apartment' of character, created out of the unusual internal spaces under
complicated oak-beamed roof surmounting an old palace. The original structural elements a
stressed, with low sloping ceilings painted a lead-grey to accentuate their plastic weight; shadowed
walls painted a dark-brown against which others painted white stand out with sparkling clarit
windows are at floor level. The chairs, upholstered in vivid colours and in black, are models
prototypes of pieces designed by the owner, architect Mario Tedeschi, Milan ITALY

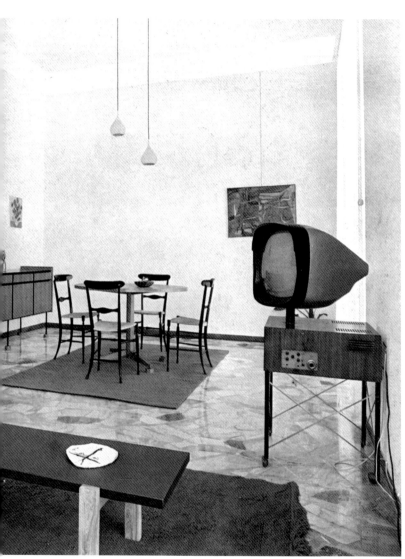

re-designed, this interior has a mosaic floor in Siena marble with washable walls painted white
pale-yellow.   The dining table is in cherrywood with rush-seated
nised dining chairs of the Chiavari 'campanino' type. The TV set, designed by Danio Montagni,
a separately mounted tube, which can be tilted and revolved. The living area is simply furnished
cane chairs, a slate-topped olive table and an upholstered bench seat with a fall-back which
verts it into a bed. Interior designed by Prof. Marcello Parigi, Chiavari ITALY

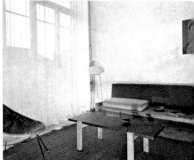

In the foreground, settee and two *Pernilla* easy chairs in bent-laminated beech with a dull plastic finish. The settee, with sprung seat and back, is upholstered in Eg Ult fabric and felt, the chairs in black leather strapping and a detachable brown sheepskin cover. The centre table is in birch with white Formica top surface, and beside the settee is a drop-leaf table with ash-bordered alder top on nickel-plated steel tube legs. The steel supported bookshelves are in untreated pine with brackets of bent, laminated birch. All are designed by Bruno Mathsson for Karl Mathsson SWEDEN ▼

Terrace of a flat in Buenos Aires forming an open-air extension to the living area. The iron-frame woven wicker chairs and stool, made on a basic oval pattern, are in a natural beige tone; the table top in pinkish-brown and beige wicker. Designed by the architect, Beppi Kraus de Newbery ARGENTINA ▶

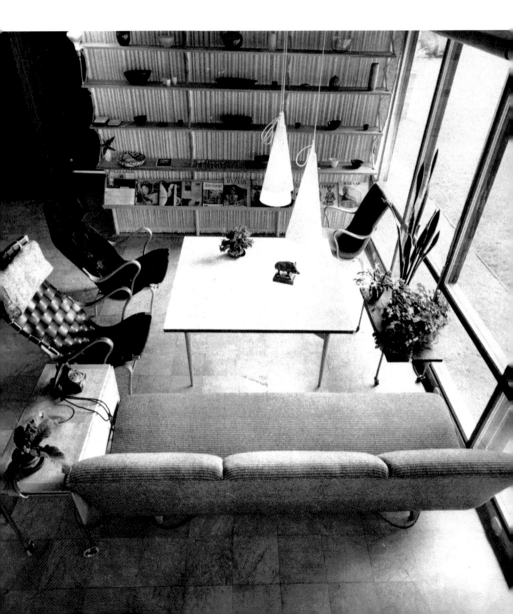

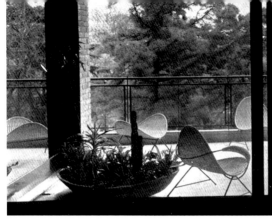

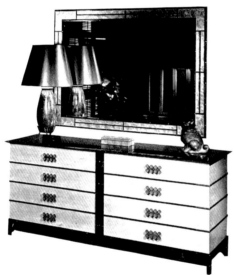

Corner bar in wild cherry with Formica surface to top shelf; the end support and ringed football bar stools are in wrought-iron. Detail from an interior designed by Jean Royère FRANCE ▼

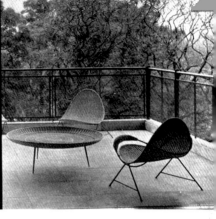

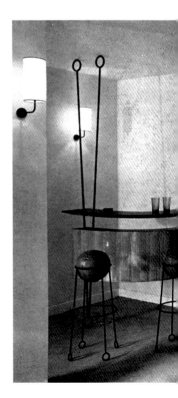

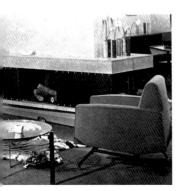

▲ Maple dresser, in veneered holly and black lacquer with bamboo and Kappa-shell framed mirror. From the Indonesian collection designed by Renzo R. Rutili for the Johnson Furniture Company USA

◀ Corner fireplace in black-lacquered tôle framed in marble, hung on a pale blue wall. The carpet is light green and the chair is upholstered in light tan. Detail from an interior designed by Raphaël SA, FRANCE

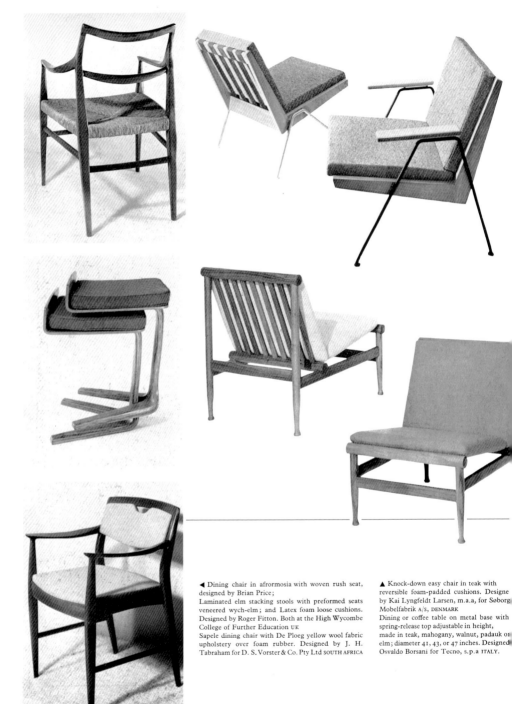

◀ Dining chair in afrormosia with woven rush seat, designed by Brian Price;
Laminated elm stacking stools with preformed seats veneered wych-elm; and Latex foam loose cushions. Designed by Roger Fitton. Both at the High Wycombe College of Further Education UK
Sapele dining chair with De Ploeg yellow wool fabric upholstery over foam rubber. Designed by J. H. Tabraham for D. S. Vorster & Co. Pty Ltd SOUTH AFRICA

▲ Knock-down easy chair in teak with reversible foam-padded cushions. Designe by Kai Lyngfeldt Larsen, m.a.a, for Søborg Mobelfabrik A/S, DENMARK
Dining or coffee table on metal base with spring-release top adjustable in height, made in teak, mahogany, walnut, padauk or elm; diameter 41, 43, or 47 inches. Designed Osvaldo Borsani for Tecno, s.p.a ITALY.

◄ *Chevron* mahogany frame chair on plastic-tipped steel legs, chrome-plated or black finish; Latex foam seat and back cushions. Designed by Robin Day, RDI, FSIA, for Hille of London UK

Low occasional table on black iron base. The top, measuring 60 × 40 inches, is in padauk with rhythmic plywood inlays. Designed by Tapio Wirkkala for Askon Tehtaat O/Y, FINLAND ▼

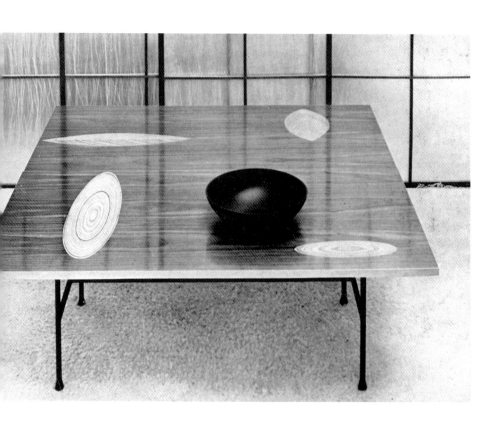

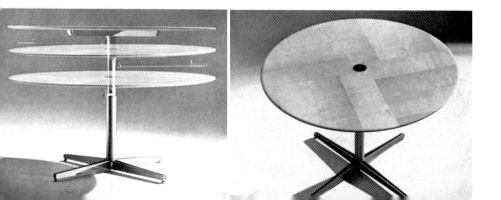

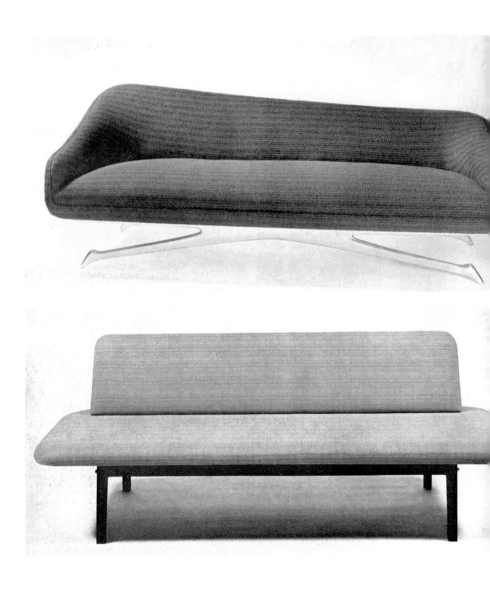

Settee with pre-formed seat 84 inches long on aluminium base, designed by Vladimir Kagan, AID. It is upholstered in fabrics designed by Hugo Dreyfuss and is made by Kagan-Dreyfuss Inc. USA

Day-bed of knock-down construction with detachable back-rest. It is 72 inches long and is made in walnut, oak, or maple with foam rubber cushioning. Designed by John M. Stene for the Brunswick Mfg Co. Ltd CANADA

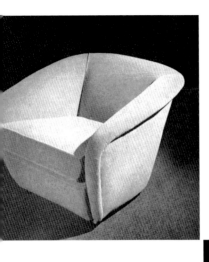

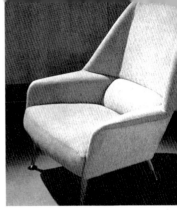

Flamingo easy chair, steel frame with Pirelli webbing on mahogany legs. It is upholstered in Latex foam and plastic foam, and is designed by Ernest Race, RDI, FSIA, for Ernest Race Ltd UK

rpheus chair and settee with beech frame upholstered bberised hair; Latex foam cushions. The settee, hich is made in two lengths, reflects the comfort of e old-time Chesterfield. Designed by Ronald Long, SIA, for R. S. Stevens Ltd UK ▲ ▶

asy chair with pre-formed seat on rubber-tipped eel legs, also available with wood underframe. esigned and made by Jens Risom Design, Inc. USA ▼

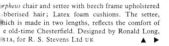

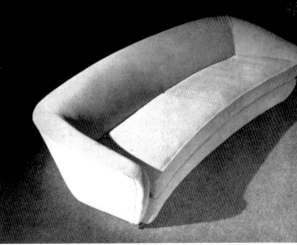

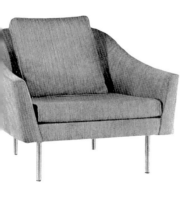

irage/Omega settee, curved beech frame with moulded atex foam back and reversible cushions, all on tension rings. Also made as a three-seat settee. Designed by . B. Keith, MSIA, for H. K. Furniture Ltd UK ▶

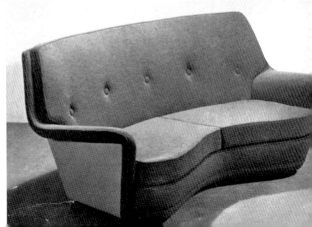

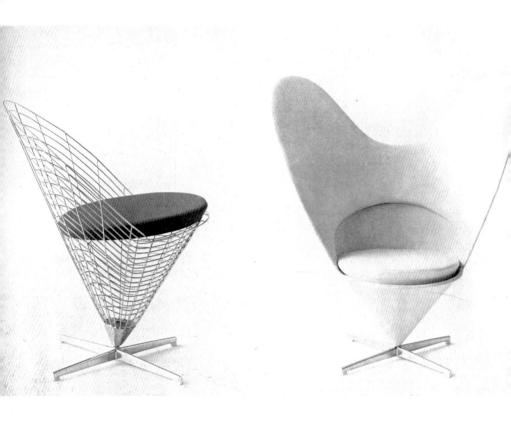

▲ Bar stool and wing chair from a range of chairs, tables and stools in thin plate steel or steel wire on stainless steel profile legs. All stresses are gathered to one point and both models revolve or remain stable at will. Upholstery is in foam-rubber with plasticised or wool covering fabrics. Designed by Werner Panton for Unika-Væv A/S, DENMARK

The Tulip high-back armchair, white moulded fibre glass shell on steel base, height 51 inches. Designed and made by Laverne Inc. USA ▶

Chromium-plated steel nylon-tipped stacking stools with painted plywood tops and leather-covered cushions. They are just over 12 inches high and 20 inches diameter. Designed by Poul Kjærholm for Ejvind Kold Christensen A/S, DENMARK ▼

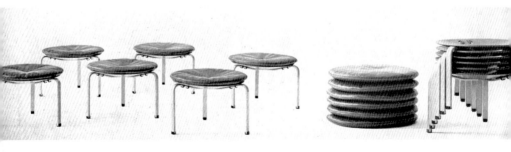

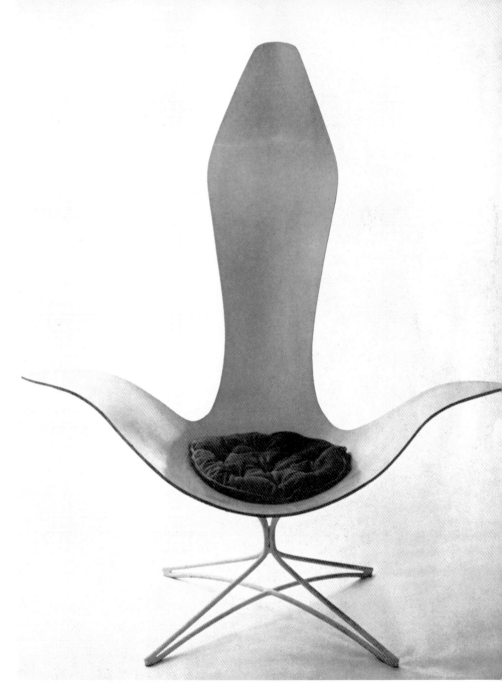

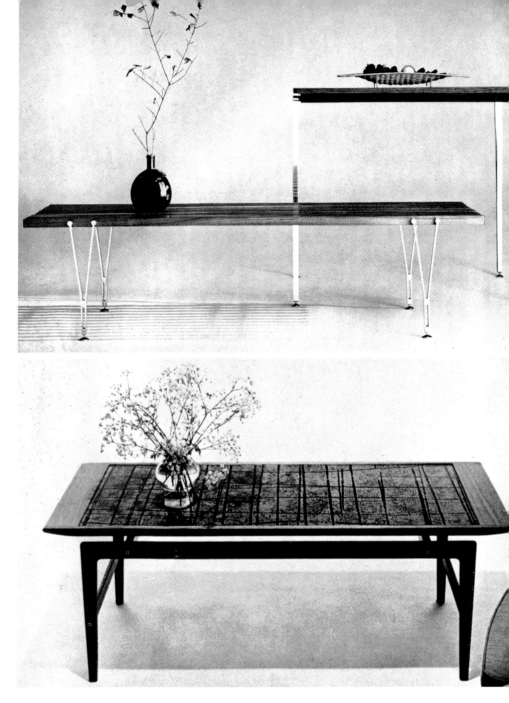

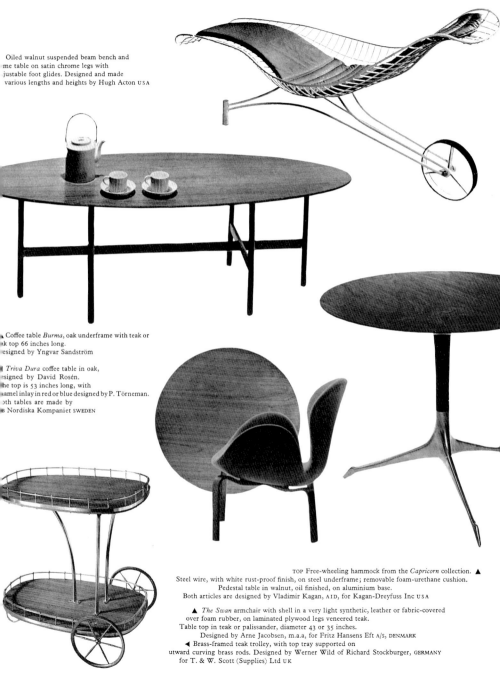

Oiled walnut suspended beam bench and ⁞me table on satin chrome legs with ⁞justable foot glides. Designed and made ⁞various lengths and heights by Hugh Acton USA

⁞ Coffee table *Burma*, oak underframe with teak or ⁞k top 66 inches long.
⁞esigned by Yngvar Sandström

⁞ *Triva Dura* coffee table in oak,
⁞signed by David Rosén.
⁞he top is 53 inches long, with
⁞amel inlay in red or blue designed by P. Törneman.
⁞oth tables are made by
⁞B Nordiska Kompaniet SWEDEN

TOP Free-wheeling hammock from the *Capricorn* collection. ▲
Steel wire, with white rust-proof finish, on steel underframe; removable foam-urethane cushion.
Pedestal table in walnut, oil finished, on aluminium base.
Both articles are designed by Vladimir Kagan, AID, for Kagan-Dreyfuss Inc USA

▲ *The Swan* armchair with shell in a very light synthetic, leather or fabric-covered
over foam rubber, on laminated plywood legs veneered teak.
Table top in teak or palissander, diameter 43 or 35 inches.
Designed by Arne Jacobsen, m.a.a, for Fritz Hansens Eft A/S, DENMARK
◀ Brass-framed teak trolley, with top tray supported on
utward curving brass rods. Designed by Werner Wild of Richard Stockburger, GERMANY
for T. & W. Scott (Supplies) Ltd UK

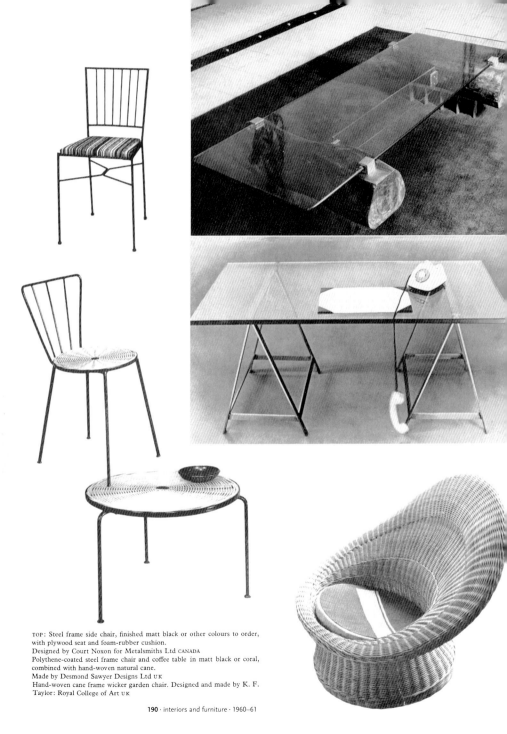

TOP: Steel frame side chair, finished matt black or other colours to order, with plywood seat and foam-rubber cushion.
Designed by Court Noxon for Metalsmiths Ltd CANADA
Polythene-coated steel frame chair and coffee table in matt black or coral, combined with hand-woven natural cane.
Made by Desmond Sawyer Designs Ltd UK
Hand-woven cane frame wicker garden chair. Designed and made by K. F. Taylor: Royal College of Art UK

◀ Low fireside table in Securit glass mounted on ebony logs. By Raphaël FRANCE
Polished steel trestle table with one-inch thick plate glass top 60 inches long. Designed by David Hicks for Hicks & Parr Ltd UK
Coffee table on black-lacquered metal legs with bevel-edge plate glass top. Designed by Max Ingrand FRANCE for Fontana Arte ITALY ▶

▼ Oiled walnut multiposition armchair with retractible aluminium footrest. Upholstered in Hugo Dreyfuss fabrics, it is designed by Vladimir Kagan, AID, for Kagan-Dreyfuss Inc. USA
Laminated high-frequency pressed shell, upholstered *Structura* weave over Latex foam, on polished metal legs. Designed by Pierre Paulin FRANCE for Wagemans & van Tuinen NV HOLLAND. The brass-ringed dull-lacquered fireirons are designed by Jens H. Quistgaard for Dansk Designs DENMARK

RIGHT, ▼ Circular occasional table in walnut, teak or cherrywood, with smoked-glass top. Made by Wilhelm Renz KG GERMANY
Oiled walnut sculptured table with elliptical plate glass top. Designed by Vladimir Kagan, AID, for Kagan-Dreyfuss Inc. USA

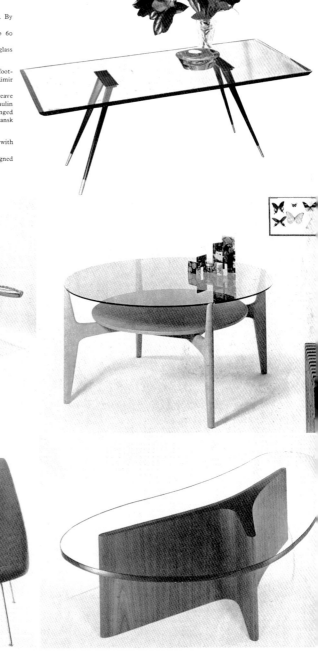

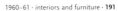

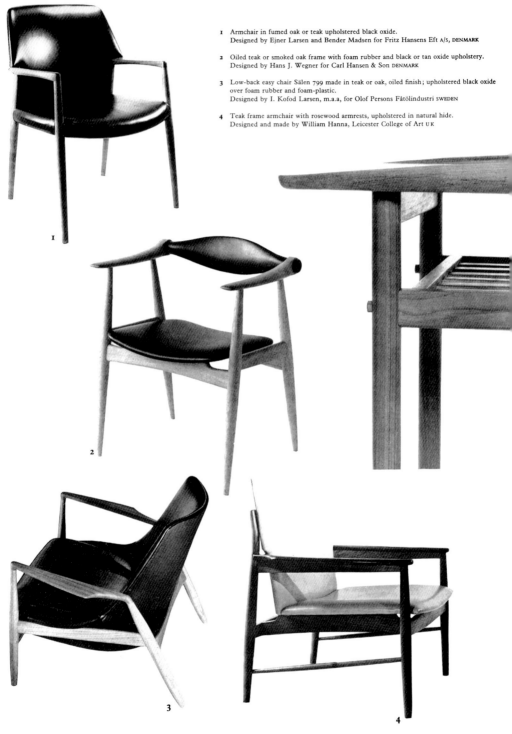

1 Armchair in fumed oak or teak upholstered black oxide.
Designed by Ejner Larsen and Bender Madsen for Fritz Hansens Eft A/S, DENMARK

2 Oiled teak or smoked oak frame with foam rubber and black or tan oxide upholstery.
Designed by Hans J. Wegner for Carl Hansen & Son DENMARK

3 Low-back easy chair Sälen 799 made in teak or oak, oiled finish; upholstered black oxide
over foam rubber and foam-plastic.
Designed by I. Kofod Larsen, m.a.a, for Olof Persons Fåtölindustri SWEDEN

4 Teak frame armchair with rosewood armrests, upholstered in natural hide.
Designed and made by William Hanna, Leicester College of Art UK

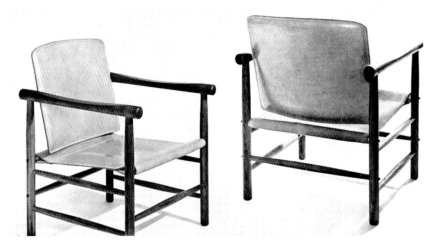

BELOW: Low coffee table in teak, walnut or rosewood with top measuring 65 inches. LEFT: Detail from an end table in the same range. Both designs are of knock-down construction. Designed by Grete Jalk for P. Jeppesen's Møbelfabrik A/S, DENMARK. Double-frame armchair in English walnut with leather-covered seat and backrest. Designed by Colin Eggleton, High Wycombe College of Further Education UK

▲ Knock-down easy chair, No. 506, made in solid teak with oxhide seat and back rest; note the flattened curve of the armrests. Designed by Kai Lyngfeldt Larsen, m.a.a, for Søborg Møbelfabrik A/S, DENMARK. BOTTOM: Easy chair on Wengé wood underframe, shell upholstered in natural leather. Designed by E. Veranneman BELGIUM

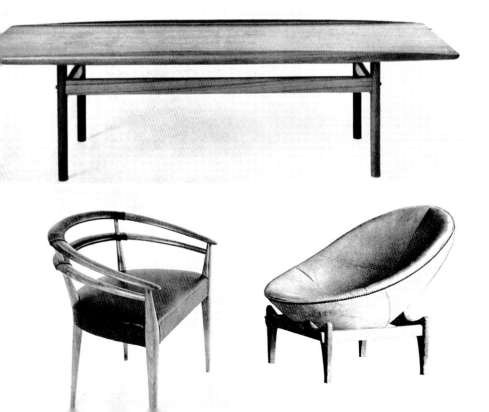

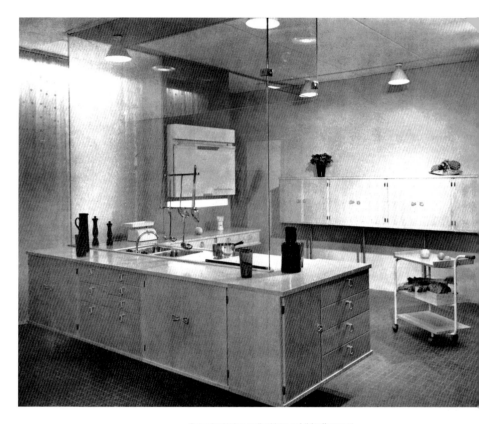

Open-plan kitchen, wall cabinets and 'island' storage/
sink unit in polished ash and stainless steel with hooded
screen of Securit glass; floor in grey ceramic tiles.
Designed by Jacques Hitier FRANCE

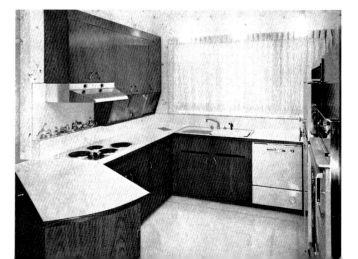

Compact small kitchen with all fitting
in; the storage cabinets are in oiled
with counter tops in Formica. Desig
Sigrun Bulow-Hube for the Aka Fu
Co. Ltd CANADA

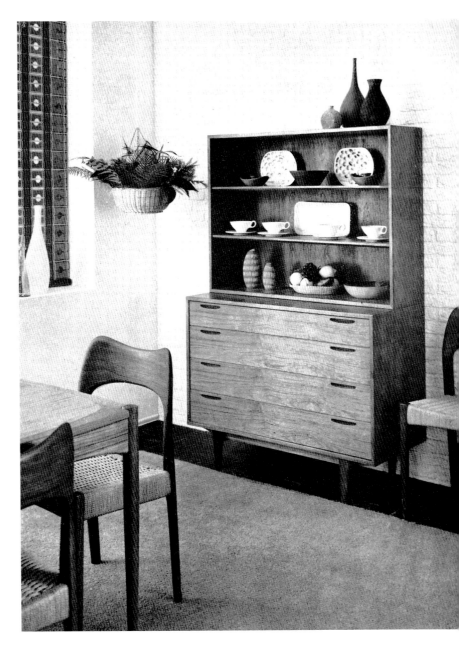

Jutland dining group in hand-rubbed oiled teak. The four-drawer chest and shelf unit (which can be used separately) is designed by Ib Kofod-Larsen, the chairs by Hovmand-Olsen of Denmark for the Selig Manufacturing Co. USA

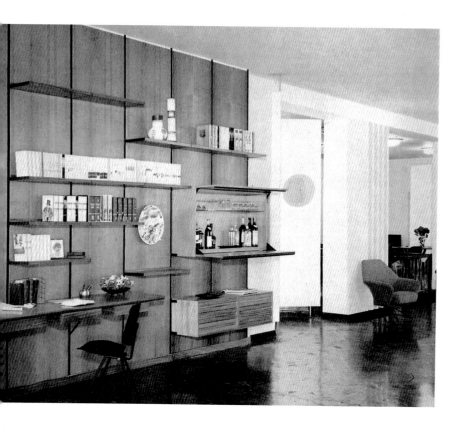

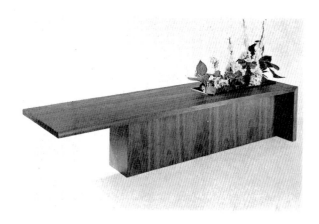

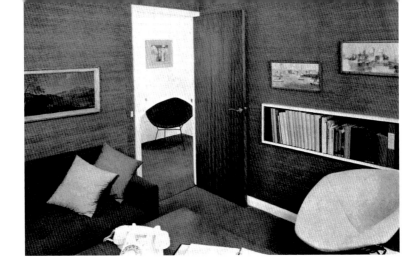

Wall elements designed for variable arrangement at y height on metal rails. They can be applied directly the wall or combined as a room divider with or ithout wood panels.   Designed by Osvaldo Borsani r Tecno s.p.a. ITALY

BELOW: Coffee table with metal plant container et in the 66-inch long top. Designed by Vladimir agan, AID, for Grosfield House USA

▲ Corner of reception room with white-framed bookshelf inset against a background of brownish/black Japanese grasscloth wallpaper.   The *Bertoia* chairs are upholstered in off-white and black, the *Vono* sofa in dark olive green with lettuce green cushions. Interior designed by Spencer & Gore UK

▼ Fireplace in brick and tile with slate top. Designed by Jean Royère; tapestry by Picart le Doux FRANCE

Chimneypiece in two tones of grey brick with white marble mantelshelf. Designed by Emile Veranneman BELGIUM   ▼

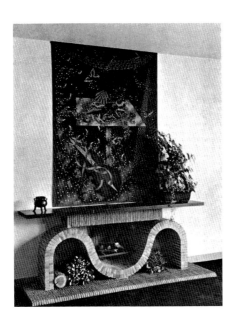

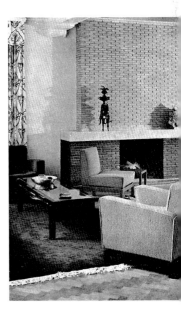

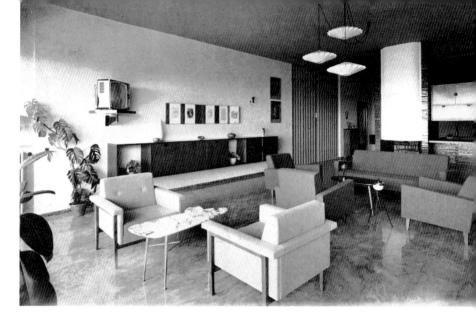

Large living room with glazed brick ceiling-height chimney piece dividing off a small dining area; opposite (not shown) is a window wall opening onto a balcony. Polished marble floor with furniture and wall fittings (which includes a bracket for the television set) in polished walnut. Divans and Pistoai chairs are upholstered in blue and light green wool fabric over foam rubber.

Dining room: table, trolley and adjustable wall elements in teak with the doors of the cabinet faced in blue and white Formica; the Chiavari chairs are upholstered in orange.

Both interiors are conversions for large villas designed by Prof. Marcello Parigi, Chiavari ITALY

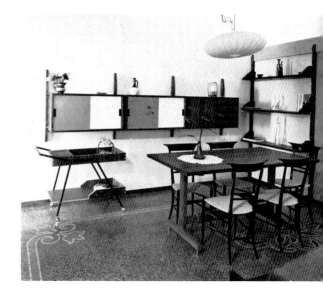

With the exception of the red-upholstered Knoll chair in the foreground, the main scheme of this living room is kept to white/grey/black with colour brilliance provided by the tropical garden seen through the picture windows. It is furnished with sculptured pieces upholstered in medium and dark grey bouclé fabrics, marble and copper-topped tables and a shelf/cabinet wall fitting on black iron tube supports for bar, radio and record player. Over the corner open hearth a black sheet iron hood. Interior designed by architect Beppi Kraus de Newbery ARGENTINA

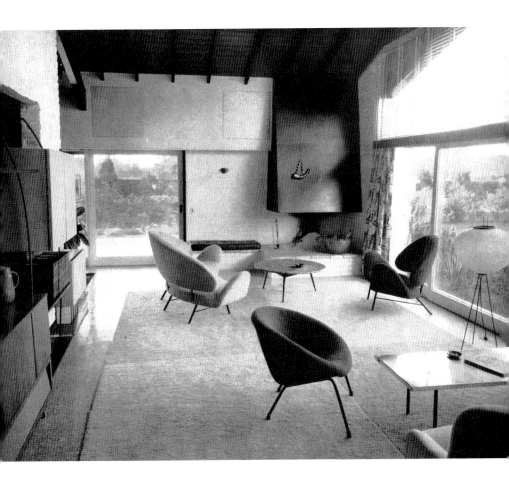

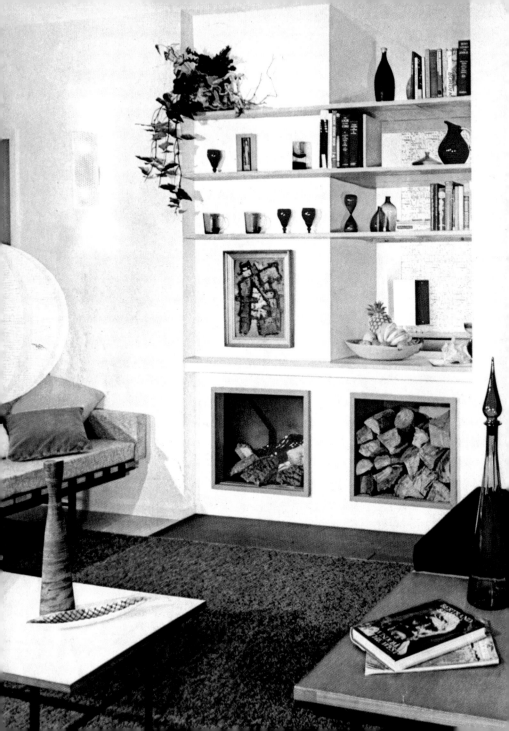

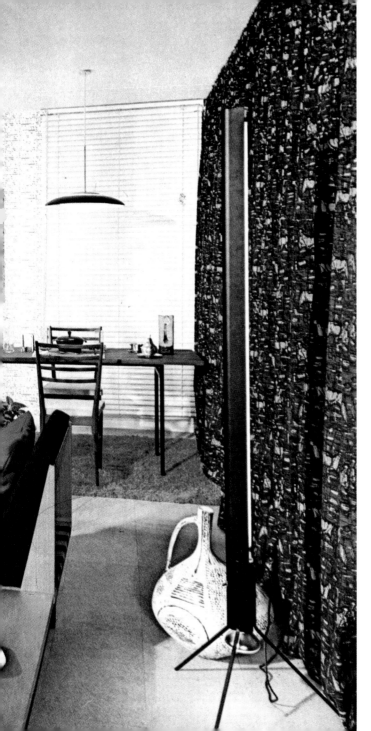

An award-winning interior scheme based on a modified open plan. The chimney piece, fitted with display shelves, forms a dividing link between the two areas. Informality in grouping, continuous curtain treatment, a vibrant colour scheme, furniture of simple lines scaled to the proportions of the room, all contribute to an air of solid comfort. The floor is in 'Jointite' cork tiles from Mundet Cork Products with Kosset carpeting;
Tumbeltwist rug from Shelley Textiles at the dining end;
Wallpaper *Night Watch* by Arthur Sanderson & Sons Ltd.
Curtains *Galloway* by Edinburgh Weavers;
Modulus seating units by Hille of London Ltd

White plastic top coffee table by Stafford Furniture Ltd; with vase by Briglin Pottery Ltd.
Fluorescent tube standard by Fluorel Ltd and stoneware wine bottle by A. & R. Duckworth Ltd.
At the dining end, a pendant in spun aluminium and opal glass by Merchant Adventurers Ltd hangs above the afrormosia dining group made by D. Meredew Ltd.
House designed by R. J. Nicol and A. M. Edwards, AARIBA; interior furnished by Busbys (Bradford) Ltd to a scheme prepared by Mrs Helen Challen.

Courtesy 'Ideal Home'

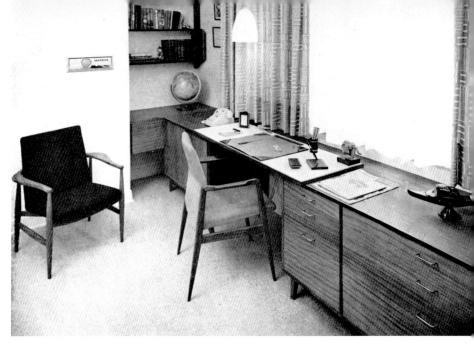

▲ Boy's study with writing shelf bridging a continuous arrangement of storage units in afrormosia. Designed by Sigrun Bulow-Hube for the Aka Furniture Co. Ltd CANADA
Demountable bedroom units from the AM8 range. In semi-matt cherry or palissander wood with bed frame lacquered black and chromium steel bases to the dressing table and glass-topped bedtable surfaced in white plastic. Designed Willy Guhl, SWB/VSI. Made by AG. vorm. Ad. Aeschlimann; steel frame cane chair made by Dietiker & Co. SWITZERLAND

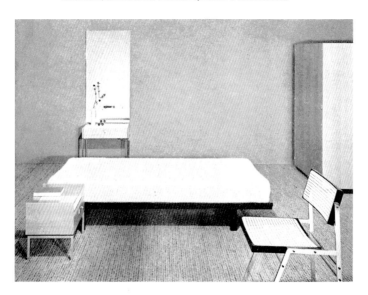

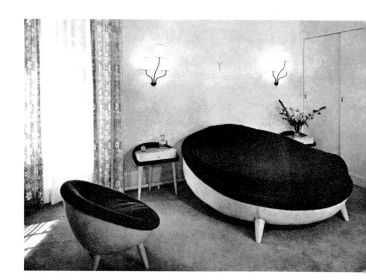

Woman's bedroom with bed, armchair and bedtables upholstered in royal blue and yellow fur velvet. Twin-bedded children's room with fitments in natural waxed oak; the black metal frame chairs are upholstered in 'Havana' plasticised fabric. Both interiors are designed by Jean Royère in collaboration with Jacques Levy Ravier FRANCE

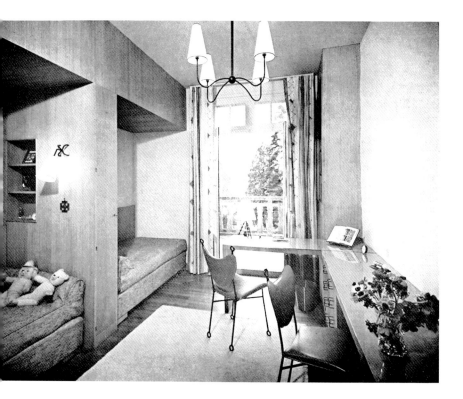

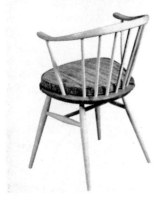

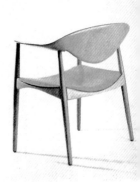

Windsor chair, solid elm with framings in beech; the foam cushion has a detachable cover and straps. Designed by Lucian R. Ercolani for Ercol Furniture Ltd UK

▼ *Stamford* panel back dining chairs in natural or oiled walnut or mahogany finishes with upholstered seats. Designed by Robert Heritage, MSIA, for Archie Shine Ltd UK

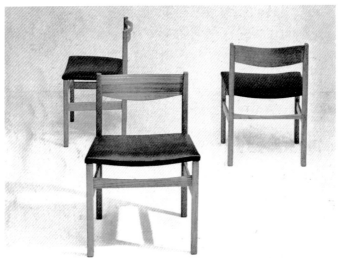

▼ Square-section steel frame chair, satin chrome finish, with back and rails in mahogany; laminated upholstered seat. Designed and made by Harry Sowden, MSIA, UK

Carver chair in solid oak, teak or ash; seat padded foam rubber with fabric cover. Designed by Carl-Axel Acking for AB Nordiska Kompaniet SWEDEN ▶

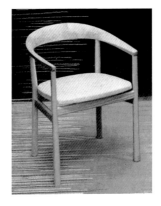

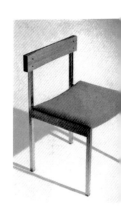

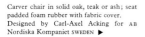

◀ Oak chair with tan leather upholstery. Designed by A. Bender Madsen and Ejner Larsen.
Made by Willy Beck DENMARK
Ebonised beech chair with seat of woven cane.
Designed by Gio Ponti ITALY.
From Conran Furniture UK ▶

Dining chair in teak, rosewood, walnut or ash with leather or fabric covered foam padded seat.
Designed by Renato Venturi for Mobili MiM s.p.a. ITALY

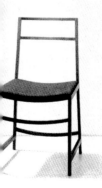

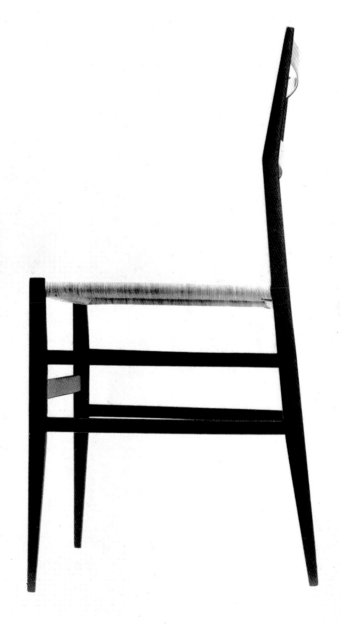

P.32, metal frame with swivel seat and adjustable back-tilt mechanism; removable cover over foam rubber upholstery. Designed by Osvaldo Borsani for Tecno s.p.a. ITALY

Marlowe, beech frame upholstered rubberised hair, with L foam cushion on rubber webbings. Designed by Ronald Long, MSIA, for R. S. Stevens Ltd UK

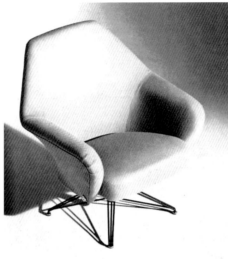

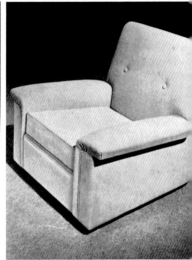

Junior, beech or teak frame with padded seat and backrest. Designed by I. Relling for West Norway Factories Ltd A/S. From Westnofa (London) Ltd UK

Aurora glass fibre shell on mahogany legs; removable cov plastic foam cushioning. Designed by W. S. Chenery, Des.RCA, for Lurashell Ltd

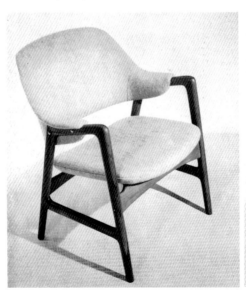

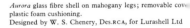

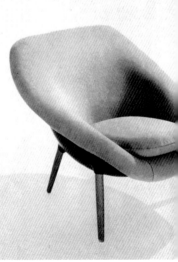

eel frame wide chair on mahogany legs; upholstered
e Ploeg yellow wool fabric over Dunlopillo.
esigned by J. H. Tabraham for R. Schultz SOUTH AFRICA

High back armchair with footrest, made in a variety of woods and a
wide range of covering fabrics.
Designed by Sigrun Bulow-Hube for the Aka Furniture Co. Ltd CANADA

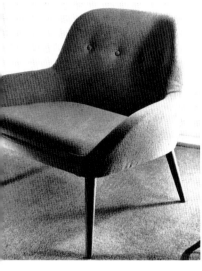

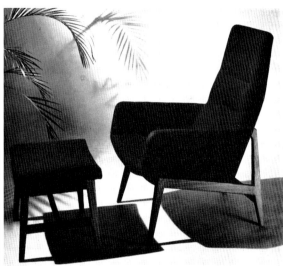

lid teak frame armchairs. Spring interior on flat
licals with polyurethane and foam rubber upholstery:
Model 152 designed by Finn Juhl, m.a.a.

▼ Model 125 designed by Edv. Kindt-Larsen, m.a.a.
There is a matching settee 56 inches wide.
Models 125 and 152 made by France & Søn A/S, DENMARK

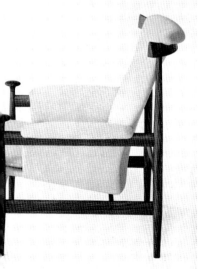

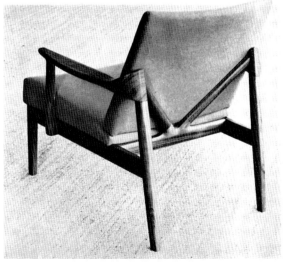

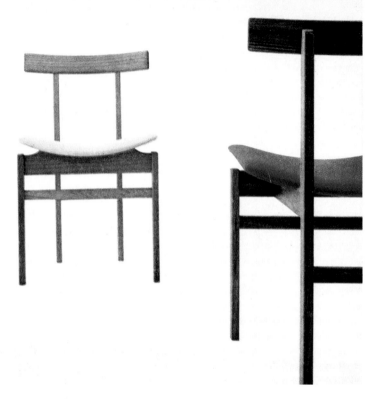

Dining chair, Model 193, in solid teak; laminated seat with upholstery pad of polyurethane. Designed by Inger Klingenberg.

Dining chair, Model 205, solid teak frame, laminated swivel back with caned panel, upholstered seat.
Designed by Arne Vodder. ▶
Both made by France & Søn A/S, DENMARK

▼ Sideboard *Hamilton* in rosewood and mahogany, Indian laurel and walnut, or teak finishes; length 90 inches.
Designed by Robert Heritage, MSIA, for Archie Shine Ltd UK

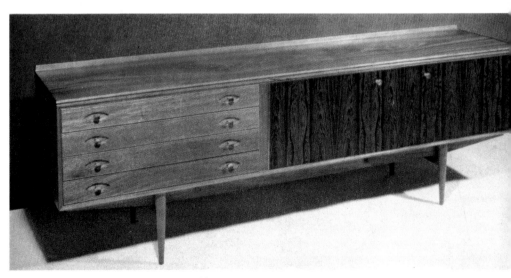

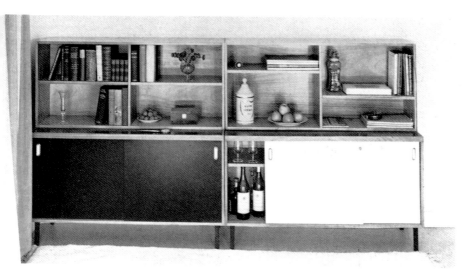

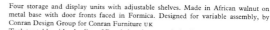

Four storage and display units with adjustable shelves. Made in African walnut on metal base with door fronts faced in Formica. Designed for variable assembly, by Conran Design Group for Conran Furniture UK

Teak tea table with edge lists of Bangkok teak; top 55 inches long with 16-inch pull-out trays in plastic or teak veneers. Designed by Tove and Edv. Kindt-Larsen for AB Seffle Möbelfabrik SWEDEN

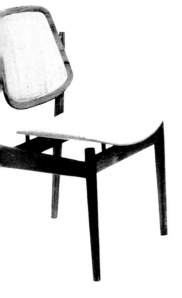

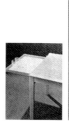

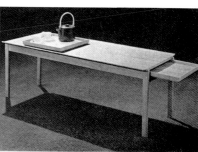

ee-drawer hall chest *Entré* in teak or oak.
gned by Erich Merten, SIR. Made by AB Dio
elindustri for Threemen AB, SWEDEN ▶

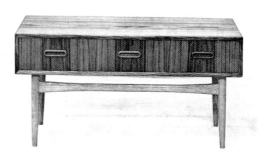

▼ Chaise longue *Eden* from the 'Paradise' suite, with foam-padded moulded light plastic curved frame; the seat, 66½ inches long, has 'No-sag' springs, with mahogany, teak or walnut finishes to the red beech legs. Designed by Kerstin Hörlin-Holmquist for AB Nordiska Kompaniet SWEDEN

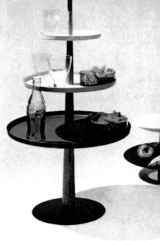

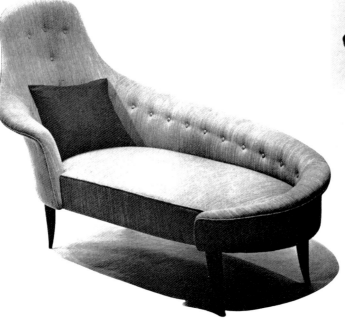

Sofa *Duello*, with laminated frame and shaped c‖ upholstered in a wide range of covering fabric‖ foam-rubber. Designed by Olof Ottelin fo‖ Stockmann-Orno FINLAND ▶

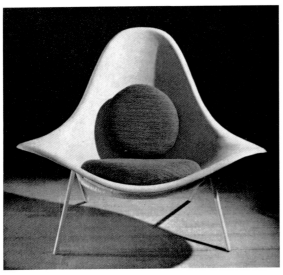

◀ Easy chair of moulded fibreglass on metal‖ Designed by Sandra Heath, student at the C‖ School of Arts & Crafts, for Heal's of London t‖

Pedestal group, chrome metal base with rev‖ foam-padded laminated chair seats, and ma‖ footrest; the table tops, 28 and 41 inches dia‖ are in rosewood or Formica. All designed by Paulin FRANCE for the *Artifort* range made by ‖ mans & Van Tuinen N V, HOLLAND ▶

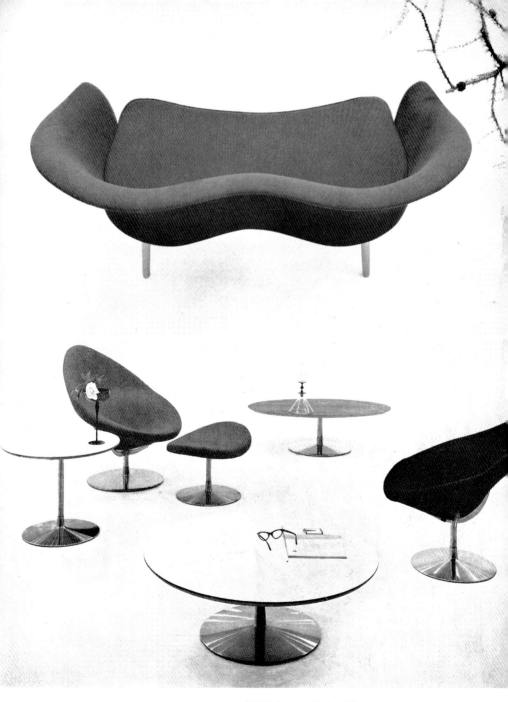

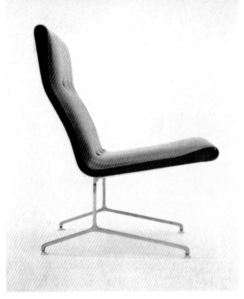

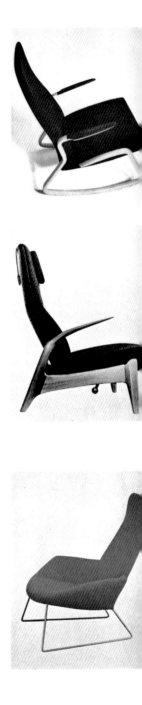

Hall chair in moulded plywood with foam rubber padding and leather upholstery; legs in stainless steel. Designed by Stefan Siwinski for Korina Designs CANADA

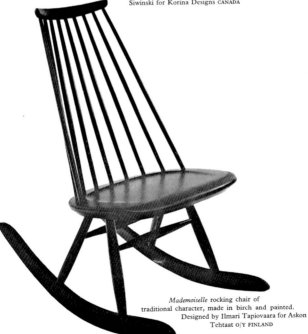

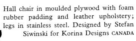

Mademoiselle rocking chair of traditional character, made in birch and painted. Designed by Ilmari Tapiovaara for Askon Tehtaat O/Y FINLAND

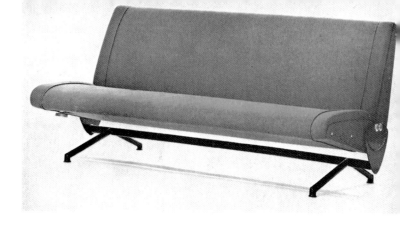

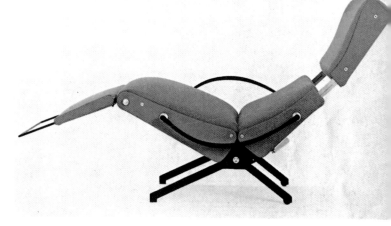

▼ Rocking chair, laminated ash frame with rosewood arms; upholstery rubber webbing and Latex foam under wool tapestry cover. Made by Gordon Gray, High Wycombe College of Further Education UK
◄ Rock'n-rest chair in polished mahogany, teak or oak; seat rockable, or fixed in any one of eight positions. A Norwegian design made by Gimson & Slater Ltd UK

Reclining chair P.40 with jointed metal frame adjustable to many positions; upholstery foam rubber with removable covers available in a wide range of colours.
TOP Settee D.70 with back and seat adjustable to any angle, reversible, or extended to make a bed by lever mechanism operated by side knob (see diagram). Underframe in stove-enamelled steel tube with brass fittings; upholstery foam-rubber with fitted removable cover. Both designed by Osvaldo Borsani for Tecno, s.p.a. ITALY

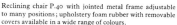

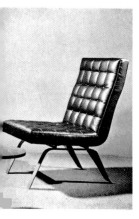

◄ ◄ Armchair, mild steel rod frame with wool fabric upholstery over foam padding. Designed by Colin Andrews, L.C.C. Technical College for the Furnishing Trades UK
◄ Hall chair, flat steel frame with welded steel rod mesh infilling to seat and back; upholstered in quilted black hide over foam rubber. Designed by Alan Hunt for H. Don Carolis & Sons Ltd CEYLON

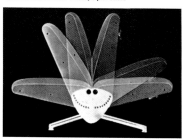

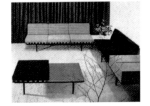

▼ ▶ Group and details from the *Form* range of interchangeable Modulus units on metal frames 28 inches wide and 56, 72 or 122 inches long. Table tops are plastic laminated or in makore; seat cushions foam rubber with zip-off covers. Designed by Robin Day, RDI, ARCA, FSIA, for Hille of London UK

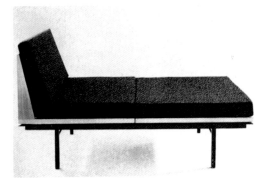

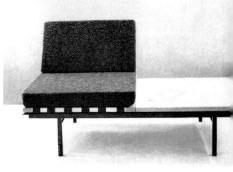

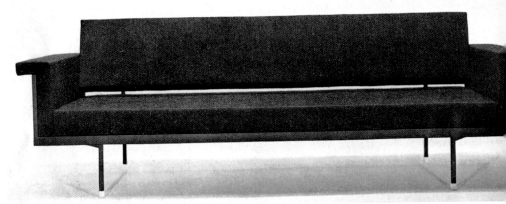

▲ *Naeko* long low settee, black iron or palissander under-frame, 89 inches long, upholstered latex foam with wool fabric covering.
Designed by Kasuhide Takahama of Japan for Gavina Poltrone ITALY

Tripos easy chair, mahogany or afrormosia seat adjustable to three positions suspended in square-section steel tube frame, fused nylon or satin chrome finish; cushions Latex and plastic foam with detachable covers. Designed and made by Ernest Race Ltd UK

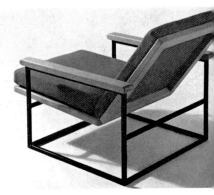

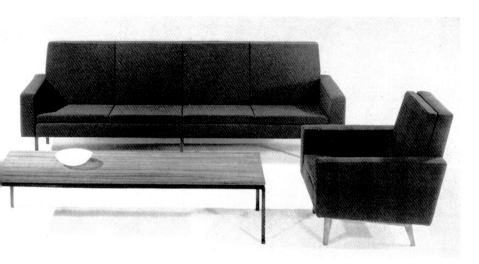

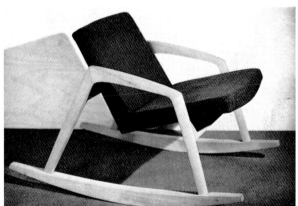

quare built armchair and settee for four
loose foam cushion seats 23 × 22 inches
xcelsa teak or metal frame. Florentine
zed frame tea table with Excelsa teak
66 inches long. Designed by Theo
apelman for A. Polak's Meubelindustrie
LAND

king chair, beech frame, plywood seat
olstered foam rubber. Designed and
e by Graham Probst, Kingston School
rt UK

Aziatica high-backed armchair and stool,
aut frame with slung seat upholstered
ish-brown wool fabric over foam rubber.
gned by Jos De Mey for Van den
ghe-Pauvers BELGIUM

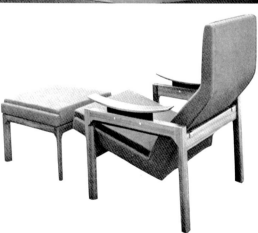

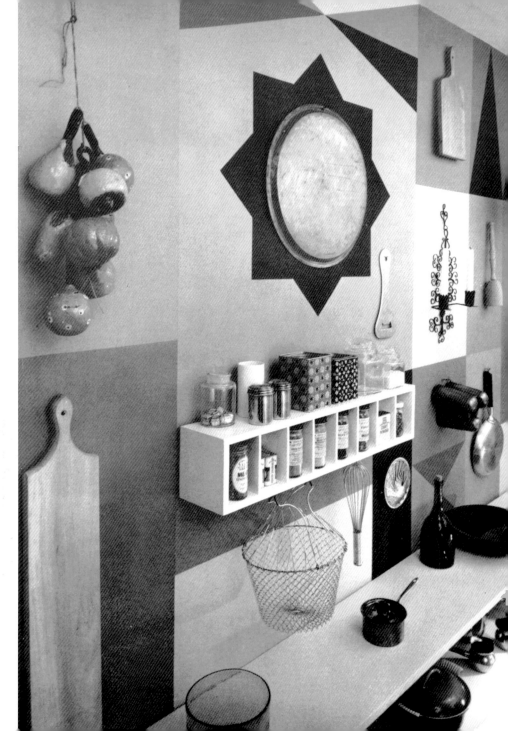

Teak chests of drawers with bevelled finger grips at the sides, recessed in the black spacer between each unit; top surfaces of teak or white plastic veneer. The continuous base is in brushed or polished chrome steel. Designed by Florence Knoll of Knoll Associates, Inc USA ▽ ▷

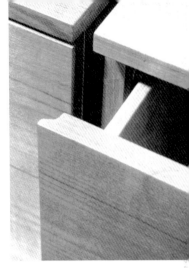

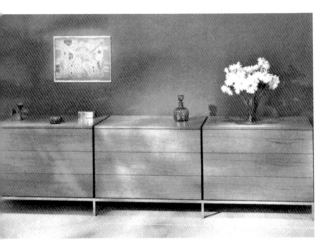

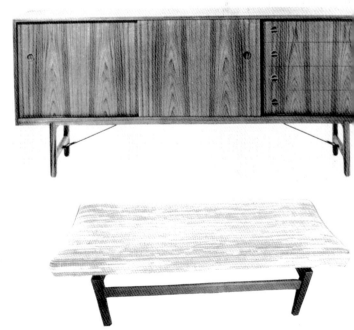

Teak sideboard lined in beech, with veneered door panels and recessed handles; 78 inches long. Designed by A. Bender Madsen and Ejner Larsen DENMARK. From Georg Jensen Inc USA

Walnut bench with seat cushion covered in a handwoven fabric of calfhide strips and wool. By Hella Skowronski USA

◁ Brilliant panels of colour frame the kitchen equipment in this New York apartment; spice shelf, chopping boards, moulds, omelet pans, salad baskets thus become part of a visual scheme. Underneath, white-lacquered shelves with a wine rack built in provide additional storage space. By Albert Herbert Design USA

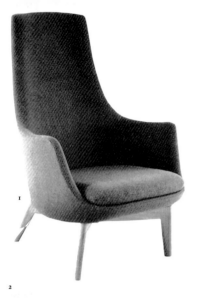

1

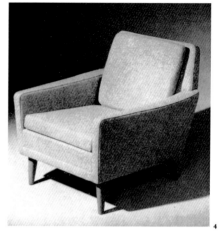

4

2

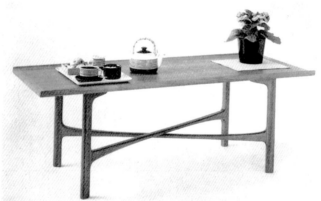

3

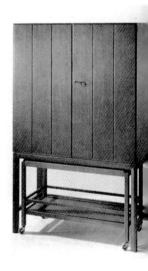

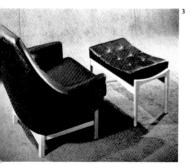

Furniture from SWEDEN

1
High back easy chair, moulded frame in poly-styrene, with base in teak. Designed by Karl Erik Ekselius for AB J. O. Carlsson

2
Coffee table *Carmel* designed by Folke Ohlsson. Made in teak and oak or in walnut by AB Svenska Möbelfabrikerna Bodafors

3
Armchair *Generalen* made entirely of foam rubber with removable foam seat cushion on rubber bands; the base is in oak. The foam-upholstered hassock *Siesta* is made in oak or in Bangkok teak. Designed by Ib Kofod-Larsen for Olof Persons Fåtöljindustri.

5
Cabinet and trolley *Signum* in mahogany, designed by Axel Larsson. for AB Svenska Möbel fabrikerna

6, 4
FOREGROUND Swivel-based *Contourett Roto* easy chairs, tubular steel and back frame with zig-zag springs, foam seat and neck pillow. Designed by Alf Svenson. BACKGROUND *Derby* group (armchair detail 4) on teak legs, upholstery based on zig-zag springs; foam-padded arms and reversible foam cushions with zipped covers. Designed by Folke Ohlsson. All made by Ljungs Industrier AB/Dux

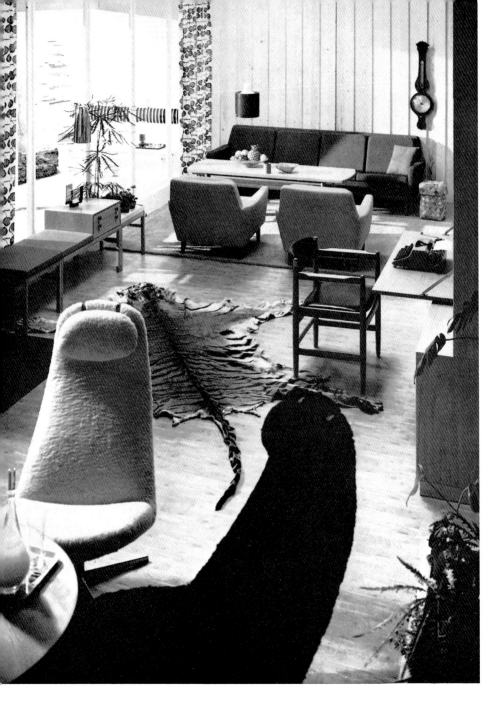

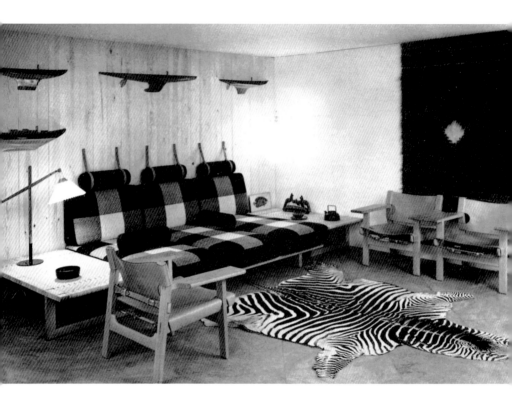

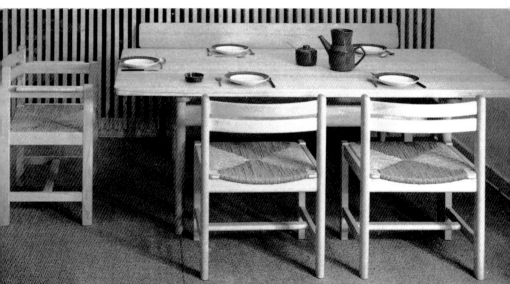

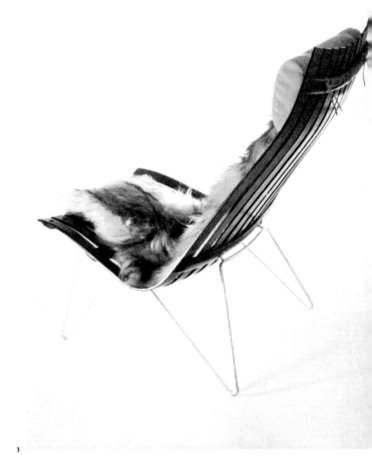

1
One-, two- or three-seater settee upholstered in brown/white large-check wool designed and woven by Lis Ahlmann has brown cylindrical cushions for the head and for knee support: as 'conveyors' they also facilitate sliding into the very deep seats. The hunting chairs are in light oak with back and seat in natural cow-hide. Made by Fredericia Stolefabrik A/S DENMARK

2
Dining table in oak or teak/oak, 62 × 32 inches, and chairs in oak and beech. Made by F. D. B. Møbler DENMARK

5
Chair and stool in light oak made by Fredericia Stolefabrik A/S DENMARK
All designed by Børge Mogensen, m.a.a.

3
Chair in moulded palissander with dyed sheepskin cover and down-filled head pillow. Designed by Hans Brattrud for Hove Møbler NORWAY

4
Chair with flag-line threaded seat and back; the steel frame cast in one piece, split, moulded and chrome-plated. Designed by Poul Kjærholm for E. Kold Christensen DENMARK

3

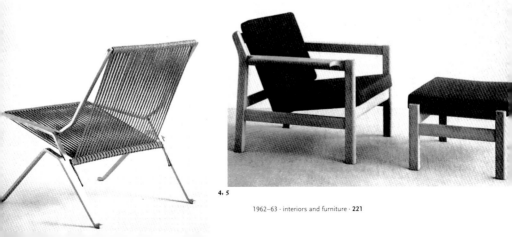

4, 5

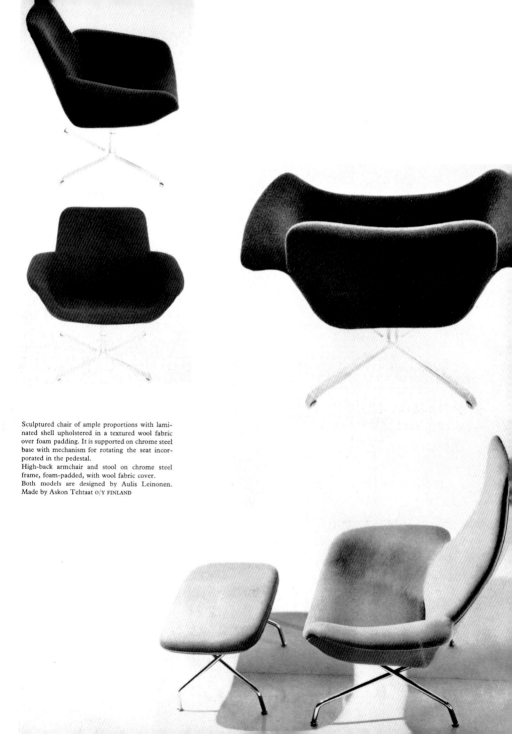

Sculptured chair of ample proportions with laminated shell upholstered in a textured wool fabric over foam padding. It is supported on chrome steel base with mechanism for rotating the seat incorporated in the pedestal.

High-back armchair and stool on chrome steel frame, foam-padded, with wool fabric cover.

Both models are designed by Aulis Leinonen. Made by Askon Tehtaat O/Y FINLAND

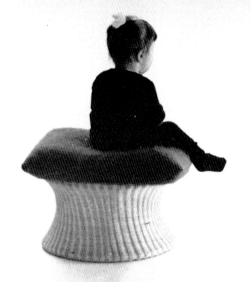

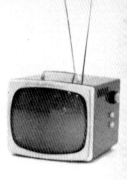

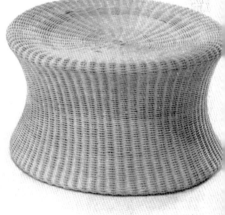

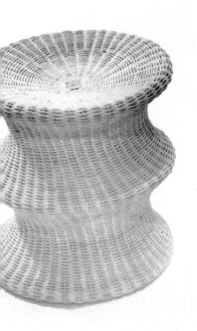

Light cane seats designed by Eero Aarnoi.
Made by Askon Tehtaat O/Y FINLAND

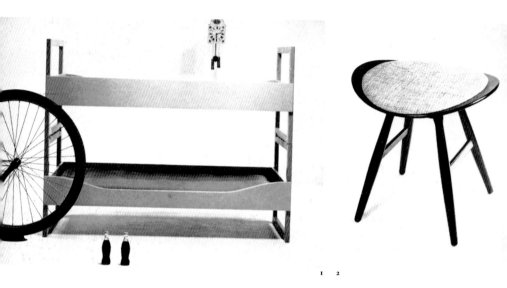

I   2

1, 2
Child's bed in painted wood. With the bunks
mounted on a hinged frame, it can be easily taken
down and transported.
Elipse tabouret in black-lacquered birch with foam
padded seat cushion.
Both are designed by Olof Ottelin for o/y Stockmann-Orno FINLAND

3
A simple and easily mounted basic furnishing
scheme of two- and three-drawer storage units in
natural pine with black lacquered sliding front
panels; steel frame moulded chair and stool
upholstered in wool fabric over foam padding.
Designed by Eero Aarnio for Askon Tehtaat o/y
FINLAND

3

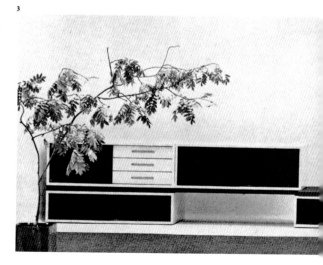

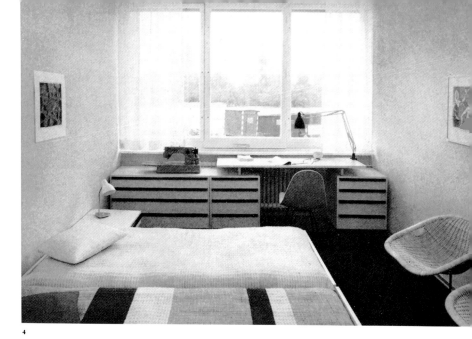

4

4
Double bedroom fitted with a sewing and work
area at the window end. The chest units ranged
along the wall are from the Freba range made by
K. H. Frei, and a removable shelf placed across
them makes a convenient desk. The moulded chair
is designed by Hans Bellman for Strässle Söhn &
Cie; the cane chairs by Wolfer & Moesch for
W. Jenny AG. Interior designed by Alfred Altherr
SWB SWITZERLAND

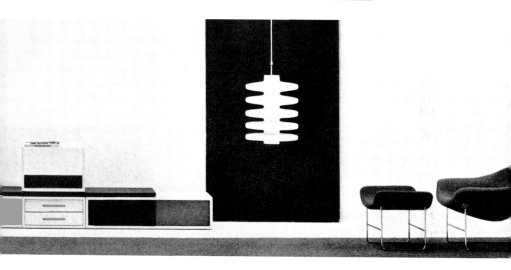

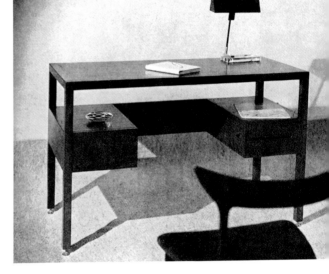

Tubular steel frame chairs with Pirelli webbing and moulded foam rubber padding. The one piece cover is in *Brynje*, a stretchable wool-nylon fabric by Unika Væv.
The chairs are designed by Pierre Paulin FRANCE for Wagemans & van Tuinen NV HOLLAND

Small three-drawer desk in imbuya. Designed by Erwin Plaut, MSIA, for Alexander Joles S. AFRICA

Metamorphose upholstered armchair on steel under-frame, from a unit range comprising one, two or four seats interchangeable with one another and with table tops in white plastic.
Designed by the Al-Veka team for Kembo Meubel-fabrieken NV HOLLAND

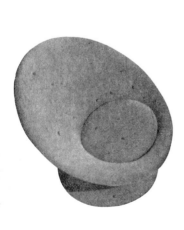

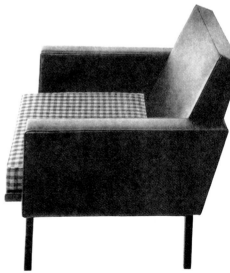

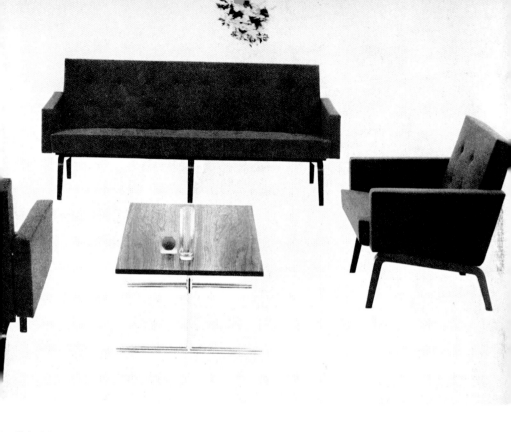

...n-padded upholstered sofa and chairs (series
...on metal or laminated plywood legs. They are
...able as one-, two-, three- and four-seater units
...or without arm supports. Table top in jaca-
...a on metal base. Designed by Theo Ruth.

...ular steel frame group (set 416) with black-
...ered side pieces and jacaranda-strip seat and
...suspension. Foam rubber cushions Vaumoll-
...covered. Designed by Kho Liang Le.

...of these groups are made by Wagemans & Van
...en NV HOLLAND

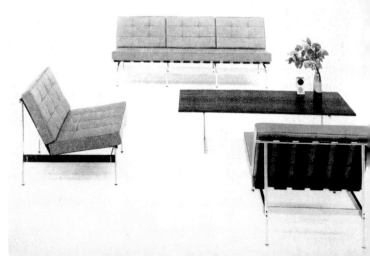

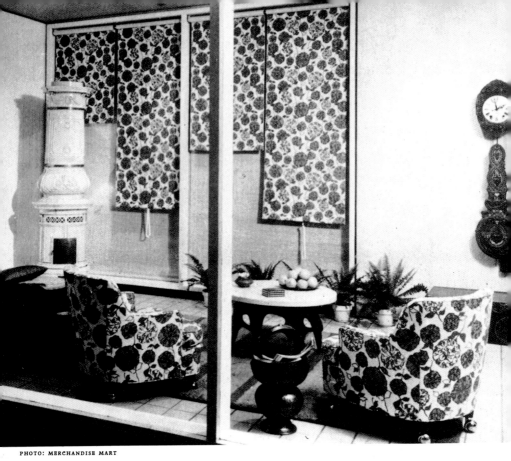

PHOTO: MERCHANDISE MART

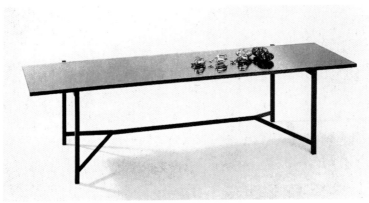

On a bright pink rug in an area of l
natural wood and within white
light-toned wood-panelled walls,
armchairs covered in a linen print
pinks and reds on a white grou
roller shades are of the same mate
Armchairs, the large black lea
pouffe and marble-topped walnut ta
all designed by Edward Wormley
A setting which uses an old Aust
white-enamelled stove, carved w
wall clock and other antique piece
Designed by Roy Klipp of John
Colby & Sons. Furniture made by
Dunbar Furniture Company USA
Coffee table model *2143*, top of
mirror crystal 149 cm long; m
underframe lacquered black. Mad
Fontana Arte ITALY
opposite
Fireplace with chimney breast
'pleated' stainless steel
Designed by Gautier-Delaye and m
by Usine-Gueunon FRANCE

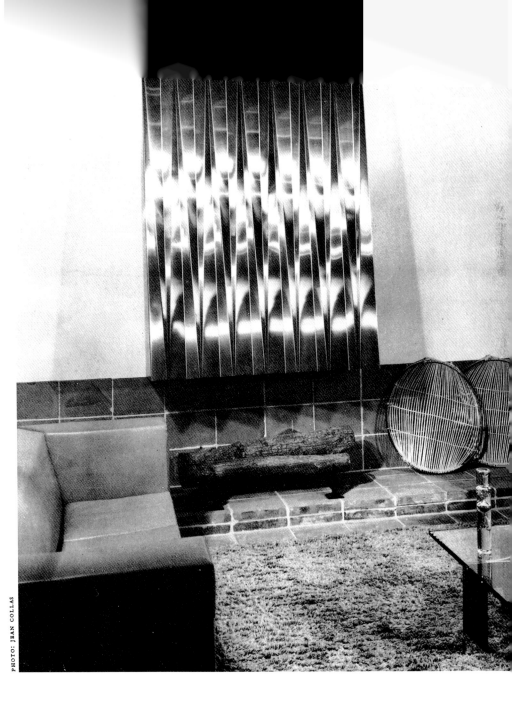

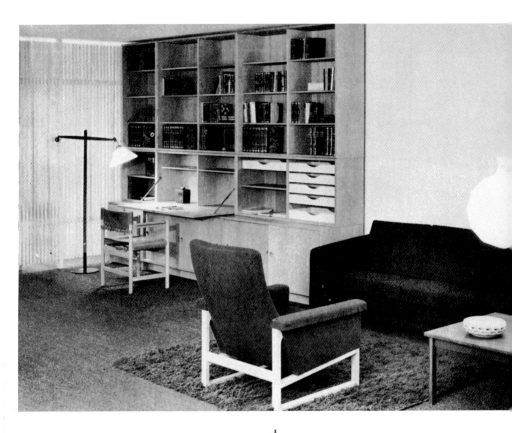

1
Storage fitting using a combination of units from the *Öresund* planned system in natural oak or teak, designed by Børge Mogensen and made by Karl Andersson & Söner SWEDEN. The settee and armchair are made by Fredericia Stolefabrik A/S DENMARK
2
Glass-topped coffee table on gilt iron frame
Designed and made by Jean Royère FRANCE
3, 5
Chrome-steel dining chair with continuous back/arm rest in teak or oak and loose latex foam seat cushion
4
Lightweight chair with moulded shell seat on a non-swivel aluminium base; overall height 96 cm
Designed by Jan Inge Hovig
6
Teak table, centre section in black oxhide or black plastic alternative finishes; 79 × 79 cm × 48 cm high
Designed by Kristian Vedel
3–6 made by Fritz Hansens Eft. A/S DENMARK

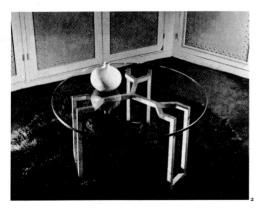

2

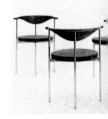

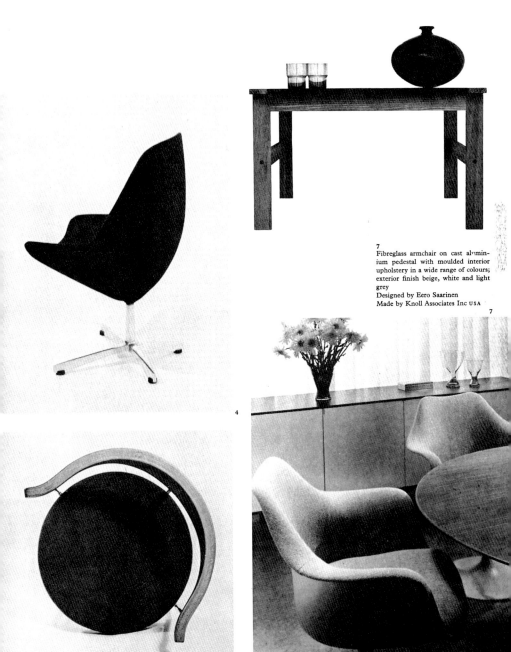

7
Fibreglass armchair on cast aluminium pedestal with moulded interior upholstery in a wide range of colours; exterior finish beige, white and light grey
Designed by Eero Saarinen
Made by Knoll Associates Inc USA

7

4

5

1
Laminated shell chair on steel tube legs; upholstered in wool fabric in a large range of colours over foam padding; overall height 73 cm
Designed by Pierre Paulin for Wagemans & van Tuinen NV HOLLAND

2
Circular table in the *Silver Line* range. Teak or rosewood top 89 cm diameter; underframe of solid teak with aluminium insert
Designed by Hvidt & Mølgaard

3
Coffee table, hand-finished teak with a 33-cm pull-out extension flap in black matt Formica. Made in two sizes, 122 and 152 cm long
Designed by Jørgen Hasse

4
Highback rocking chair, oiled teak hand-finished frame with loose seat cushion; wool fabric, p.v.c. or hide upholstery
Designed by Ole Wanscher
2–4 made by C. W. France & Søn A/S DENMARK

5
Sofa *SA 30* with buttoned back and seat cushions, and jacaranda coffee table on metal base
Designed by Karl Erik Ekselius
Made by J. O. Carlsson SWEDEN

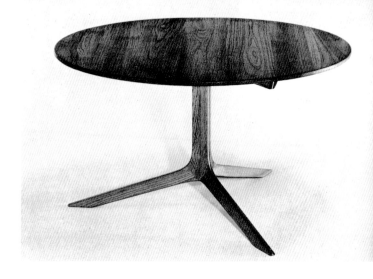

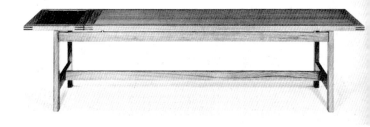

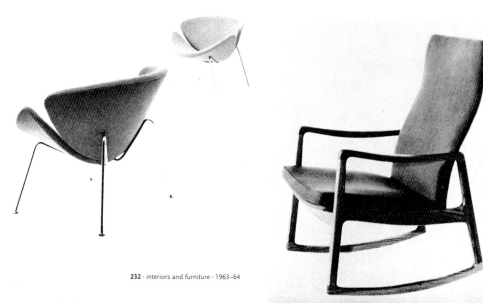

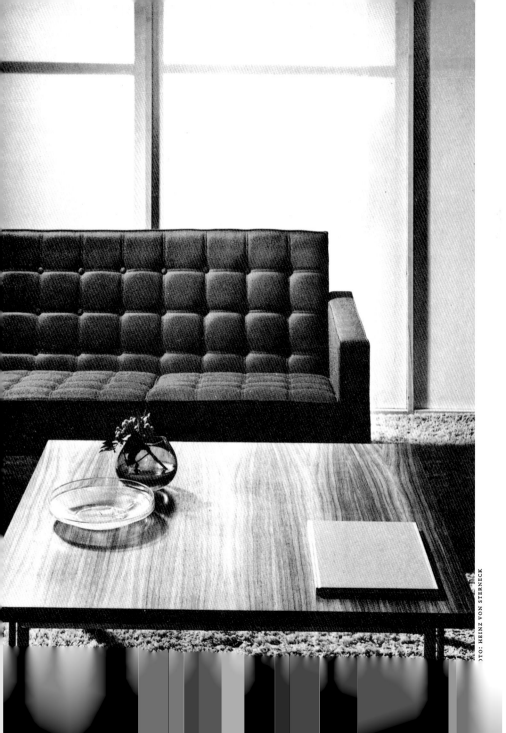

PHOTO: HEINZ VON STERNECK

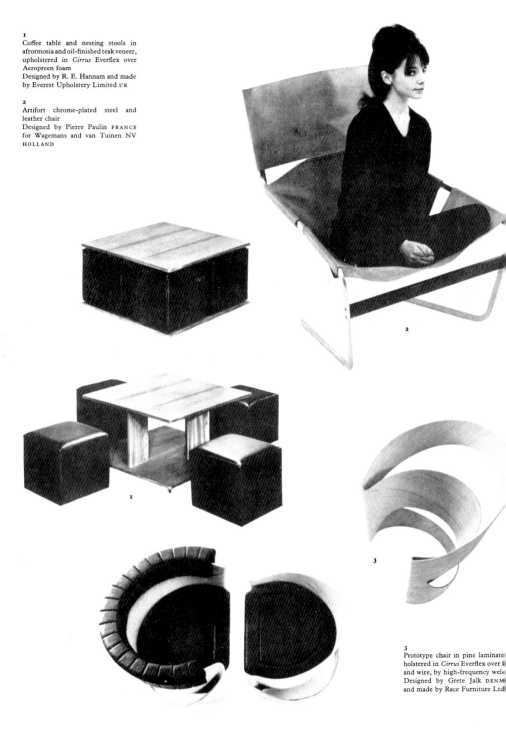

1
Coffee table and nesting stools in afrormosia and oil-finished teak veneer, upholstered in *Cirrus* Everflex over Aeropreen foam
Designed by R. E. Hannam and made by Everest Upholstery Limited UK

2
Artifort chrome-plated steel and leather chair
Designed by Pierre Paulin FRANCE
for Wagemans and van Tuinen NV
HOLLAND

2

1

3

3
Prototype chair in pine laminate holstered in *Cirrus* Everflex over f and wire, by high-frequency wel
Designed by Grete Jalk DENM
and made by Race Furniture Ltd

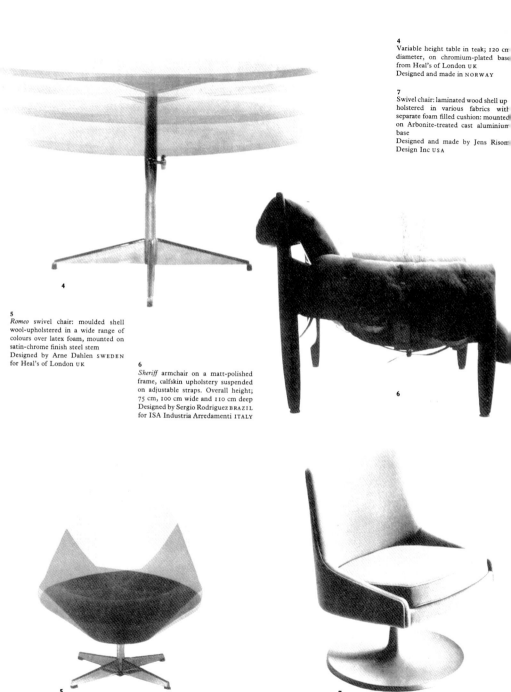

4
Variable height table in teak; 120 cm
diameter, on chromium-plated base
from Heal's of London UK
Designed and made in NORWAY

7
Swivel chair: laminated wood shell up
holstered in various fabrics with
separate foam filled cushion: mounted
on Arbonite-treated cast aluminium
base
Designed and made by Jens Risom
Design Inc USA

5
Romeo swivel chair: moulded shell
wool-upholstered in a wide range of
colours over latex foam, mounted on
satin-chrome finish steel stem
Designed by Arne Dahlen SWEDEN
for Heal's of London UK

6
Sheriff armchair on a matt-polished
frame, calfskin upholstery suspended
on adjustable straps. Overall height;
75 cm, 100 cm wide and 110 cm deep
Designed by Sergio Rodriguez BRAZIL
for ISA Industria Arredamenti ITALY

1
All-in-one unit in walnut: alternatively
doors can be cloth finished: overall
height 190 cm
Designed and made by Mobili MIM
s.p.a. ITALY

2
Bunk or single beds in square section
steel tube with chromium fittings,
beechwood guard rail and imitation
leather panels at head and foot; 76 ×
178 or 203 cm and 76 or 90 × 203 cm
Designed by Frank Guille for A.F.
Buckingham Ltd UK

3
International range of bedroom units
using fine matt-finished cherry wood
with Formica laminated plastic top
surfaces. Shown here on plain carpeting by J. Crossley & Sons Ltd with a
rug from Designs of Scandinavia and
curtains made by Edinburgh Weavers.
Unit Furniture designed by Gunther
Hoffstead for Uniflex UK

PHOTO JEFFRYES

4
Bed in solid wood on steel feet with
Perlon tension support; 100 × 200 cm
or 90 × 190 cm
Designed by Ernst Kirchoff for Casa
GmbH W. GERMANY

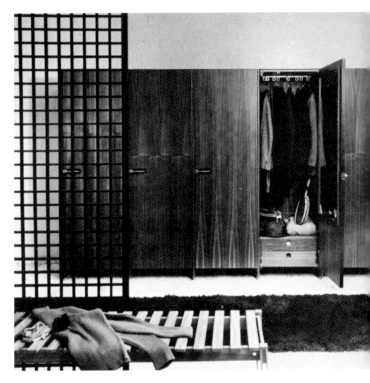

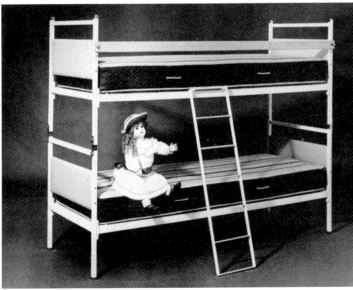

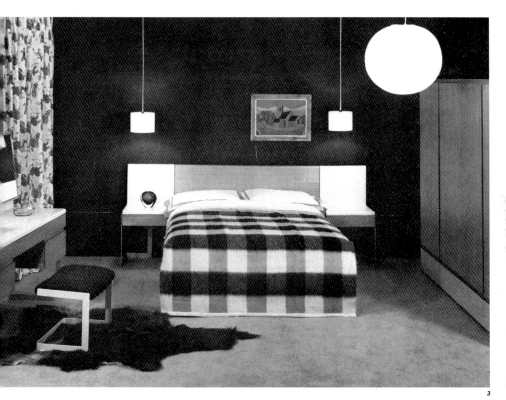

3

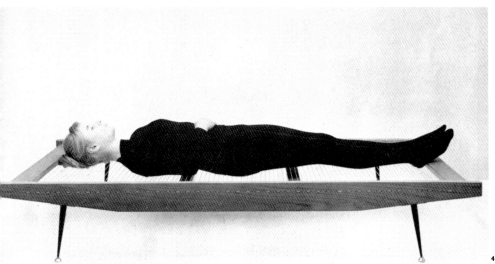

4

1, 2
Lower or higher table in solid teak or
wenge with natural finish; top surface
154 × 50 cm
Designed by arch. Harald Roth for
Casa GmbH W. GERMANY

3, 4
Zelda tables in walnut and palissander
also with red or white lacquer finish;
80 × 80 cm, 26 or 54 cm high
Designed by Sergio Asti and Sergio
Favre for Poltronova ITALY

5
'Lady' armchair and dining-chair from
the *Outline* range in ¼-inch steel rod
finished in resistant black lacquer with
corduroy velvet cushions in hot pink,
turquoise, curry or fir green
Designed by John Risley and made by
Luger Manufacturing Corpn for
Raymor USA

6
Stool of natural or dyed leather woven
on walnut frame; 51 cm square
Designed and made by Jere Osgood
for America House USA

7
Stool in chromium-plated steel with
hide seat; 58 × 42 cm, 45 cm high
Designed by Esko Pajamies for J.
Merivaara OY FINLAND

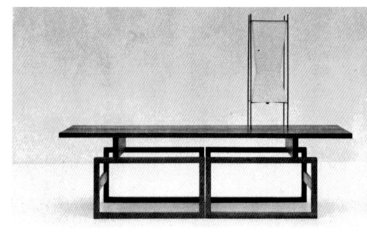

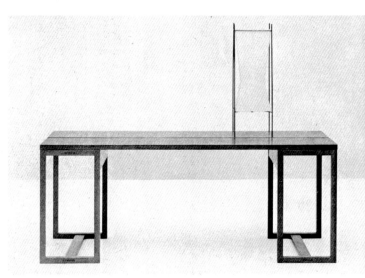

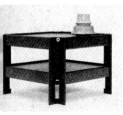

3

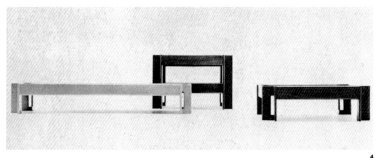

PHOTOS 1, 2 WILLI MOEGLE
PHOTOS 3, 4 MARI
PHOTOS 7, 8 PIETINEN
PHOTO 9 STRUWING

4

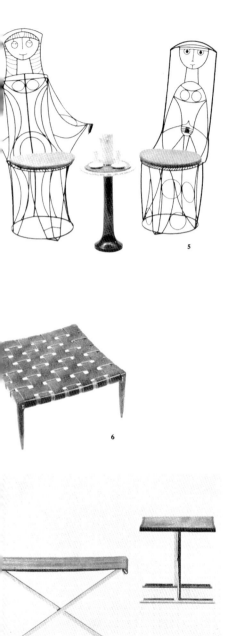

8
Bonzo swivel chair from laminated wood with loose foam rubber cushions covered in real or imitation leather: mounted on chromium-plated steel; overall height 73 cm
Designed by Toivo Korhonen and Esko Pajamies for J. Merivaara OY
FINLAND

9
Dining-chairs in finest Swedish Kalmar pine with natural finish
Designed by Kai Lyngfeldt Larsen arch.m.a.a. for Søborg Møbelfabrik A/S DENMARK

5

6

7

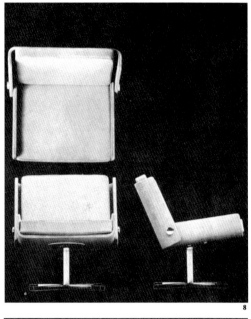

8

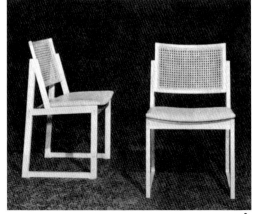

9

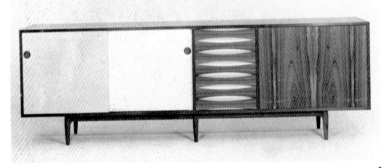

1
Settee from a lightweight shell
holstered in fabric or oxhide
foam rubber on an aluminium I
140 × 68 cm, 76 cm high
Designed by Arne Jacobsen for J
Hansens Eft. A/S DENMARK

2
Sideboard in teak or palissander c
bined with white plastic finished de
250 × 47 × 80 cm
Designed by Arne Vodder for P. C
Sibast I/S DENMARK

3
Sideboard 1307 with white-lacque
concave-formed doors (also avail
in mahogany): lined with ahorn: n
feet 340 × 52 cm, 96 cm high
Designed by Antoine Philip
FRANCE
for Behr Möbelfabrik W. GERMAN

4, 5
Three-legged chair in natural be
with seat in woven impregnated p
cord; 57 × 57 cm, 72 cm high
Designed by Mogens Lassen for I
Hansens Eft DENMARK

6, 7
Dining-chairs in teak, upholstere
woollen weave
Designed by Grete Jalk for P.
pesens Møbelfabrik A/S DENMAR

8, 9
Artifort chair No. 042, 'easel' frame
chrome-finish steel
Artifort chair No. 040 in chro
plated steel with rosewood strips
Both chairs upholstered in Syn
leather-cloth or Lisboa knitted fa
over pre-formed shells
Designed by Geoffrey Harcourt
Wagemans and van Tuinen
HOLLAND

10
Selsdon chair with cantilevered fr
of satin-chrome finished steel
anodized aluminium: upholstered
Bridge of Weir hide, in vari
colours
Designed by William Plunkett
William Plunkett Ltd UK

PHOTOS 1, 4, 5 STRUWING
PHOTO 3 BUSCHE
PHOTOS 8, 9 GEWEST
PHOTO 10 BEDFORD LEMERE

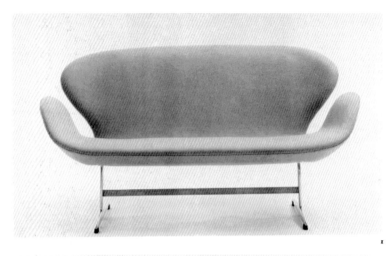

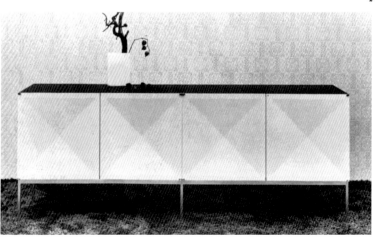

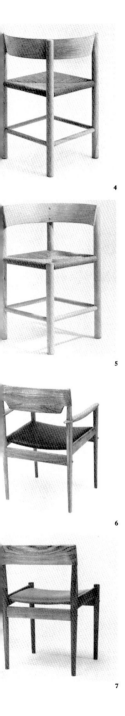

4

5

6

7

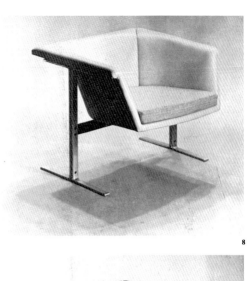

8

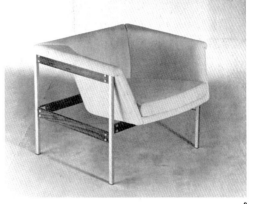

9

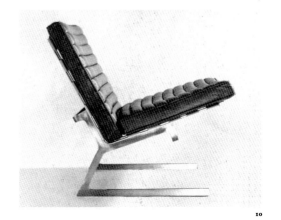

10

Informal folding tables and
chairs, natural beech
Designed by Hans J. Wegner for
Johannes Hansen DENMARK

Cot or play-pen in painted birch,
white, blue, rose or yellow:
122 × 84 × 56 cm
Designed by Pirkko Stenros and made
by Muuramen Huonekalutehdas O/y
for Artek O/y AB FINLAND

Hobbies stand in painted ash,
diameter 80 cm
Designed by J. C. Colombo for
G. B. Bernini & Figli ITALY

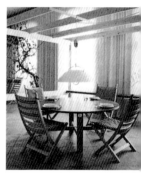

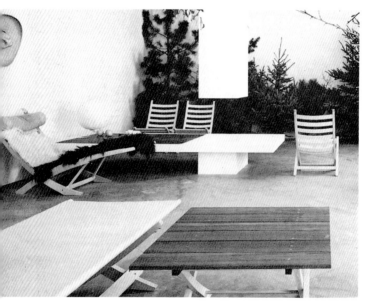

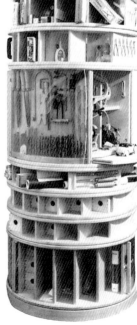

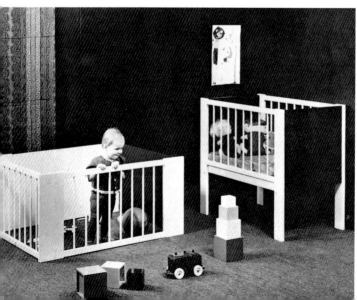

satile frame with attachments
gned by Hans von Klier for
estante ITALY

Shinto-ritual-inspired tea table in
laminated oak veneers
at bottom of page seat in natural oak
worked in a traditional way
(with end-section)
Both designed and made by Riki
Watanabe, Q Designers JAPAN

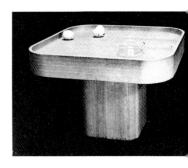

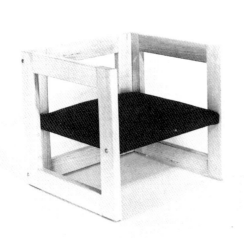

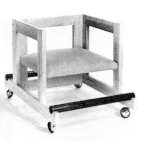

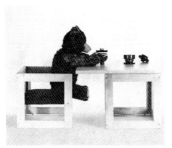

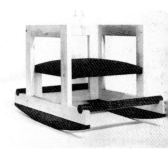

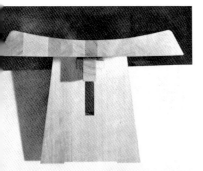

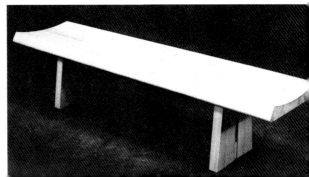

Demountable chair in aluminium and
leather
Made by Palini s.r.l. ITALY

Convertible settee: chrome rails,
black-enamelled support frame
upholstered in Den Blaa fabric
Made by Design Associates UK

Caori Japanese-inspired low table,
incorporating drawers, shelves and
central hatch: wood frame lacquered
red or charcoal, polished brass top
Designed by Vico Magistretti ITALY

Wassily a new version of a famous
model in chromium finished steel
tube with coach hide in tan, dark
brown or black
Designed by Marcel Breuer FRANCE
Both at Aram Designs Limited UK

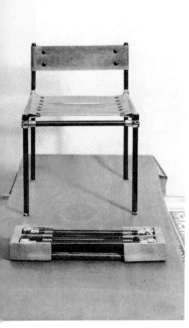

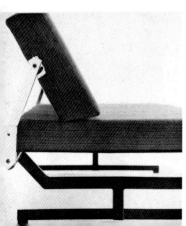

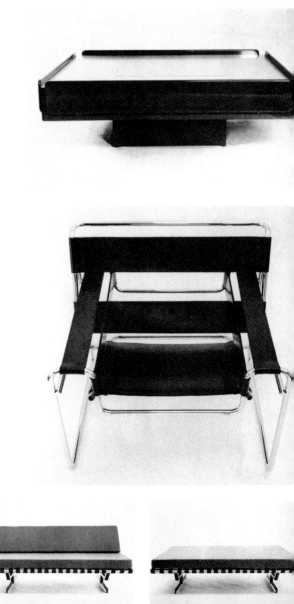

...nchair of rectangular sections,
...a of steel cords wrapped in foam
...ber and upholstered in black
...la leather cloth
...igned by Vico Magistretti for
...i di Amedeo Cassina ITALY

...ir and ottoman, steel with steel
...e mesh
...igned by Darrell Landrum for
...rd Inc USA

Terry circular table, the top
veneered palisander, base of
polished spun aluminium or brass
41 cm high, 80 cm diameter
Aram Designs Limited UK

Chair TU 515 of chrome-finished
oval steel tube, woven cane seat
Designed by Antti Nurmesniemi for
J. Merivaara O/y FINLAND

Table base of black-painted steel
for a variety of circular tops, 70 cm
high
Designed by Vico Magistretti for
Figli di Amedeo Cassina ITALY

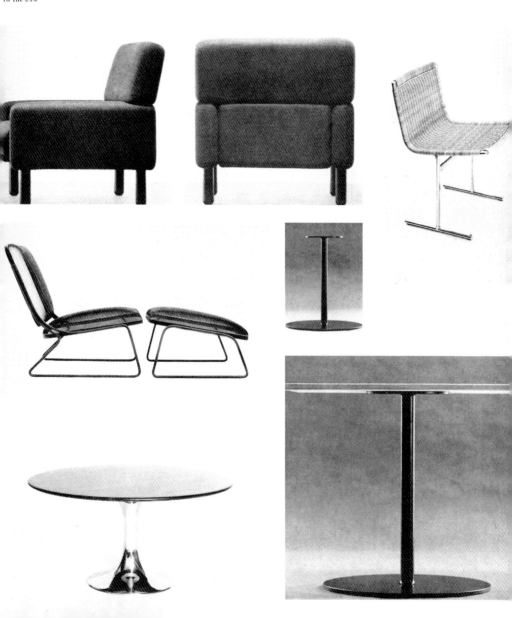

Wall units of macoré, teak,
mahogany or walnut, allied to
plastic foil in black, white or clear
colours: overall 366 × 223 cm high
Made by Erwin Behr Möbelfabrik
W. GERMANY

Summa Wall Fix demountable units
in oak, overall width of shelf
101 × 30 cm deep
Made by Conran & Co Ltd UK
Bentwood chair, cane back and seat
Made by Ligna CZECHOSLOVAKIA

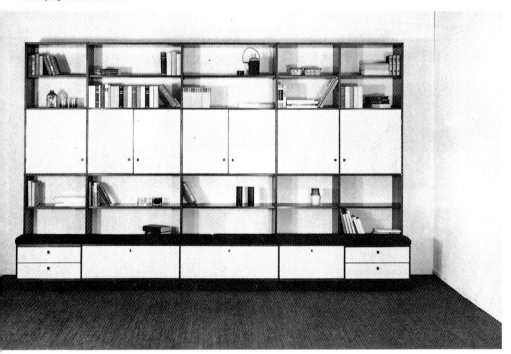

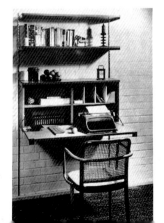

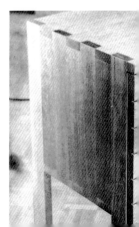

eboard B 45 in rosewood, interior
naple, on legs of chrome-finished
l, 248 × 55·5 × 80 cm high
igned by Dieter Waeckerlin
TZERLAND for Erwin Behr
belfabrik W. GERMANY

ble-topped sideboard in teak,
rmosia or rosewood
× 46 × 74 cm high
igned by Robert Heritage for
hie Shine Ltd UK

eboard (and detail) in solid
ogany 183 × 43 × 70 cm high
igned by G. E. Schlup for
E. Schlup & Co SWITZERLAND

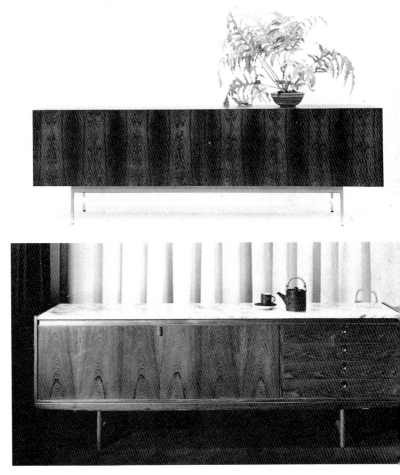

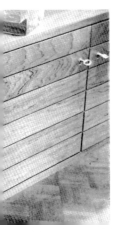

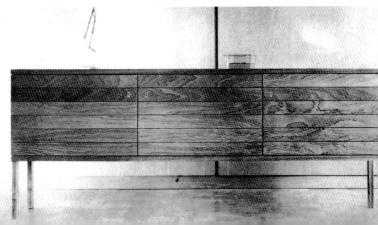

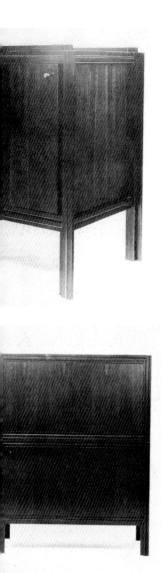

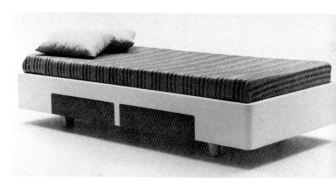

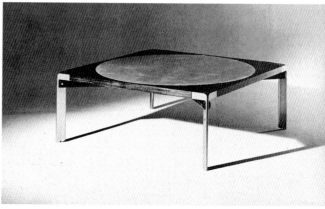

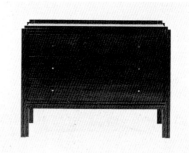

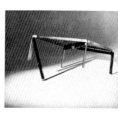

Metal framed, red lacquered
cabinet and chest
Designed by Carlo de Carli for
Sormani ITALY

Bed lacquered white with drawer
lacquered in contrast colours
Designed by Cesare Casati for
Arflex SpA ITALY

Card table, with baize disc,
reversing to leather, set in
rosewood top: aluminium frame
with foldaway legs, leaving shorr
ones for a table 40 cm high
Designed by Eugenio Gerli for
Tecno SpA ITALY

photographs Clari

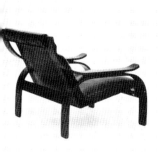

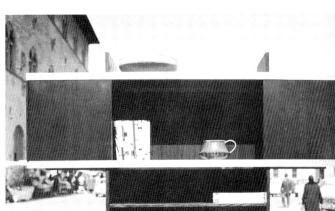

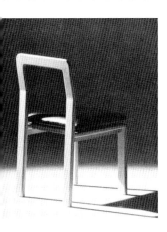

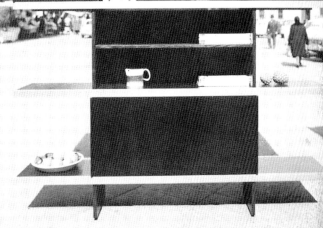

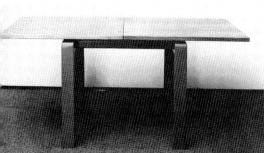

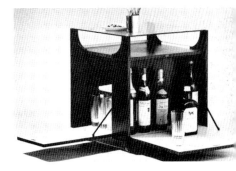

photographs Clari

adline chair laminated walnut,
 upholstered or lacquered wood
 textile
 igned by Marco Zanuso for
 ex SpA ITALY

 ir and dining-table; table top of
 nut or palisander natural finish;
 nes laminated wood with black,
 nge, green or white lacquered
 .h: top 80 cm square, extending
 60 cm long
 igned by Cesare Casati for
 ex SpA ITALY

Shelf unit: ash or walnut
Designed by Angelo Mangiarotti
for Poltronova ITALY

Cocktail bar/table: a cube of
rosewood lined with white plastic
and glass-topped
Designed by Bruno Munari for
Stildomus Selezione ITALY

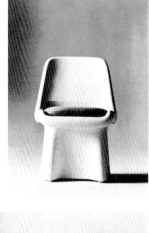

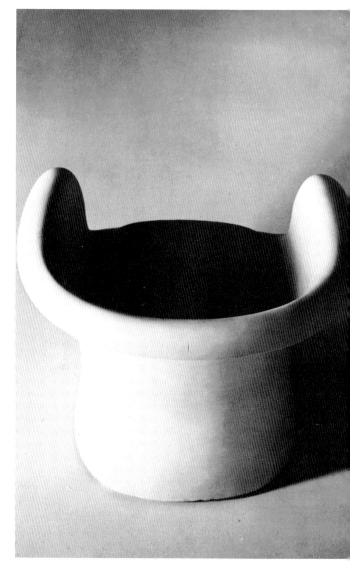

Chairs and foot stool, moulded in
expanded polystyrene
Unique pieces designed by Angelo
Mangiarotti for Figli di Amedeo
Cassina ITALY

Sofa with space in its body for
bottles, glasses, books etc; foam
rubber cushions suspended on
rubber webbing, detachable
lacquered wood frame on metal
structure with integral cigarette
lighter: overall length 275 cm
Designed by Casati & Hybsch for
Arflex SpA ITALY

Wall system building up to an
combination of music-and-cock
unit/writing desk/bookshelves
natural finished walnut or
palisander: each unit 184 × 80
Designed by Joe Colombo for
Arflex SpA ITALY

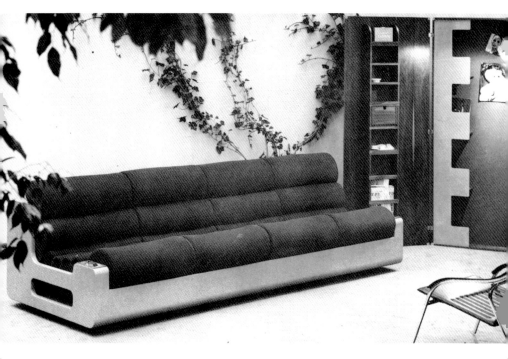

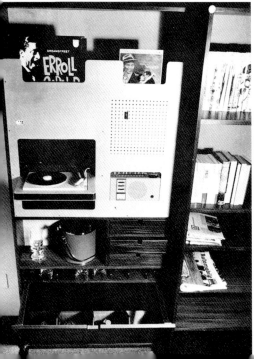

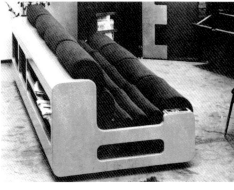

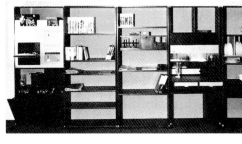

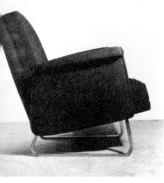

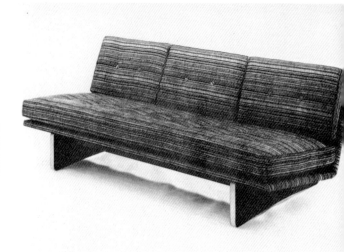

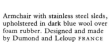

photograph d'Oliveiro

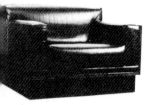

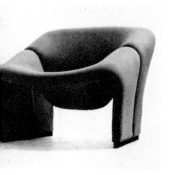

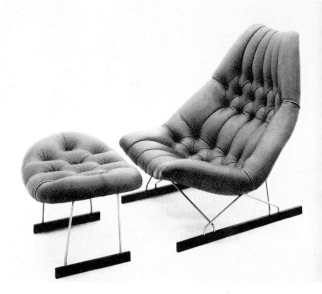

Armchair with stainless steel sleds, upholstered in dark blue wool over foam rubber. Designed and made by Dumond and Leloup FRANCE

Cousso massive chair: palisander frame upholstered in leather over latex foam. Designed by G. Van Rijk for Epeda SA BELGIUM

Folded metal frame chair upholstered in knitted fabric over foam rubber, with rubber straps: overall width 76 cm. Designed by Pierre Paulin for Artifort HOLLAND

Spring upholstered settee on wooden frame, covered with black/white weave: overall width 180 cm Designed by Kho Liang Ie

Chair and foot stool, upholstered in various coloured hide over foam rubber on a moulded shell with metal base.
Designed by Geoffrey D. Harcourt
Both made by Artifort HOLLAND

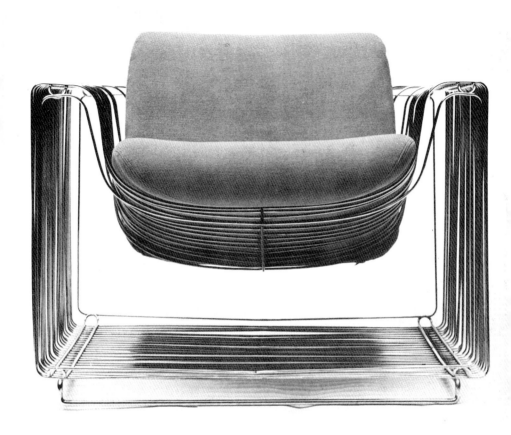

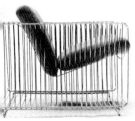

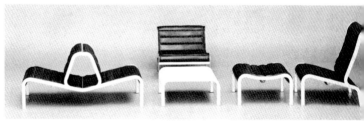

ctrac cage-for-comfort from
rome steel wires suspending
ex foam interchangeable
hions

Chairs and ottomans with foam-
section upholstery on square
section steel frames; the table in
pressed wood
All designed by Olivier Mourgue
for Airborne International FRANCE

photographs Berdoy

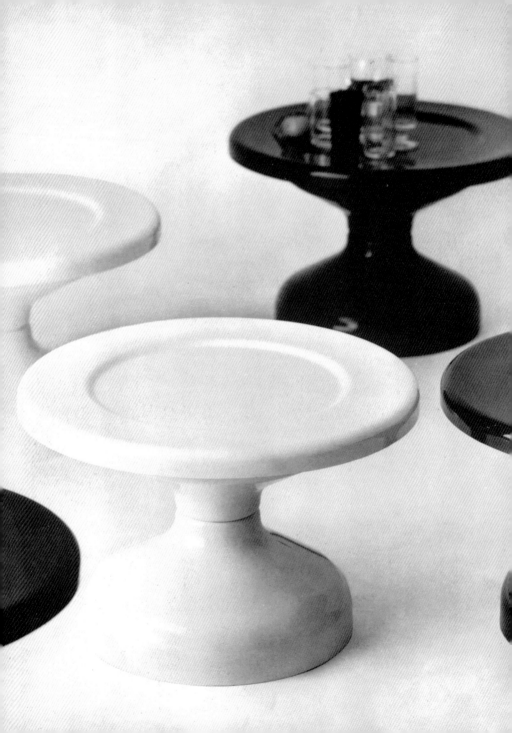

table in polyester resin, white,
ge, bordeaux or green, 60 cm
eter × 38 cm high
gned by archs. A. & P. G. Castiglioni
artell s.r.l. *Italy*

e chair, swivelling glass fibre shell
olstered with polyfoam
padded with Dacron
ions, red, orange, black or white
m diameter × 120 cm overall height
gned by Eero Aarnio for Asko Oy
and

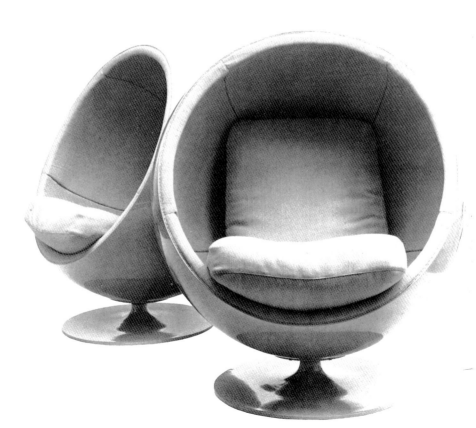

Springtime demountable chairs, two-seater sofa and square or rectangular table, solid plywood lacquered red, black or white with matching or contrast cushions, based on 65 or 104 × 75 cm seat unit: *right,* details
Designed by Marco Zanuso for Arflex s.p.a. *Italy*

Storage-wall: details of television compartment and disc shelving: to the right, the wall closed
Designed by Raphaël *France*

centre
922 armchair, wood frame upholstered in fabric, leather or simulated leather over foam rubber: series includes two- or three-seater settee
Designed by Vico Magistretti for Figli di Amedeo Cassina *Italy*

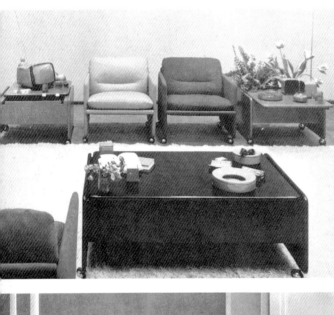

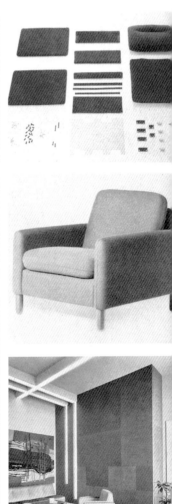

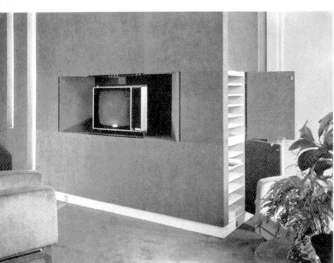

5 self-standing shelf units, bent
wood lacquered black, red or white,
r 75 × 37 × 27 cm
gned by A. Vittoria for Tecno s.p.a.

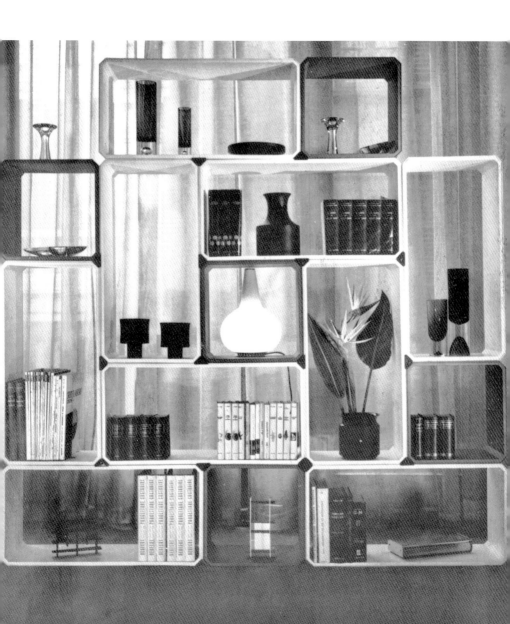

London Combination corner chair 632
which with chairs 630 *right* and the
higher 631 can be utilised in many
formal arrangements, moulded-foam on
laminated wood and solid timber,
suspended on special chromed cast-iron
link-frames or as single units
Designed by Geoffrey D. Harcourt for
Artifort *Holland*
4700 chair, natural beech with
adjustable tilt back: there is a
matching side-table and a round
occasional table in the series
Designed by Arne Jacobsen m.a.a.
for Fritz Hansen *Denmark*

centre
Cloisonacc sound-reducing, dividing
screen, felt-lined corrugated card
in many colours with self or
contrasting linings, 165–300 cm
high × 30 extending to 150 cm
Designed by Pierre Blyweert and made
by Usines de Graux/Slosse *Belgium*

Amersham chair, natural beech with
utile seat designed by Børge
Mogensen m.a.a. (*Denmark*) for Finmar
Ltd *England*

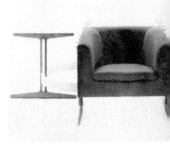

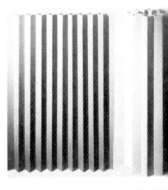

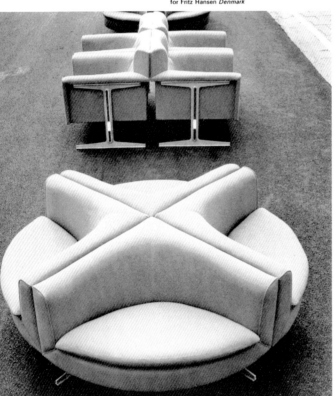

Strüwing

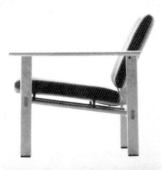

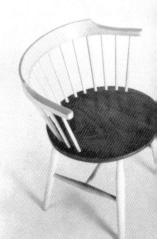

series chairs, stools and stands
nated beech, lacquered red, white
ue
gned by Verner Panton and made
ebruder Thonet AG *W. Germany*

 lounge chair of laminated birch,
uspended seat upholstered in
er over foam rubber layer, vinyl-
red hand-rests, overall height 79 cm
gned by Ilmari Lappalainen for
 Oy *Finland*

780/784 low and high backed chairs,
tubular frame, upholstered in foam
rubber and knitted fabric, on iron
base
Designed by Pierre Paulin for Artifort
Holland

Göllner

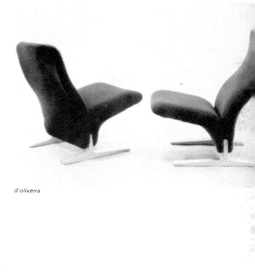

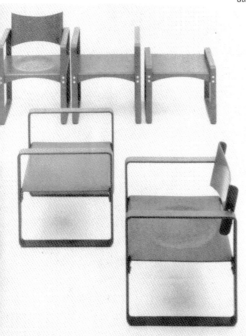

d'oliveira

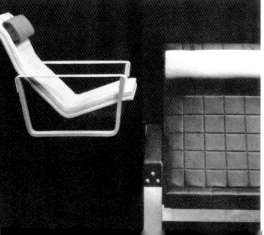

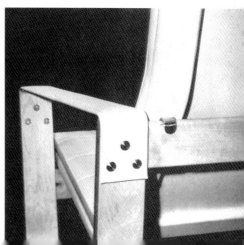

Bent plywood chair with steel
spring suspension upholstered in
leather over foam rubber
Designed by Joe C. Colombo for
Comfort di Milano *Italy*

Canada armchair in laminated wood,
natural walnut or palisander finish
or lacquered white, red or black
with hide or plaid woven upholstery
Designed by A. O. Borsani for Tecno
s.p.a. *Italy*

Simone three-seater, fibre-glass frame
upholstered in black hide, the body
accommodating radio, stereophonic
controls, cigarette case with lighter and
ashtray and a compartment for beer
bottles: the whole being mounted on
wheels
Designed by Cesare Casati and Enzo
Hybsch for Comfort di Milano *Italy*

Borsani

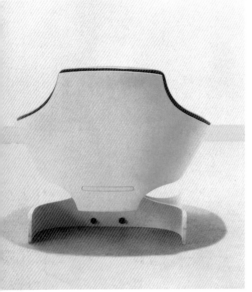

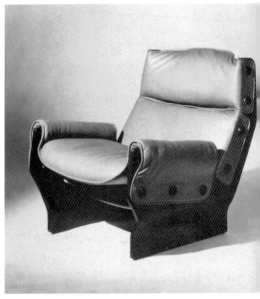

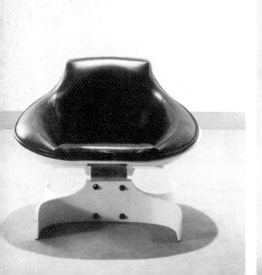

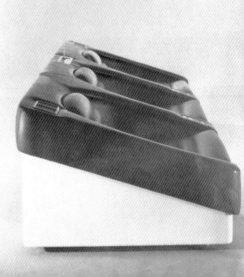

Centro bookcases, subdued palisander
78 cm square × variable height
(here 210 and 110 cm)
Designed by arch Claudio Salocchi
for Sormani s.r.l. *Italy*

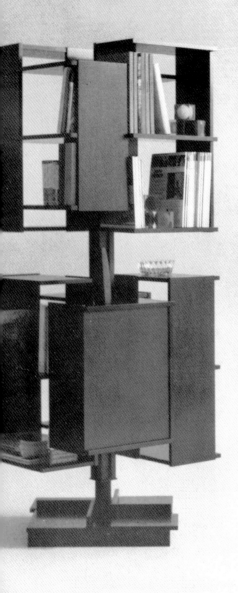

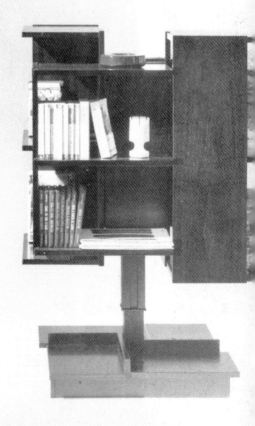

Demetrio 70 tables of reinforced resin
surfaced with Riformite in white,
red or black, 70 × 70 × 30 cm high:
a smaller version 45 × 45 × 23 cm
high can be paired as shown
Designed by Vico Magistretti for
Studio Artemide *Italy*

Table in polyester resin, white,
orange, bordeaux, grey, black,
with or without adjustable
stainless steel supports, 120 cm
diameter
Designed by archs. Anna Castelli
and J. Gardella for Kartell s.r.l. *Italy*

Telephone drum-table in red, white
or black plastic
Designed by Emma Schweinberger and
made by Studio Artemide *Italy*

Magazine, book and record stand,
each having three elements of black
or red enamelled steel, 30 × 30 × 30 cm
overall
Designed by Enzo Mari and made by
B. Danese *Italy*

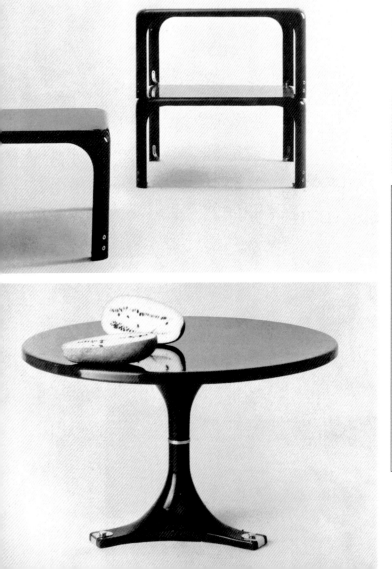

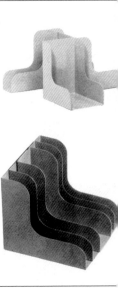

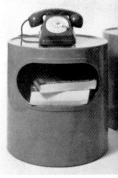

...lf unit in polyester resin,
...te, red, green, blue or black
...cm wide × 30 cm deep
...signed by arch. M. Siard for
...tell s.r.l. *Italy*

...*ow and seen on title pages*
...nchairs in laminated wood with
...cial varnishes white, orange,
...en or black, overall height
...cm: available also with PVC-
...vered back and seat cushions
...signed by Joe C. Colombo for
...tell s.r.l. *Italy*

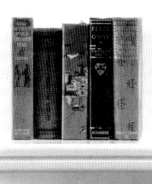

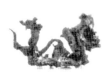

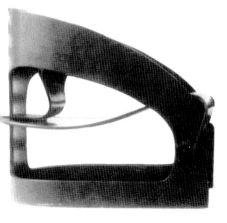

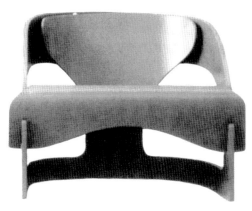

Deep-storage fitment in black-stained beech, 91 × 182 × 243 cm high: the twin horizontals accommodate strip lighting Designed and made for Timothy Rendle *England*

Quartetto demountable table, besla stone and chrome-steel 1 m square × 40 cm high Designed by Bruno Morassutti and made by Bernini *Italy*

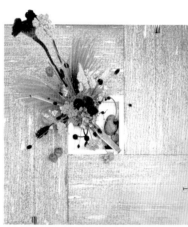

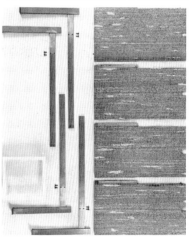

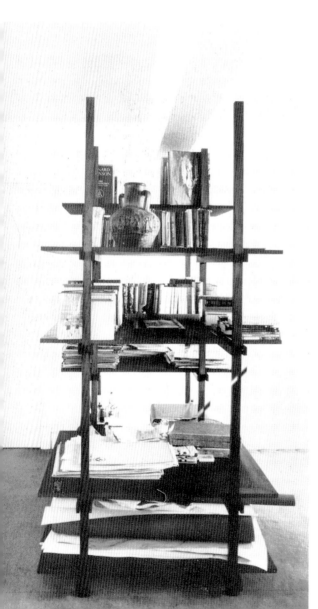

20 series: part of a related range in
olid and bent plywood walnut,
alisander or elm, the upholstered items
with Arciflex and Dacron-filled
ushions, covered leather, simulated
eather or fabric: tables (basic unit size)
2·5 × 72·5 × 39 cm high
Designed by Afra and Tobia Scarpa for
igli di Amedeo Cassina *Italy*

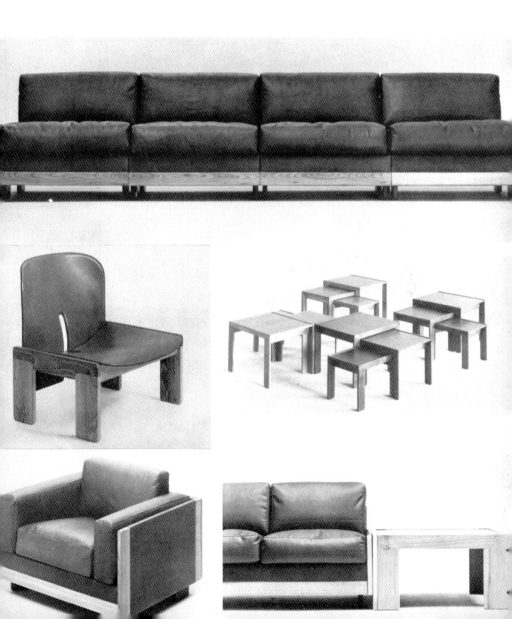

A single block mini-kitchen on wheels:
the polished or lacquered wooden
cube houses oven, spit and grill,
refrigerator, space for 6 place settings
of tableware, cutlery and glasses, for
cooking equipment and recipe books
Designed by Joe C. Colombo for Boffi
Italy

Golf Club 1002 sofa, chair, table
and stool based on wooden box-shapes
with separate wool-filled leather-covered
cushions, all pieces moving on wheels
Designed by Joe C. Colombo for Comfort
Italy

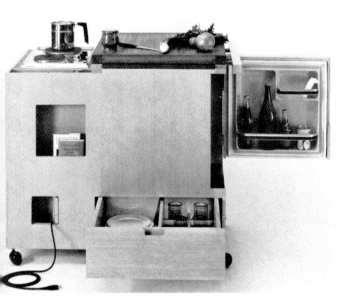

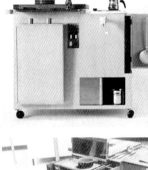

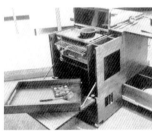

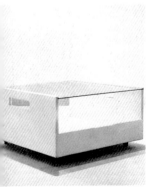

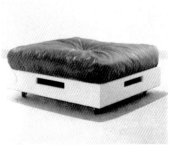

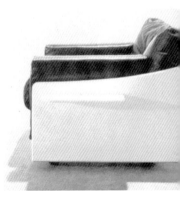

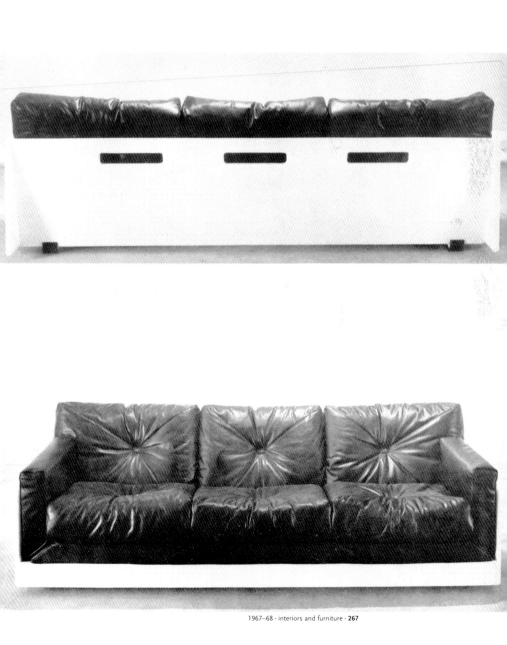

989 sofa, foam-rubber-covered frame
with down and Diolen fleece-filled
seat cushions, loose back and arm cushions
natural hide and to order in other colours
or materials 257 × 77 × 94 cm
Designed by Edelhard Harlis for Hans
Kaufeld *W. Germany*

Sofa, beech-framed with ply panels,
polyether squabs and Terylene
fleece-filled cushions, covered hide
or fabric, 190 × 71 × 84 cm
Designed by David Pye for Greaves &
Thomas *England*

Schmölz-Hoth

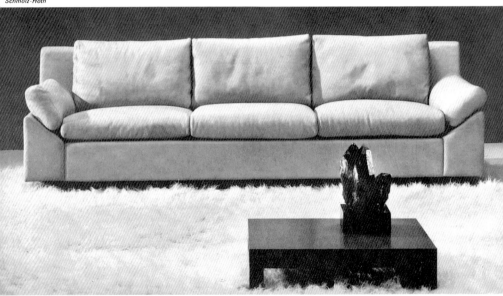

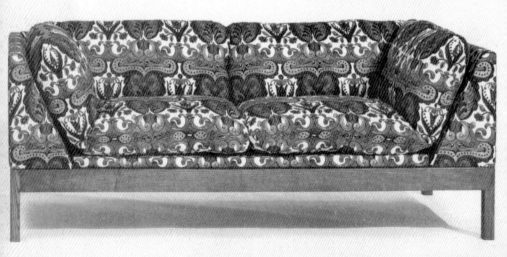

neleontti wood-framed sofa with No-
springs, Dacron-filled cushions
ered black/white Mari fabric, natural
e or other fabrics 180 × 80 × 65 cm
signed by Torsten Laakso and made
Oy Skanno AB *Finland*

o sofa and chairs upholstered
h polyether and foam rubber over
sag springs, the glass-topped
le with chrome-plated steel frame
signed by Lindau/Lindekrantz for
glund & Søner *Sweden*

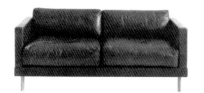

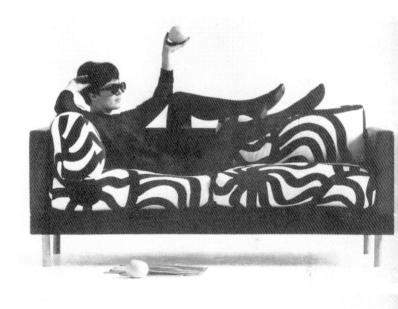

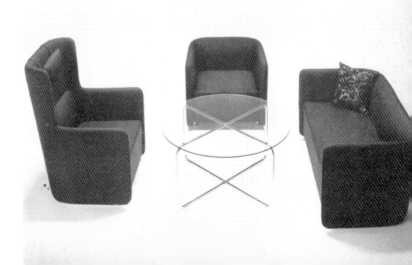

bottom
Tomotom chairs and table, part of
a range of dining, playroom and
nursery furniture, tough chipboard
lacquered vivid red, blue, yellow,
green, purple, black or white with
matching or contrasting PVC-
covered cushions
Designed by Bernard Holdaway and
made by Hull Traders Ltd *England*

Selsdon table and *Coulsdon* chair
mild steel frames, chromed or
dark grey nylon coated, with
plate glass: chairs upholstered
in polyfoam over rubber webbing
Designed and made by William
Plunkett Ltd *England*

Pann seagrass stool for indoor or
outdoor use, with a bright felt cushion
Designed by Mirja Panula for
Velsa Oy *Finland*

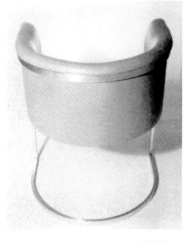

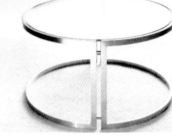

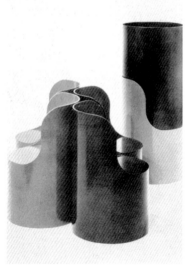

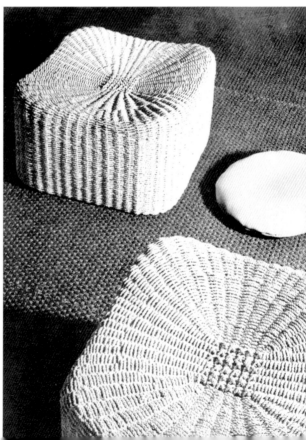

ple rocker in lacquered plywood,
elstered wool fabric over
ether chip foam: for outdoor
PVC covered upholstery over a
-fibre frame
ototype designed and made by
d Goodship *England*

mbly of three basic units,
elstered on wooden frame with
gs and polyether foam and
c covered Latex foam cushions
gned by N. K. Hislop and
abson for Gimson & Slater Ltd
and

Experimental garden furniture,
bright-lacquered iron
Designed and made by arch. Otto
Rottmayer *Czechoslovakia*

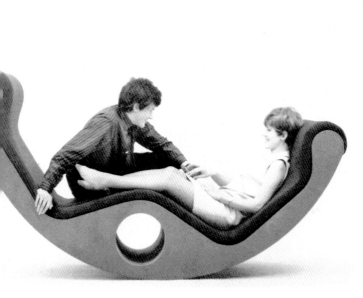

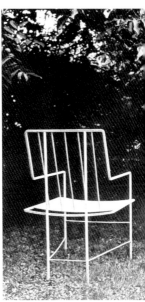

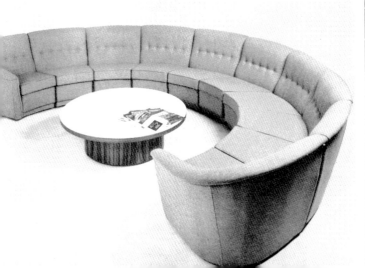

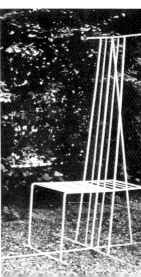

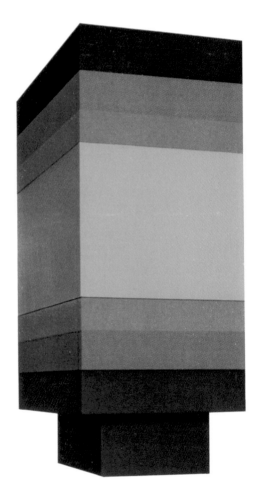

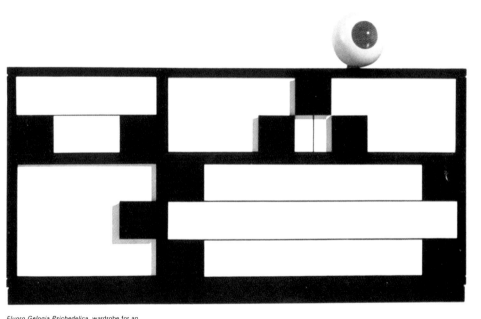

Fluoro Gelogia Psichedelica, wardrobe for an
environment from a series of studies in Print
laminated plastic
Designed by Ettore Sottsass jr for Poltronova
Italy

Chest in wengé with white glossy panels
150 × 76 × 50 cm deep.
Designed and made by Ico and Luisa Parisi
Italy

1, 2
Cini Boeri one- or two-seater element from
flexible polyurethane foams, the base protected
by tough resinous net
Designed by Cini Boeri
Gaia armchairs, fibre glass/polyester resin

moulded with constant-thickness wal
form agreeable with or without light
cushioning: white, red, mustard, dark
80 × 80 × 70 cm high
Designed by Carlo Bartoli
Both for Arflex SpA *Italy*

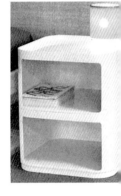

1 3 4 5
2   6

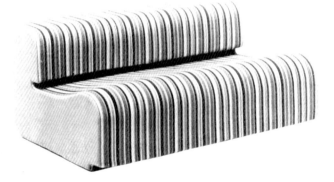

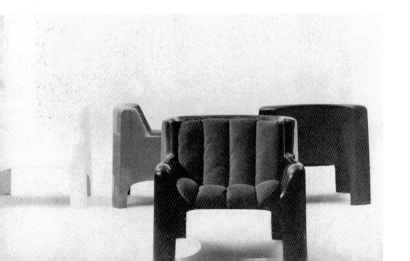

3, 4
Occasional table and bed in polyester resin, the table, black or white, designed by Anna Castelli: the bed white, orange, bordeaux, green, sky blue. Designed by M. Siard Both made by Kartell s.r.l. *Italy*

5
RZ 62 chair, glass fibre/polyester resin shell, grey or matt black with down-filled cushions covered hide or fabric: a settee is built from chair units Designed by Dieter Rams for Vitsøe & Zapf *W. Germany*

6
Elisse suspended sideboard, lacquered wood and plastic laminates with drawer fronts in anodized aluminium: 75 cm wide overall Designed by Claudio Salocchi for Sormani SpA *Italy*

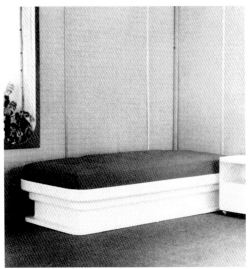

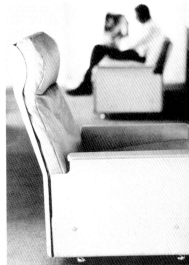

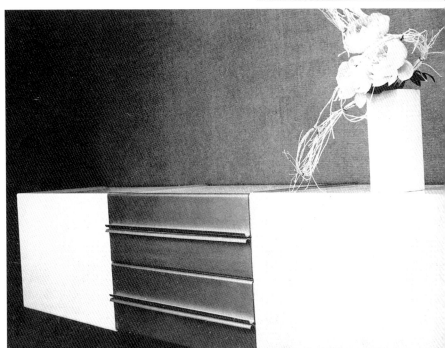

Chair, stool (also table), anodized solid aluminium
frames upholstered over foam rubber with
toning fabric, off-white/grey/Lurex, specially
woven by Unika Vaev, or custom choice
Designed by Grete Jalk for Fritz Hansens Eft
Denmark

bottom row, left to right
Stainless tubular steel upholstered with
woollen weave over foam rubber, 70 cm high
Designed by H. Verelst for Novalux *Belgium*

Tubular stainless steel chair with bright
sailcloth or natural or black hide seat and back
85 cm high
Designed by Herbert Jutzi for Baumann/Schindler
Switzerland

Habitat dining chair, reinforced plastic shell
fabric covered on bright-chromed steel tube frame
Designed by Dudas Kuypers Rowan Ltd for
Interiors International Ltd *Canada*

Tiered table, 1267 white lacquered b
chrome steel swivel base, 50 × 50 cm
Designed by arch. Giebisch
Cocktail cabinet/table 1236, pre-form
plywood lacquered light grey, white c
50 × 50 cm
Designed by arch Laprell
Both made by W. W. Interart *W. Ger*

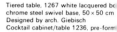

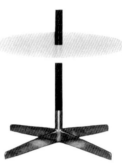

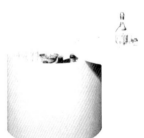

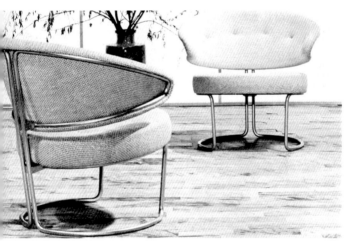

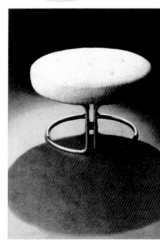

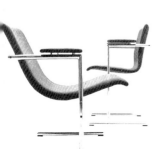

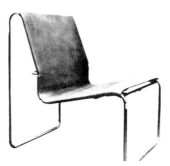

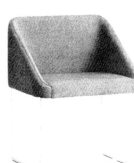

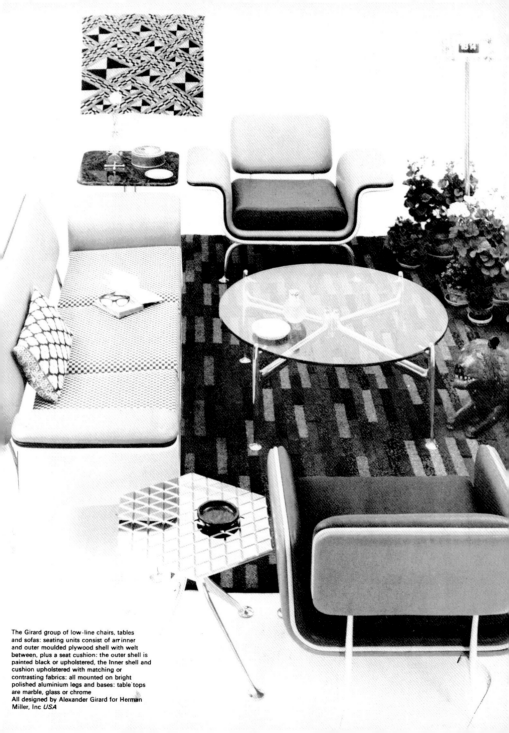

The Girard group of low-line chairs, tables
and sofas: seating units consist of an inner
and outer moulded plywood shell with welt
between, plus a seat cushion: the outer shell is
painted black or upholstered, the inner shell and
cushion upholstered with matching or
contrasting fabrics: all mounted on bright
polished aluminium legs and bases: table tops
are marble, glass or chrome
All designed by Alexander Girard for Herman
Miller, Inc *USA*

1–3
Stool and chairs: tubular frames upholstered
with Unika Vaer *Ellipse* over elasticized webbing and
polyether foam, respectively 62, 130, 90 cm
deep × 61 × 60 cm: the high-backed version
(also available with long seat) 91 cm high
Designed by Verner Panton for Storz and Palmer
W. Germany

4
Floor Seat 577, tubular frame and foam rubber
upholstered with woollen stretch fabric, 90 × 85
× 61 cm high
Designed by Pierre Paulin for Artifort *Holland*

5
Chepa steel tube framed chair upholstered with
elasticized fabric over foam rubber: 63 cm high ×
80 × 80 cm
Designed by G. Vanrijk for Beaufort *Belgium*

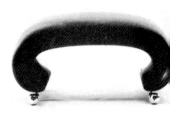

1

4

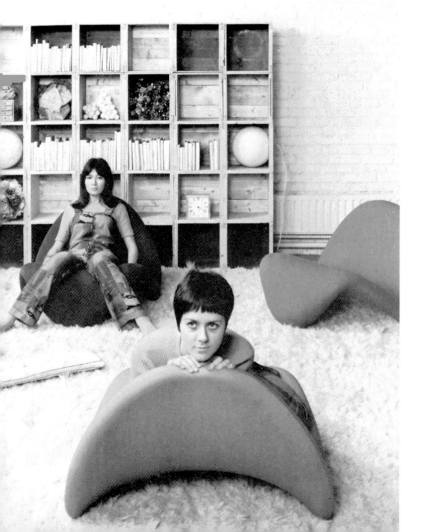

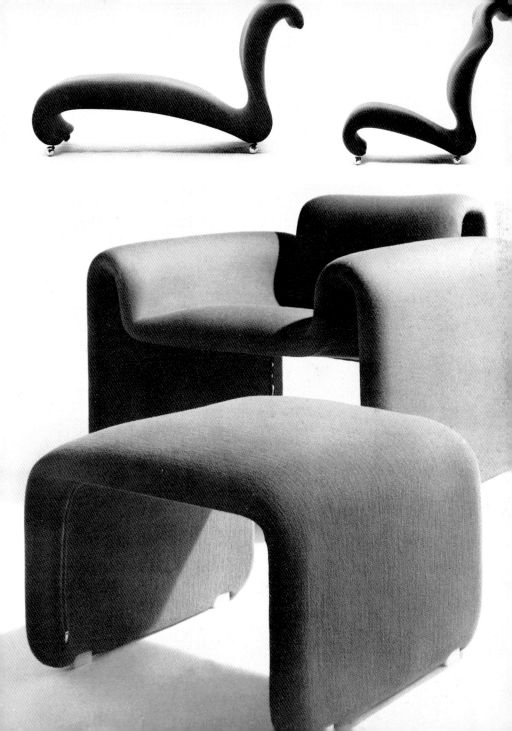

1
Hammock chair 24, cane-wrapped stainless
steel, with adjustable cushion: 155 cm overall
length
Designed by Poul Kjaerholm for E. Kold
Christensen A/S *Denmark*

2
RL.1 chair woven hide seat and back on satin
anodized aluminium or stainless steel frame
Designed by Ross Littell *Denmark* for I C F de
Padova *Italy*

3, 4
Slimline desk, walnut or rosewood 63·5 × 132
cm high folding to 15·5 cm deep
Designed by Vladimir Kagan for Kagan-
Dreyfuss, Inc *USA*

1 3 5 6
2 4 7 8

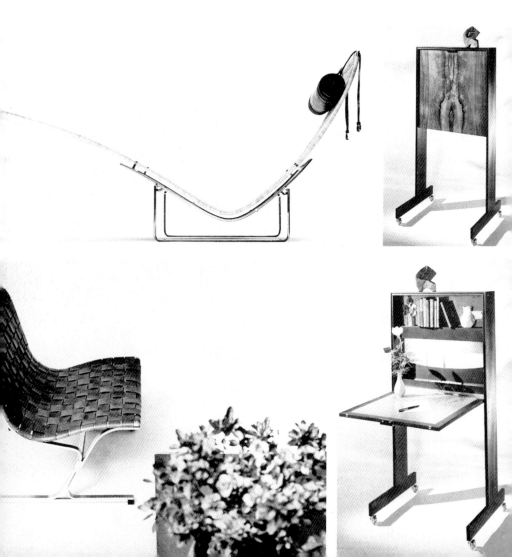

5, 6
Carlotta Young Play KD chair, beech with gloss
aniline finish in okapi, colibri, acapulco, safari,
bengali or siviglia: polyurethane-filled cushions
have specially designed covers: 88 cm wide
Designed by Afra and Tobia Scarpa for Figli
di Amedeo Cassina *Italy*

7
Assymetric chair, ash with back rests lacquered
13 shades of blue/green
Designed by Peter Karpf, made by Willy Beck
Denmark

8
Easy chair and stool in the Habitat group
(see also page 76) from rotational cast linear
polyethylene, shell covered with a thin layer
of foam rubber and upholstered: hide, fabric or
synthetic covered cushion
For outdoor use, shells are left uncovered
Designed by Dudas Kuypers Rowan Ltd for
Interiors International Ltd *Canada*

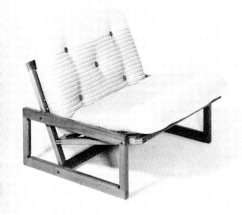

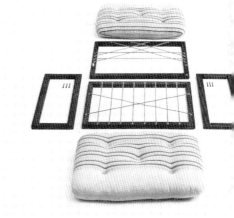

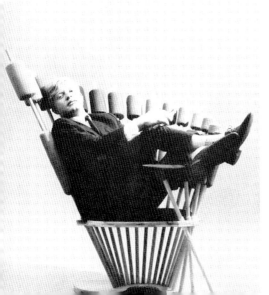

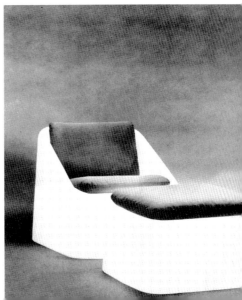

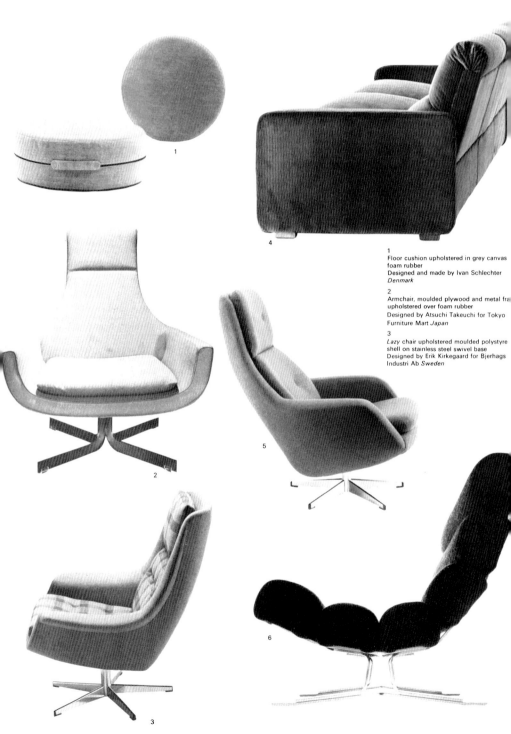

1
Floor cushion upholstered in grey canvas
foam rubber
Designed and made by Ivan Schlechter
Denmark

2
Armchair, moulded plywood and metal fra[...]
upholstered over foam rubber
Designed by Atsuchi Takeuchi for Tokyo
Furniture Mart *Japan*

3
Lazy chair upholstered moulded polystyre[...]
shell on stainless steel swivel base
Designed by Erik Kirkegaard for Bjerhags
Industri Ab *Sweden*

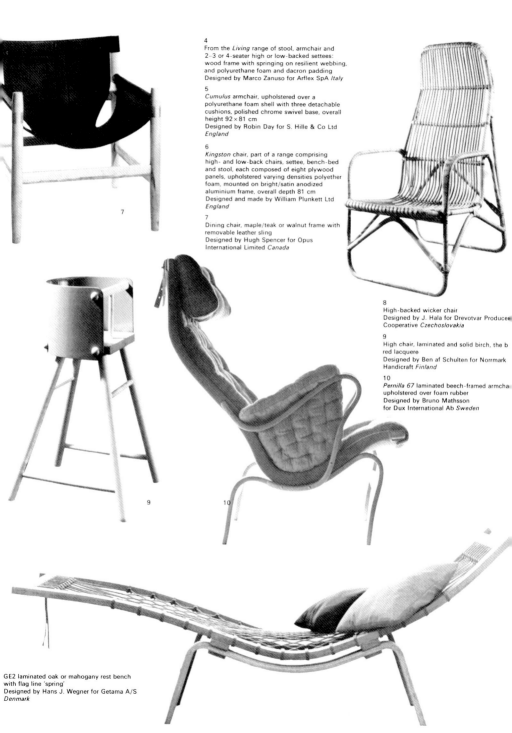

4
From the *Living* range of stool, armchair and
2–3 or 4-seater high or low-backed settees:
wood frame with springing on resilient webbing,
and polyurethane foam and dacron padding
Designed by Marco Zanuso for Arflex SpA *Italy*

5
Cumulus armchair, upholstered over a
polyurethane foam shell with three detachable
cushions, polished chrome swivel base, overall
height 92 × 81 cm
Designed by Robin Day for S. Hille & Co Ltd
England

6
Kingston chair, part of a range comprising
high- and low-back chairs, settee, bench-bed
and stool, each composed of eight plywood
panels, upholstered varying densities polyether
foam, mounted on bright/satin anodized
aluminium frame, overall depth 81 cm
Designed and made by William Plunkett Ltd
England

7
Dining chair, maple/teak or walnut frame with
removable leather sling
Designed by Hugh Spencer for Opus
International Limited *Canada*

8
High-backed wicker chair
Designed by J. Hala for Drevotvar Producer
Cooperative *Czechoslovakia*

9
High chair, laminated and solid birch, the b
red lacquere
Designed by Ben af Schulten for Norrmark
Handicraft *Finland*

10
Pernilla 67 laminated beech-framed armcha
upholstered over foam rubber
Designed by Bruno Mathsson
for Dux International Ab *Sweden*

GE2 laminated oak or mahogany rest bench
with flag line 'spring'
Designed by Hans J. Wegner for Getama A/S
Denmark

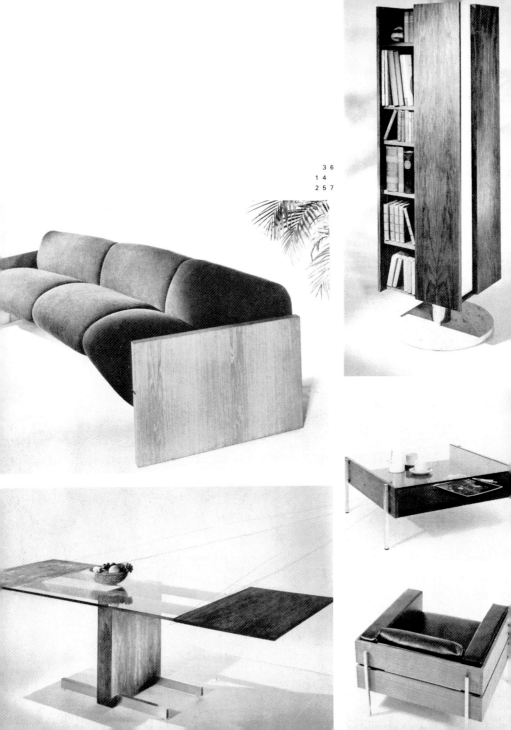

1
Tangent Cubis sofa, plank legs of oak, walnut
or rosewood, upholstered leather, vinyl or
fabric: overall length 208 cm
2
Glass-topped dining or conference table, oak,
walnut, rosewood or ebony-stained plinth with
matching or marble extensions: overall 50·5
× 137 cm and custom sizes: all on satin
aluminium stretchers
3
Revolving bookcase pillar and light panel, oak,
walnut or rosewood on polished aluminium/
travertine or slate/brass pedestal
All designed by Vladimir Kagan for Kagan-
Dreyfuss, Inc *USA*

4, 5
Forum table and chair, solid rosewood on
chrome steel square-section tube: plate glass
table top, black pvc-covered shelf 93 × 88 ×
38 cm high: chair with polyether, feather
and down-filled cushions
A matching settee is available
All designed by Robin Day for S. Hille & Co
Ltd *England*

6
Model 275, three-dimensionally moulded
laminated wood, lacquered orange, black or
white, approximately 85 cm high overall
Designed by Verner Panton for Gebruder Thonet
AG *W. Germany*

7
Working chair in laminated beech and clear acryl
Designed by Peter Karpf for Jørgen Christensen
Denmark

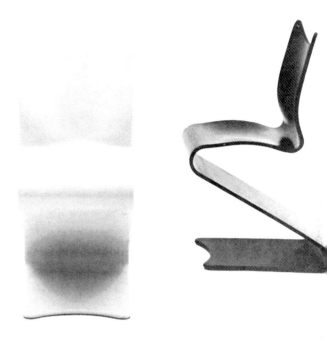

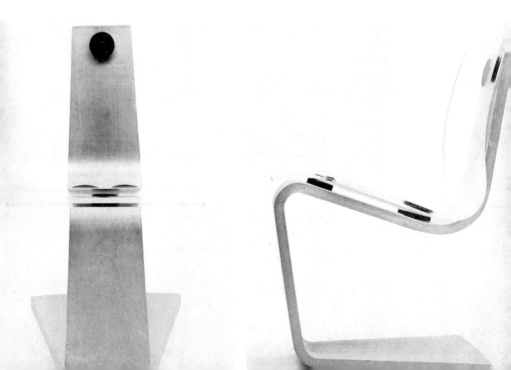

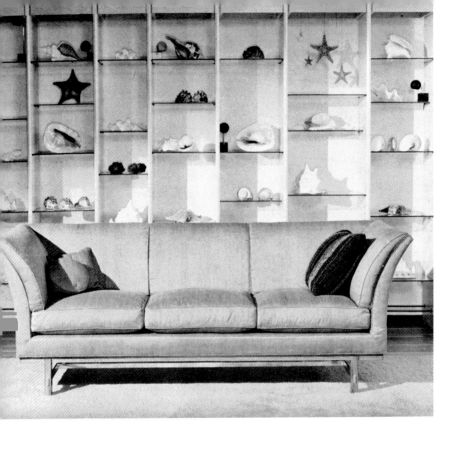

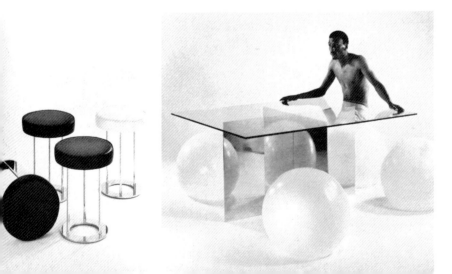

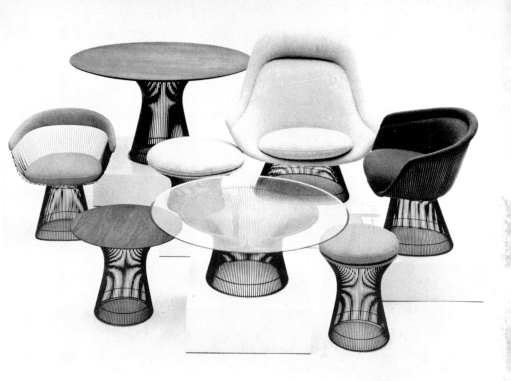

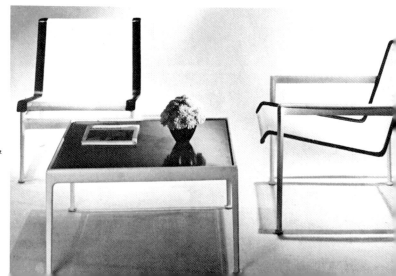

sofa, solid timber frame with exposed
ase and brass stretchers, down-filled
ushions, rubber-filled back cushions :
9 overall x 84 high
ned by Edward J. Wormley for the
ar Furniture Corporation, *USA*

ools, polished chrome steel base
ems, wood seat upholstered over
cm 42 high
ed chrome and glass table :
8 × 101 × 76 high
designed by Paul Mayen for Habitat
SA

r Collection, wire with foam rubber
stery in fibreglass shell seats on tension
netal finished dark copper oxide, or (except
hair and lounge chair) silvery nickel.
ned by Warren Platner
e Collection, indoor/outdoor group
es long chairs, dining and coffee tables
hairs, aluminium frames plastic coated
or white, table tops red-orange, yellow,
r brown porcelain enamel, resilient
ng' seats Dacron, all completely
erproof
ned by Richard Schultz
de by Knoll Associates, Inc *USA*

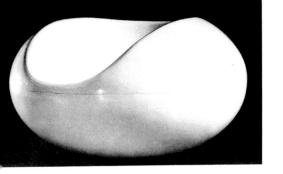

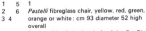

1 5
2 6
3 4

1
Pastelli fibreglass chair, yellow, red, green, orange or white : cm 93 diameter 52 high overall
Designed by Eerio Aarnio for Asko Oy, *Finland*

5
Malitte: five elements form a pattern of floor seating or slot together into a giant puzzle-sculpture : polyurethane foam covered green felt : cm 160 × 160 × 63
Designed by Echaurren Matta for Gavina, *Italy*

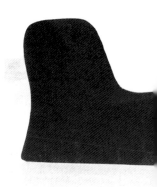

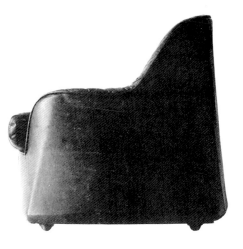

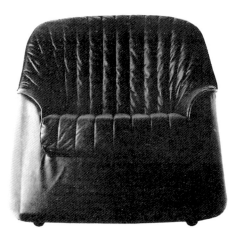

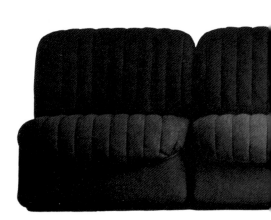

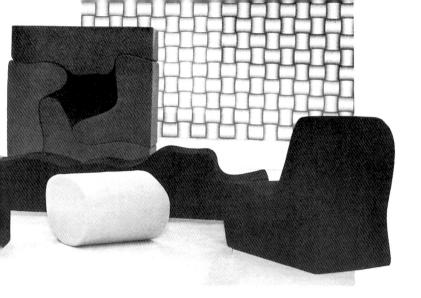

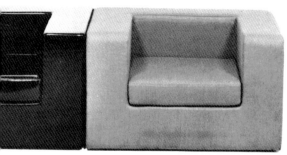

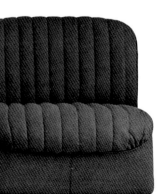

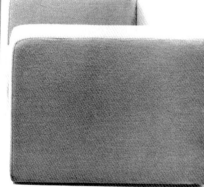

2, 3, 4
Ciprea armchair and 3 armless chairs formed
from injected foam polyurethane ; base of
expanded polystyrene vacuum moulded ;
leather, artificial leather or fabric covering
Designed by Afra & Tobia Scarpa for Cassina,
Italy
6
Throwaway foam rubber shape covered pink,
black, white, red, yellow, lilac, pale blue or
orange PVC
Designed by Willie Landels for Zanotta Poltrone,
Italy

1, 2
Opus 22 range of bedroom fitments, from
particle board, hardwood and hardboard,
doors matt white lacquer or American
walnut finish, all other surfaces white lacquer:
basic module cm 56 × 225 × 61
Designed by Walter Müller, *Switzerland*
for The Stag Cabinet Company Limited,
England
3
Wardrobe units with screen-fold doors, matt
light grey laminate surfaces: cm 203 × 296
high × 41 or 63 deep: 62.5 wide, extending
by modules of 12.5 cm
Designed by H. Gugelot for Wilhelm Bofinger,
W Germany

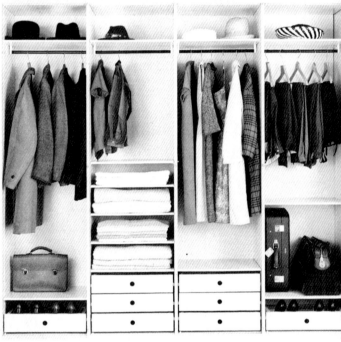

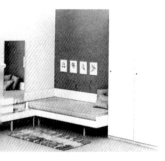

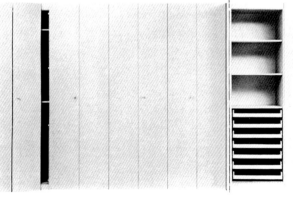

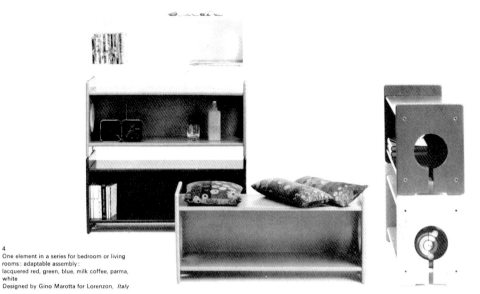

4
One element in a series for bedroom or living
rooms: adaptable assembly:
lacquered red, green, blue, milk coffee, parma,
white
Designed by Gino Marotta for Lorenzon, *Italy*

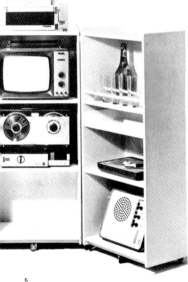

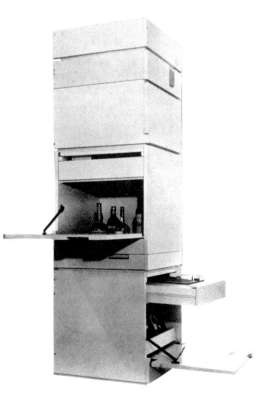

5
Folding storage unit: lacquered white, beige
or with wood finishes
Designed by Giovanni Offredi for Alberto Bazzani
Italy
6
Euro 2 stacked vertically: the three elements of
the series can also be arranged as horizontal
storage, drinks' and music cabinets, as bedside
tables and in other combinations: compressed
plywood lacquered white, aubergine, red,
emerald or shocking pink or natural: basic
module cm 57 × 57 × 57
Designed by Carlo Vigano for Cesare Nava, *Italy*

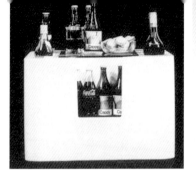

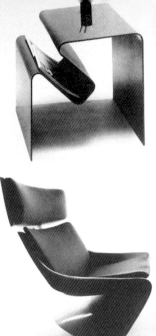

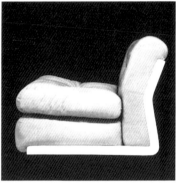

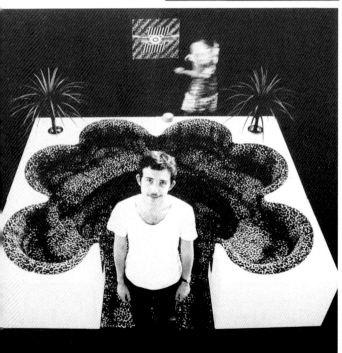

1
Drinks' cabinet/trolley incorporating ice-box:
fibreglass, white, black or orange
Designed by Sergio Mazza for Studio Artemide
Italy
3
Amanta chair, white, red, yellow, orange or
black Fibrelite shell, with foam rubber and
fibrefill cushions covered fabrics or leather
Designed by Mario Bellini for C + B *Italy*
5
Safari divan group: white PRFV structures with
Pirelli foam rubber upholstery, leopard fabric
covered: here, two sofas each cm 130 × 130,
two chairs each cm 85 × 85 and a carpet
Designed by Archizoom for Poltronova, s.r.l.
Italy
2
Form magazine/end table, shaped from a
ribbon of high gloss acrylic red, black or
white: cm 46 × 46 × 46
Designed by Andrew Ivar Morrison for
Stendig Inc, *USA*
4
Easy chair, resilient glass-fibre-reinforced
polyester, upholstered solid colour woollen
weaves over foam rubber
Designed by Steen Østergaard for A/S France
& Son, *Denmark*

1 4
2 5 6 7
3 8

6
Marcel armchair/sofa/seat units: dense foam
rubber structure with anodised aluminium
frames and connecting elements, covered
heavy wool military cloth: basic seat unit
cm 60 × 80 × 35
Designed by Kazuhide Takahama for Gavina,
Italy
7
Dollaro table, polystyrene stamped low relief
white with red, white, black, green, silver or
blue top: cm 70 diameter
Designed by Franco Angeli for Mana Art
Market, s.r.l. *Italy*
8
Bauletti games'-boxes/drinks' trolleys, natural
preformed plywood with red and yellow pattern
stain resist finished
Designed by R. Pamjo, R. Toso, N. Massari
for Stilwood, *Italy*

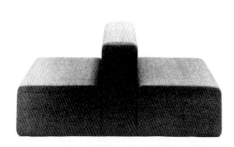
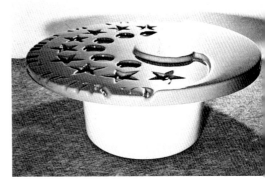
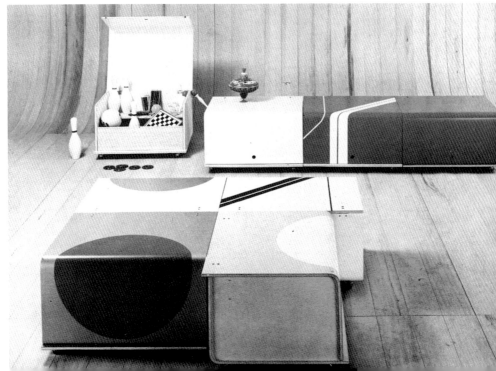

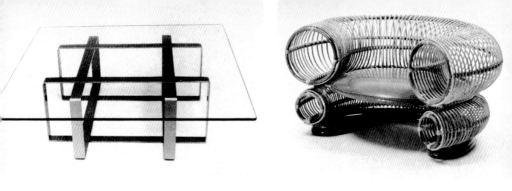

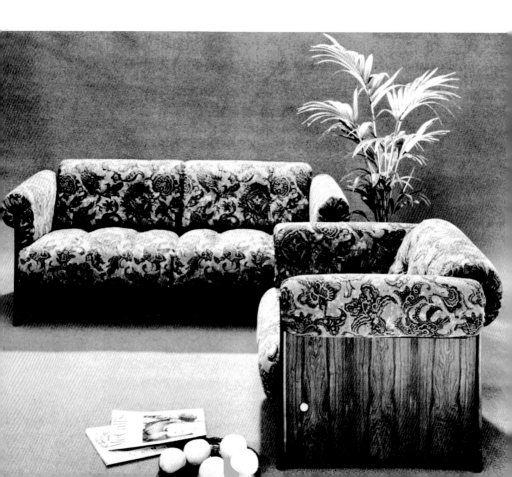

1
Glass-topped table, frame of metal hoops,
stove-enamelled colours or polished :
cm 108 × 108 × 30.5 high
Designed by John Monk for Datum Furniture
Limited *England*
2
Armchair, giunco with foam rubber cushion
Designed by Giovanni Travasa for Bonacina *Italy*
3
Buster two-seater and easy chair, laminated
wood with white lacquer or rosewood finish :
pre-formed upholstery units are demountable :
chair : cm 67 high × 83 deep × 93 wide
Designed by Ake Nilsson for Dux International
Mobel Ab *Sweden*
4
Group S420 silver-or matt-finished ball and rod
frames allow various arrangements : upholstery
specially woven by Unika Vaev, three colourways
Designed by Verner Panton for Gebruder
Thonet GmbH *W. Germany*

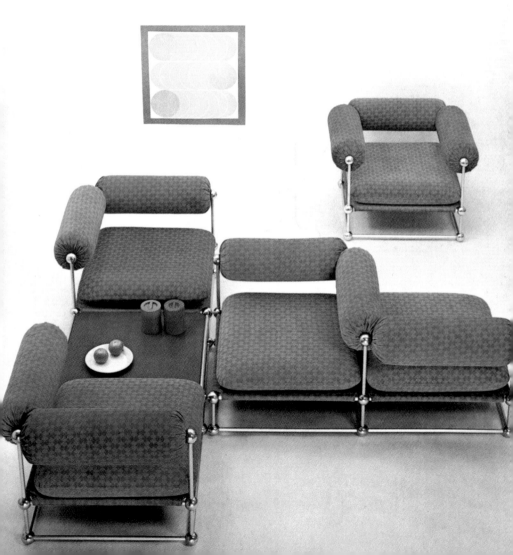

Items in a packaged series: chipboard
texture-stained, table tops lacquered:
green/lemon/grey or red/black: round tab
cm 100 diameter, with overlaid top
cm 160 diameter
2, 3 oblong table cm 189 × 39.5 with two
dropped leaves: arm chairs, longer benche
with/without arms also available: all piece
have visible screws locking into cross nuts
Designed by Bard Henriksen, *Denmark* and
made by Ums Pastoe, *Holland*, Mobel Fisk
Norway

Stowaway storage system: five units locat
on pins, mount into any desired combinati
plinth and boxes stained dark brown, back
shelves, drawers, doors natural beech: bas
unit size cm 50.3 × 50.3 × 35.6
Designed and made by Conran & Compan
Limited *England*

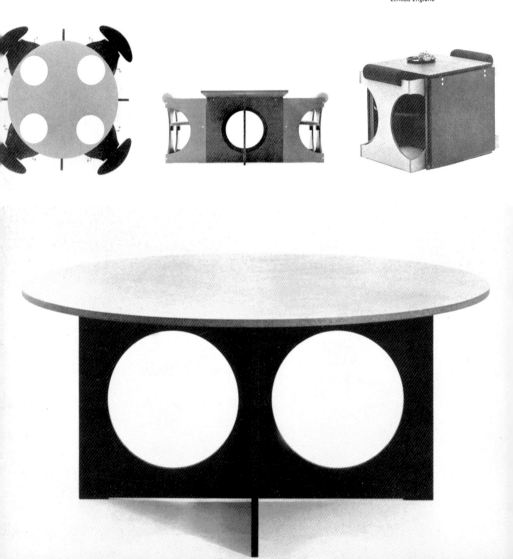

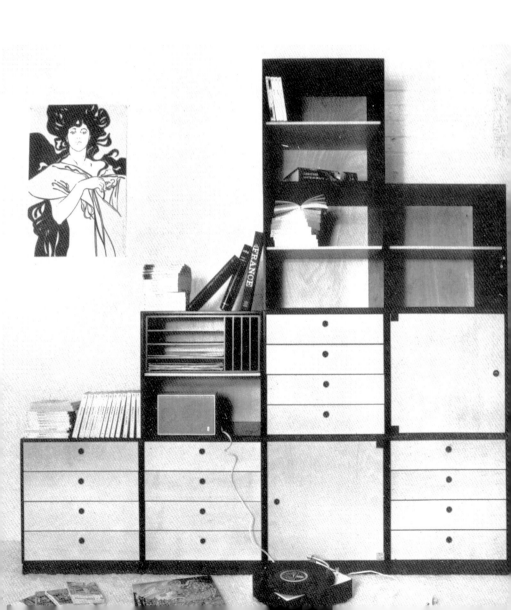

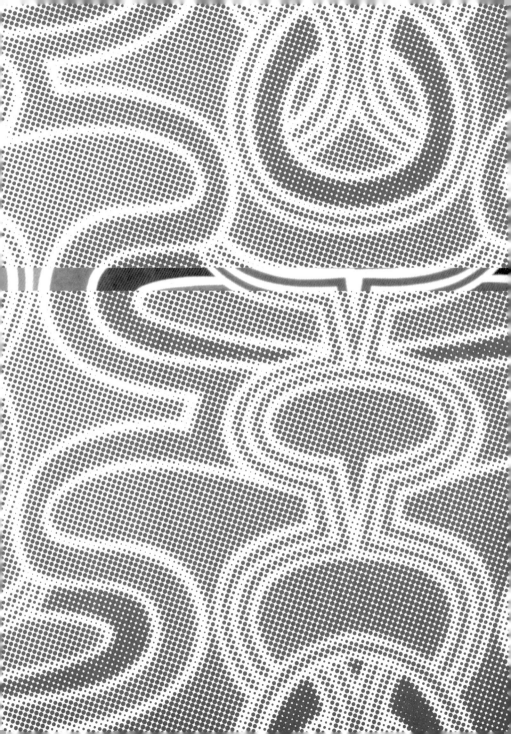

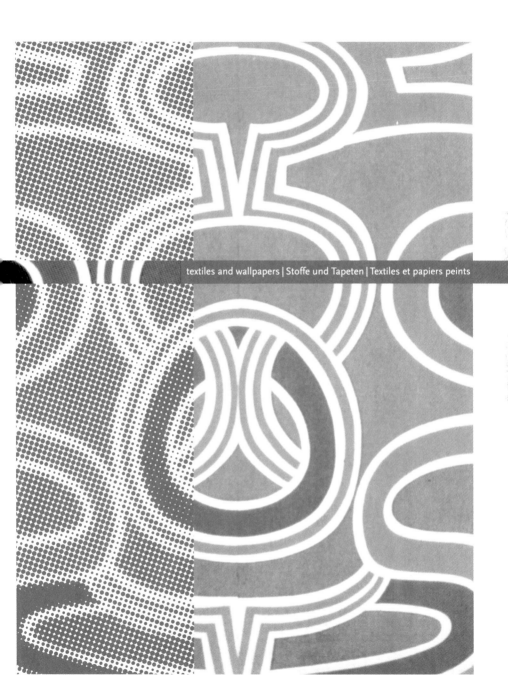

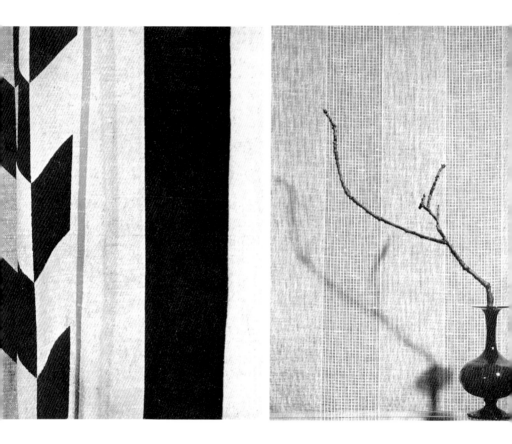

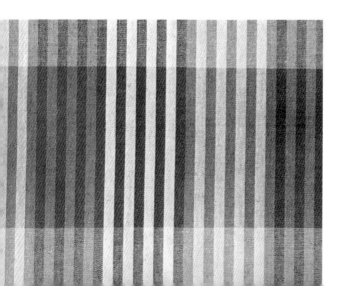

▲ *Peru* drapery fabric in Belgian linen with single or double stripe pattern in brown and orange on oatmeal. The design, inspired by traditional Peruvian rugs, is by Suzanne Huguenin SWITZERLAND for the Knoll International fabric range made by Knoll Textiles Inc. USA

A drawn-thread effect transparent white casement fabric in linen and cotton. Designed by Age Faith-Ell for AB Claes Håkansson SWEDEN

◄ Brown shadow-stripe drapery fabric in an all-cotton weave from the Cotil range. Designed by Vibeke Klint for A/S C. Olesen DENMARK

►

TOP: *Grotto* rayon/cotton texture weave in several colourways including red/burgundy/black; olive green/lemon/white; forest green/blue.
Designed by Tibor Reich, FSIA, for Tibor Ltd UK

Open weave transparent casement fabric in linen thread.
By Leinenweberei Baumann & Co. SWITZERLAND

Media casement fabric, a cotton/rayon/mohair sheer weave in blue, gold or natural. The rhythmic pattern formed by the filling stripes breaks, but does not destroy, the vertical effect created by the fancy weave. Designed by Marie Howell for David and Dash USA

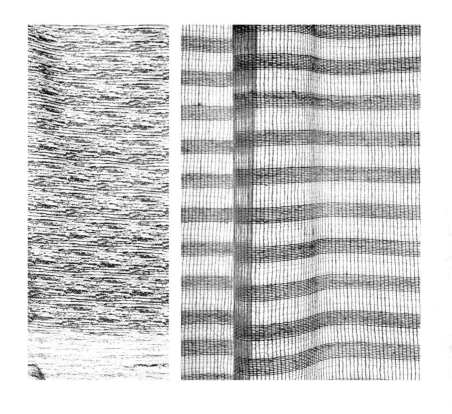
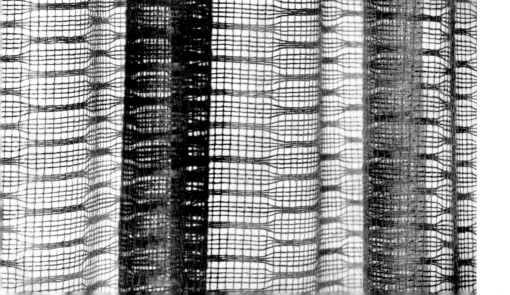

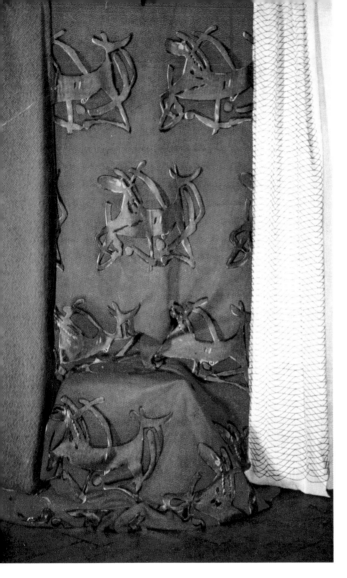

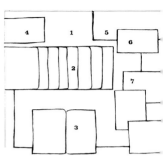

1 *Crosh* linen weave, 50 inches wide, Sanforized sh finish. Made by The Old Bleach Linen Co. Lt

2–3 *Rothes* slub weave in cotton, linen, wool/rayor viscose staple; and *Broadford* wool/rayon texture we Both fabrics are 50 inches wide and are from the Glamis range made by Donald Bros Ltd UK

4 A heavy Irish linen weave, 52 inches wide, in colourways. From Conran Fabrics UK

5 *Ancona* cotton and rayon weave with a knitted e 50 inches wide. Designed by Tibor Reich, FSIA, i in a wide range of colours by Tibor Ltd UK

6 'London shrunk' all cotton spiral repp, 48 inches v Made in a range of 15 colours by W. H. Foxton Lt

7 *Le Bosquet* by Shirley Craven and *Golden Harve* Althea McNish, two large-scale designs from the '] Present' range, hand-screen-printed in glowing co on 50-inch cotton satin by Hull Traders Ltd UK

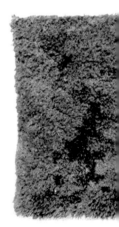

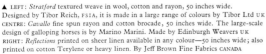

▲ LEFT: *Stratford* textured weave in wool, cotton and rayon, 50 inches wide. Designed by Tibor Reich, FSIA, it is made in a large range of colours by Tibor Ltd UK CENTRE: *Cavallo* fine spun rayon and cotton brocade, 50 inches wide. The large-scale design of galloping horses is by Marino Marini. Made by Edinburgh Weavers UK RIGHT: *Reflections* printed on sheer linen available in any colour—50 inches wide; also printed on cotton Terylene or heavy linen. By Jeff Brown Fine Fabrics CANADA

All wool rug (68 × 32 inches) from a colourful range, each individually designed and hand-knotted by Renata Bonfanti ITALY ▶ FAR RIGHT: Linen and cotton sheer-weave, 50 inches wide. A Stuttgarter Gardine fabric, also available in yellow or natural. From Danasco Ltd UK

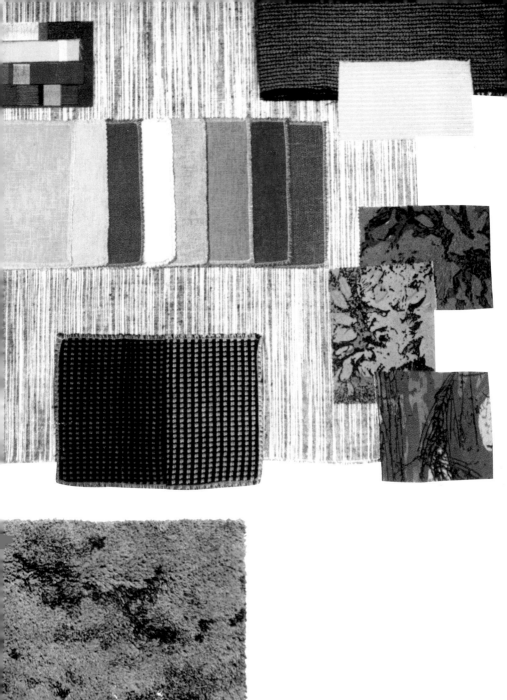

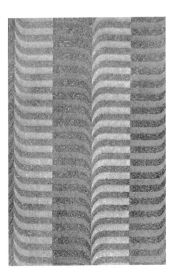

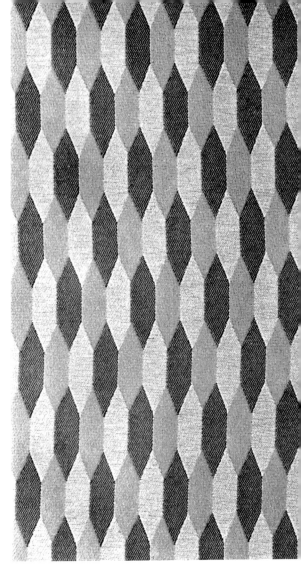

Brandon rayon and Lurex drapery fabric in blue, green, stone, beige, gold; 50 inches wide. Designed by Frank Davies, MSIA, for Warner & Sons Ltd UK

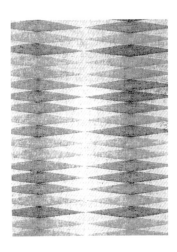

Anthracite/grey/sand weave, cotton warp, linen weft with pattern in wool; 50 inches wide. Designed by Lennart Svefors for AB Claes Håkansson SWEDEN

Biarritz rayon/nylon multicoloured hexagonal faille available in fourteen colourways; 54 inches wide. By Boris Kroll Fabrics Inc. USA

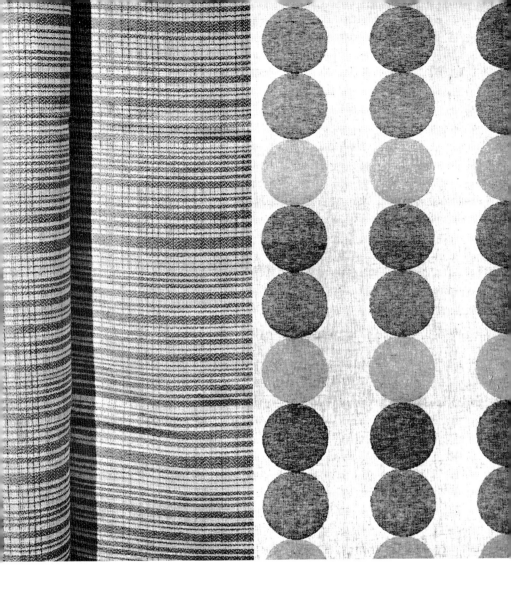

Linen weave in a wide range of colours;
55 inches wide.
By Worb & Scheitlin AG, SWITZERLAND

Anthracite/grey/sand weave, cotton warp, linen weft with pattern
in wool; 50 inches wide.
Designed by Brita Ahlgren for AB Claes Håkansson SWEDEN

Salix screenprint on cotton, 48 inches wide; green, blue, brown, grey and red are other colourings. Designed by Annika Malström.
Radja stripe screenprint on cotton, 48 inches wide, available in nine colourways. Designed by Viola Gråsten.
Both fabrics made by Mölnlycke Väfveri AB, SWEDEN
CP 4051 heavy cotton screenprint, 48 inches wide; also in grey/slate blue, red/pink, violet/turquoise tones.
By David Whitehead Fabrics Ltd UK

Cosmorama hand-screenprinted 'Everglaze' chintz, 50 in wide; also in pink/green and blue/green on white.
By Arthur Sanderson & Sons Ltd UK
Arden cotton/wool texture weave, 48 inches wide, availab eleven colourways.
Designed by Tibor Reich, FSIA, for Tibor Ltd UK

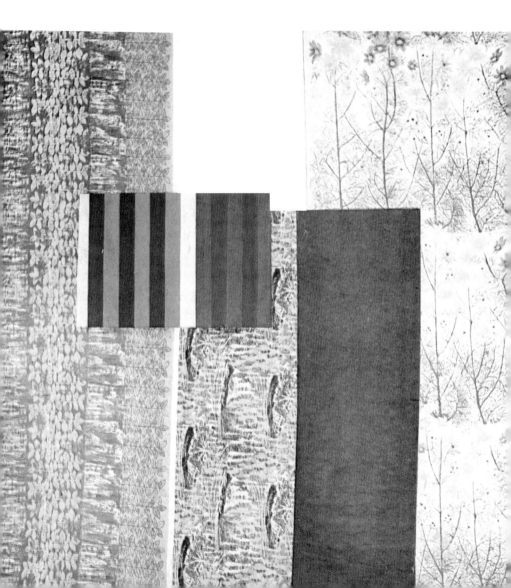

...age hand-screenprint on cotton tweed, 48 inches wide; green,
..e, and grey are other colours.
..signed by Trevor Bates for Edinburgh Weavers UK
..flower hand-screenprinted 'Everglaze' chintz, 48 inches wide;
..9 in blue/green on white.
.Arthur Sanderson & Sons Ltd UK
..tella four-colour leaf print on cotton, 50 inches wide. Designed
.Ute E. Jansen for Textildruckerei Oberursel GmbH GERMANY

Akarana cotton-satin hand-print 48 inches
wide; also with the poppy motif in purple
or lemon. Designed by Althea McNish for
Liberty & Co. Ltd UK
Monstera large leaf screenprint on stain and
crease resistant glass fabric, 46 inches wide,
available in four colourways. Designed by
Tootal Studios for Vetrona Fabrics Ltd UK
Atlanta heavy cotton-satin four-colour
print, 48/50 inches wide. A 'Time Present'
fabric in three colourways designed by
John Drummond for Hull Traders Ltd UK

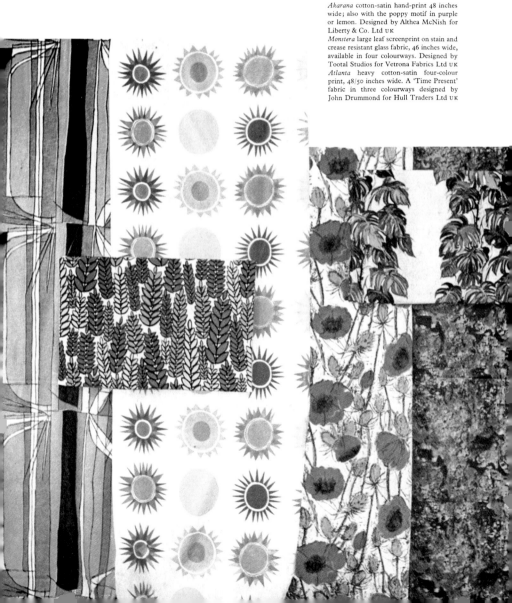

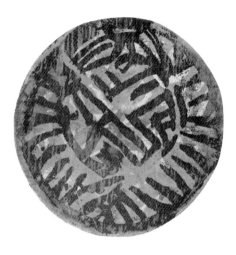

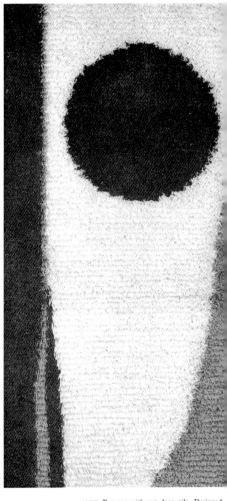

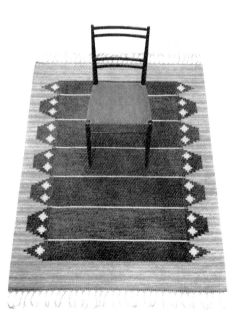

ABOVE Rya rug with cut deep pile. Designed
Mary Beatrice Bloch for Væveboden DENMARK
                                    Photo Jørn Frea
Handwoven Röllakan rug in wool combined w
spun rayon, linen and goathair. Made in f
colour combinations and in sizes 78 × 45 inc
and 94 × 67 inches. Designed by Rakel Carland
Carlanders Väveri AB, for Eric Ewers AB SWEDE

OPPOSITE Duveteen applique wall hanging, 72
41 inches. Conceived as a 'painting in fabric',
colours are related to the colour scheme of
particular room. Each is individually designed a
made by Jettie Penraat USA

LEFT Circular wool rug, 72 inches diameter,
Dresden Axminster quality. The design, a chron
tic arrangement of colour in a subtle blending
tobacco brown tones, is by Lisa Gronwall SWED
Made by Carpet Trades Ltd UK

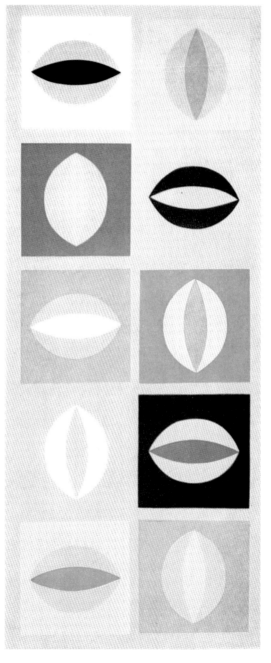

1, 2
Pesula 881, Indian cotton 48 inches wide, and *Pferd 73* a heavy cotton with 24-inch repeat. Printed by Mech. Weberei Pausa AG for Emtex GmbH GERMANY

3, 4
Naturlarä fine cotton print, 36 inches wide, sanforized finish; available in seven colourways. Designed by Marianne Mandelius; *Duo* two-tone medium weight cotton, 50 inches wide, sanforized finish; available in a range of fourteen colourings. Designed by Annika Malmström. Both made by Mölnlycke Väfveri AB SWEDEN

5, 6
Satula and *Pyöryläinen* cotton prints, 48 inches wide, available in several colourings. Both designed by Maija Isola for Printex O/Y FINLAND

7, 8
Tobago screenprint on crepe cotton, 48 inches wide, available in four colourways. Designed by Althea McNish, Des.RCA, MSIA;
Country Bunch cotton roller-print, 48 inches wide, in five colourways. Designed by Barbara Brown. Both made by Heal Fabrics Ltd UK

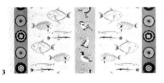

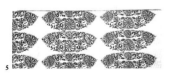

3

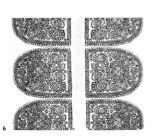

5

6

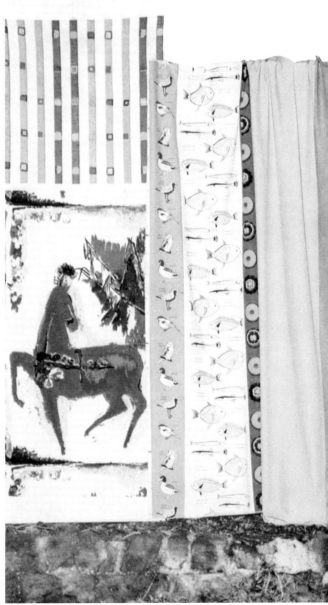

1

3

4

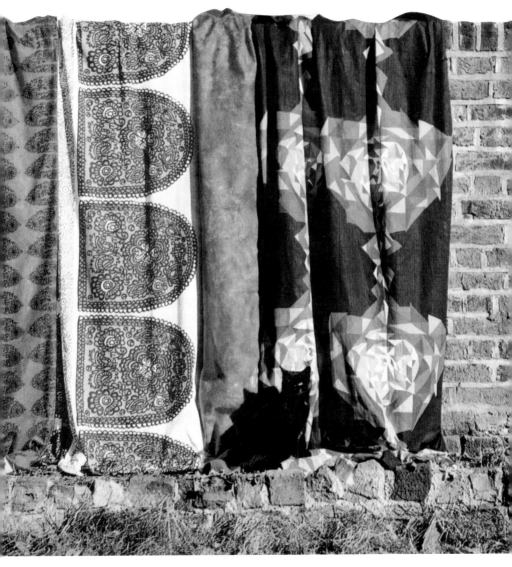

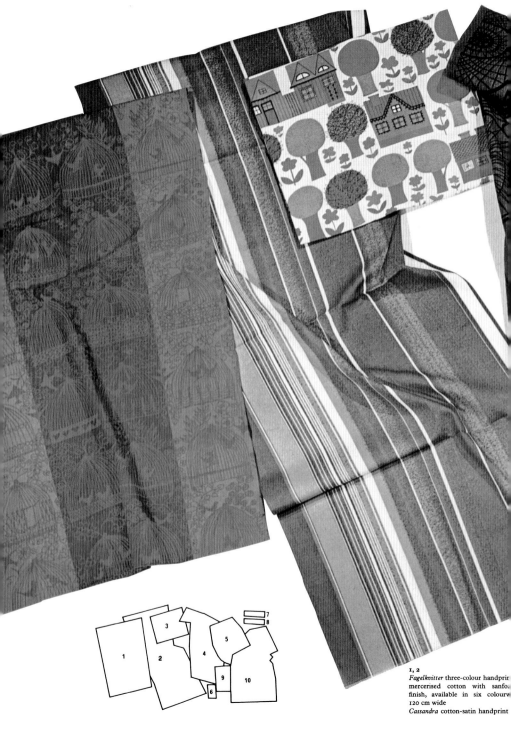

1, 2
Fagelkvitter three-colour handprin[t]
mercerised cotton with sanfo[r]
finish, available in six colour[s]
120 cm wide
Cassandra cotton-satin handprint

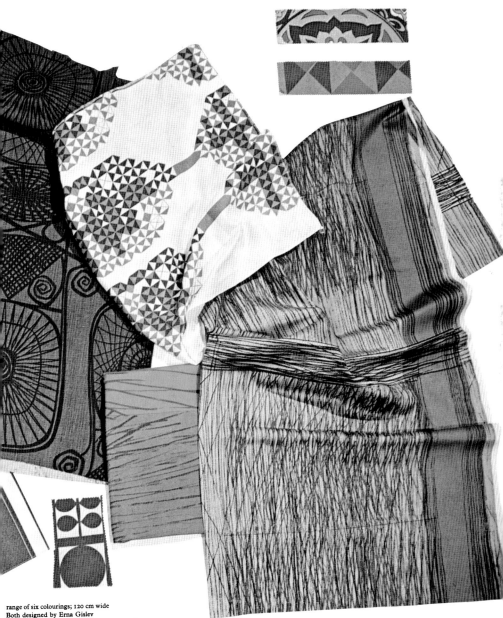

range of six colourings; 120 cm wide
Both designed by Erna Gislev

3
Smdstad a gay nursery handprint on mercerised cotton; 91 cm wide. Four colourways
Designed by Annika Malmström

4
Korgfläta linen handprint, available in a range of seven different colourways
Designed by Viola Gråsten. All for Mölnlycke Väfveri AB SWEDEN

5
Crystal Rosebank roller print on textured cotton; in six colourways; 127 cm wide
Designed by Dorothy Mathew for Turnbull & Stockdale Ltd UK

6
Grille cotton screenprint; 122 cm wide. Seen in repeat on page 87
From Heal Fabrics Ltd UK

7, 8
Bianca and *Arabella* cotton hand-screenprints; 122 cm wide. *Bianca* seen in repeat on page 86
Designed by Shirley Conran for Conran Fabrics Ltd UK

9, 10
Two from a range of designs screen-printed on heavy cotton-satin; 120 cm wide; ten colourways are available
Designed by Leo Wollner for Mech. Weberei Pausa AG GERMANY

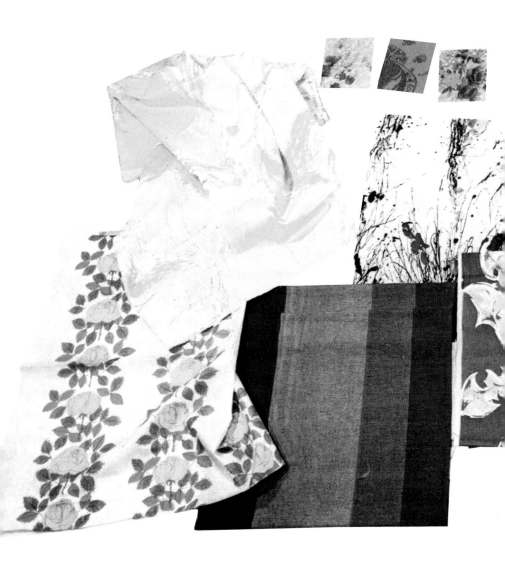

1, 8
Pastoral designed by James Morgan, *Struan* designed by Peter McCulloch: 'Time Present' screenprints on heavy cotton-satin; 122 cm wide; each is available in three colourways. For Hull Traders Ltd UK

2
Rosita screenprint on fine glazed cotton; 91 cm wide; in seven colourways
Designed by Annika Malmström.
For Mölnlycke Väfveri AB SWEDEN

3, 5
Two colourways from the *Angelique* range of screenprints on cotton-satin; 128 cm wide
Designed by Pascaline Villon
4
Chandernagor screenprint on dobby cotton in four colourways
Designed by Laureat Stève
All for Boussac de Paris FRANCE

6
September Garland screenprint on poplin; 122 cm wide. Availabl three colourways. From A Sanderson & Sons Ltd UK

7
Baltic Stripe heavy rayon weav many colourways and several s of pattern; 122 cm wide. Mad Cavendish Textiles Ltd UK

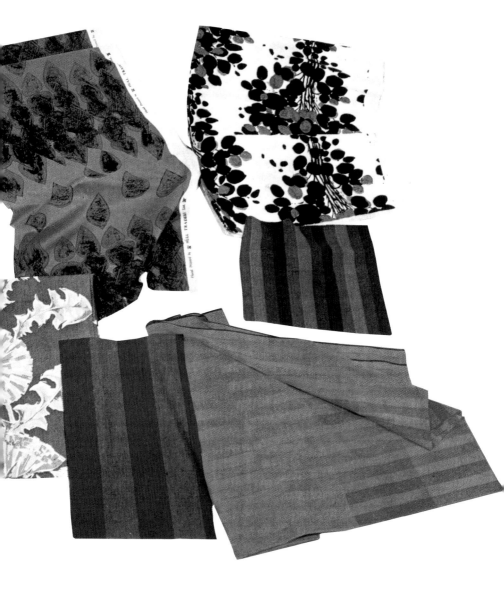

10
Woven cotton stripe, range *373/45*, in four colourways; 152 cm wide

12, 13
Fine cotton weaves, ranges *374/35* and *392/65*, each in four colourways; 132 cm wide

All designed by Uhra Simberg for Finlayson-Forssa FINLAND. From Danasco Fabrics Ltd UK

II
ox and *Perla* two screenprints on avy cotton
ade by Danasco Fabrics Ltd UK

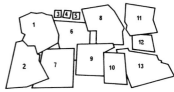

1
Kakoset wall tapestry in tradi**
'täkänä' double hollow-weave:
yarn in khaki/brown on green/p**
100 × 180 cm
Designed by Maija Kolsi-Mäke**
Helmi Vuorelma O/Y FINLAND**

2
Fästmansgåva screenprint on fine
lin with sanforised finish: availa**
four colourways
Designed by Beret Helena R**
Made by Borås Wäfveri A/B for
Sörensen AB SWEDEN

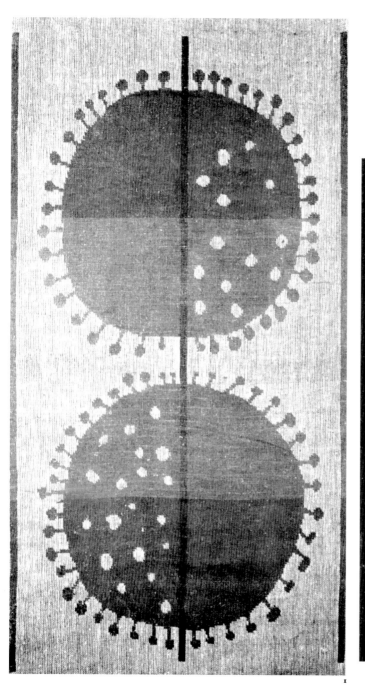

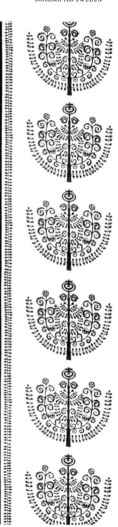

1

3
Korppa, another 'täkänä' design, the hollow-weave technique producing counterchange effects on the reverse: linen yarn in light/dark purple with bright red/dark blue; 47 × 140 cm Designed by Maija-Liisa Forss-Heinonen for Helmi Vuorelma O/Y FINLAND

4
Fireside Evening machine-made rya rug; 184 × 138 or 276 × 184 cm Designed by Ritva Puotila Made by O/Y Finnrya A/B FINLAND

PHOTOS 1, 3 KUVAKIILA
PHOTO 4 PIETINEN

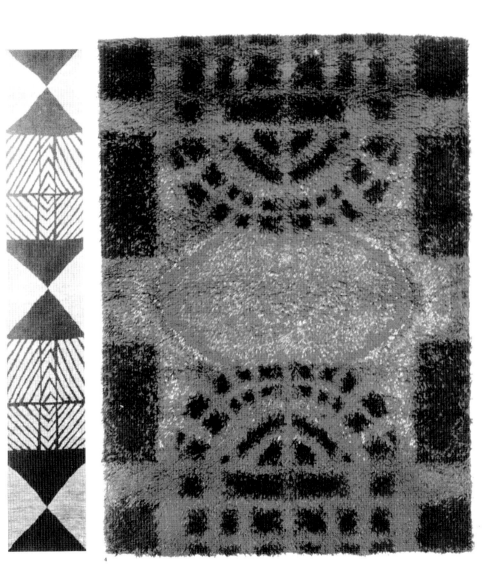

4

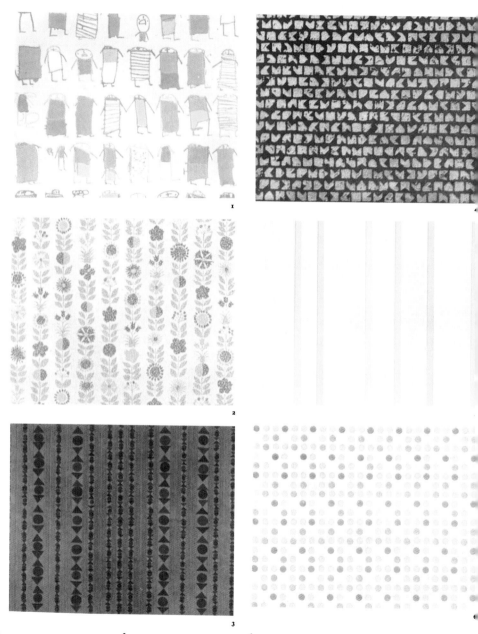

1
Plastic coated nursery wallpaper 43182 designed by Edward Veevers: also available in pink/blue/yellow

2
Floral stripe 43186 designed by Derek Healey: three colourways are available, one on black ground

3
Geometric stripe 43202 designed by Pamela Kay: in three colourways

4
Mosaic 43196 designed by Edward Veevers: metallic gold on matt brown paper, copper on grey, pale yellow or pale grey on white

5
Vertical stripe 43173, a plastic coated paper available in three colourways Designed by Roger Nicholson

6
Discs 43195, plastic coated and available also in blue/grey pastel tones on white. Designed by Paul Hugener

All these papers are in the Pa. Mondo Collection made by The Paper Manufacturers Ltd UK Matching or co-ordinating fabric available in the Bevis range m factured by Simpson & Godlee L*

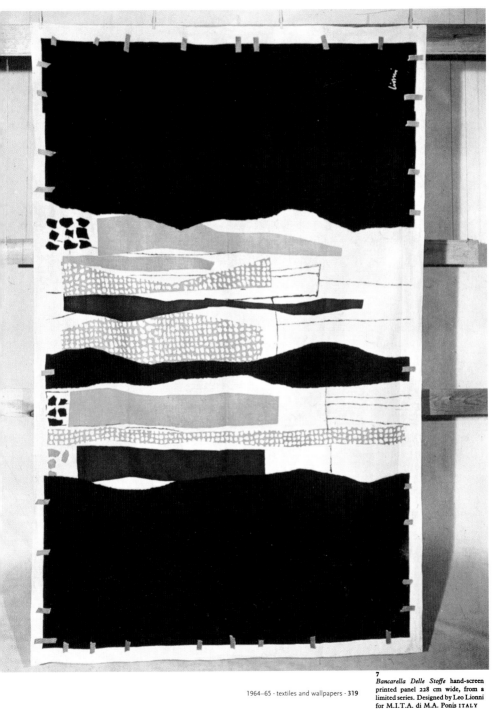

7
Bancarella Delle Stoffe hand-screen
printed panel 228 cm wide, from a
limited series. Designed by Leo Lionni
for M.I.T.A. di M.A. Ponis ITALY

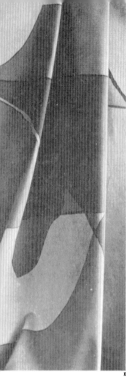

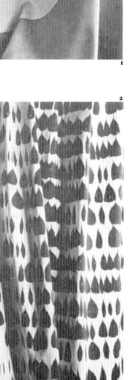

1
Shape screenprint on heavy cotton
satin; 122 cm wide: purple/brown/
terracotta, grey/brown/gold and green/
peacock/red
Designed by Shirley Craven

2
Queen of Spain one-colour screenprint available in three colourways on
white cotton and in three colourways
on dyed cotton satin—red/orange,
blue/green and green/blue
Designed by Michael Taylor
Both Time Present fabrics made by
Hull Traders Ltd UK

3
Oresund three-colour weave in fine
cotton, available in eight colourways;
150 cm wide
Designed by Tove Kindt-Larsen for
Gabriel DENMARK

4, 6
Love in Idleness and *Master Tuggie's*:
screenprints on heavy cotton; both
available in three colourways; 122 cm
wide
Both designed by Gillian Farr for
Conran Fabrics Ltd UK

5
Loto screenprint on 100% linen or
linen/cotton. Available in ten colourways—predominant tone of reds,
greens, blues, browns, violet or grey;
also yellow/orange, dark brown/grey-
blue and clear beige; 130 cm wide
Made by Falconetto ITALY

7
Tapestry print on mohair/rayon/cotton
Royale cloth: four colourways; 122
cm wide
Designed by Ballatore & Larsen
Design Corporation for Jack Lenor
Larsen Inc USA

8
Heavy cotton two-tone repp; 122 cm
wide, available in thirty-four colours:
Made by Liberty & Co Ltd UK

9, 10
Bellmansro and *Fästmansgåva* screen-
prints on fine sanforised cotton; 90 cm
wide: one seen in repeat on page 80
Designed by Beret Helena Ruuth
Produced by Boras Wäfveri A/B for
A.E. Sörenson AB SWEDEN

11
Patience screenprint on heavy cotton;
122 cm wide, available in many colours
and designs
Made by Liberty & Co Ltd UK

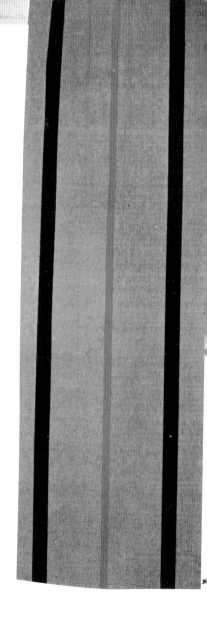

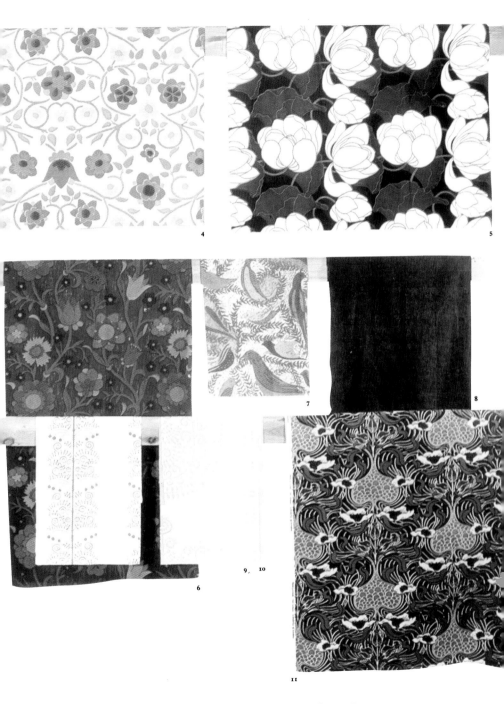

4

5

6

7

8

9 , 10

11

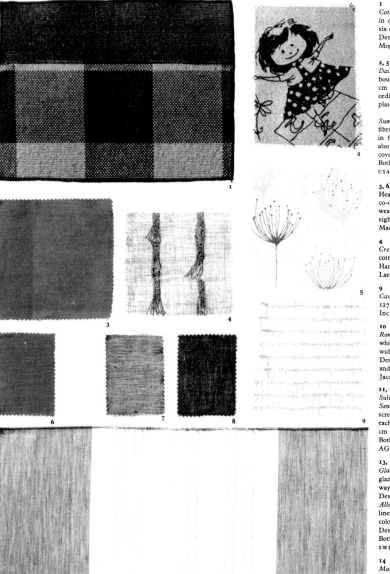

1
Cotil 742: 100% wool upholstery
in check and matching plain w
six colourways; 130 cm wide
Designed by Lis Ahlmann and
Mogensen for A/S C. Olesen DEN

2, 5
Daizy Maizy print on fibr
bouclé, or on fortisan or cotton
cm wide: design available also a
ordinated wallpaper with wa
plastic and other finishes

Summer Silk print on fibreglass b
fibreglass Neptune, fortisan or
in fifteen colourways; 122 cm
also available as co-ordinated
covering
Both for Laverne International
USA

3, 6, 7, 8
Heavyweight cotton repp, availa
co-ordinated checks and two
weaves: thirty-four colours inc
eight checks; 122 cm wide
Made by Liberty & Co Ltd UK

4
Crescendo sheer weave, natural
cotton/metallic thread; 127 cm
Handwoven in Italy for Jack
Larsen Inc USA

9
Casablanca mohair/rayon/cotton
127 cm wide for Jack Lenor I
Inc USA

10
Roman 100% cotton weave i
white and four colourways; 1
wide.
Designed by Elsa Lagersson-
and Nils Gröndahl for A/B
Jacquardväveri SWEDEN

11, 12
Sulina designed by Karin Mori
Senassi designed by Ulrike Rhon
screenprints on indanthren c
each available in six colourways
cm wide
Both made by Mech. Weberei
AG W. GERMANY

13, 15
Glad Påsk 21/414 screenprint o
glazed cotton; 91 cm wide: four c
ways
Designed by Erna Gislev
Allegro 25/848 screenprint on
linen/cotton weave; 120 cm wid
colourways
Designed by Annika Malmströ
Both for Molnlycke Väfveri
SWEDEN

14
Mantilla screenprint on cotton
Designed by Maija Isola for D
Fabrics Ltd UK

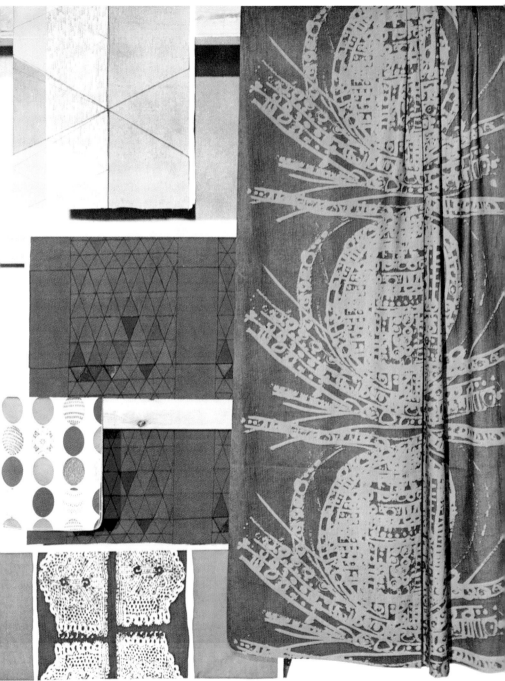

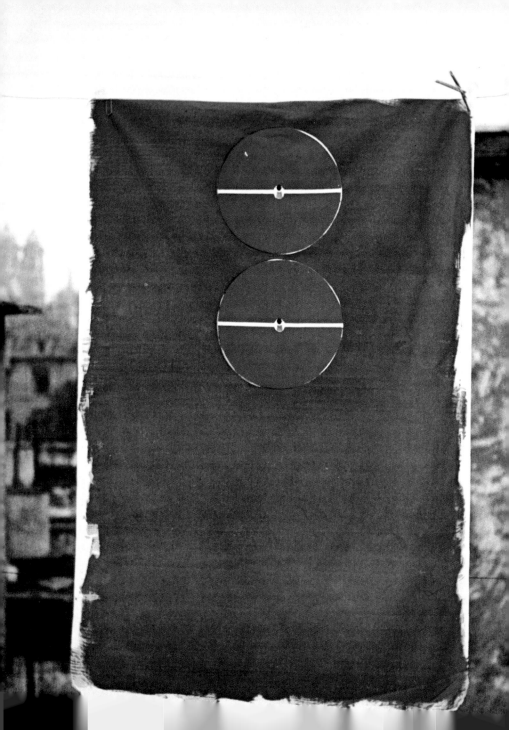

of a series of panels, printed
 wood on to thick linen
120 cm
gned and printed by Guiseppe
ie ITALY

Ristiretki an all-wool rya rug
110 × 168 cm
Designed by Raija Gripenberg
for Helmi Vuorelma O/y FINLAND

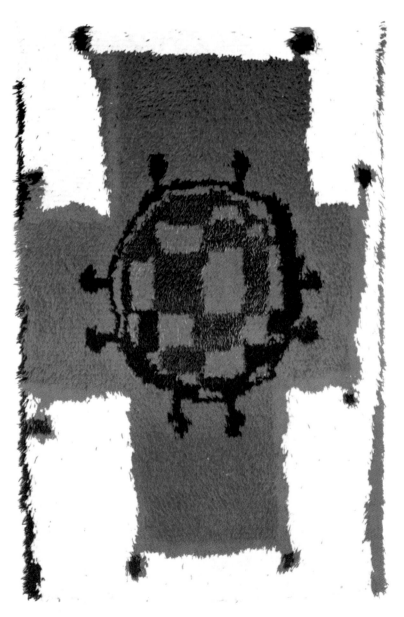

Figment glass-fibre weave in green,
orange, black or gold on white
122 cm wide
Designed by Estelle and Erwine
Laverne for Laverne International
Ltd USA

Slingöga 80% linen/20% cotton
sheer, 150 cm wide, available in
and four neutral or light colours
Designed by Gerd Stenberg for
AB Marks Jacquardvävveri SWEI

A woven solid/open stripe in
Fiberglas Beta yarn, available in
white or tan, 122 cm wide
Designed by Marie Howell of
Howell Design Associates for
Qual-Fab, Inc USA

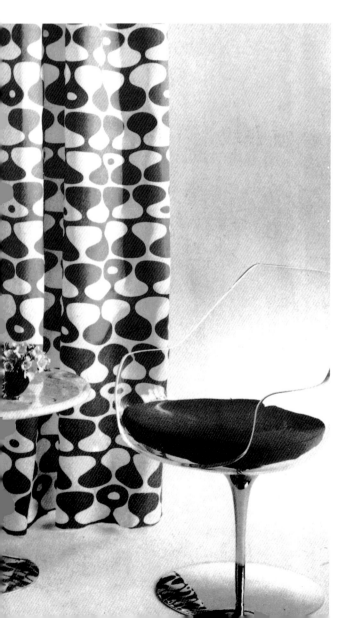

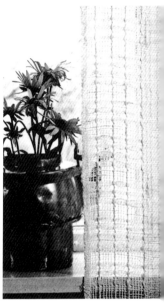

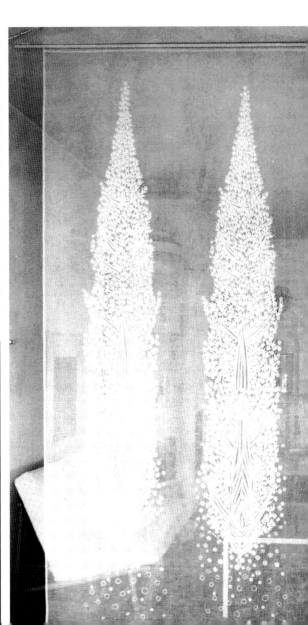

Parcypress room-divider: etch-print
on cotton, 127 cm wide, white only
Designed by Astrid Sampe for
NK Inredning SWEDEN

...ay a Rovana knit casement
...onze or white; fireproof,
...d damp resistant
...a large-scale design flock
...d on organza
...22 cm wide and made for
...enor Larsen Inc USA

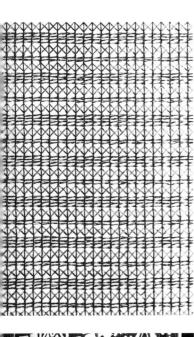

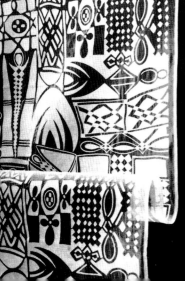

1 *Prince of Quince* screenprint on heavy cotton/linen cloth in three colourways and black/white 122 cm wide
Designed by Juliet Glynn-Smith for Conran Fabrics Ltd UK

2 *January* print in several colourways on 100% cotton, 122 cm wide

3, 4 *Tristripe* and *Diamonds*, a 15 cm repeat stripe and a four-colour print, both on Belgian 100% cotton cloth 122 cm wide

2, 3, 4 designed by Alexander Girard for Herman Miller Textiles USA

5 *Morven* a 100% linen, 124 cm wide in colours matching *Chroma* plain Wilton carpet: part of a series of co-ordinating carpets and weaves
Designed by Ian Miller for Thomson Shepherd & Co Ltd and Crest Weaving Co Ltd UK

6 *Jackanapes* screenprint on cotton cloth in two colourways 122 cm wide
Designed by Juliet Glynn-S for Conran Fabrics Ltd UK

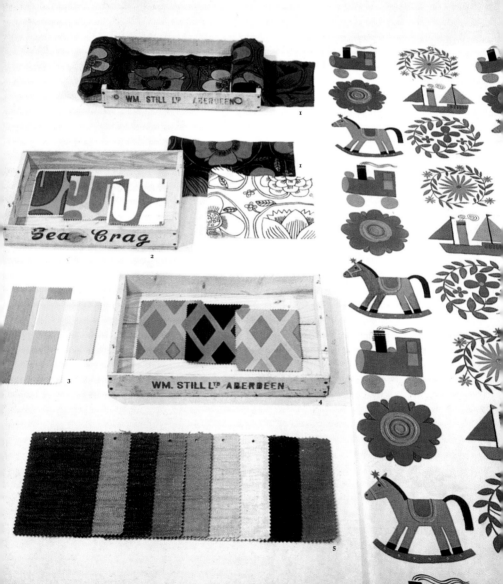

järter Ess screenprint on fine
iron cotton, 90 cm wide
colourways
gned by Erna Gislav for
nlycke Hemtextil AB SWEDEN

8 Fine 100% cotton woven checks
in five colourways, 152 cm wide
Designed by Uhra Simberg for
O/y Finlayson-Forssa AB FINLAND

9 *Moidart* a 'Time Present' screenprint
on heavy cotton-satin, 122 cm wide
available in four colourways
Designed by Peter McCulloch for
Hull Traders Ltd UK

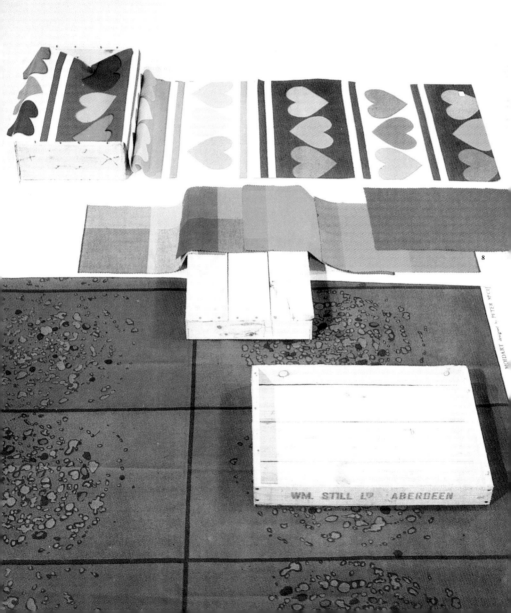

8

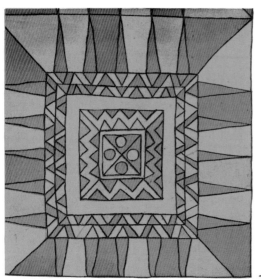

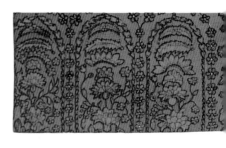

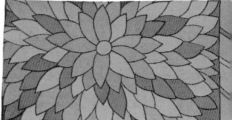

Nomoi screenprint on Dolan:
8 colourways: 120 cm wide
Designed by Leo Wollner for
Weberei Pausa AG W. GERMANY

Bali printed stripes on sanforized
100% cotton in 5 colourways:
119 cm wide
Designed by Erna Gilev for
Mölnlycke Hemtextil SWEDEN

Daisy Chain screenprint on cotton
poplin in 5 colourways:
122 cm wide
Designed by Pat Albeck for
Cavendish Textiles Ltd UK

Numea screenprint on Dolan:
8 colourways: 120 cm wide
Designed by Leo Wollner for
Weberei Paussa AG W. GERMANY

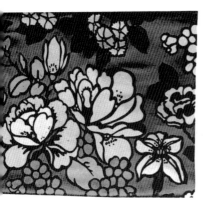

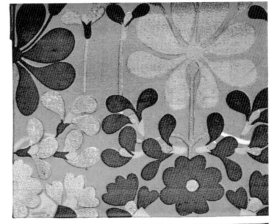

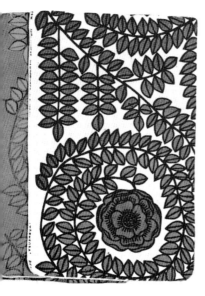

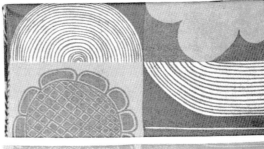

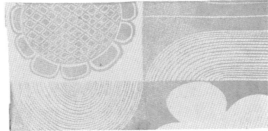

Chanelle screenprint on cotton satin in 4 colourways: 122 cm wide
Designed by Gillian Farr for Bernard Wardle Fabrics UK
seen in repeat on page 97

Törnrosa screenprint on 100% textured weave cotton 8 colourways: 145 cm wide
Designed by Viola Grasten for Mölnlycke Hemtextil SWEDEN

Florentina screenprint on shrink resistant, cotton crepe in 5 colourways: 122 cm wide.
Designed by Jyoti Bhomik
Imprint screenprint on shrink resistant cotton crepe in 4 colourways: 122 cm wide
Designed by Ian Logan

Both made by Heal Fabrics Ltd UK

AD Photography

Rondo all wool rug also in yellow
or green: 305 cm diameter
Designed by Agnethe Gjoedvad
Unika Vaer DENMARK

▷

Melting Snow hand-made wool
rug: 150 × 120 cm
Designed and manufactured by
Atelje Airi Snellman-Hänninen
FINLAND

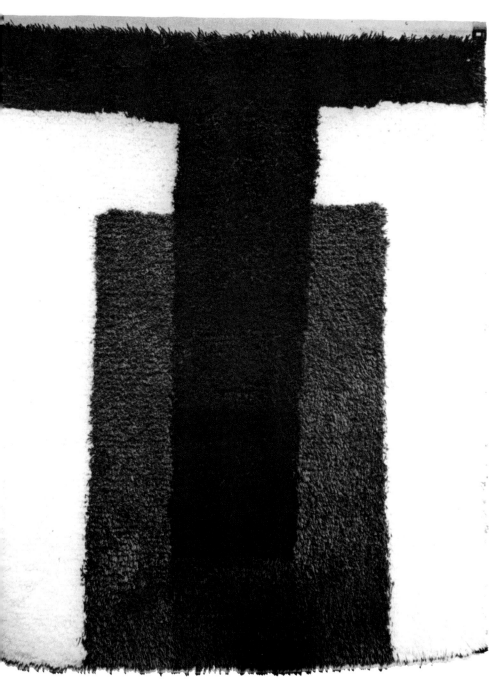

Ziggy-Zaggy screen-print on heavy plain cotton 4 colourways 120 cm wide Designed by Shirley Craven and made by Hull Traders Ltd *England*

Chan-Chan 100% cotton, tie-dyed upholstery or curtain weave, flame, flamingo (shown) amberviolet, bluewhite, 137 cm wide Designed and produced in Kenya by Eliza Willcox for Jack Lenor Larsen, Inc *USA*

Euclide hand screen-print on heavy 100% hemp, 100 cm wide Designed by Alberto Locatelli for Locatex s.r.l. *Italy*

Bellona heavy satin-faced cotton rep pre-shrunk and vat dyed in altogether about 42 colours 127 cm wide Design by Shirley Craven for Hull Traders Ltd *England*

Gran Canyon, Caldonia and *Acapo* hand screen-prints on cotton/line cloth All designed by Alberto Locatelli for Locatex s.r.l. *Italy*

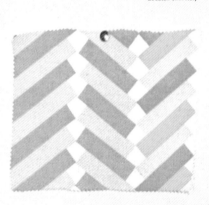

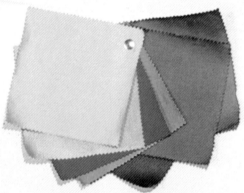

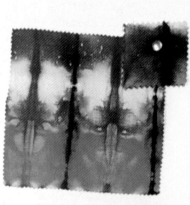

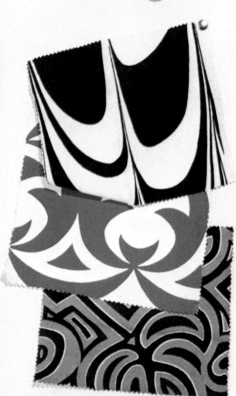

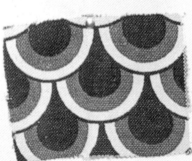

in *Kettle* and *Cabbage* two of
es of tea towels, 100% Irish
printed many bright colours
hite 78 × 53 cm
ned by Ornella Noorda (*Italy*)
onran Fabrics *England*

eau *Beardsley* from a series
ated printed trays and
-mats, black/white only
ned and made by Xlon Ltd
nd

Numeri cotton panels printed in
blue and green on turquoise and
three reds on white ground
Designed by Ornella Noorda
Zebra pillow panel in black and
white only
Designed by Anna Fasolis
both produced by Ornella Noorda *Italy*

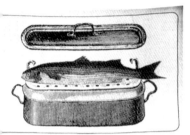

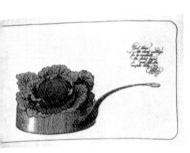

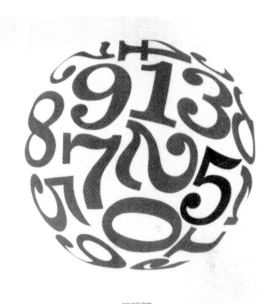

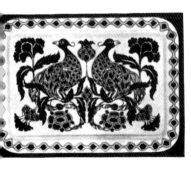

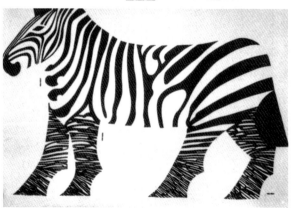

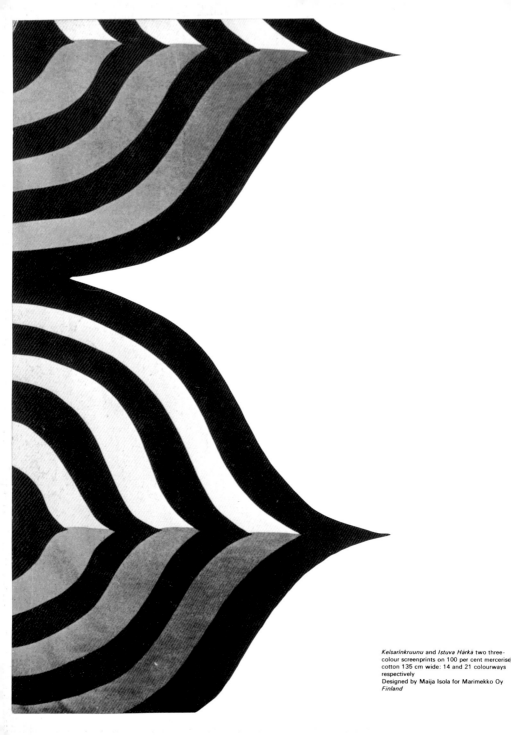

Keisarinkruunu and *Istuva Härkä* two three-colour screenprints on 100 per cent mercerise cotton 135 cm wide: 14 and 21 colourways respectively
Designed by Maija Isola for Marimekko Oy
Finland

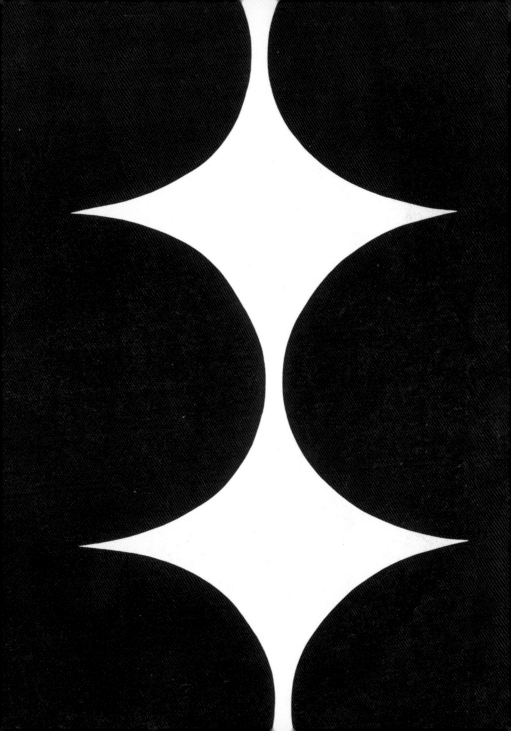

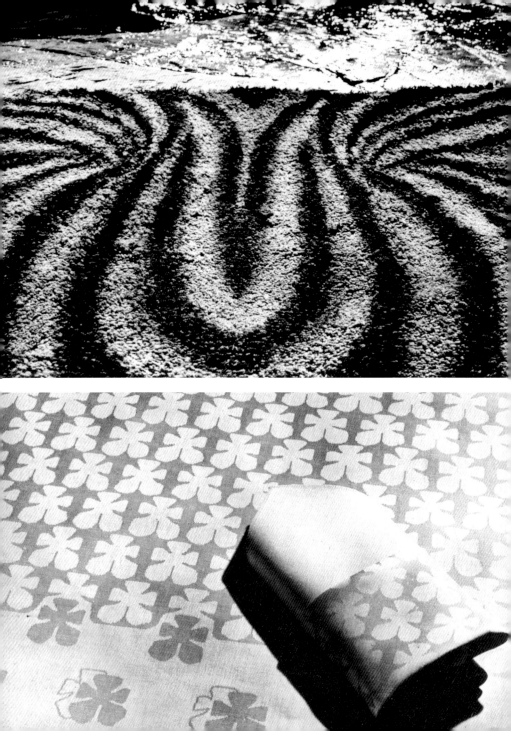

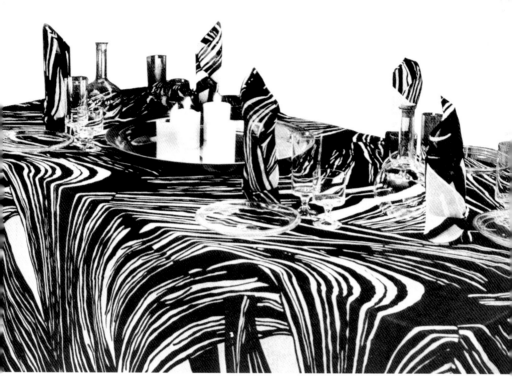

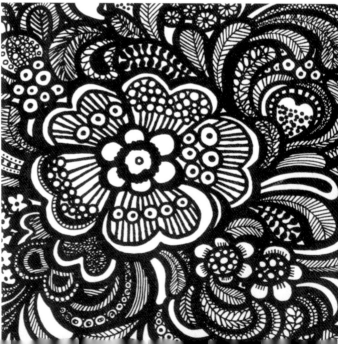

t (waves) all-wool carpet, blue-violet
2·5 m to 10 × 10 m
gned by Ritva Puotila for Oy Finnrya Ab
nd

okki and *Viol* damasks, gold, blue, rose,
ral or white, the cloth 130 × 130 or 150
0 cm
gned by Dora Jung

a screenprint on cotton 180 cm wide, the
kins printed on cotton voile, 10 colours
gned by Marjatta Metsovaara
for Oy Tampella Ab *Finland*

*en*print on cotton satin, black/white and
other colourways 140 cm wide
gned by Raili Konttinen for Porin Puuvilla
inland

2, 3, 4

Fret black, white, red or blue screenprir
on natural hessian
Designed by David Bishop
Phulwari and *Jaal* two of a series of tra
Indian designs handblocked colour-fas▊
100% cotton 91 cm and 122 cm wide
All for The David Bishop Company *Eng▊*

5, 7
Screenprints on cotton cretonne
5 designed by Margit Steiner
7 designed by Anne Fehlow
each with 4 colourways, all 120 cm wi▊
Made by Mech. Weberei Pausa AG *W.*

1
Complex a screen print on cotton satin 122 cm
wide 4 colourways
Designed by Barbara Brown for Heal Fabrics
Limited *England*

6
Istuva Härkä three-colour screenprint o▊
mercerized cotton 21 colourways 135 c▊
Designed by Maija Isola for Marimekko
Finland

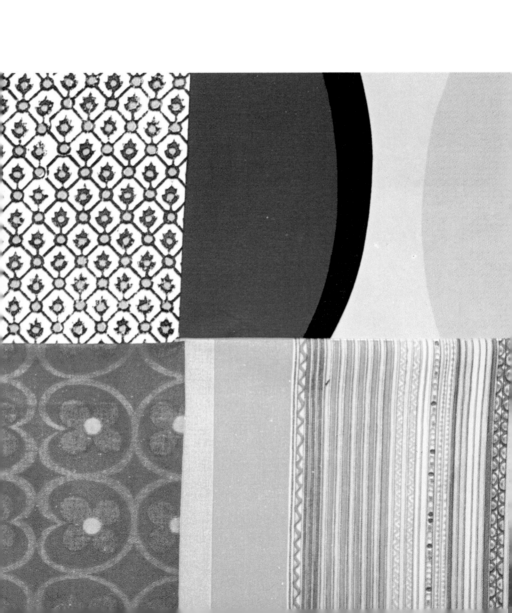

Adriaco all wool rug, cm 137 × 183
Designed by Ritva Puotila, machine-made
by Oy Finnrya Ab, *Finland*

Signal screen-printed 100% cotton, four
colourways : cm 122 wide
Designed by Peter McCulloch for Heal
Fabrics Limited, *England*

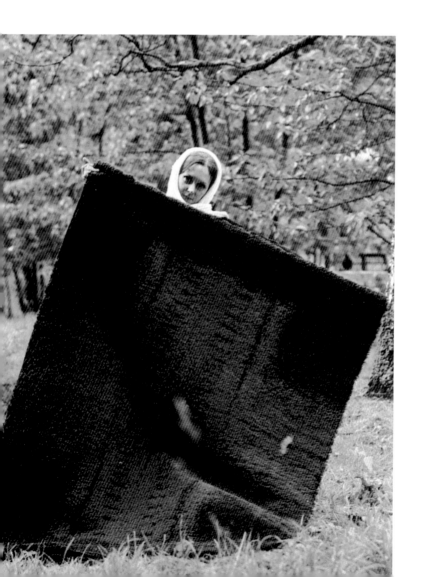

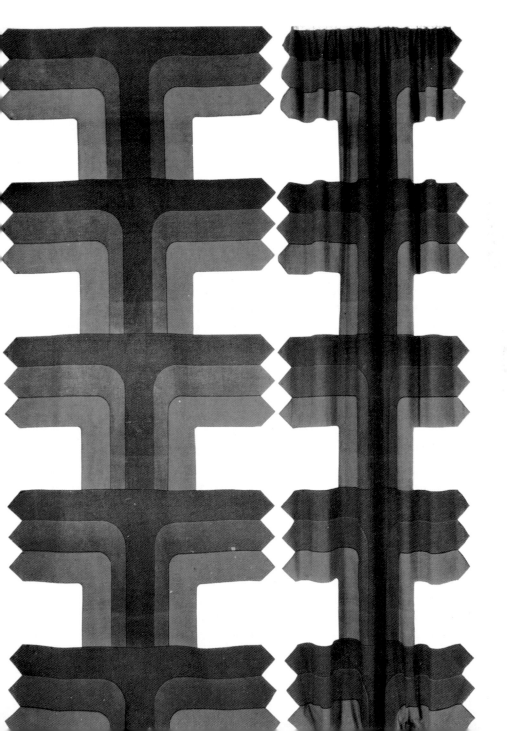

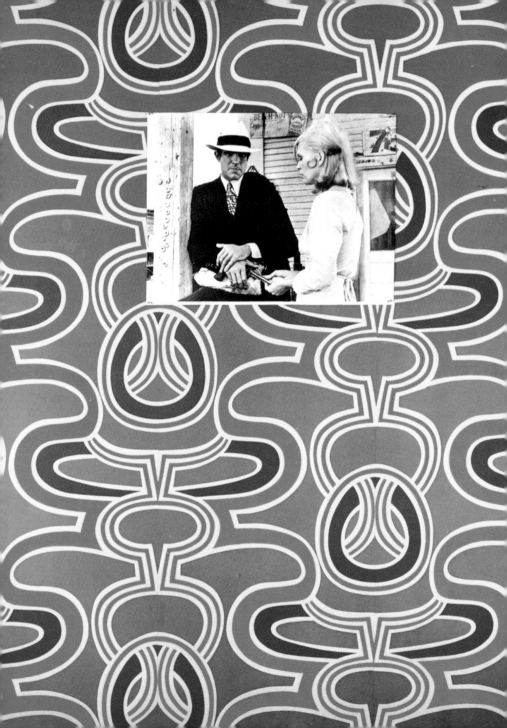

hand-screen printed wallpaper from the
dio 8 range: cm 56 wide
gned by Judith Cash for The Wall Paper
ufacturers Limited, *England*

at Night lithograph cm 51 × 67
oward Hodgkin, *England*
a range of prints at the Alecto Gallery,
don

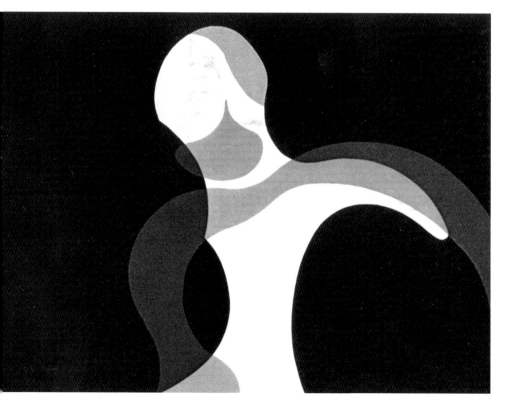

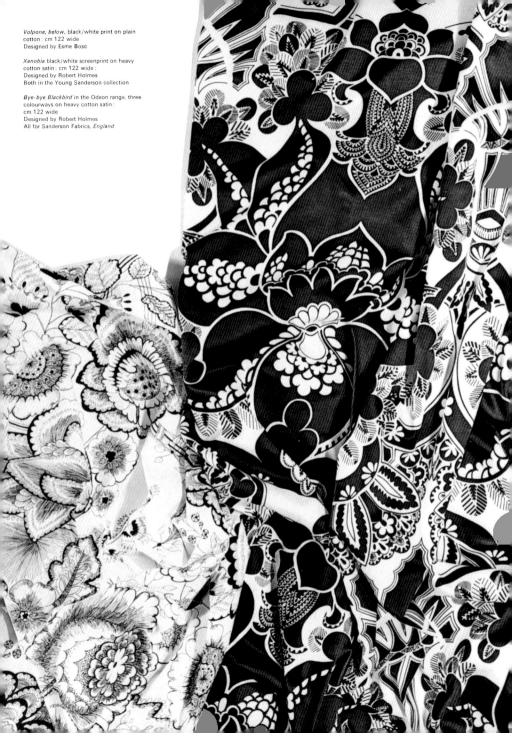

Volpone, below, black/white print on plain
cotton : cm 122 wide
Designed by Esme Bosc

Xenobia black/white screenprint on heavy
cotton satin : cm 122 wide :
Designed by Robert Holmes
Both in the Young Sanderson collection

Bye-bye Blackbird in the Odeon range, three
colourways on heavy cotton satin :
cm 122 wide
Designed by Robert Holmes
All for Sanderson Fabrics, *England*

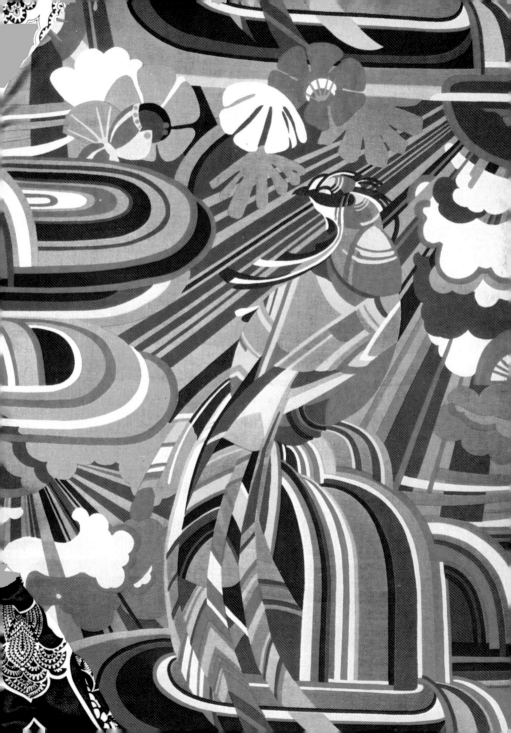

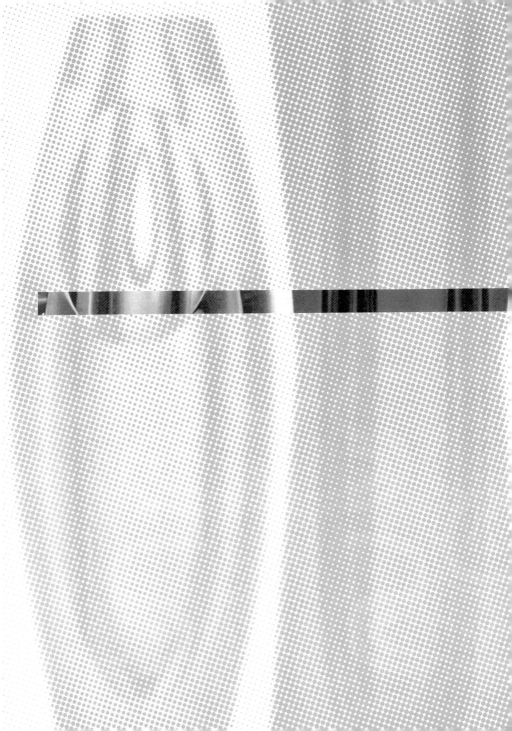

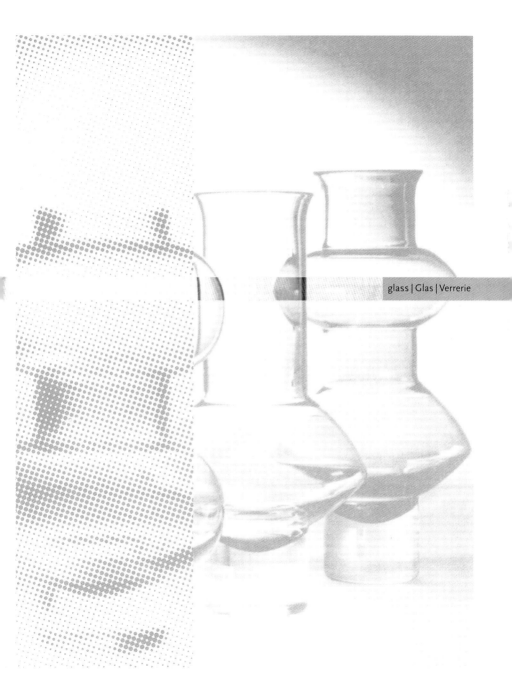

glass | Glas | Verrerie

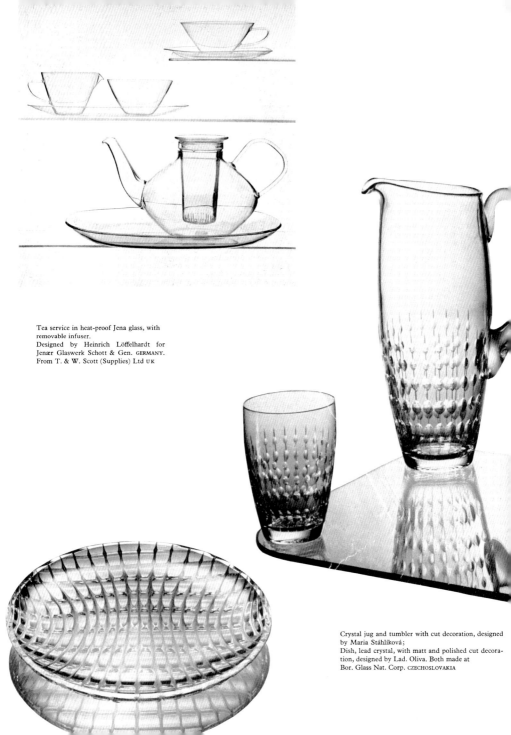

Tea service in heat-proof Jena glass, with removable infuser.
Designed by Heinrich Löffelhardt for Jenær Glaswerk Schott & Gen. GERMANY.
From T. & W. Scott (Supplies) Ltd UK

Crystal jug and tumbler with cut decoration, designed by Maria Stáhlíková;
Dish, lead crystal, with matt and polished cut decoration, designed by Lad. Oliva. Both made at Bor. Glass Nat. Corp. CZECHOSLOVAKIA

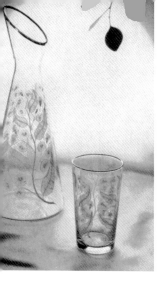

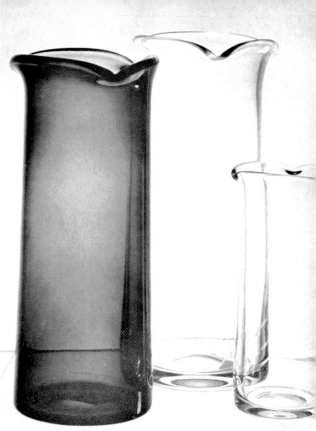

'Giraffe' water jug and tumbler from the *Calypto* service in bent glass with imprinted milk-white design of eucalyptus leaves and flowers. Designed by W. M. Harris, Royal College of Art, for W. E. Chance & Co. Ltd UK

Thick crystal jugs, clear and coloured; unique pieces designed by Grethe Meyer and Ibi Trier Mørch for A/S Kastrup Glasvaerk DENMARK ▶

Clay-infused crystal tumblers, designed by Masakichi Awashima for the Awashima Glass Company Ltd JAPAN ▼

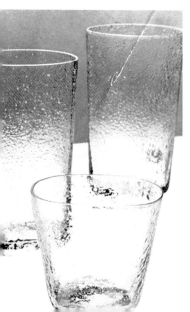

Crystal water set, intaglio-cut, designed by E. Baxter for James Powell & Sons (Whitefriars) Ltd UK

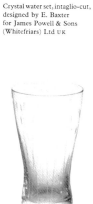

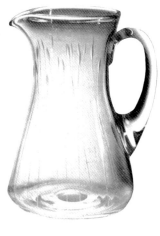

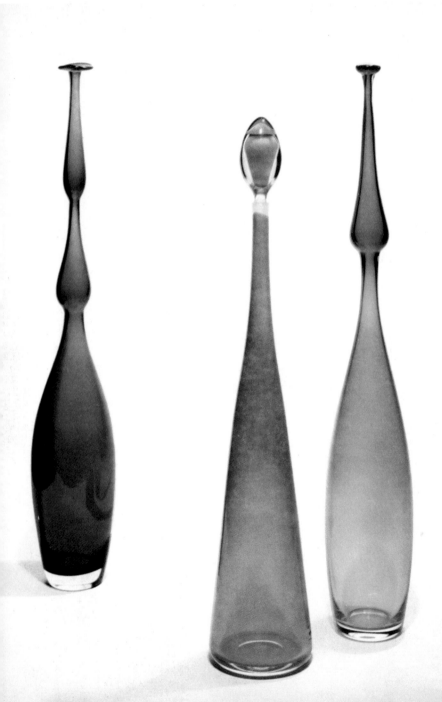

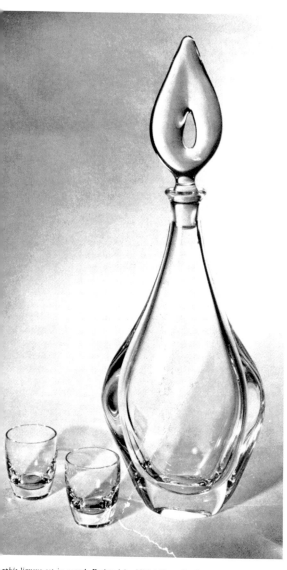

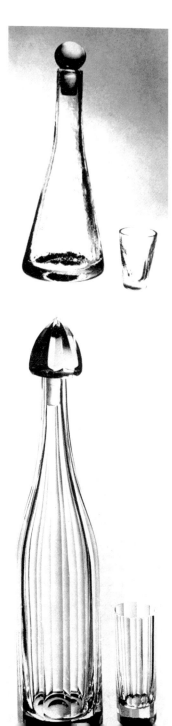

rphée liqueur set in crystal. Designed by Michel Daum for Daum
allerie de Nancy FRANCE

)loured crystal bottle vases with clear base. About 29½ inches high,
is a unique piece designed by F. Meydam for NV Koninklijke
abriek Leerdam HOLLAND

► Clay infused crystal decanter and beaker designed by Masakichi
hima for the Awashima Glass Co. Ltd JAPAN

-crystal decanter and glass with cut decoration. Designed by Vicke
strand for AB Kosta Glasbruk SWEDEN ►

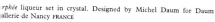

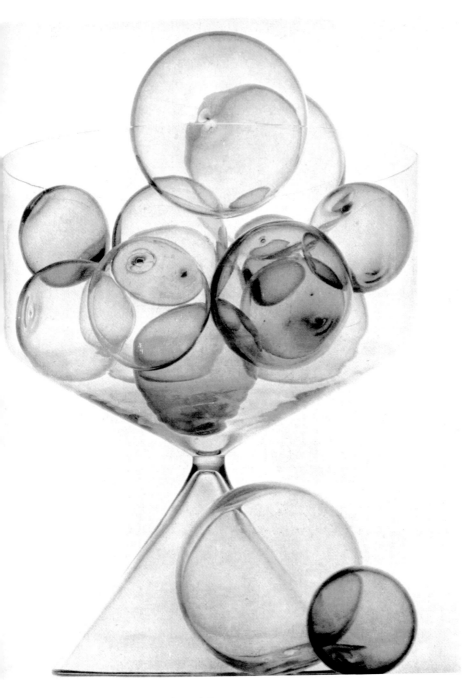

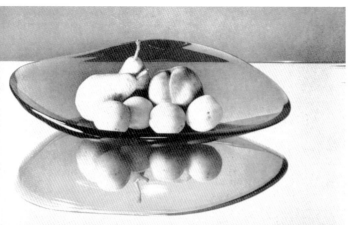

OPPOSITE: Vase in thin-walled blown crystal from the *Ypsilon* series with coloured air-filled glass spheres.
Designed by Mona Schildt for AB Kosta Glasbruk SWEDEN

Shallow fruit bowl in coloured crystal, with curved edge; overall width 13½ inches.
Designed by Max Ingrand FRANCE for Fontana Arte ITALY

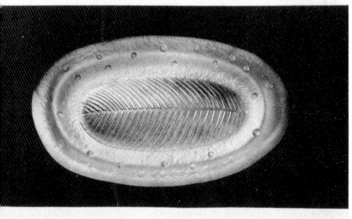

Platter of thick rough glass, sand-blasted and polished, diameter 17 inches.
Designed and made by Max Ingrand FRANCE

Thin-walled blown crystal bottle vases, clear or coloured.
Designed by Ingeborg Lundin for AB Orrefors Glasbruk SWEDEN

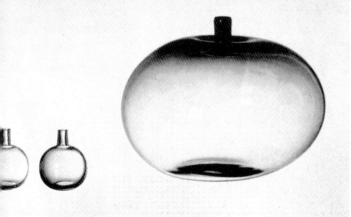

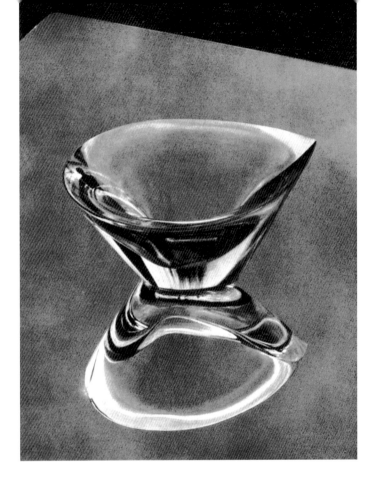

Lead crystal bowl with colour suspended in the body of the glass. Designed by Tapio Wirkkala for Karhula-Iittala Glassworks FINLAND

Two-colour large crystal plates, triangular, oval and square shapes, designed by Timo Sarpaneva for Karhula-Iittala Glassworks FINLAND ▶

Opaline glass bowls with transparent etched bands in acquamarine and blue, or in grey and amber, 14 inches diameter. Designed by Dino Martens for Vetreria Rag. Aureliano Toso ITALY ▼

Free-hand lead crystal bowl, 23 inches diameter. Designed by Vicke Lindstrand for AB Kosta Glasbruk SWEDEN

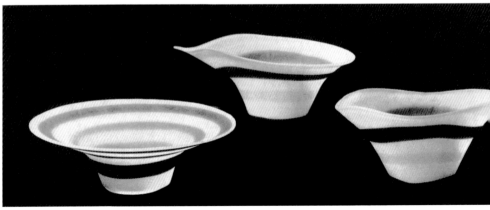

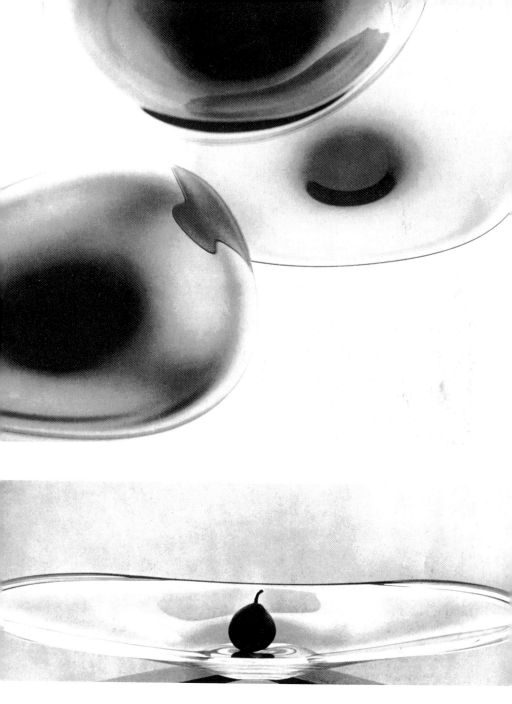

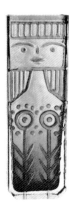

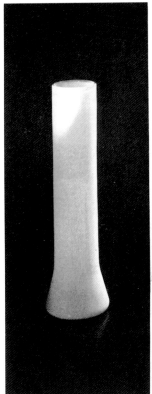

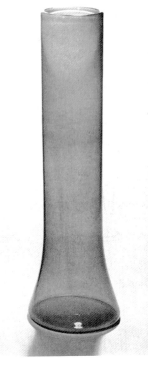

Antique green vase with rough cut relief decoration. Designed by Victor Berndt for AB Flygsfors Glasbruk SWEDEN
▶ Vases from a series executed in clear colours; about 16 inches high. Designed by F. Meydam for NV Koninklijke Nederlandsche Glasfabriek Leerdam HOLLAND
▼ Bottle vases, 13 inches high, and pedestal bowl in transparent turquoise glass. Designed by Enrico Bettarini for La Fenice ITALY
Horses in clear crystal, smoke, olive green. Designed by Jaakko Niemi for Wärtsiläkoncernen A/B Notsjö Glasbruk FINLAND

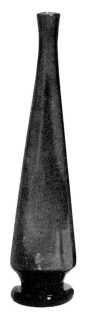

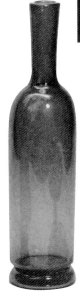

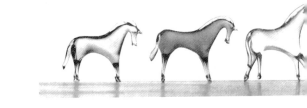

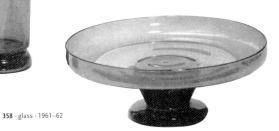

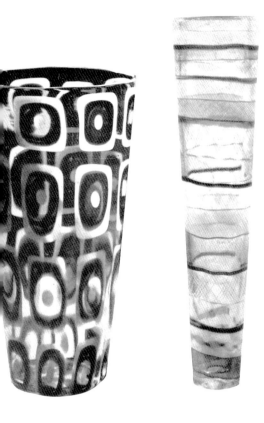

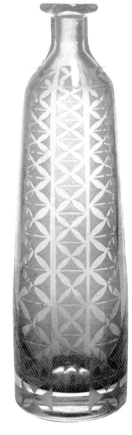

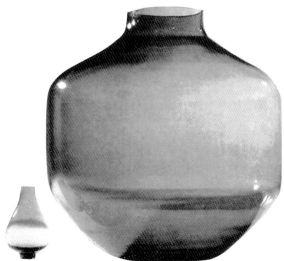

ABOVE, LEFT TO RIGHT
Vase composed of large fused pieces of
white and acquamarine transparent glass;
13 inches high.
Designed by Ercole Barovier for Barovier &
Toso ITALY
Floor vase, 21½ inches high, with *Zanfirico*
banded decoration in soft colours.
Unique piece designed by Dino Martens
for Vetreria Aureliano Toso ITALY
Lead crystal bottle with amber inside casing
and sand-blast decoration; 12 inches high.
Designed by George Elliott, Royal College
of Art; made by K. Wainwright at Stour-
bridge School of Art UK
◀ Floor vase, about 15½ inches square,
and matching specimen vase in green, blue,
steel, gold or amethyst transparent glass.
Designed by R. Stennett-Willson, MSIA,
for Lemington Glassworks UK

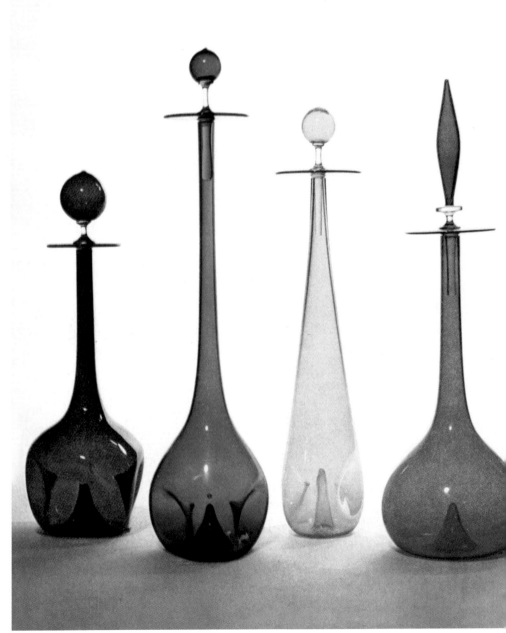

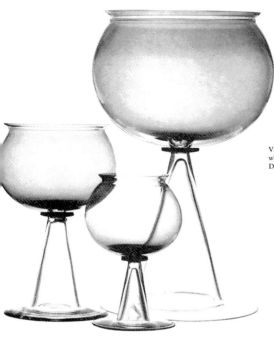

Vases in amethyst or dark indigo soda glass, with blown, clear white stems; 9, 6 and 14½ inches high.
Designed by Kjell Blomberg for Gullaskrufs Glasbruks AB, SWEDEN

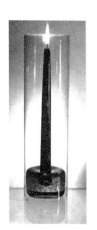

Candleholder in heavy crystal with shade in blue, ruby or clear crystal; 11 inches high.
Specimen vases with trapped bubble, made in amber, Arctic blue, ocean green, twilight or clear crystal; 8½ inches high.
Designed by W. J. Wilson, FSIA, for James Powell & Sons (Whitefriars) Ltd UK

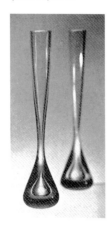

loured crystal bottle vases; 13¾, 17 and 18¼ inches high.
ned by Ermanno Toso for ria Fratelli Toso ITALY

Floor vase in transparent coloured glass, 23½ inches high.
Designed by Josef Hospodka for Borské sklo n.p. CZECHOSLOVAKIA

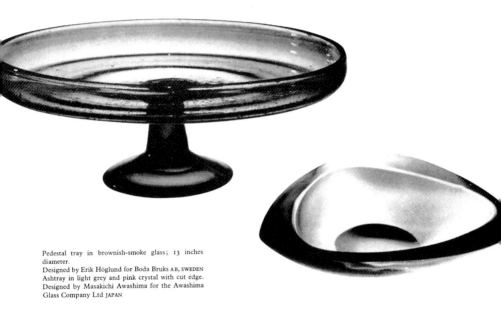

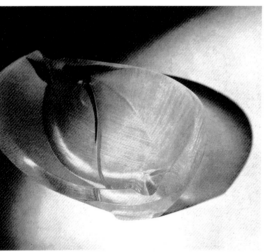

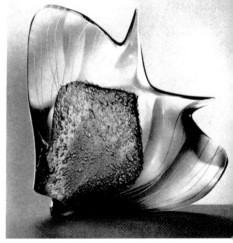

Pedestal tray in brownish-smoke glass; 13 inches
diameter.
Designed by Erik Höglund for Boda Bruks AB, SWEDEN
Ashtray in light grey and pink crystal with cut edge.
Designed by Masakichi Awashima for the Awashima
Glass Company Ltd JAPAN

Ashtray *Phillippines*, engraved crystal; 7 inches
diameter.
Designed and made by René Lalique & Cie FRANCE
Fish in clear crystal with air-filled body and engraved
veining; about 10 inches high.
Designed by Stanislav Honzík for Borské sklo n.p.
CZECHOSLOVAKIA

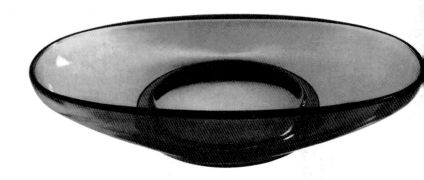

Flint glass dish in coloured glass, as shown, or clear; width overall
12½ inches. Designed by John Cochrane, MSIA, with Milner Gray,
RDI, FSIA, of Design Research Unit for Geo. Davidson & Co. Ltd UK
Dark topaz cased crystal bowl, 16 inches diameter, and greenish-
yellow dark topaz shell.
Designed by Flavio Poli for Seguso Vetri D'Arte ITALY

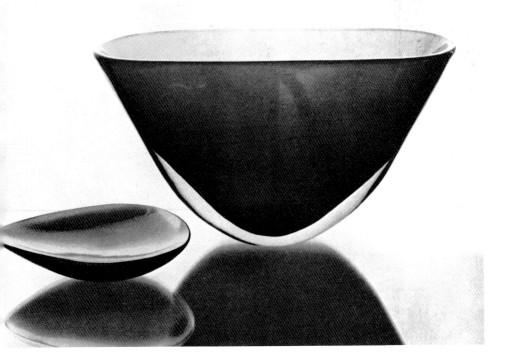

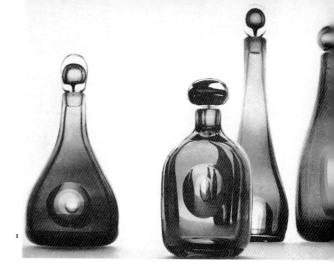

1

1
Crystal decanters with a colour layer suspended in the body of the glass; in individual colourings with contrasting stoppers.

These and the thick crystal vases **3** and **4** OPPOSITE are from the *Ventana* series in which a prism-like effect is obtained by a variation of the 'doubling technique' with coloured layers encased within clear crystal and a 'window' then cut to the coloured core. Each piece is unique, varying in size from 4 to 9 inches high. Designed by Mona Morales-Schildt. Made by AB Kosta Glasbruk SWEDEN

2
Clear crystal paperweights with colour inlay; the tallest is 7 inches high. Designed by Mona Morales-Schildt. Made in a limited series by AB Kosta Glasbruk SWEDEN

Photos Beata Bergström

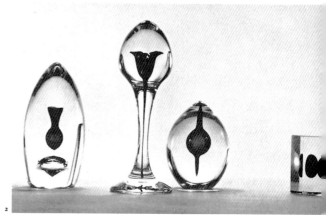

2

3

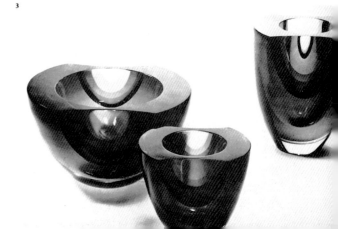

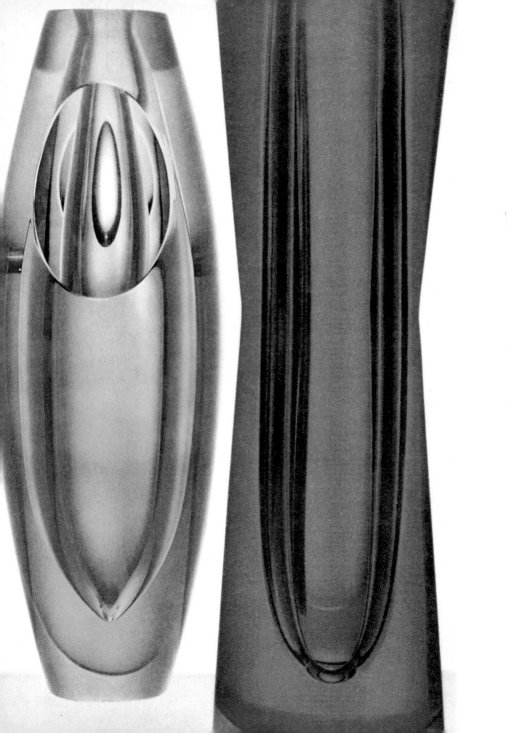

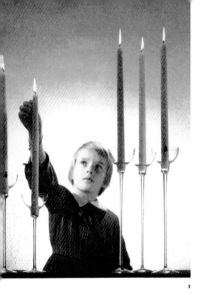

1

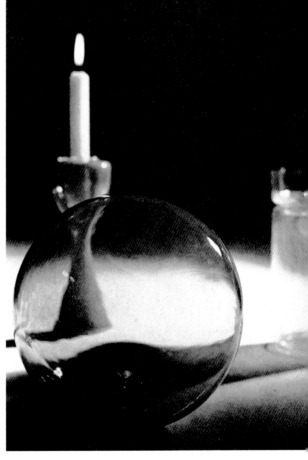

1
Slender candleholders in crystal, named 'Grete'
after the little girl; 5, 9, 12 and 14 inches high.
Designed by Per Lütken for Holmegaards
Glasværk A/S DENMARK
2
Candlestick, ball and covered jar, transparent and
opaline glass in various colours. Designed by Angelo
Barovier for Barovier & Toso ITALY
3
Coloured glass vase and bowl, in blue, green,
brown, silver and grey. Designed by Gunnar Ander
for AB Lindshammars Glasbruk SWEDEN
4
Crystal vases with fine linear engraved decoration.
Designed by Ludvika Smrčková. Made by Borské
sklo, n.p. CZECHOSLOVAKIA

3

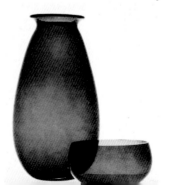

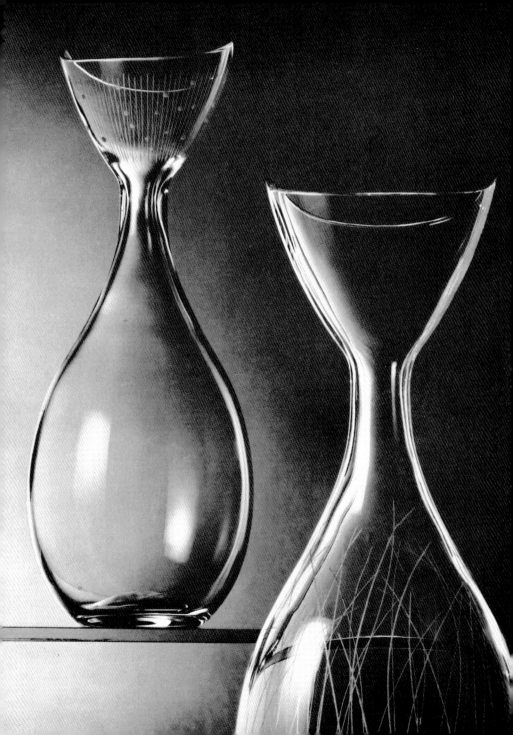

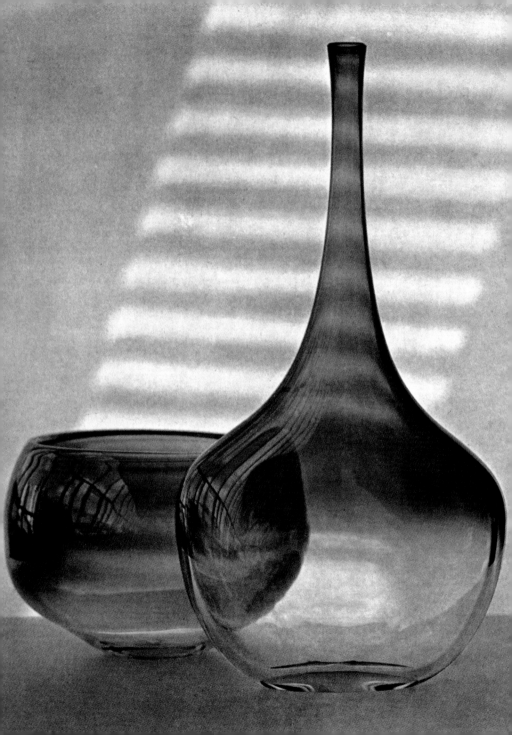

and vase, handblown in light
; vase 45 cm high
ned by Bengt Orup for
ohansfors Glasbruk SWEDEN

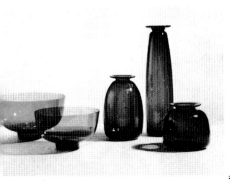

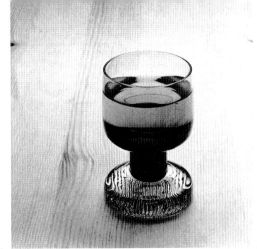

2

3

blue glass handblown bowls,
with optics; tallest vase 36 cm
ned by Jacob E. Bang for
:astrup Glasværk DENMARK

y glass, blown cup in smoke grey,
formed clear crystal base
e' savings bank vases, blown
e glass with air bubbles trapped
: body; 12 cm overall
lesigned by Göran Wärff for
bergs Glasbruk SWEDEN

al ashtrays, pressed glass; dia-
r 12 cm
ned by Masakichi Awashima for
oshida Glass Mfg Co Ltd JAPAN

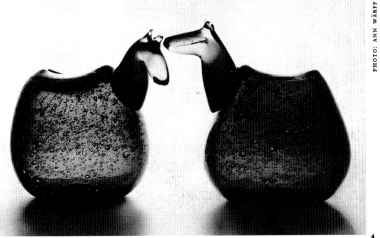

4

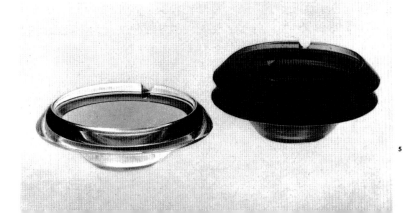

5

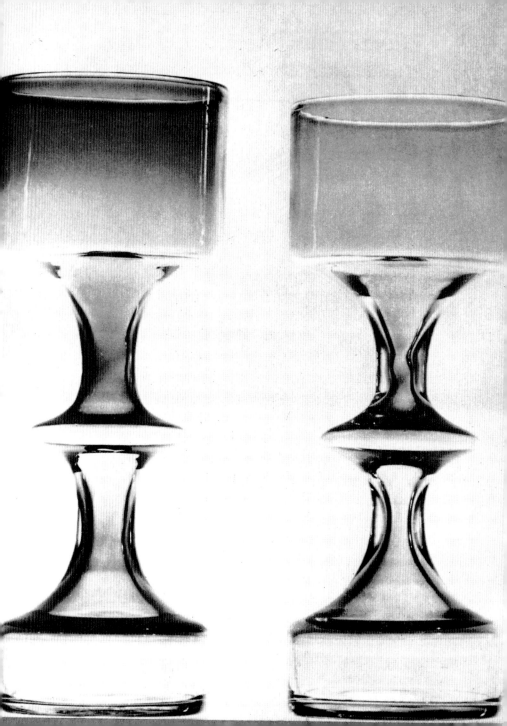

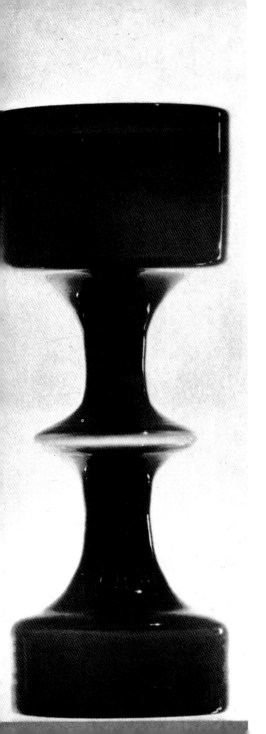

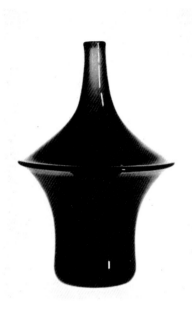

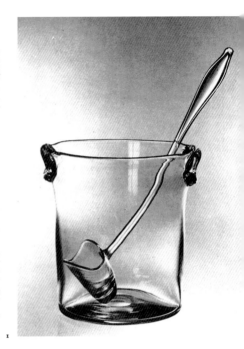

1

1
Leerdamunica deep blue crystal vase;
25 cm high
Designed by F. Meydam for
NV Koninklijke Nederlandsche Glas-
fabriek 'Leerdam' HOLLAND
2
Punch bowl in clear crystal, grey and
blue; 20 cm high
Designed by Nils Landberg for
AB Orrefors Glasbruk SWEDEN

3
Wine and beer glasses in greyish-green
glass with trapped air bubbles
Designed by Erik Höglund for Boda
Bruks AB SWEDEN
4
Hand-ground thick crystal ashtray
with colour inlay
Designed by Max Ingrand for Fontana
Arte ITALY

PHOTOS 1, 5: ARCHIEF LEERDAM
3: BEECHES STUDIO, 7: SUNDAHL

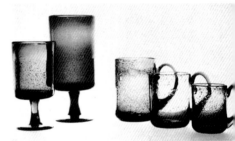

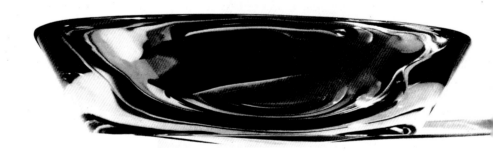

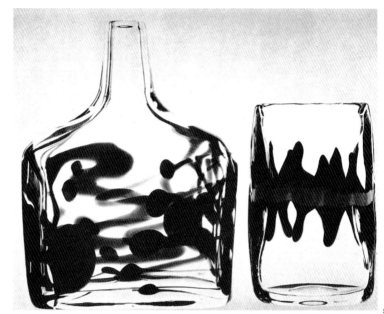

damunica unique clear crystal
s with colour inlay
igned by F. Meydam for
Koninklijke Nederlandsche Glas-
riek 'Leerdam' HOLLAND

ar crystal vases; 16 and 12 cm high
igned by Nils Landberg for AB
efors Glasbruk SWEDEN

es in steel grey, copper green or
ve green crystal; 10, 22 and 11 cm
1
igned by Tom Möller for Reijmyre
sbruk SWEDEN

el edge crystal vases with cut
oration, clear and smoke grey; 23
1 15 cm high
igned by Ingeborg Lundin for AB
efors Glasbruk SWEDEN

5

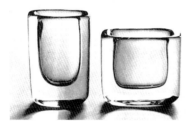

6

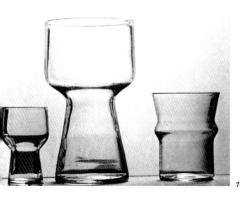

7

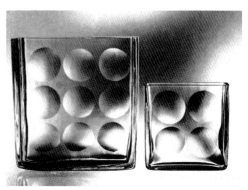

8

1
Cocktail shaker and glasses in clear
crystal. Designed by Nils Landberg
2, 3
Ingeborg barware service in clear
crystal, blue and grey
Expo clear crystal vase with copper
wheel engraved decoration; 23 cm high
Designed by Ingeborg Lundin
4
Rocamadour thick-walled clear crystal
vase; 50 cm high
Designed by Michel Daum for Daum
Cristallerie de Nancy FRANCE
5
Expo high polished clear crystal vases
with cut decoration; 20 and 12 cm high
Designed by Sven Palmqvist
7
Hock glasses in clear crystal
Designed by Nils Landberg
1–3, 5, 7 all for AB Orrefors Glasbruk
SWEDEN

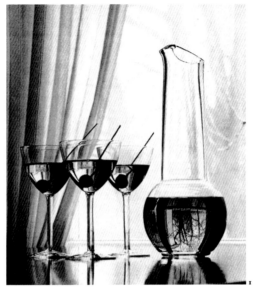
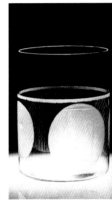

1

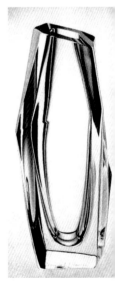

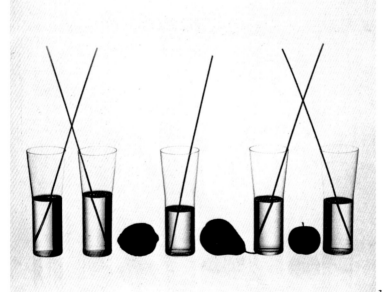

2

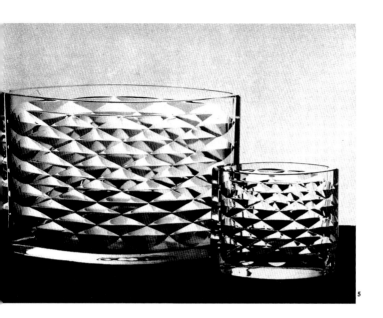

5

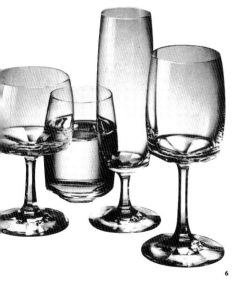

6

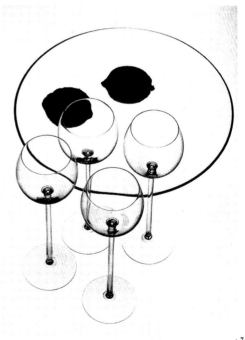

... and wine glasses in clear crystal
... ut decoration
... ned by Miloš Filip (UBOK) for
... varské sklo n.p. ČSR
... O: JINDRICH BROK

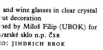

· 7

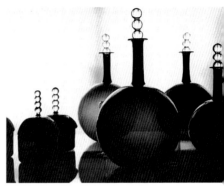

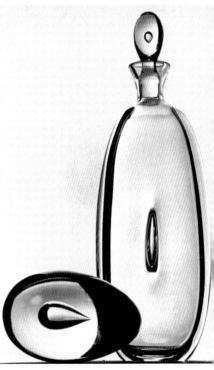

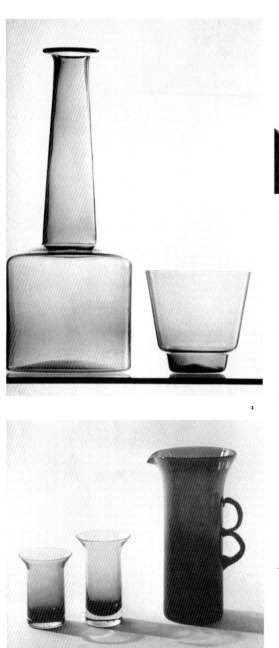

PHOTO 1 PIETINEN
PHOTO 2 GIORGIO CASALI
PHOTO 3 ERKKI VAALLE
PHOTO 5 ANNELIES SCHOLT
PHOTO 6 WAHLBERG
PHOTO 7 GEORGES VERCHEV

decanter and glass in blue or lilac
crystal
Designed by Timo Sarpaneva for
Karhula-Iittala Glassworks FINLAND

jug and glasses, hand-made blown
glass Series 408/9/10 in green or
amethyst with interior crystal coat,
giving a soft effect
Designed by Sergio Dello Strologo for
Sestante ITALY

covered jars and bottles, hand-blown
various colours
Designed by Nanny Still for Riihimäen
Lasi O/Y FINLAND

decanter and paper weight in full-
lead crystal
Designed by Vicke Lindstrand for
A/B Kosta Glasbruk SWEDEN

whisky decanter and glass, blown and
cut crystal
Designed by A.D. Copier for NV
Koninklijke Nederlandsche Glasfabriek 'Leerdam' HOLLAND

wine carafe and glasses, thin-walled
clear crystal
Designed by Asta Strömberg for A/B
Strömbergshyttan SWEDEN

whisky and aperitif tumblers Murcie
crystal with solid base
Designed by Z. Busine for S.A. Manu-
facture de Boussu BELGIUM

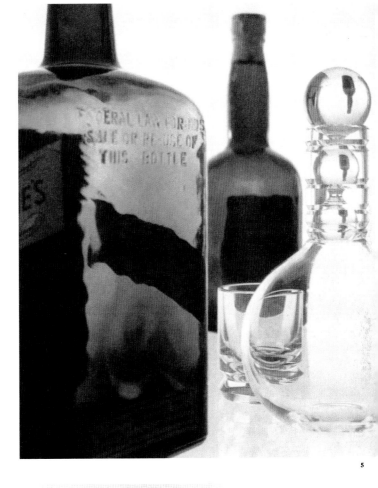

5

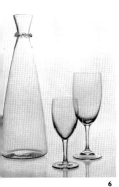

6

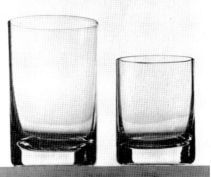

7

Light blue vase in the Ravenna technique; 24·5 cm high
Designed by Sven Palmqvist for A/B
Orrefors Glasbruk SWEDEN

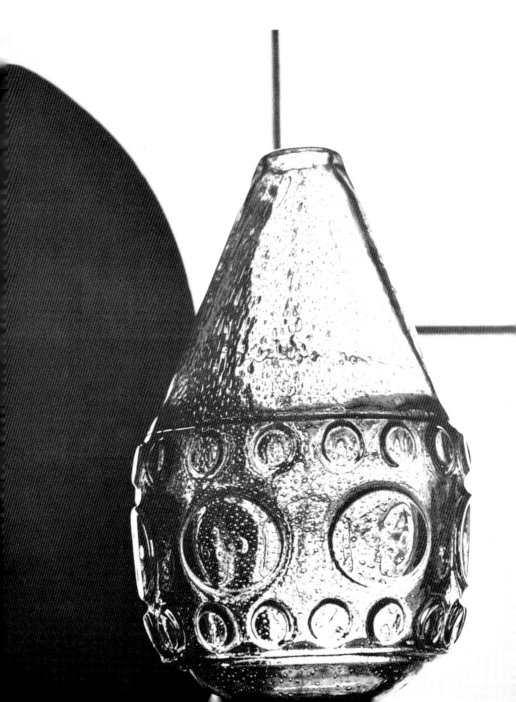

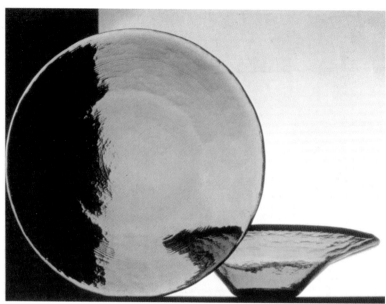

1
Plate and bowl in hand-mou
glass; 38 cm and 25 cm diameters
Designed by Göran Wärff for P
bergs Glasbruk SWEDEN

2
Pedestal bowls in blown glass; 1
and 24 cm high
Designed by Lojo Linssen for
Koninklijke Glasfabriek 'Leerd
HOLLAND

3
Decanter 42 cm high, and jars
blown glass
Designed by Pavel Hlava (UBOK
Decanter made at Zeleznobro
Sklo, n.p.; jars at Borské Sklo,
CSSR

PHOTO 1 ANN WÄRFF
PHOTO 2 ANNELISE SCHOLTZ
PHOTO 3 LUMÍR ROTT

1

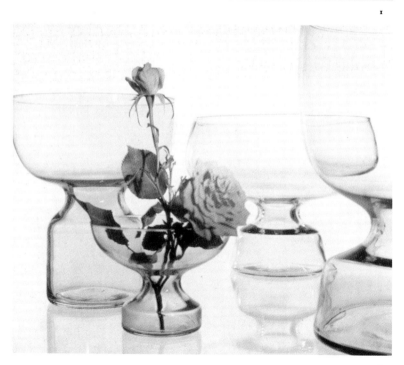

2

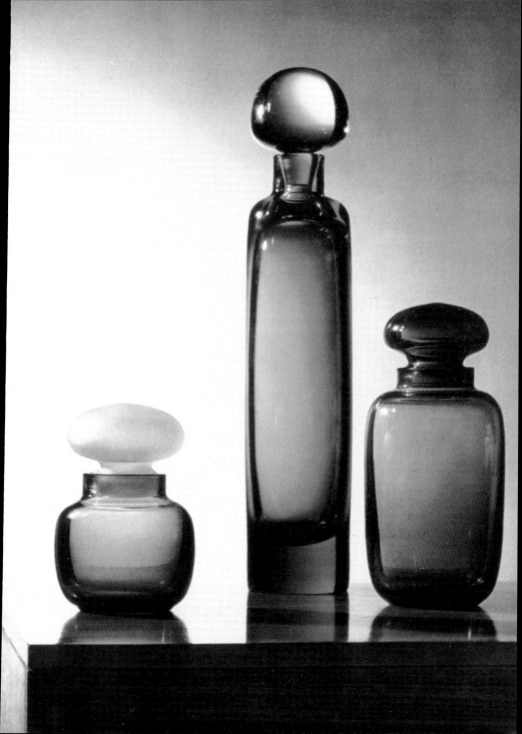

Crystal glass vase blown into a burnt mould, 22 cm high, clear or smoke-grey
Designed by Timo Sarpaneva for Karhula-Iittala Glassworks FINLAND

Tulip-shaped wine glasses
Designed by Claus Josef Riedel for Tiroler Glashütte AUSTRIA

Dark brown fruit bowls
Designed by Benny Motzfeldt for Hadelands Glassverk NORWAY

Olympia vases, lead crystal, surface etched, the base cut and polished
tallest 33 cm high
Designed by Claus Josef Riedel for Tiroler Glashütte AUSTRIA

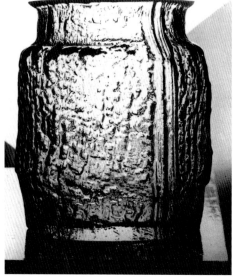

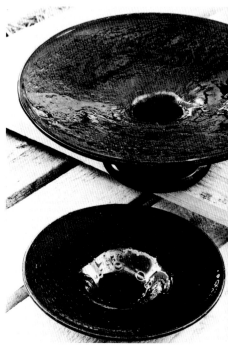

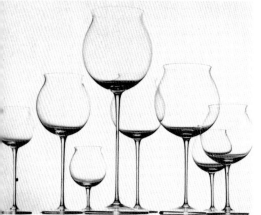

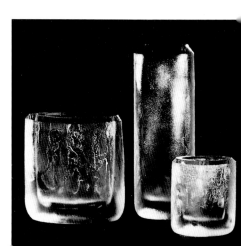

ured vase with metal sheet
n the walls of the glass, 35 cm
a unique piece
gned by Pavel Hlava, UBOK
ké sklo, n.p. CZECHOSLOVAKIA

bowl in brown glass edged
blue, 15 cm high
gned by Göran Wärff for
a Glasbruk AB SWEDEN

Covered jars in smoke-grey glass
with lids in cut clear crystal, 16·5 cm,
7·5 cm and 12 cm high
Designed by Gunnar Ander for
Lindshammars Glasbruk AB
SWEDEN

Tall thin-waisted vases, 32 cm high
Designed by Mona Morales-Schildt
for Kosta Glasbruk AB SWEDEN

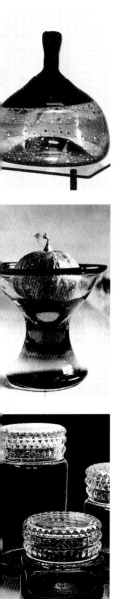

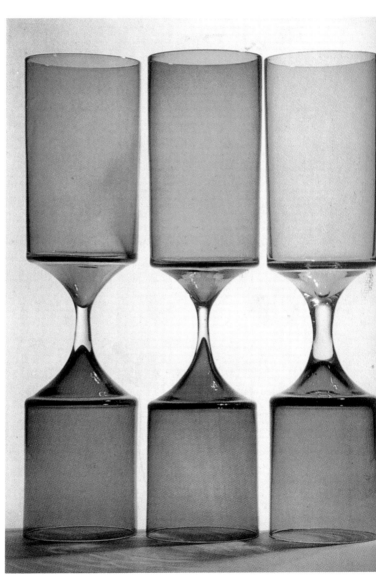

Hock glass in hand-blown crystal
15 cm high
Designed by Michel Daum for Daum
Cristallerie de Nancy FRANCE

Viking carafe in blue or green
antique glass, largest size 1 litre
capacity
Designed by Ole Winther for
Holmegaards Glasvaerk A/S
DENMARK
Crystal bottles about 30 cm high
Designed by Masakichi Awashima
for Awashima Glass Company Ltd
JAPAN

Classic glass tumblers, clear am
midnight-blue, green or smoke
25, 22 and 18 cl capacities
Designed by Dumond & Leloup
for S.A. Markhbein FRANCE
Brandy glass and goblet of Shiz
trickle-glass
Designed by Masakichi Awashi
for Awashima Glass Company
JAPAN

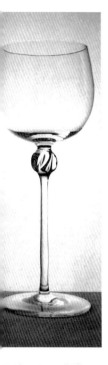

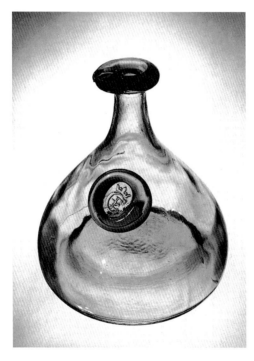

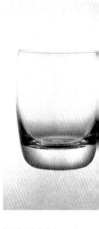

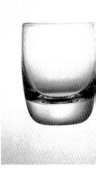

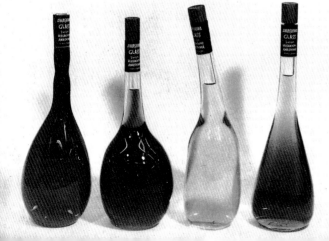

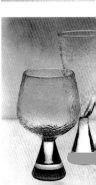

oso crystal tumblers and mixer,
mixer 55 cl capacity
gned by Vicke Lindstrand for
a Glasbruk AB SWEDEN

n-blown crystal glasses, 5 to 35 cl
:ities
gned by Bengt Orup for
inge Glashytta SWEDEN

Pitcher and tumbler in smoke-blue
glass, the pitcher 800 cc capacity
the tumbler 180 cc
Designed by the Industrial Arts
Institute for Sasaki Glass Company
Ltd JAPAN

Bowls in clear crystal or ruby
pressed glass, 11 and 18 cm diameter
Designed by Gunnar Ander for
Lindshammars Glasbruk AB
SWEDEN

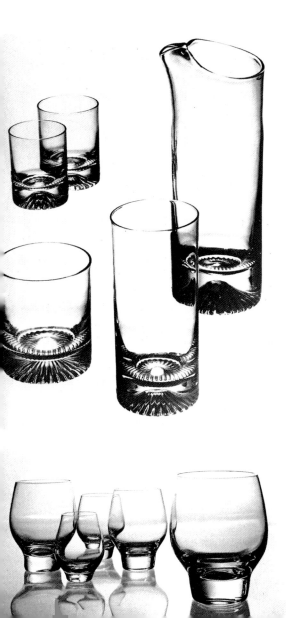

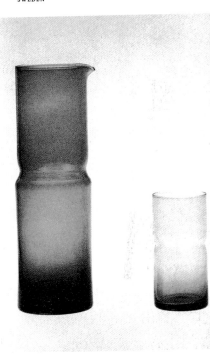

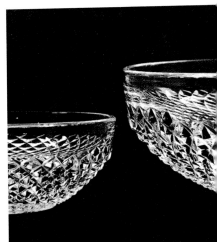

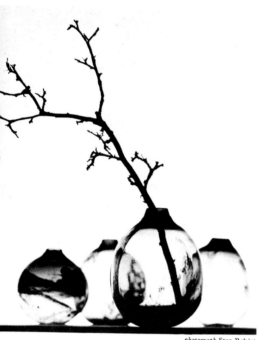

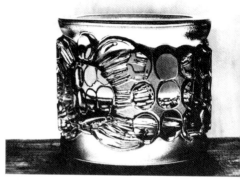

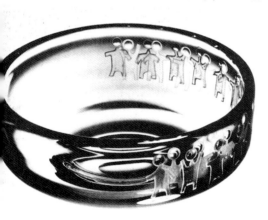

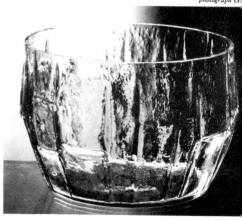

Vase in clear grey glass with black
blisters: 40 cm high
Designed by Eva Englund for
Arvid Böhlmarks Lampfabrik
SWEDEN

Unique bowl in engraved clear
crystal 30 cm diameter
Designed by Ove Snadeberg for
Kosta Glasbruk AB SWEDEN

Blasted crystal bowl 18·5 cm
diameter
Designed by Bertil Vallien for
Boda Bruks AB SWEDEN

Series 1609 bowl, clear or indigo-
blue crystal: 19 cm diameter
Designed by Christer Sjögren for
Lindshammars Glasbruk AB
SWEDEN

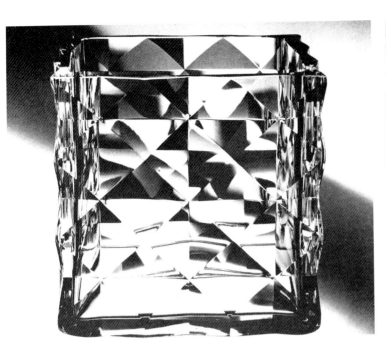

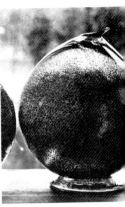

photograph Sten Robért

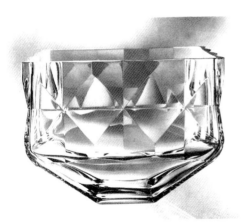

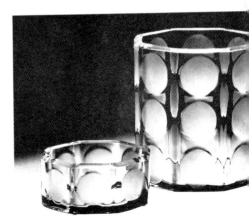

Heavy crystal bowls with cut
decorations, 20 and 15 cm high
Designed by Sven Palmqvist for
Orrefors Glasbruk AB SWEDEN

Bowl and vase in clear cut crystal:
vase 23 cm high
Designed by Ingeborg Lundin for
Orrefors Glasbruk AB SWEDEN

top Vases in blue-grey cased crystal
23 cm high
Designed by Ann & Göran Wärff
for Kosta Glasbruk AB SWEDEN

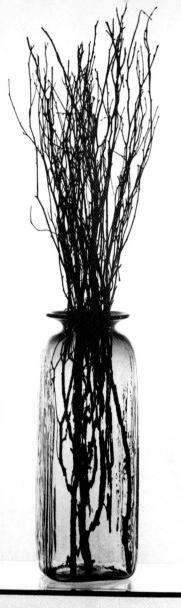

Bottle-jars handcrafted in olive,
crystal, turquoise, honey, peacock
or tangerine: approximately
26 cm high
Designed by Joel Philip Myers for
Blenko Glass Co USA

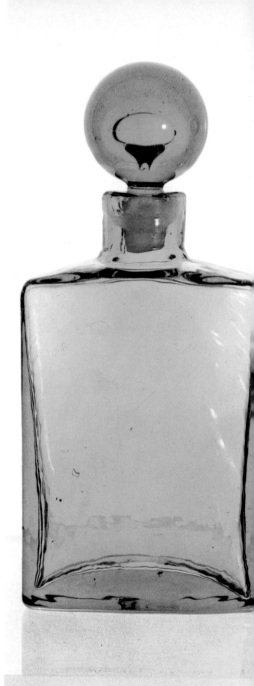

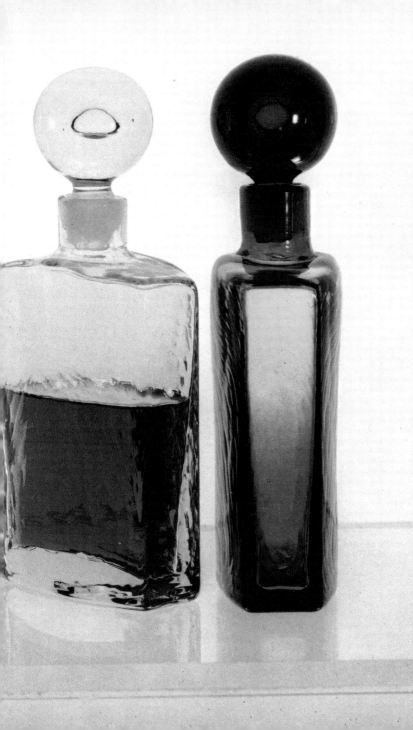

Set of stacked vases, household
glass
Designed by Alfred Seidl for
Stölzle Glasindustrie AG *Austria*

Hand blown vase, clear crystal
on smoke-green 20 cm high
Designed by Nobuyasu Sato for
Sasaki Glass Co Ltd *Japan*

Windhat bowl, blown household
glass, clear and sea-blue, 36 cm diameter
Designed by Tamara Aladin for
Riihimäen Lasi Oy *Finland*

Vases K.7024/5 antique grey glass
with small bubbles the larger 29 cm high
Designed by Severin Brørby for
Hadelands Glassverk *Norway*

Large dish machine spun, blue,
honey, olive, crystal, 31 cm diameter
Designed by Joel Philip Myers
and made by Blenko Glass Co *USA*

Parisini

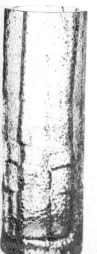

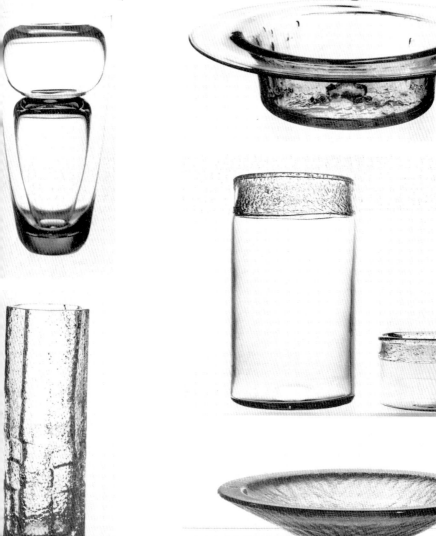

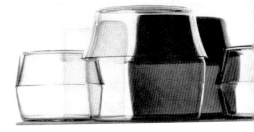

Covered bowls, mould blown, clear blue,
green grey and crystal 7–10 cm high
Designed by Naoto Yokoyama for
Noritake Co Ltd *Japan*

Two of a series of opal crystal goblets
from 18 to 28 cm high
Designed by Gunnar Cyrén for
AB Orrefors Glasbruk *Sweden*

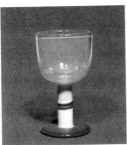

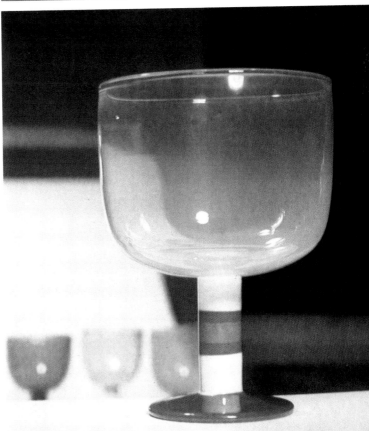

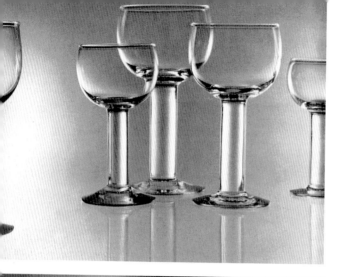

BS 2100 crystal stemware with
solid stems designed by Gunnar Cyrén
PS 2114 stemware with air bubbles
Designed by Sven Palmqvist
All made by AB Orrefors Glasbruk *Sweden*

Bowl from the *Sargasso* series,
blister glass 15 cm high
Designed by Notsjoe Glass/Kaj Franck
for Oy Wärtsila AB *Finland*

Moonstone series handblown bowls
and candleholders
Designed by Per Lütken for Kastrup
and Holmegaards Glasvaerker A/S *Denmark*

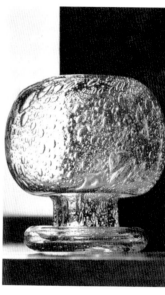

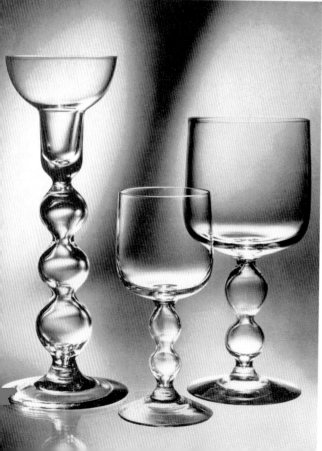

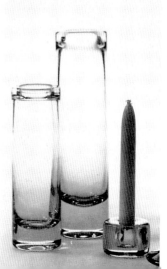

Bowl in the *Patina* series, engraved
decoration with a specially soft
antique effect 30 cm diameter
Designed by Vicke Lindstrand for
AB Kosta Glasbruk *Sweden*

Expo DU 198–64 crystal bowls,
clear or grey, red-brown in
overlay 20–22 cm high
Designed by Ingeborg Lundin for
AB Orrefors Glasbruk *Sweden*

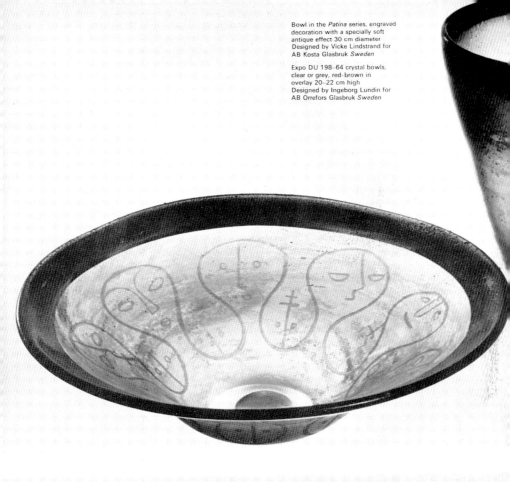

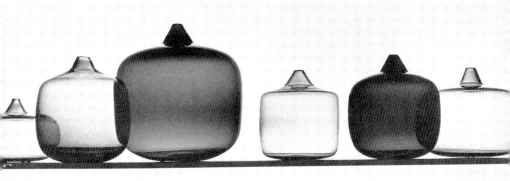

Kaja (shimmer) cut crystal with various coloured 'shade' 18 cm diameter
Designed by Tamara Aladin for Riihimaën Lasi Oy *Finland*

Sunrise cut crystal vase 27 cm high
Designed by Erkkitanio Siiroinen

Turmalin cut crystal vase with green or blue 'shade'. 18 cm diameter
Designed by Nanny Still
both for Riihimaën Lasi Oy *Finland*

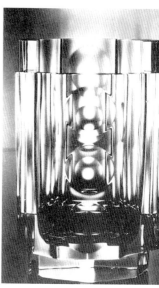

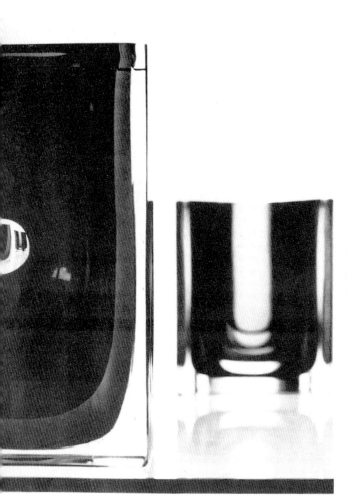

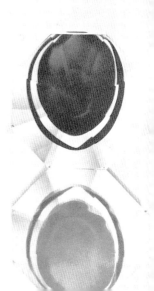

sed glass tumblers
gned by Kaj Franck and made
y Wärtsilä AB *Finland*

ntella decanter and mug, blown
household glass with blue or
red tops, jug 1 litre capacity
gned by Nanny Still for Riihimaën
Oy *Finland*

w, right
ora decanters and tumblers in
ead crystal with cut olives
gned by Mona Morales-Schildt
B Kosta Glasbruk *Sweden*

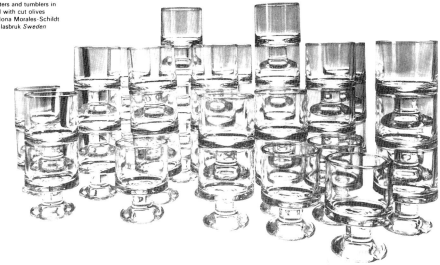

Sten Robert

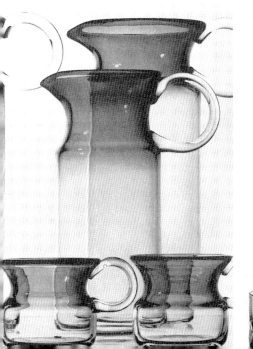

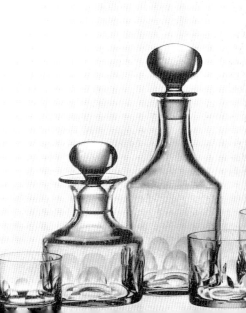

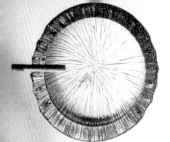

Ash tray in the *Cascade* series in clear crystal
Designed by Yukio Ito

Decanter and tumbler in clear crystal from a series of table glass including stemware in various sizes
Designed by Denji Takeuchi/Nobuyasu Sato/Yuuji Takahashi

Tivoli series, tumblers, water pitcher, ice pail and decanter in smoke-green crystal, taller tumbler also available, pitcher 1 litre capacity
Designed by Denji Takeuchi/ Yuuji Takahashi

opposite
Ash tray in smoke-green glass 20 cm diameter
Designed by Denji Takeuchi

Wine decanter and glasses in clear crystal, decanter 72 cl capacity
Designed by Denji Takeuchi

All made by Sasaki Glass Co Ltd
Japan

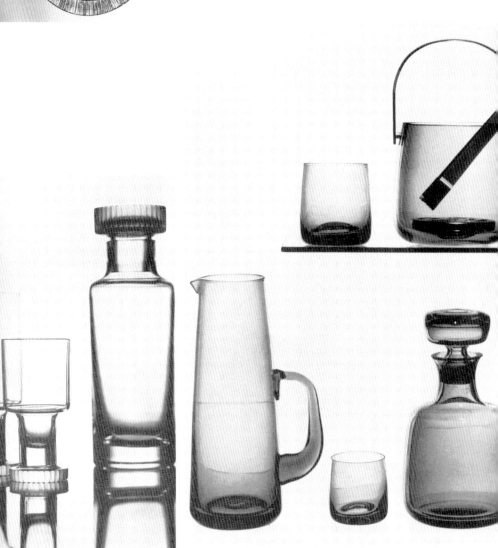

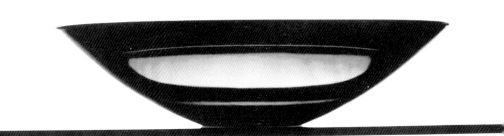

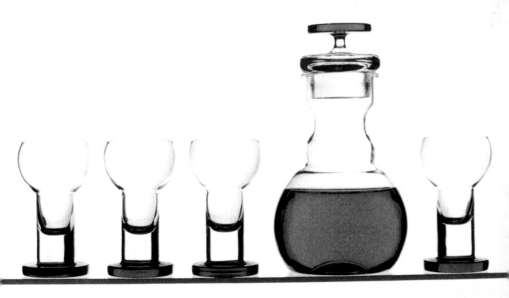

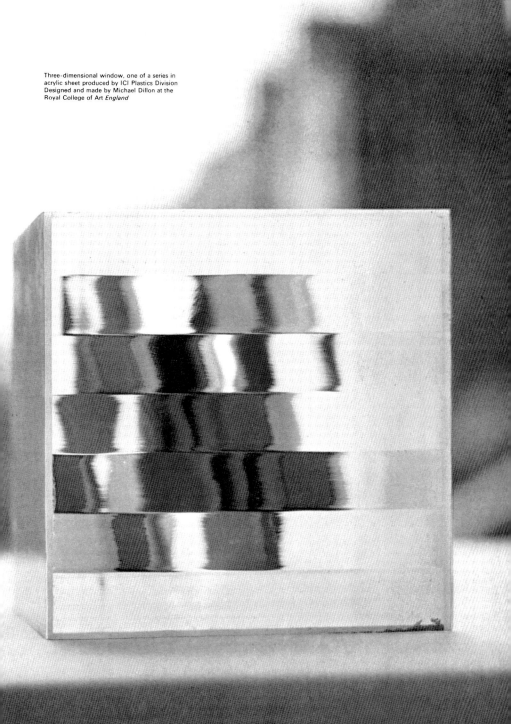

Three-dimensional window, one of a series in
acrylic sheet produced by ICI Plastics Division
Designed and made by Michael Dillon at the
Royal College of Art *England*

Fused glass panel approximately 30 × 30 cm:
one of a series
Designed by Alfred R. Fisher for Whitefriars
Glass Limited *England*

Candleholders, mould-blown clear glass
31·5 and 18 cm high
Designed by Timo Sarpaneva for Iittala
Glassworks *Finland*

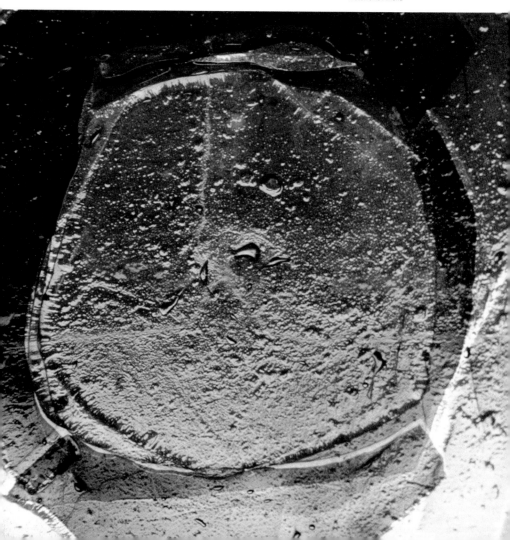

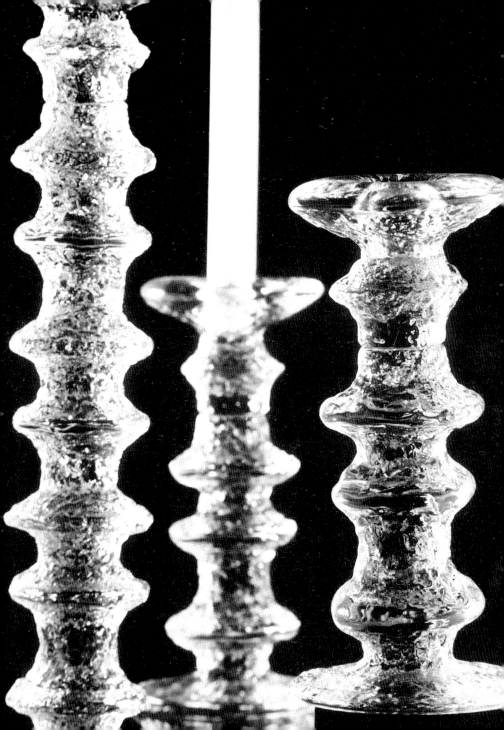

Doorstop, hand-made crystal approximately
6 × 9 cm
Paperweight, hand-made crystal approximately
6 × 6 cm
Both designed by Ronald Stennett-Willson for
King's Lynn Glass Ltd *England*

Candlesticks in full-lead crystal
Designed by Mona Morales-Schildt for Ab
Kosta Glasbruk *Sweden*

Labyrinth clear and violet cut crystal 20 cm
diameter
Designed by Aimo Okkolin for Riihimaen Lasi
Oy *Finland*

▷

Glass Tree clear lead crystal, with
green balls, cast and glued: wood
60 × 48 cm
Designed by Bengt Edenfalk for S
Glasbruk Ab *Sweden*

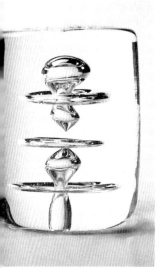

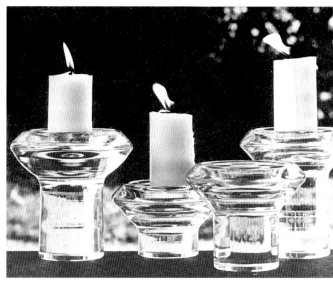

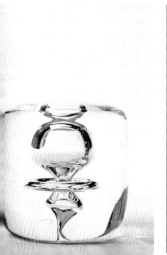

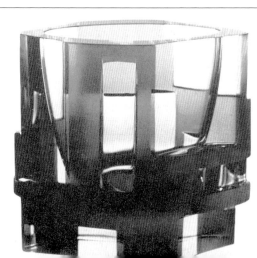

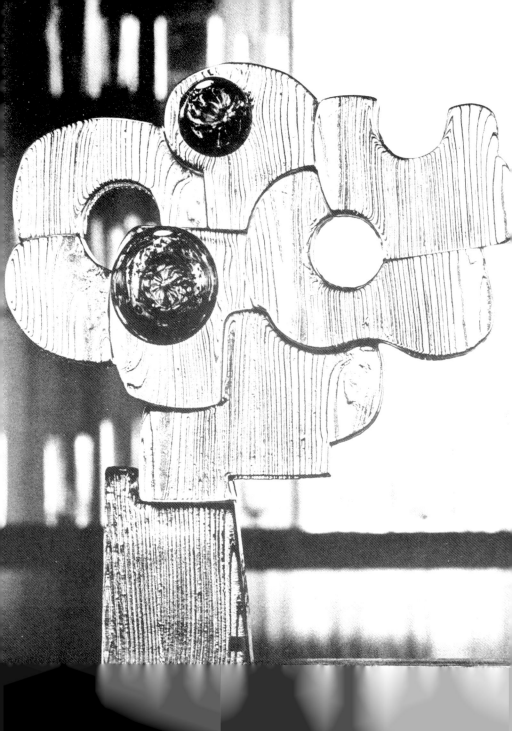

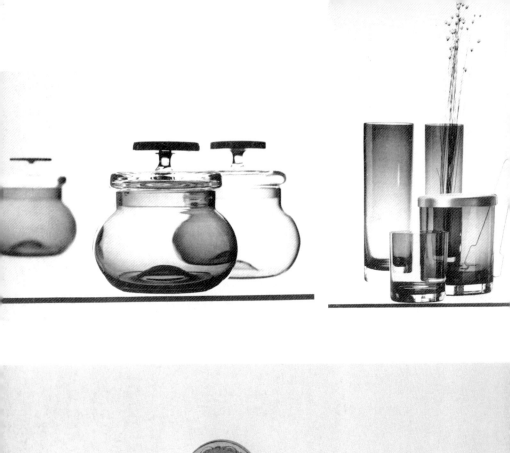

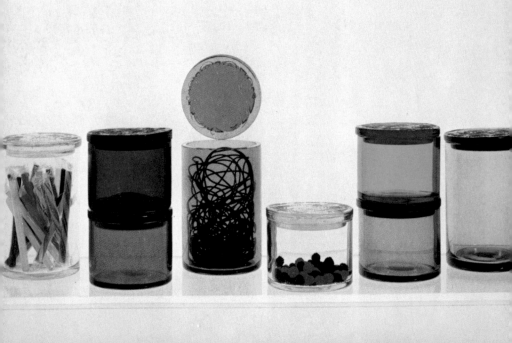

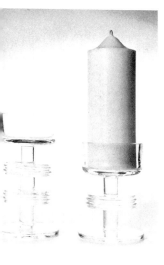

ly jars in ruby, blue or green with clear
al covers, 13 cm high
ned by Denji Takeuchi
s, ice pail and tumbler, part of a series
ding jugs, ashtray and cigarette box all in
e/clear crystal cased glass, the vases
m high
ned by Nobuyasu Sato and Norimichi
da
or Sasaki Glass Company Limited *Japan*

dcrafted jars from 11 to 20 cm high
ned by Joel Philip Myers for Blenko Glass
pany *USA*

d-made crystal candlesticks, 12·5 and
m high
ned by Ronald Stennett-Willson for King's
Glass Limited *England*

ware, straw glass, plain crystal
ned by Vera Liskova for Carlsbad Glass/
er N.C. *Czechoslovakia*

er set, ship's decanter and decanter, part
range of hand-blown crystal
ned by Frank Thrower for Dartington
s Limited *England*

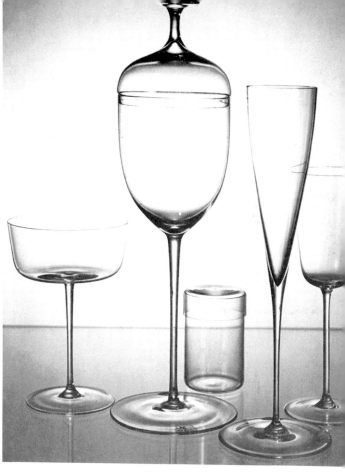

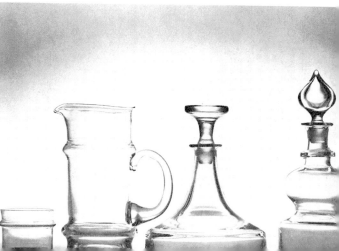

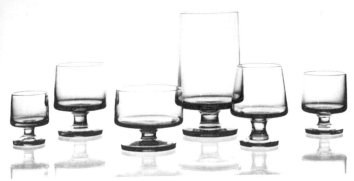

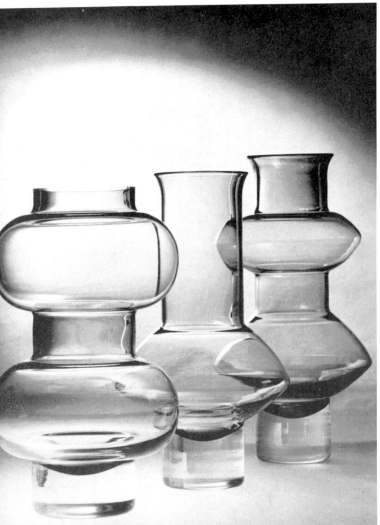

1
Stub handmade soda glass, flint or smoke
Designed by Ibi Trier Mørch for Kastrup and
Holmgaards Glassworks *Denmark*
2
Two-toned vases crystal with olive, amber
or ocean blue: about cm 23 high
Designed by Bo Borgstrom for Åseda
Glasbruk Ab *Sweden*
3
Coat-hangers/striped decorative discs:
cm 11 and 13 diameter
Designed by Yóji Fusamae for Joetsu
Crystal Glass Company Limited, *Japan*
4, 6
NS 2130 goblets in clear crystal
Tumbler and decanter in clear cut crystal
Both designed by Nils Landberg for
Ab Orrefors Glasbruk, *Sweden*
5
Nut bowls; mould-blown glass, cm 10 diameter
Designed by Naoto Yokoyama for Joetsu
Crystal Glass Company Limited, *Japan*

1 3 4 5
2   6

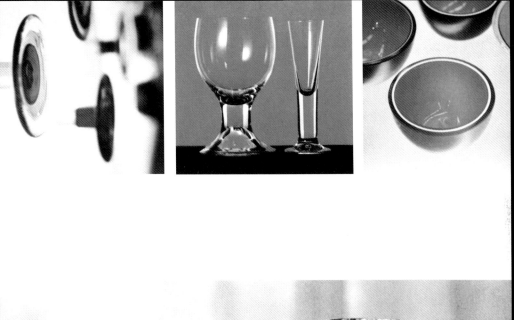

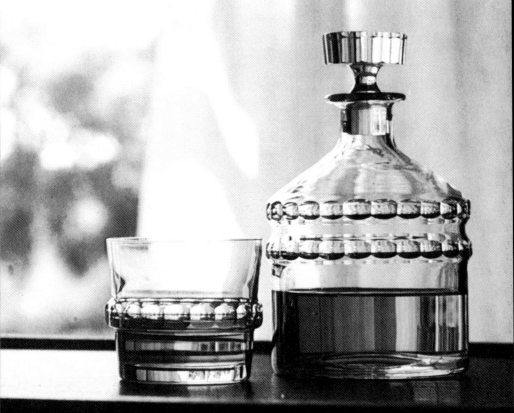

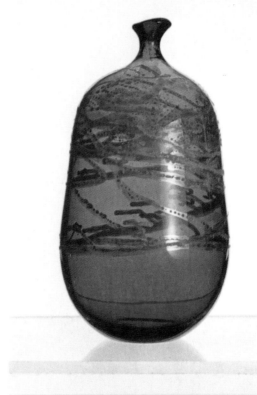

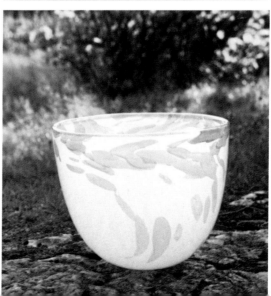

1
Vase in off-hand blown glass, purple lead
glass with silver on surface : cm 18.4 × 33.3
Designed by Joel Philip Myers for
Blenko Glass Company *USA*
2
Bowl in full crystal, in floating colour
technique : cm 23 high
Designed by Rolf Sinnemark for Ab Kosta
Glasbruk, *Sweden*
3
Vase, layered and cut colour, opal/crystal/
blue/red : cm 22 high
Designed by Vratislav Sotola for Borske sklo
n.p. Novy Bor. *Czechoslovakia*

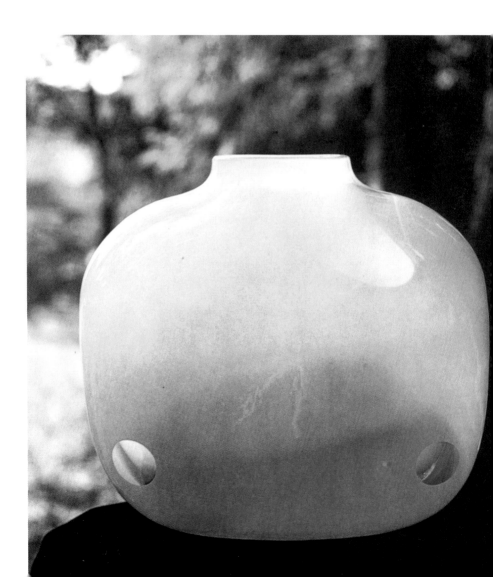

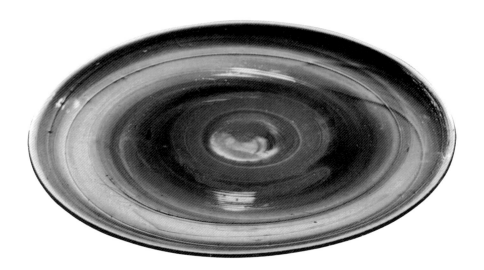

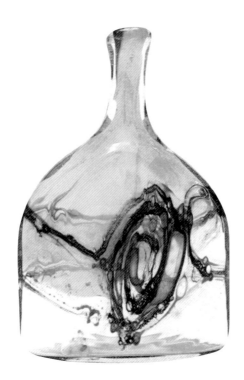

1
Plate free hand-blown, surface fumed
cm 41.7 diameter
Designed and made by Gerald Rollason
at the Royal College of Art, *England*
2
Soda glass bottle, free hand-blown shape
approximately cm 38 high
Designed and made by Sam Herman, *Engla*
3
Off-hand blown vase, reverse blown crystal
cased on yellow: cm 29.2 × 17.8
Designed and blown by Joel Philip Myers
for Blenko Glass Company, *USA*
4
Vase, off-hand and mould-blown, blue
yellow, green, red, amber and crystal:
cm 21.6 × 36.9
Designed by Joel Philip Myers for Blenko
Glass Company, *USA*
5
Glass form with inset brass filings:
cm 35.6 × 25.4
Designed and made by Marvin B. Lipofsky.
USA

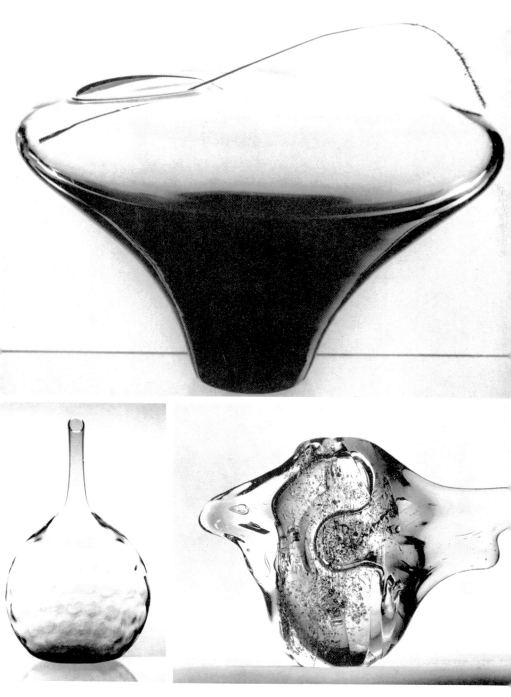

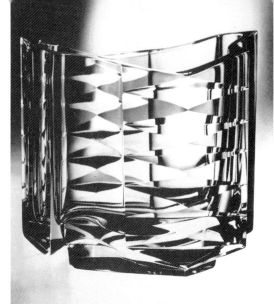

1
2 3 5
  4

1
Konto cut crystal vase, clear and neoblue
cm 25 high
Designed by Erkkitapio Siiroinen for Riihim
Lasi Oy, *Finland*
2
Grapponia blown bottle in clear, mossgree
and neoblue: cm 18.5 high
Designed by Nanny Still for Riihimäen Lasi
Finland
3
Tiara bowl, hand pressed and fire-polished
soda glass: cm 10.2-22.8 diameter
Designed by Kjell Blomberg for Gullaskrufs
Glasbruks Ab, *Sweden*
4
Stellaria from a range of plates and dishes
in hand-pressed and fire-polished soda glas
cm 10.2-30.5 diameter
Designed by Kjell Blomberg for Gullaskrufs
Glasbruks Ab, *Sweden*
5
Kajo cut crystal vases, five colours:
approximately cm 18 high
Designed by Tamara Aladin for Riihimäen
Lasi Oy, *Finland*

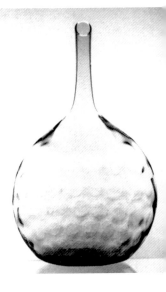

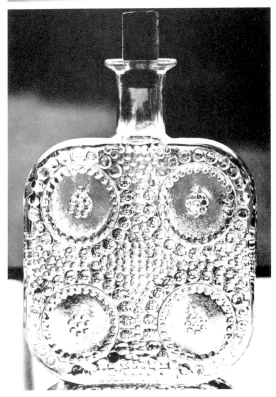

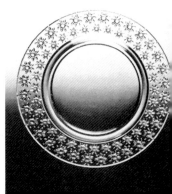

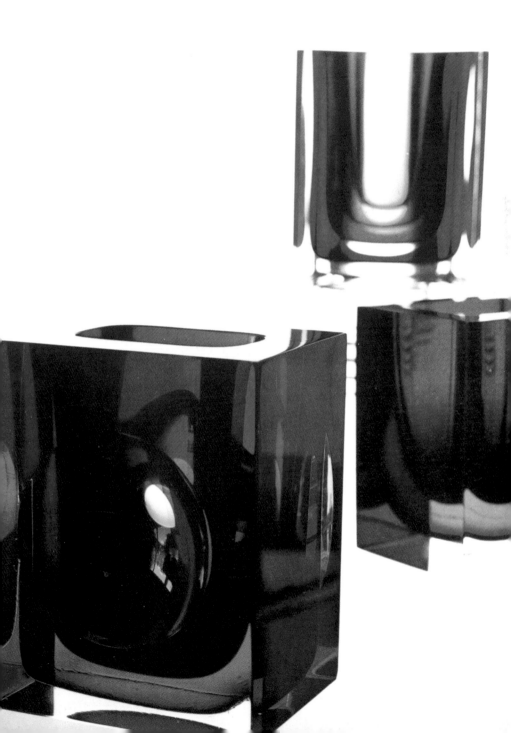

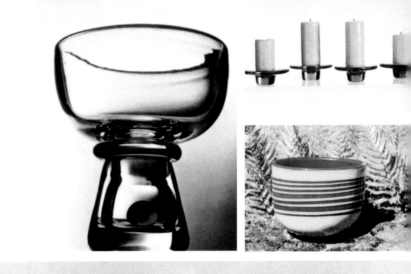

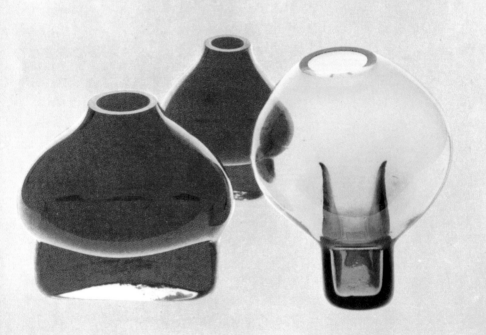

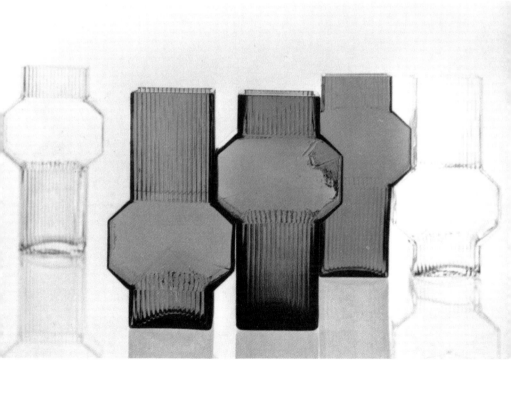

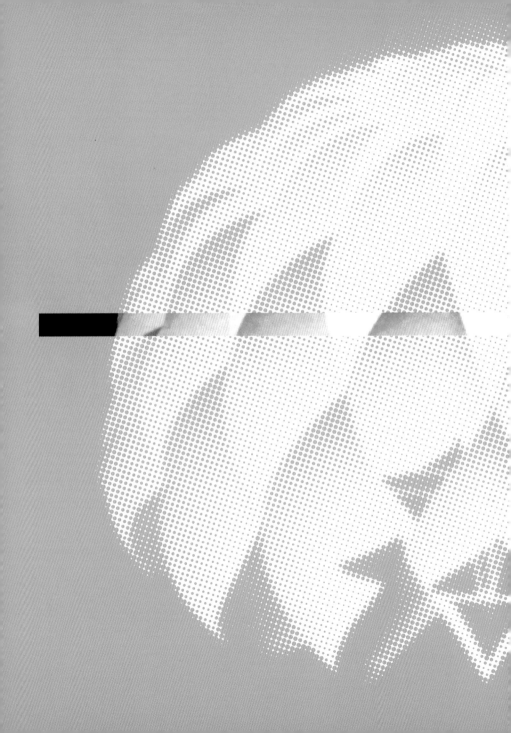

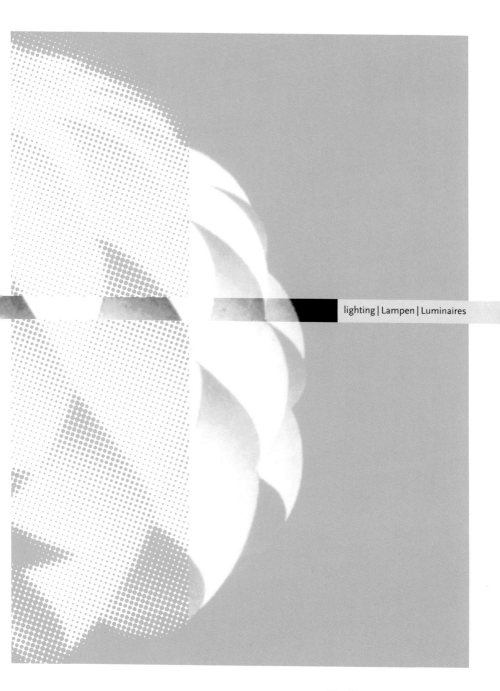

lighting | Lampen | Luminaires

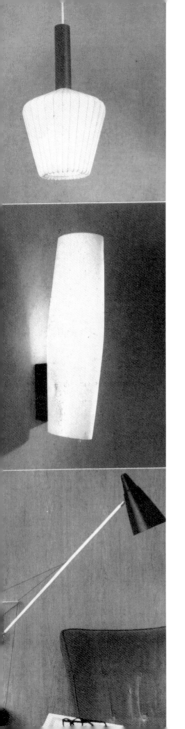

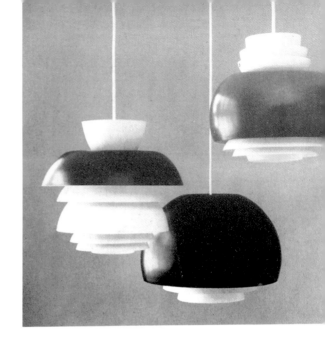

▲ White opal glass louvred pendants with lacquered aluminium shades.
Designed by Jørn Utzon, m.a.a for Nordisk Solar Co. A/S, DENMARK
'Snowflower' table lamp of white opaline glass on fir block mount, designed by G. L. de Snellman-Jaderholm. Shade made by Karhula-Iittala Glassworks FINLAND ▶
Lantern table light of smoke-coloured glass in metal frame. Designed by Victor Berndt for AB Flygsfors Glasbruk SWEDEN ▼

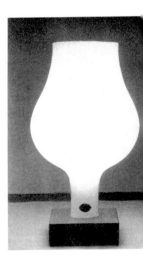

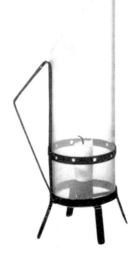

◀ FAR LEFT: White Chrysaline pendant on matt black aluminium 'stem'. Designed by Beverly Pick, FSIA, for W. S. Chrysaline Ltd UK
Satin etched white opal glass wall light on aluminium mount with matt black exterior finish. Designed by R. Reynolds, MSIA, for The General Electric Co. Ltd UK
Aluminium wall fitting adjustable in a hemisphere; lacquered shade available in several colours, boom and mount in white or black eggshell finish with brass details. Designed by Yarborough-Homes, MMSIA, of Cone Fittings Ltd UK

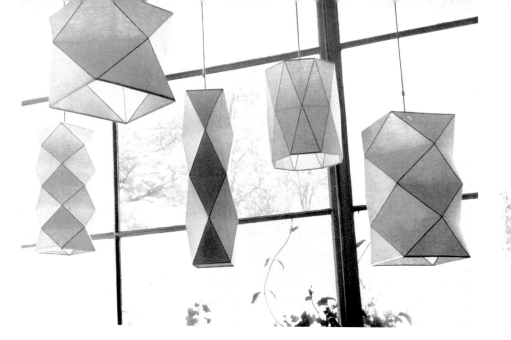

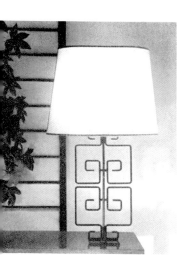

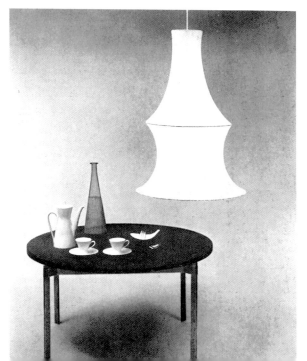

'Harlequin' pendants with shades made of chintz in
different colours. Designed by Hans Bergström, SIR,
for Ateljé Lyktan SWEDEN

Black wrought-iron table lamp with gold fibre-glass
fabric shade. Designed by John Crichton; base made
by Panoma Wrought Iron Ltd, shade by Max Robert-
son NEW ZEALAND

Vinyl-sprayed fish net eye-level pendant—one of
several shapes designed by George Nelson for the
Howard Miller Clock Co. USA

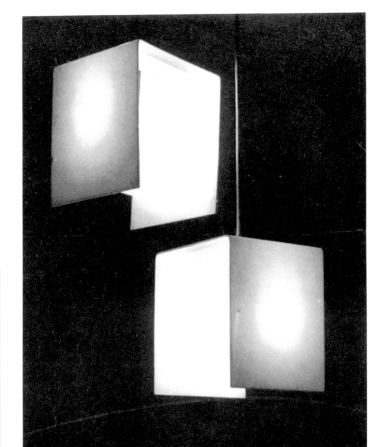

Hanging lamps of folded Perspex
designed by Yki Nummi for
o/y Stockmann-Örno FINLAND

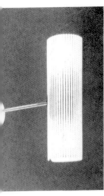

▲ Satin brass wall bracket with
washable *Gaylite* shade in white,
red/white or blue/white stripes.
▶

Metal ceiling unit in matt black
with polished brass reflector.
Both from the *Variform* range
designed by R. Reynolds, M S I A,
for The General Electric Co.
Ltd UK

Pendant, shades light grey/lilac,
light grey/moss green or satin
copper/black, with nylon louvre.
Designed by Bent Karlby for
A/S Lyfa DENMARK

Open-base globe pendant in
white flashed opal glass on anodised aluminium suspension. Designed and made by Troughton
& Young (Lighting) Ltd UK

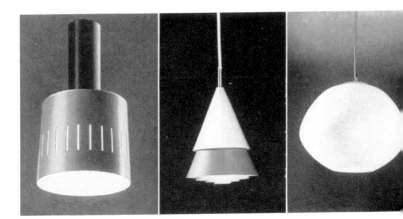

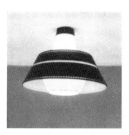

Achilles and *Apollo* from the Olympus range of light fittings in Pearlstone satin opal glass with eggshell finish pierced aluminium coloured reflectors. Made by Falk Stadelmann & Co. Ltd UK ▲ ▶

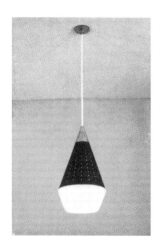

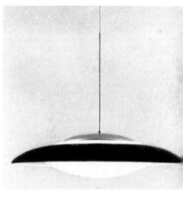

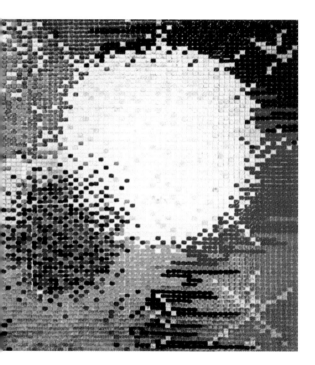

▲ *Sunburst* translucent Bohemian glass mosaic panel on plate glass lit from behind. Designed by Grace Grover for Dennis M. Williams Ltd UK

Wide spherical pendant of white opal glass with spun aluminium reflector available in six colours. It provides both upward and downward light and is designed by Paul Boissevain, MSIA, for The Merchant Adventurers Ltd UK

Ceiling fitting of coloured and uncoloured acrylic glass unities arranged in two layers. Designed by Hans Bergström for Ateljé Lyktan AB SWEDEN ▶

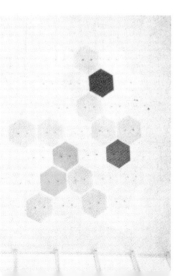

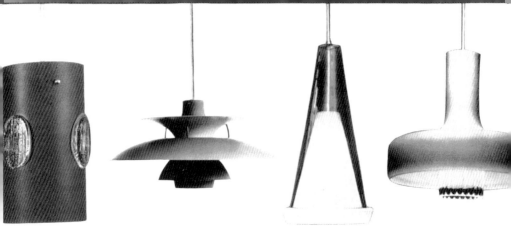

1 Lacquered glass with clear crystal medallions. Designed by Victor Berndt for AB Flygsfors Glasbruk SWEDEN

2 Metal pendant, shades lacquered red, lilac, white or blue outside, white inside, with inner shade in red.
  Designed by Poul Henningsen for Louis Poulsen & Co. A/S, DENMARK

3 White opal glass with outer shade in red, green, blue, or smoke-glass. Designed by Sven Middelboe for Nordisk Solar Co. A/S, DENMARK

4 Two-part fitting: matt opal glass over inner shade in clear lead-crystal. Designed by Heinrich Fuchs for Phönix GmbH GERMANY

5 Matt white etched glass shade, designed and made by Hesse-Leuchten GERMANY

6 Cascade effect multiple fitting, white opal shades with polished brass cups on black cord suspension: 8 Matt white etched-stripe opal glass fitting. Both are designed by Rudolf Hollman for Oswald Hollman Ltd UK

7 Two-piece shade of convex acid-polished glass on black-lacquered suspension. Designed by Max Ingrand FRANCE for Fontana Arte ITALY

9 Black wrought-iron standard with ivory rhoidoid lanterns edged in black. Designed by Jean Royère FRANCE

10 Stoneware lantern, turquoise glaze. Designed by Gerd Bøgelund for The Royal Copenhagen Porcelain Manufactory A/S, DENMARK

11 Black-lacquered iron frame standard with brass-ringed Triplex opal 'egg', 27 inches diameter: 12 Black-lacquered iron pedestal terrace lamp with four anti-dazzle discs lacquered white and red, and top refractor. Both are designed and made by Stilnovo, s.r.l. ITALY

13 Brass desk lamp with anodised aluminium shade.
  Designed by L. Summers: The Royal College of Art UK

14 Polished wood standard, acid-polished diffusing glass cone, polished brass ring. Designed by Max Ingrand FRANCE for Fontana Arte ITALY

15 Matching floor and desk lamps in metal, lacquered black or grey.
  Designed by Arne Jacobsen, m.a.a, for Louis Poulsen & Co. A/S, DENMARK

16 Metal standard with Perspex reflector in white and light yellow. It is adjustable in the horizontal and vertical planes—the diagram shows one of the several positions. Designed and made by Stilnovo, s.r.l. ITALY

9   10   11   I

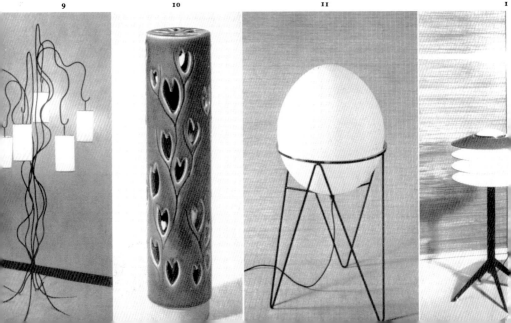

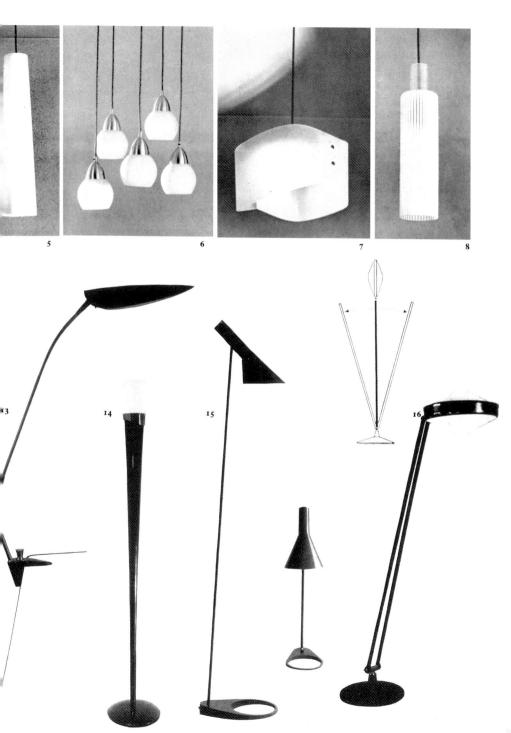

5

6

7

8

3

14

15

16

Pendants
1 Cylinder in satin opal glass
and lacquered metal in a
range of eight colours.
By Handelsonderneming
Willem Hagoort HOLLAND
2 *Triplex Opal* satin glass globe
for four lamps with lacquered
reflector. By Stilnovo ITALY
3 Perspex white opal circular
bowl for three lamps with
transparent outer shade
4 White satin etched opal
inner cylinder with coloured
spiral-decorated outer glass;
metalwork in satin brass.
Both designed by J. Hildred,
MSIA, for the General Electric
Co. Ltd UK

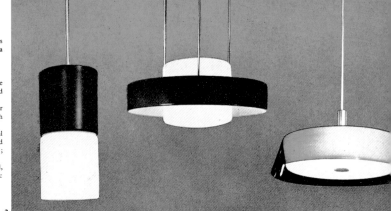

1, 2, 3

4, 5, 6

5, 6 Spun aluminium 'Drums'
lacquered in a range of eight
colours, inside white with
white opal louvre.
Designed by R. Boissevain,
MSIA, for Merchant Adven-
turers of London Ltd UK
7 Lamp ringed with twenty-
eight rectangular glass reflectors on black lacquered
metal mount; 8 square ceiling
fitting with bowl in satin
etched glass and a bevelled
thick glass, framed in white
lacquered metal.
Both by Fontana Arte ITALY
9 Cylinder in white opal glass
with coloured outer globe.
By Carl Fagerlund for AB
Orrefors Glasbruk SWEDEN

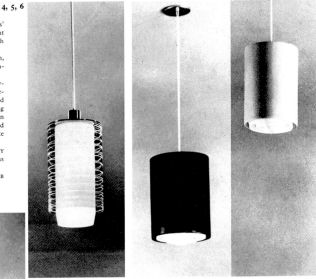

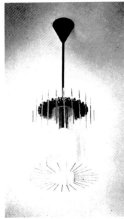

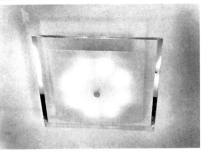

7 8

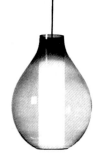

9

10

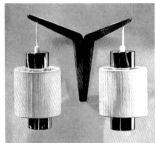

10 Teak wall bracket with copper pendants and bound ramie shades. By Holm Sørensen & Co. DENMARK
11 Twelve lamp candelabra in polished brass and oxidised steel. By Stilnovo, s.p.a. ITALY
12 Pendants in acrylic glass, transparent and white opal, with added coloured pieces. Designed by Hans Bergström for Ateljé Lyktan SWEDEN

11

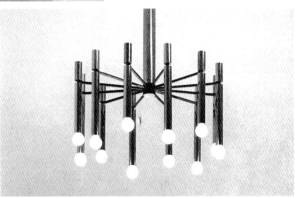

12

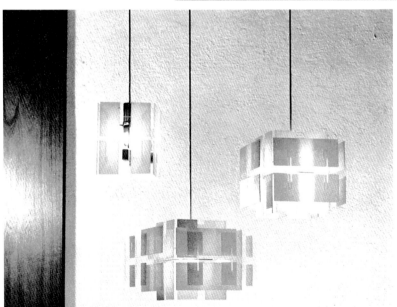

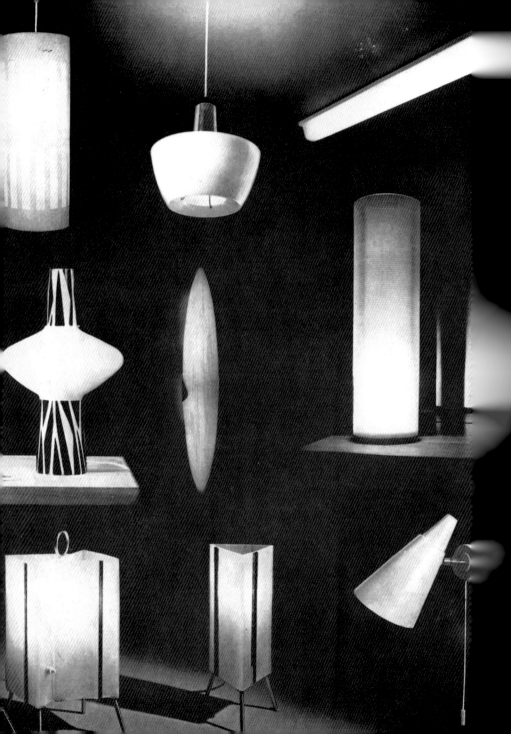

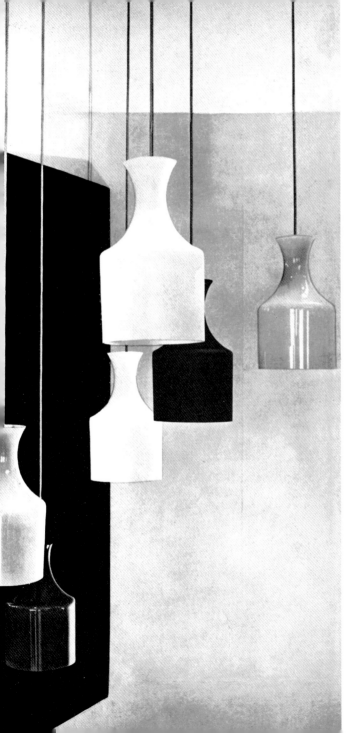

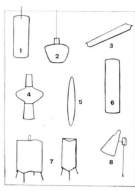

1 Cylinder pendant, 14 inches deep, made from two sheets of ingres paper. Designed by Peter Hjorth and Arne Karlsen, m.a.a., for Interna DENMARK

2 Pendant in aluminium anodised silver with moulded plastic diffuser; diameter 12 inches

3 Ceiling fitting in moulded opal Perspex with white metal mount; for 60 or 48 inch fluorescent tubes. By Troughton & Young (Lighting) Ltd UK

4 Table lamp in satin Triplex opal glass with fired black decoration, or in plain white; 15 inches high. Designed by Uno Westerberg for AB Arvid Böhlmarks Lampfabrik SWEDEN

5 Wall bracket in plexiglass on gilded brass mount; 23½ inches high. By Arlus SA, FRANCE

6 Cylindrical plastic table lamp with mahogany base and vertical rail carrying inner air-cooling aluminium reflector; 19 inches high. By John D. Stewart, MSIA, UK

7 Table lamps, single or with ring link, in white translucent glass with coloured stripes, on gilded brass mount; 15 and 17 inches high. Designed by Angelo Barovier for Barovier & Toso ITALY

8 Wall light in spun aluminium shade in various colours, ball joint stem and cord pull aluminium anodised warm brass. By Cone Fittings Ltd UK

◀ Pendants in opal glass, white or grey. Designed by Lisa Johansson-Pape for O/Y Stockmann-Orno FINLAND

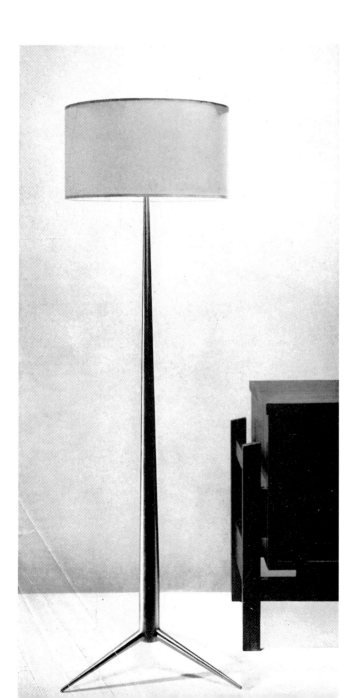

◄ Floor lamp with polished
stem and base.
Designed and custom made by F
Veranneman for E. Langui BEL◄
photo Atelier Ph

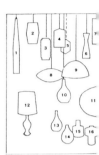

1, 2 *Umbrello* and *Botte* Vi
Italian glass pendants. F
J. Wuidart & Co. Ltd UK
3 Cylindrical pendant, opal g
with slotted brushed cop
shade. From the Rimini serie
Falk Stadelmann & Co. Ltd
4 Square grey-green Orre
Swedish glass pendant. F
J. Wuidart & Co. Ltd UK
5 Spanish brass lantern f
Homeshade Company Ltd u
6 German matt opal etched p
dant. From Heal's of London
7 Yellow glass cylinder light
Hiscock Appleby & Co. Ltd
8 Japanese Noguchi rice pa
pendant. From Primavera U
9 Danish domed copper pend
Louisana. From Danasco Ltd
10 Satin opal glass pendant v
green overglass. By Frede
Thomas & Co. Ltd UK
11 Spanish collapsible globe s
in wood veneers held by wro
iron rings. From Heal's
London UK
12 Table lamp with deep pa
ment shade on white china b
From G.B. Lamps UK
13 Matt white opal glass penc
By Troughton & Young Ltd
14 *Fiasco* green Italian glass
dant by Vistosi. From J. Wui
& Co. Ltd UK
15 Squat light blue glass pend
From Danasco Ltd UK
16 White opal glass pendant
blue overglass. By Frede
Thomas & Co. Ltd UK
Courtesy 'Ideal H

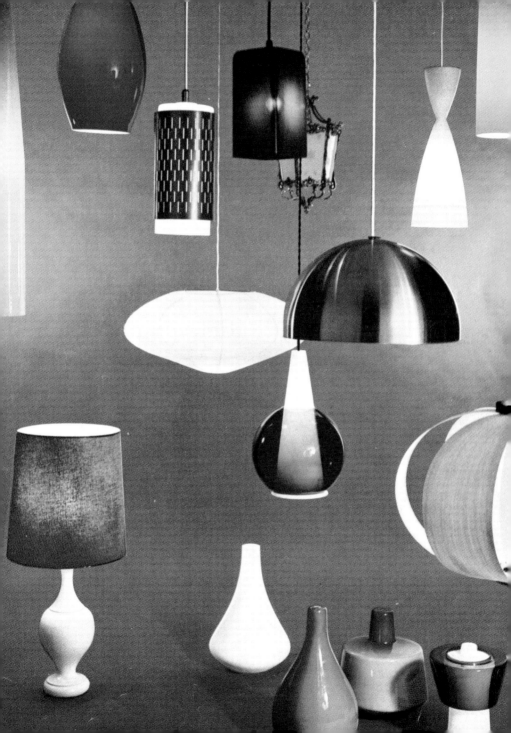

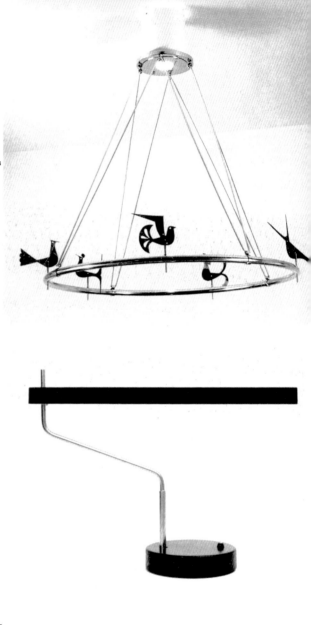

3

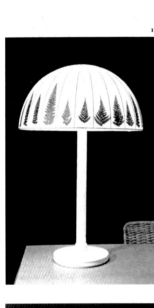

1

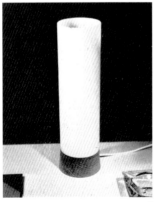

2

1
Table lamp with shaft and foot of natural pine or white-painted hardwood; plasticised shade with natural leaf inlay.
Designed by Hans-Agne Jakobsson and Arne Nilsson for Hans-Agne Jakobsson AB SWEDEN

2
Cylinder table lamp, 8 or 12 inches high, white satin finish shade on waxed hardwood base. F a range designed by John D. M. Brown, MSIA Plus Lighting Ltd UK

4
Desk lamp, black lacquered metal base and sl with polished chrome rotating arm. Designe Stahel for Telle-Büromöbel AG SWITZERLAND

5

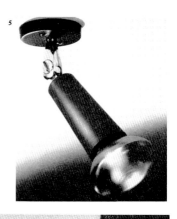

g ceiling fitting, diameter 38 inches, with
hed brass decorative birds; spotlight in centre
yed white matt finish. Designed by Tommi
inger for Parzinger Originals Inc USA

stable spot lamp for ceiling or wall, semi-matt
k finish with chromium universal joint. De-
ed and made by Troughton & Young Ltd UK

delabra of white-enamelled metal, with glass
les in blue, green, red or clear; the candlesticks
detachable from the base. Designed and made
Jans-Agne Jakobsson AB SWEDEN

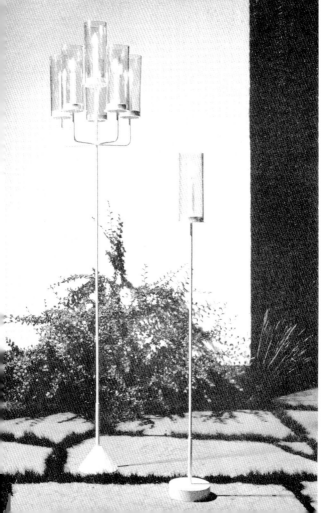

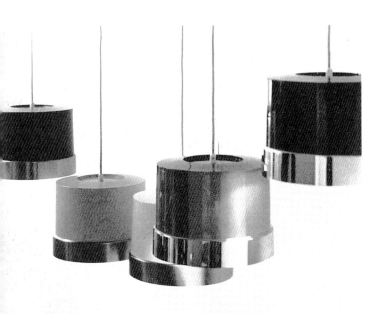

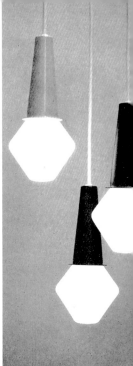

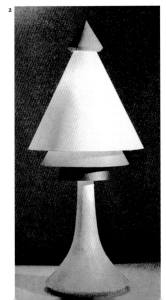

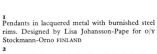

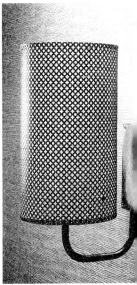

1
Pendants in lacquered metal with burnished steel rims. Designed by Lisa Johansson-Pape for O/Y Stockmann-Orno FINLAND

2
Maple table lamp with tiered card shade in three tones of the same colour. Designed and made by Lisbeth Brams DENMARK

3
Lacquered metal and white opal bulb pendants. Designed by Tapio Wirkkala for Idman FINLAND

4
Wall lamp, copper mount with black pink-lined perforated metal drum shade. Designed by John Crichton. Made by E. West & Co NEW ZEALAND

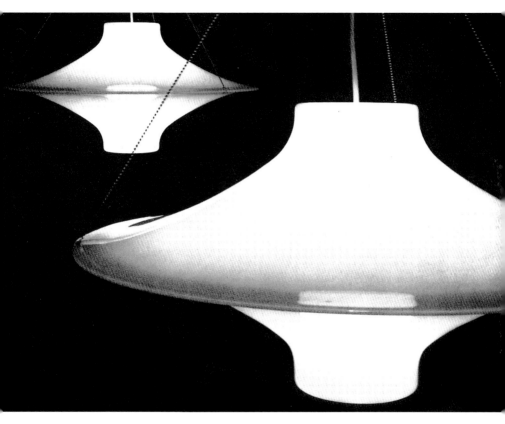

6

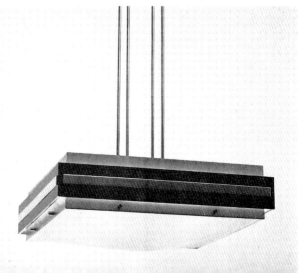

e opaline glass pendants. Designed by Yki
mi for O/Y Stockmann-Orno FINLAND

-lamp pendant, black and white lacquered
frame with engraved frosted crystal diffuser;
s polished brass. Designed and made by
ovo s.p.a. ITALY

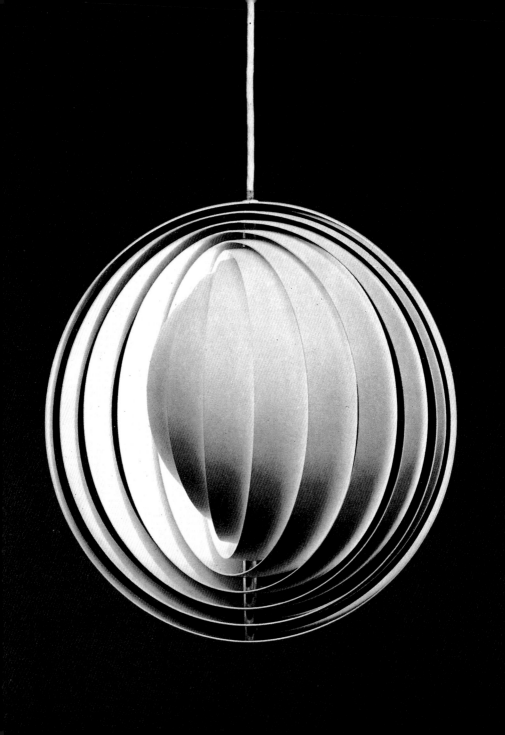

Pendant of adjustable white metal
rings; 35 cm diameter
Designed by Verner Panton for Louis
Poulsen & Company A/S DENMARK

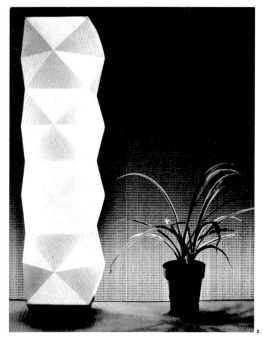

PHOTO: WERNER ERIK

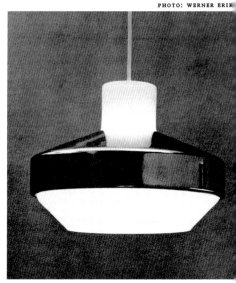

1
Facet table lamp, 66 cm high, of creased and folded white polypropylene with mahogany end caps Designed by Roger McClay for Cone Fittings Ltd UK

2
Pendant of opal glass with lacquered brass shade; 26 × 20 cm Designed by Göran Wärff for Böhlmarks Lampfabrik SWEDEN

3, 4
Tube pendant with louvre *TL1432* in flashed white opal glass; 25 and 30 cm diameter
Ceiling unit *1643C* in matt white opal glass; 25 cm diameter. From the

Opalight Range A light fittings metal details in aluminium and satin silver, or pale gold to order Designed by Paul Boissevain Merchant Adventurers Ltd UK

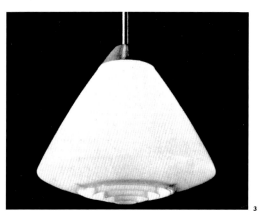

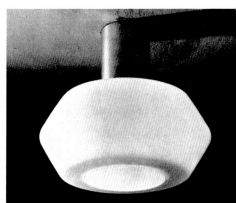

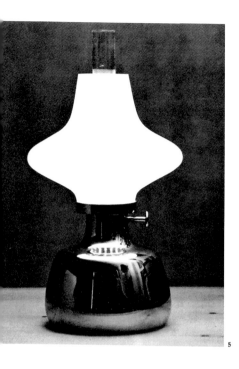

5

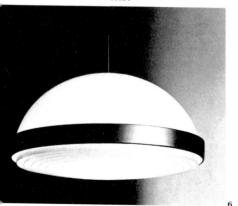

TO: ALDO BALLO

6

7
Table, ceiling and floor lamps with shades of white-enamelled aluminium slats; 20 cm diameter; 50, 32 and 77 cm high respectively
Designed and made by Hans-Agne Jakobsson AB SWEDEN

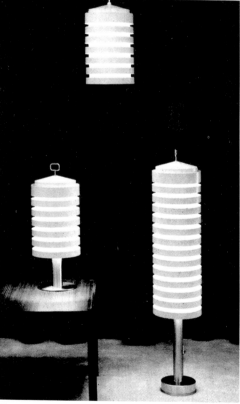

6
amp, 32 cm high, of opal glass a brass base gned by Henning Koppel for s Poulsen & Company A/S MARK

Pendant with opal Perspex reflector and white plastic louvre, finished with satin nickel-plated brass; 46 cm diameter
Designed and made by Stilnovo s.p.a. ITALY

7

PHOTO: OVEHALLIN, WAHLBERG

1963–64 · lighting · 437

1, 2
Matt white corrugated opal glass
cylinder pendants *F609/610*
White flashed satin-opal pendant
F667/R3 with burnished copper drum
reflector. Designed by A. B. Read.
Made by Troughton & Young
(Lighting) Ltd UK

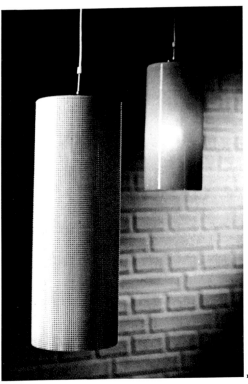

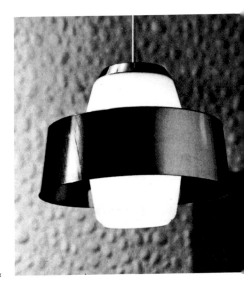

3, 4
White flashed satin-opal cone shade
F/66 and tapered shade *F/65* with
metal details stove-enamelled black
Designed for the *Harlequin* series of
interchangeable fittings and made by
Troughton & Young (Lighting) Ltd UK
5
Six-light fluorescent unit *136A* with
61 cm and 122 cm tubelights on matt
white spun aluminium mount; arms
anodised satin silver, or pale gold
Designed by Paul Boissevain for
Merchant Adventurers Ltd UK

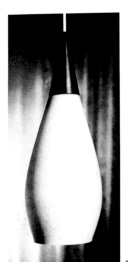

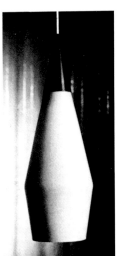

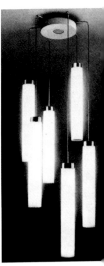

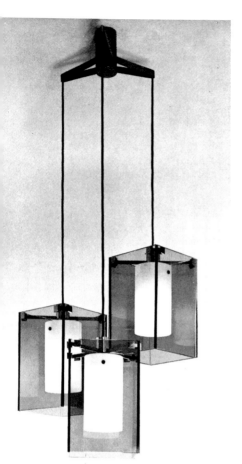

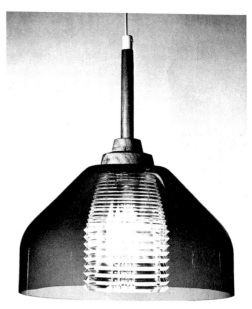

8

6

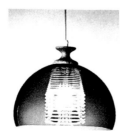

ple pendant fitting *2210* with
ke-grey glass shades, 63 × 50 cm,
satin-opal diffuser; metal details
uered brass
igned and made by Fontana Arte
LY
, **9**
dant series *L2218/2216/2220* with
r brown shade over inner cylinder
lear crystal; 30 and 22 cm diameter
igned by Victor Berndt. Made by
Flygsfors Glasbruk for Svenska
ips AB SWEDEN

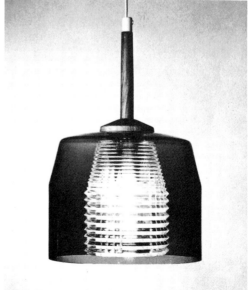

7

9

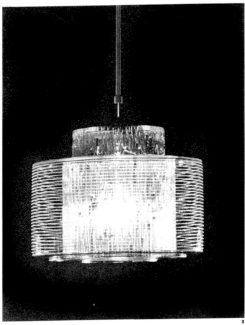

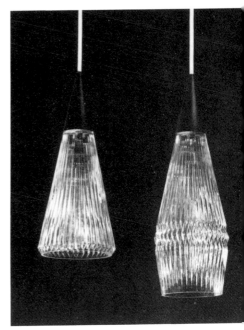

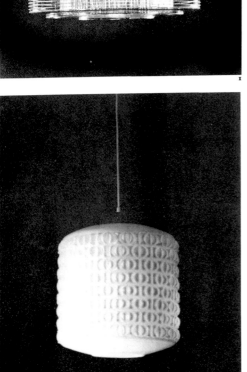

1, 2
Corona and Cordoba pendants: *Corona*
in clear glass, crystal decor with inner-
glass crystal, moulded decor 27·5 cm
diameter. *Cordoba* opal cased glass
with satin etched finish 30 cm
diameter
Designed and made by Peill &
Putzler Glashuttenwerke GmbH w.
GERMANY

3
Pendants in clear crystal and satin-
black finished metal
Additions to the *Harlequin* range for
Troughton & Young Ltd UK

4
Hall mirror-light in etched opal glass;
width overall 61 cm (the position of
the mirror and grey textured panel
be reversed)
Made by Osram (General Electric
Ltd) UK

5
Wall bracket F700, random patt
pressed clear crystal; 25 cm diame
In the Mondolite range designed
Troughton & Young Ltd UK in
junction with Peill & Putzler G
huttenwerke GmbH w. GERMAN

6
Opal globe pendants with white c
over-shades of stretch fabric over s
wire; 23, 28, 33 and 38 cm square
Designed and made by Raymor M
Division USA

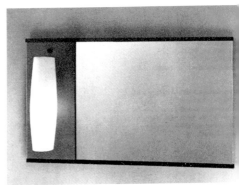

PHOTO: FOX

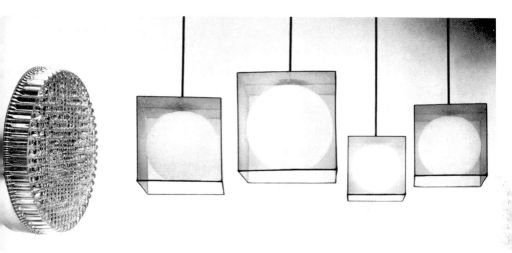

5

6

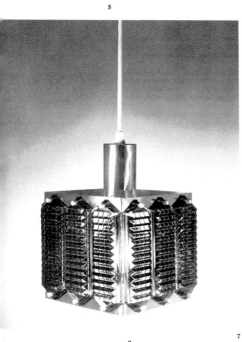

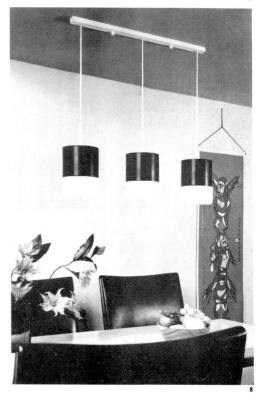

8

7

rism-cut clear amber glass pendant
with brass mounting; 18 cm square
Designed by Victor Berndt for AB
Flygsfors Glasbruk SWEDEN

Triple ceiling fitting with opal glass
shades and crystal glass reflection:
mounted on black anodised aluminium; 15 cm diameter
Designed and made by Staff & Schwarz
W. GERMANY

8

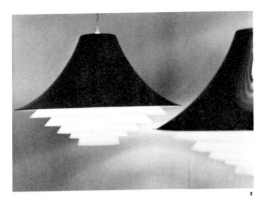

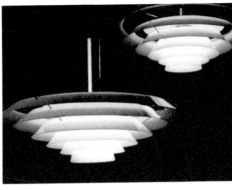

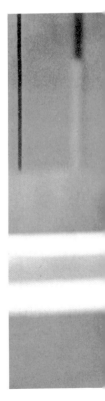

1, 2, 3
Acrylic pendants
Series R5823 in black and white; 55
cm diameter
Series 64–478 in pastel or alabaster
colours on polished aluminium suspension; 55 cm diameter
Series 64–474 in neutral light brown
or dark brown/white; 22 cm diameter

All designed by Yki Nummi

4
Pendants Series 61–044 in grey, blue
grey or Havannah brown glass with
matt interior; 19 cm diameter

5
Metal pendants transparent-lacquered
Series R5792: darkest green or milk-
white with matt transparent acrylic
rims and white louvre; 34 cm diameter

6
Lacquered metal shades Series 61–019
and 30–019 for pendant or floor fittings: champagne transparent-lacquered centre, banded in warm grey or
sand brown; 44 cm diameter. The
floor lamp is adjustable in height
All designed by Lisa Johannson-Pape

All fittings made by Stockmann-Orno
FINLAND

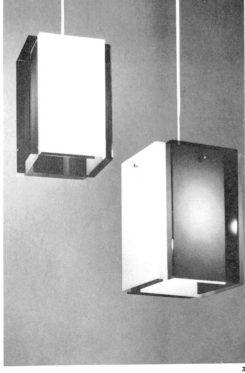

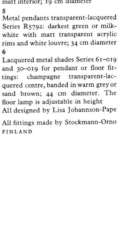

PHOTOS PIETINEN

3

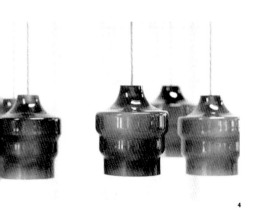

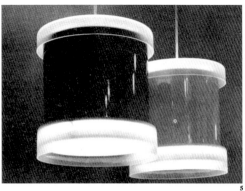

4

5

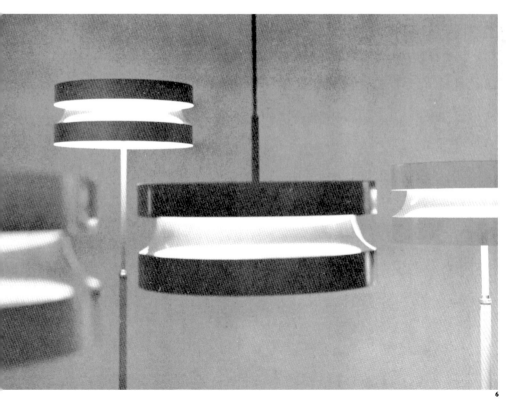

6

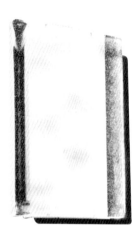

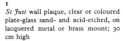

I
St·Just wall plaque, clear or coloured
plate-glass sand- and acid-etched, on
lacquered metal or brass mount; 30
cm high
Designed and made by Max Ingrand
FRANCE

2
Floor lamp Model 1085 of transparent
Perspex with black anodised alumi-
nium; 160 cm high. Designed by Gino
Sarfatti

3
Wall lamp Model 244 on metal spring
extension with ceiling attachment;
shade in smoked Murano glass
Designed by Ico Parisi
Both for Arteluce ITALY

4
Pendant Model 1246 for two lamps
black-enamelled and brushed copper
reflector over exterior bowl in engraved frosted crystal and inner bowl
in white satin-opal Triplex glass; 62
cm diameter
Designed and made by Stilnovo spa
ITALY

5
Pendant Model 2259 in plate-glass on
brass suspension oxidized gun-metal
grey: 43 cm high
Designed and made by Fontana Arte
ITALY

PHOTO JEAN RIATIGRAITI

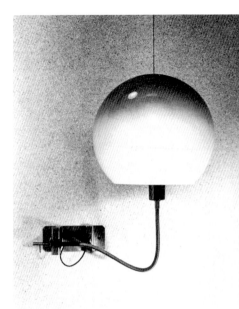

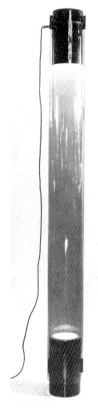

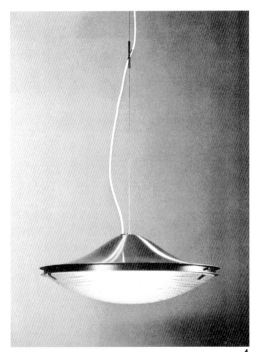

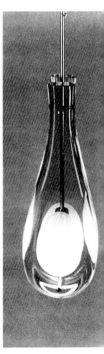

2

4

444 · lighting · 1964–65

6
Brushed copper pendant with inner shade of dark red or smoked acrylic Designed by Sergio Asti, S. Favre for Kastell ITALY

7
Pendant Model 2118 in black lacquered aluminium with green or smoked Murano glass. Designed by Sergio Asti

8
Floor lamp 1086, anodised metal, with shade on swivel bracket; full height 120 cm
Designed by Gino Sarfatti
Both for Arteluce ITALY

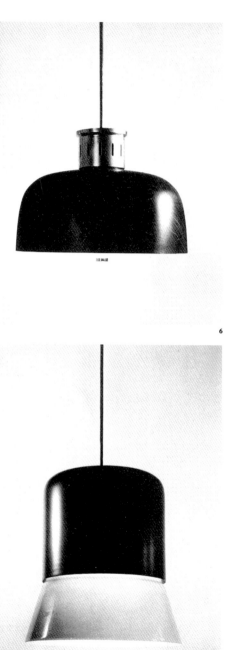

6

7

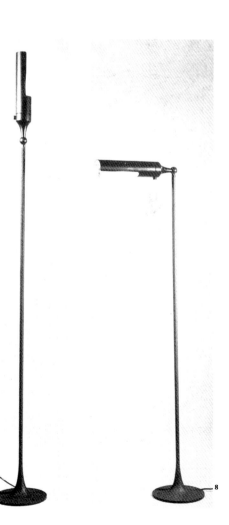

8

Pendant shade of sliced bamboo/rattan, purple-red or natural, 75 cm deep
Designed by Industrial Arts Institute made by Kawai Kogyo K.K. JAPAN

Pendant or floor lamp, vinyl-chloride sheet assembled with acrylic pleats: opaque white, 33 cm deep
Designed by Industrial Arts Institute and made by Yamada Shomei K.K.
JAPAN

Adjustable fittings in black-sprayed aluminium, brass mountings, matt black iron stand; respective overall heights 47 cm, 148 cm (also available with 2-lamp mounting), and 50 cm
Designed and made by H. & F. Beisl
W. GERMANY

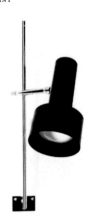

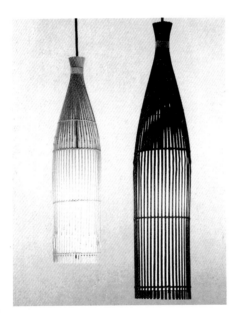

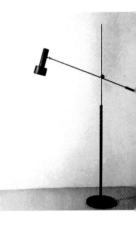

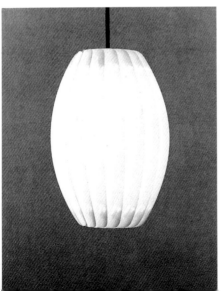

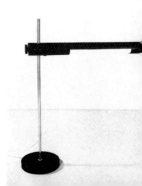

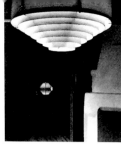

ies 2150 fitting, spun aluminium
m stove-enamelled pearl-grey,
'ow, scarlet, matt black or white;
anodised finishes with moulded
al-white louvre, illuminating
wards and downwards

w Series 2160 fittings for walls
ceilings (recessed or semi-
cessed) matt black stove-enamelled
minium drums with internal
 le grid for downward, concealed,
ht

ies 2150 and 2160 both made by
erchant Adventurers UK

Pendant and floor lamps in fine-
grained natural pine veneers
53 and 26 cm diameter
Designed by Hans-Agne Jakobsson
for AB Ellysett SWEDEN

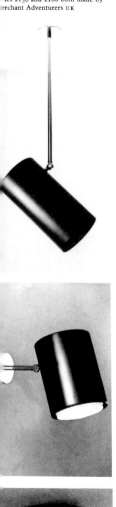

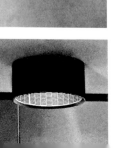

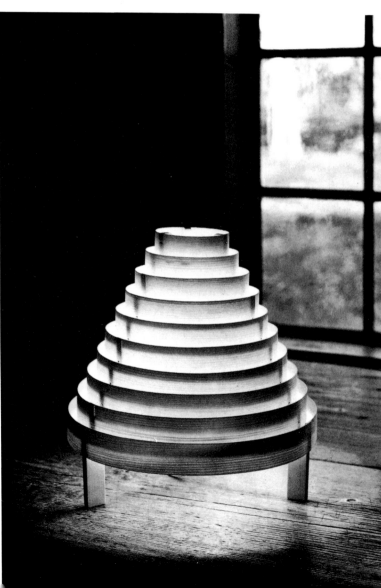

Table lamp 10,054 in satin-opal
glass, the stem chromed brass on a
cubic metal base, lacquered black,
white or grey, 53 cm high overall
Designed and made by Max Ingrand
FRANCE

Nizza pendant of satin-opal and
crystal lead, 30 cm diameter
Designed and made by Peill &
Putzler Glashüttenwerke W. GERMANY

Table lamp with tipping head in black,
white or deep red, polyester finish
35 cm high
Designed by Umberto Riva for
Kartell-Binasco ITALY

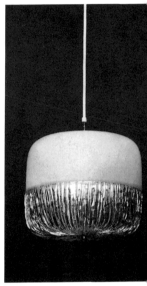

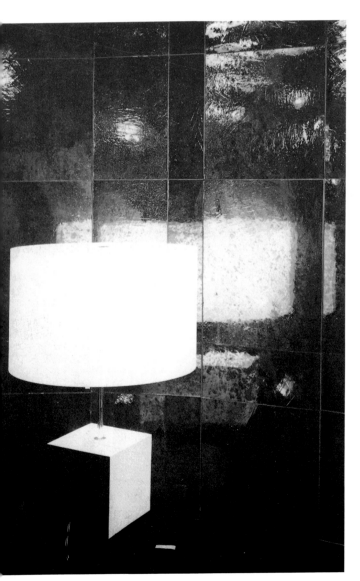

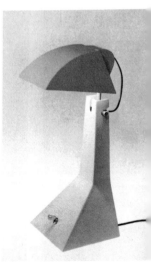

ants, series 66–112 in white opal
with red or white acrylic bowls
n diameter
gned by Lisa Johansson-Pape for
Stockmann-Orno AB FINLAND

r, table or wall fitting, the
rotating through 360°; in
er or metal painted black or
e
gned by Mauri Almari for
an O/y FINLAND

Brierley cylindrical fitting in amber,
smoke, amethyst or crystal glass
about 30 cm deep
Designed by George Elliott for
Stevens & Williams UK

Table lamp in brass,
leather-cased stem
Designed and made by Carl Auböck
AUSTRIA

Table lamps, series 40–040 in metal
sprayed red, blue or white, 52 cm high
Designed by Yki Nummi

Pendants, series 61–164 in colour-
sprayed metal, with white acrylic
rims, 56 cm diameter
Designed by Svea Winkler
Both for O/y Stockmann-Orno AB
FINLAND

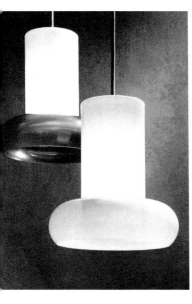

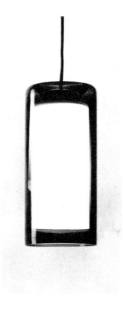

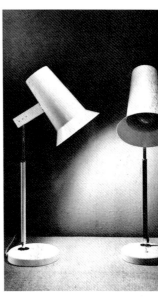

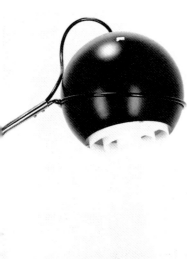

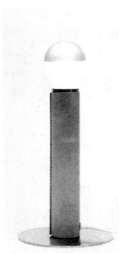

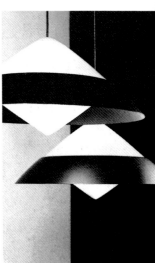

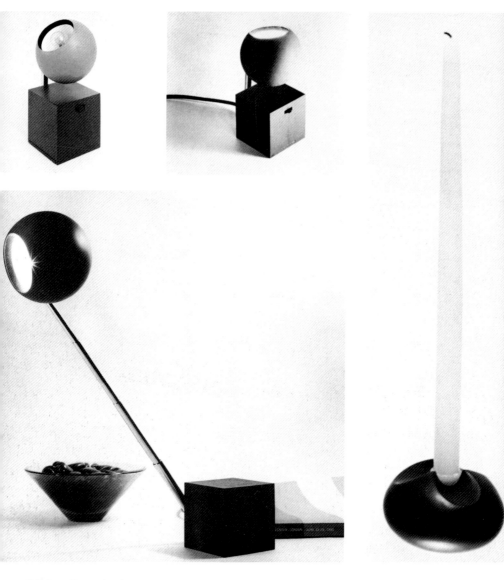

Table lamp with stamped metal
shade, moulded plastic base; white,
black or brown: metal telescoping
arm extends to 15 cm
Designed by Lax Design Associates
for Lightolier Inc USA

Bulb-like candleholder; porcelain
with various coloured glazes: 11 cm
high
Designed by Industrial Arts
Institute and made by Tasendo Co
Ltd JAPAN

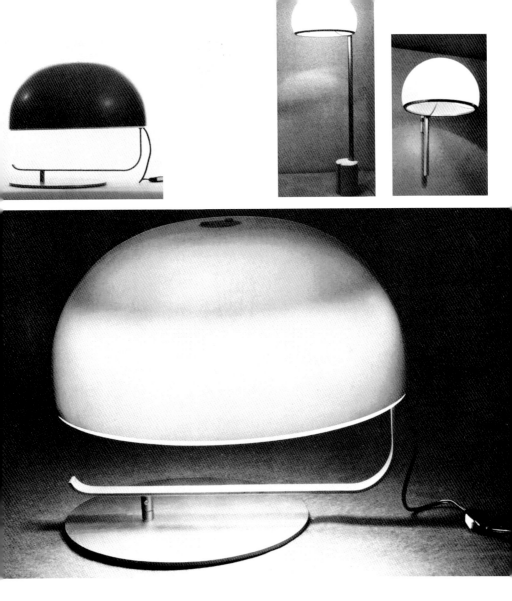

able lamp varnished iron frame,
opal or coloured Perspex shade:
3 cm diameter
Designed by Marco Zanuso for
O-Luce ITALY

top Wall or standard lamp with white
concrete base: nickel matt brass
column: opal Perspex shade
Designed by Gregotti Meneghetti
Stoppino for Arteluce SA ITALY

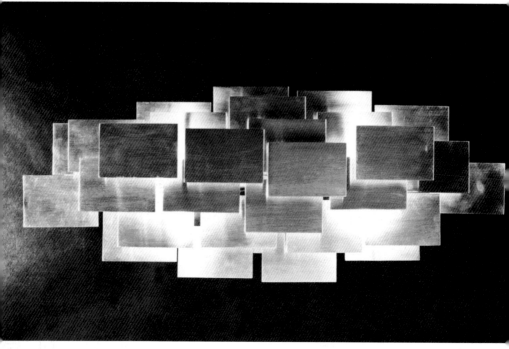

photograph Schnakenburg

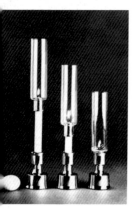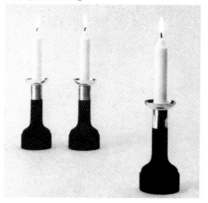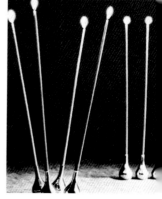

Staccato 100 fitting satin
chrome, silvered or lacquered
finish: plates built up to required
size; this one 60 × 24 cm
Designed and made by Johann
Faltermaier W. GERMANY

Magic Lantern candle holders of
brass finished metal overall height
29 cm
Designed by Jens Quistgaard for
Dansk Designs DENMARK

Candlesticks of stained beech and
polished or silver-plated brass;
total height 16 cm
Designed by Hans Bølling for
Torben Ørskov & Co DENMARK

Onion candlesticks, silver plated or
solid brass; tapers in 13 colours
Designed by Jens Quistgaard for
Dansk Designs DENMARK

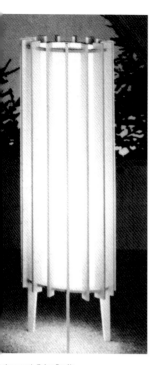

photograph Color-Studio

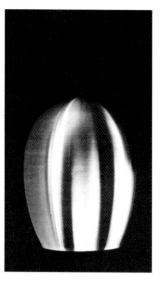

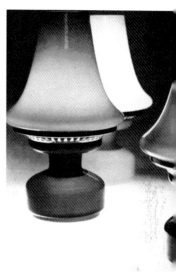

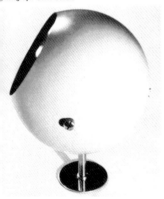

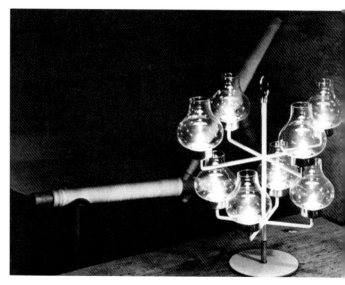

Tema floor lamp, kalmar-pine with inner linen shade, available also as table or pendant fitting: 78 cm high
Designed by Ib Fabiansen for Fog and Mørup A/S DENMARK

Table lamp with orange metal shade and alux reflector, nickel arm and flange: total extension 28 cm
Designed by E. Graae and H. Helgar for Louis Poulsen & Co A/S DENMARK

Pendant lamp in aluminium: 36 cm deep
Designed and made by A. A. Gruberts Sønner DENMARK

Cluster lamp, black vion and lacquered brass with clear glass bowls; available also as pendant or standard
Designed by Anders Pehrson for Ateljé Lyktan AB SWEDEN

top
Table lamp; base and shade of opal, amethyst, yellow, olive green or turquoise glass; available as wall fitting or nested pendant arrangement: 34 cm high
Designed and made by Hans-Agne Jakobsson AB SWEDEN

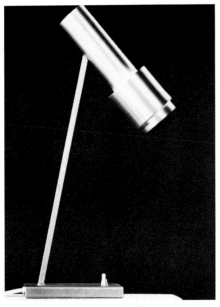

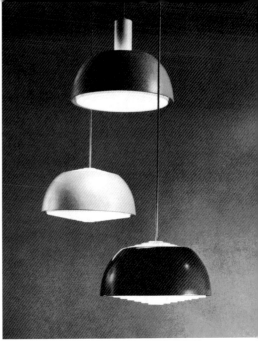

photograph Gravett

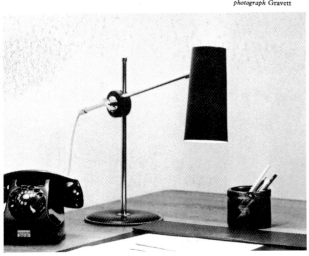

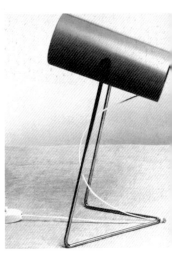

Table lamp lined with copper
emitting white light, or aluminium
emitting lilac light: 46 cm high
Designed by Bent Nordsted for
H. A. Gruberts Sønner DENMARK

Adjustable lamp of black leather,
chrome and jacaranda: 36 cm high
Designed by Anders Pehrson for
Ateljé Lyktan AB SWEDEN

Pendants MA 3460 white plastic
louvres and spun aluminium stove-
enamelled grey, red, blue; 30 and
48 cm diameter
Designed by Paul Boissevain for
Merchant Adventurers Ltd UK

Wall or table lamp, steel tube
frame with steel cylinder in six
colours lined white: overall height
27 cm
Designed by John Brown for
Plus Lighting Ltd UK

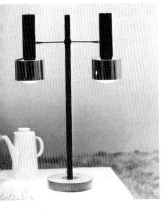

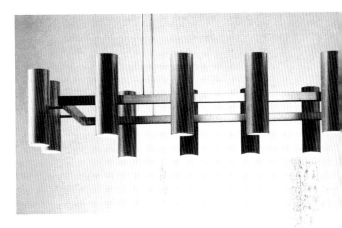

photographs Hooker

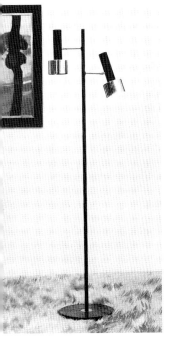

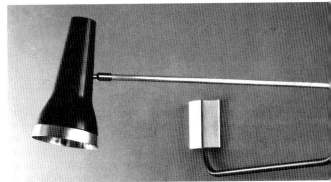

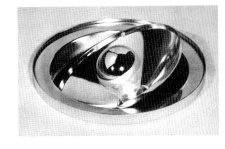

Table and standard spot lamps
with reflectors (rotating only) and
arm of copper, chrome or brass
on square section tube, mahogany
base: overall height 61 and 148 cm
Designed by John D. M. Brown
for Plus Lighting Ltd UK

Pendants spun aluminium drums
finished black or grey; aluminium
extrusions: mounted size to order
Designed by Paul Boissevain for
Merchant Adventurers Ltd UK

Double hinged swinging arm wall
light, adjustable reflector, rim and
outer arm, anodized aluminium;
shade white, black or colours:
maximum extensions 91 cm
Designed by E. Cooke for Cone
Fittings Ltd UK

Recessed fitting soffit ring finished
polished, anodized aluminium,
reflector tips and rotates: overall
width 28 cm
Designed and made by Courtney,
Pope Ltd UK

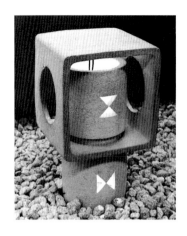

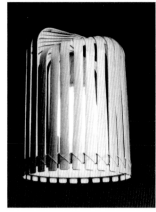

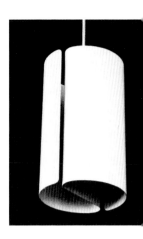

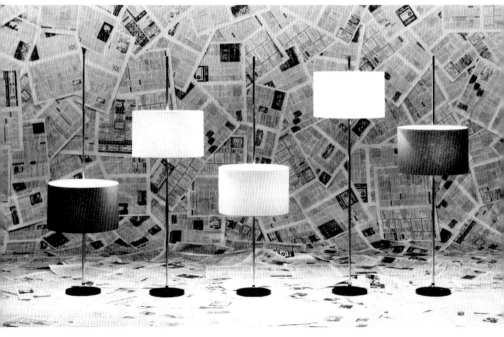

Garden lamp in yellow stoneware, demountable: 60 × 30 cm
Designed by Mosuke Yoshitake for Ōmi Kagaku K.K. JAPAN

Standard 1161–5 with chrome column and lampholder adjustable up to 160 cm; shade in white, graphite, yellow, brown or red, linen lined
Manufactured by Staff Leuchten
W. GERMANY

top
Pendant lamp of natural sliced bamboo: 22 cm diameter
Designed and made by Design Center Shizuoka JAPAN

top
Pendant lamp from bent metal sheet, silver-grey or rose-pink finish: 22 cm diameter
Designed and made by Design Center Shizuoka JAPAN

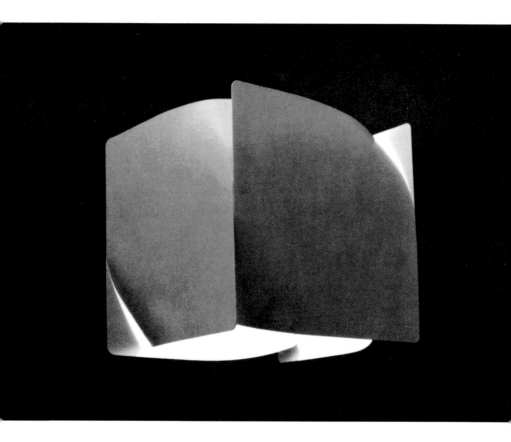

dant made with four bent sheets
ron with silver-grey lacquered
sh: 22 cm cube
signed and made by Design
ter Shizuoka JAPAN

All-white glass dome light 40 cm high
Designed by Sergio Asti and made
by Arteluce *Italy*

Table lamp of reinforced plastic
material, white or red, 55 cm diameter
Designed by an architectural
group and made by Artemide *Italy*

Opaline white globe with moplen support
in amarant, blue, ebony black
26 cm diameter × 23 cm high
Designed by Joe Colombo and made
by Kartell s.r.l. *Italy*

White smoked glass on metal base
50 cm diameter
Designed by Angelo Mangiarotti

Blue aluminium with white smoked
glass diffuser 45 cm diameter × 40 cm high
Designed by Leonardo Ferrari and
Franco Mazzucchelli Tartaglino
Both made by Artemide *Italy*

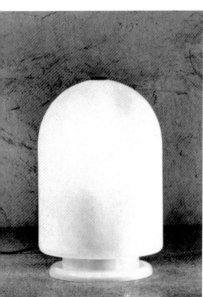

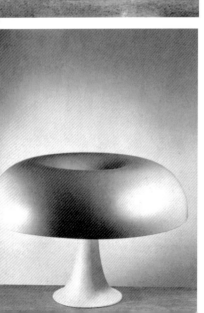

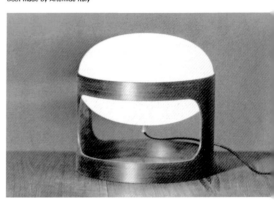

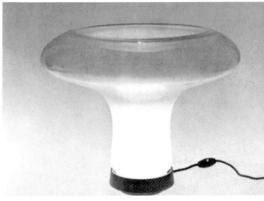

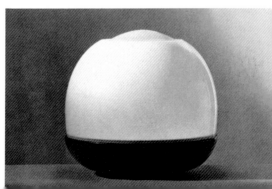

chrome brass standard with opaline
diffuser 175 cm high × 48 cm diameter
designed by Emma Schweinberger Gismondi,
made by Artemide *Italy*

Table lamp, metal lacquered white,
sand or sky blue: revolving
light 12 cm diameter
Designed by Vico Magistretti and
made by Artemide *Italy*

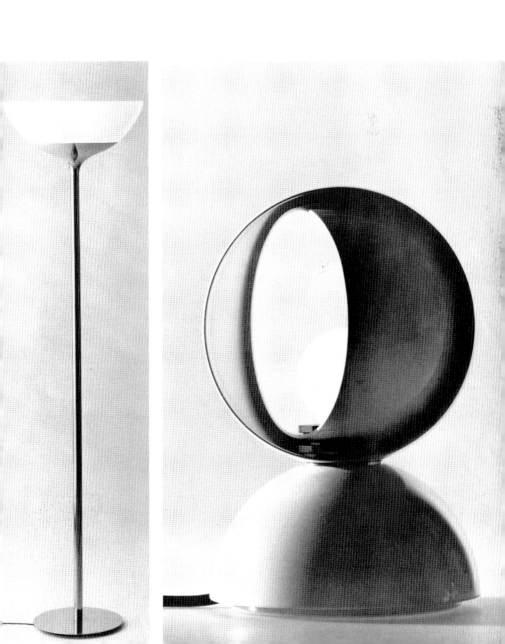

Flower illuminator of enamelled
anti-rust treated metal, pillar
and roof dark green 68 cm high ×
18 cm square
Designed and made by Hans-Agne
Jakobsson AB *Sweden*

Table lamp, bent iron sheet lacquered
light or dark grey, 18 cm diameter
Designed and made by Design Center
Shizuoka *Japan*

Stoneware garden lamp, 50 cm
diameter
Designed by Mosuke Yoshitake
and made by Tokyo Craft Co *Japan*

opposite
Wall-mounted swinging and
extendable fitting, grey metal and opal
glass, extends to 110 cm × 28 cm overall
Designed by Josef Hurka and made
by Napako *Czechoslovakia*

Group of table lamps, acrylic tube cased
in bamboo, lacquered iron sheet and
plywood respectively mounted on
iron rims 18, 20 and 18 cm diameter
All designed and made by the Design
Center Shizuoka *Japan*

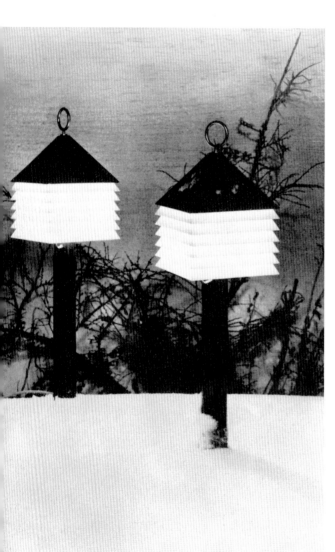

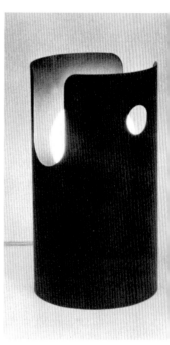

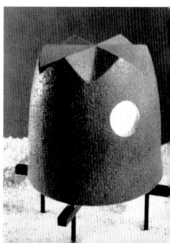

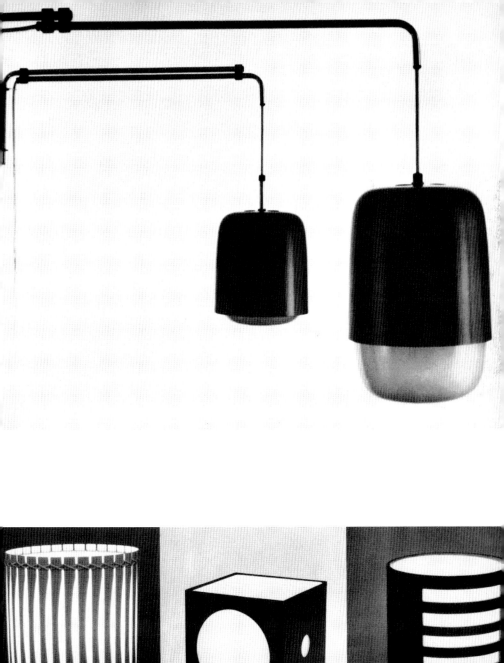
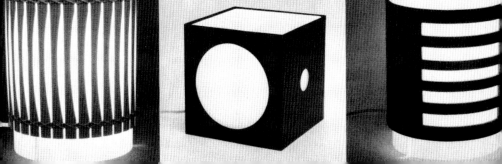

Ragusa pendant, lead crystal with matt/bright relief, 26 cm deep Designed and made by Peill & Putzler Glashüttenwerke *W. Germany*

Tuikku lanterns, blown glass in four colours 22 cm high Designed by Nanny Still for Riihimäen Lasi Oy *Finland*

Table lamp, milk-white acrylic on aluminium disc 22 cm high Designed by Industrial Arts Institute and made by Kawai Kogyo KK & Tokyo Jushi KK *Japan*

Erkki Vaalle

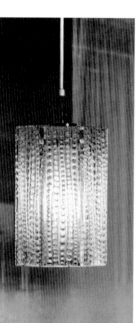

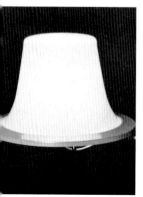

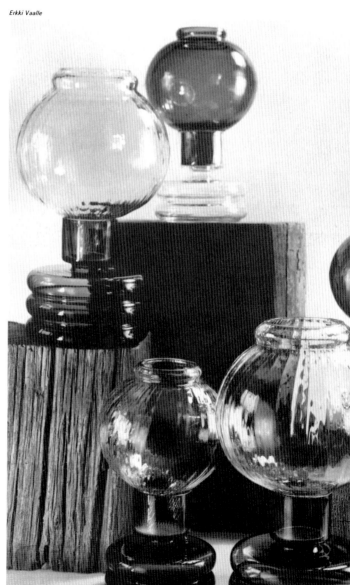

dant, wall-mounted, table
standard fittings, satin
dized aluminium with opal and
ke-grey acrylic bowls
igned by Robert Welch and made
Lumitron Ltd *England*

Pendant coloured acrylic with
metal rim-reflector, 15 cm diameter
Designed by Lisa Johansson-Pape
Wall-mounted fittings in white and
coloured acrylic, 15 cm diameter
Designed by Yki Nummi
bottom left
Wall fitting, colour sprayed metal,
18 cm diameter
Designed by Svea Winkler
All made by Oy Stockmann Orno
Finland

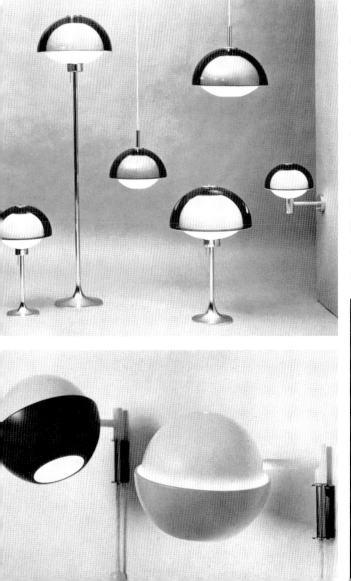

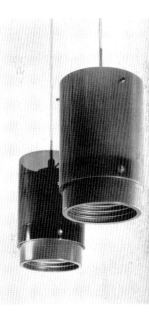

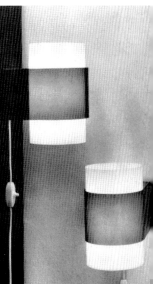

Pendant, black-lacquered and chromed metal with Perspex reflector, green, white, grey 60 cm diameter
Designed by Pieter de Bruyne *(Belgium)* for Arteluce *Italy*

SEN/18 one of a range of low-glare, baffle grid units available also as ceiling mounting or recessed fittings, enamelled blue-grey and white
Designed and made by Courtney, Pope (Electrical) Ltd *England*

Model 1090 demountable floor lamp in Ondolux 1·22 m high
Designed by Gino Sarfatti for Arteluce *Italy*

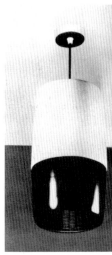

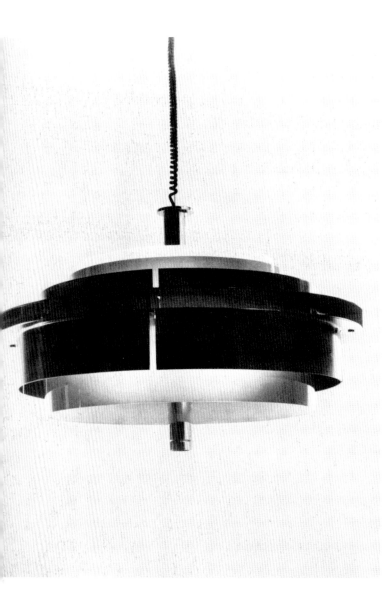

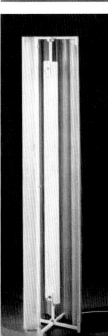

e-standing lamp, table or floor model,
ckelled brass stem with black-lacquered
uminium reflectors, bright diffusers
s and 145 cm high

oor lamp with swinging, tipping and
volving bar, nickelled brass and
ack-lacquered aluminium, 135 cm high
th designed and made by Beisl
uchten KG *W. Germany*

Wall-light, single, double or triple
mounted, satin silver, light gold or
copper finished aluminium with flashed
opal, clear amethyst or smoke shades,
projection 20 cm
Simple-to-fix wall light, the white opal
cylinder fitted with a sleeve in one of
many colours. Available, mounted on a
stem of anthracite moulded plastic and
bar and fitting of anodised aluminium
Both designed by E. Cooke Yarborough
for Conelight Limited *England*

Trombone one of a series,
chrome stems and tipping cylinders
of matt aluminium 51 cm high
Designed by Jo Hammerborg for
Fog & Mørup *Denmark*

Table-spot-lights in nickelled
brass and black-lacquered aluminium
23 cm high
Designed and made by Beisl Leuchten KG
W. Germany

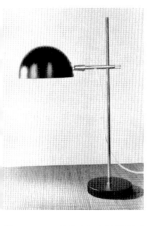

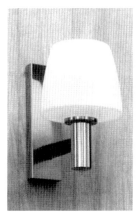

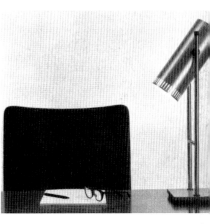

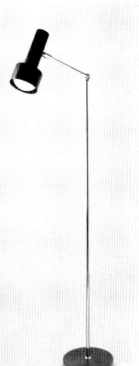

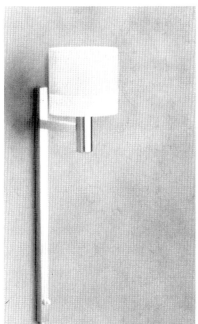

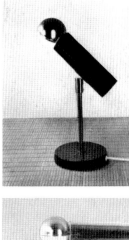

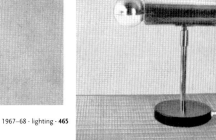

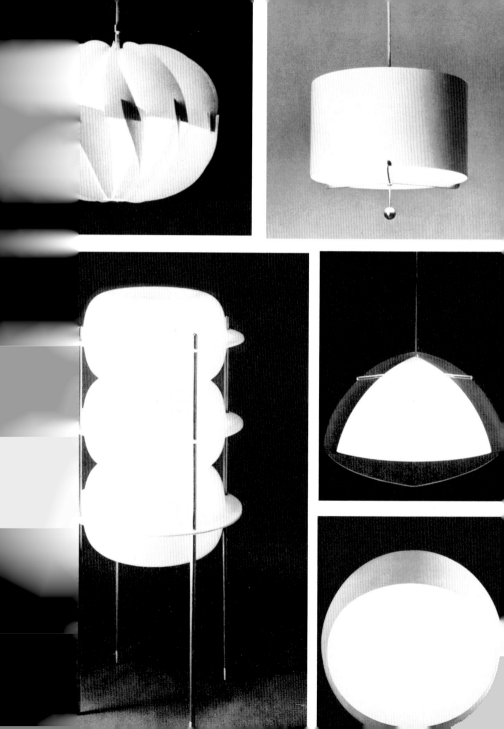

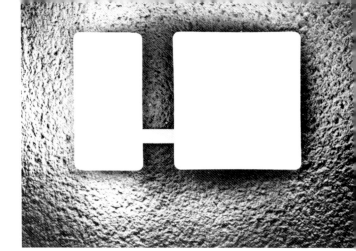

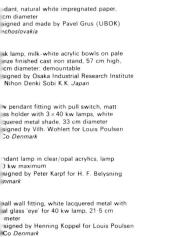

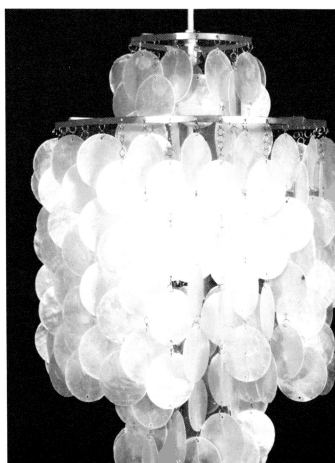

…dant, natural white impregnated paper,
…cm diameter
…signed and made by Pavel Grus (UBOK)
…choslovakia

…sk lamp, milk-white acrylic bowls on pale
…nze finished cast iron stand, 57 cm high,
…cm diameter: demountable
…signed by Osaka Industrial Research Institute
…Nihon Denki Sobi K.K. *Japan*

…v pendant fitting with pull switch, matt
…ss holder with 3 × 40 kw lamps, white
…quered metal shade, 33 cm diameter
…signed by Vilh. Wohlert for Louis Poulsen
…Co *Denmark*

…ndant lamp in clear/opal acryhcs, lamp
…) kw maximum
…signed by Peter Karpf for H. F. Belysning
…nmark

…all wall fitting, white lacquered metal with
…al glass 'eye' for 40 kw lamp, 21·5 cm
…meter
…signed by Henning Koppel for Louis Poulsen
…Co *Denmark*

…ie of a series of weatherproof box fittings for
…erior or exterior walls, graphite with satin
…al glass, here 20 × 20 cm + 20 × 11 cm
…erall
…esigned and made by Staff Leuchten GmbH
…*Germany*

…handelier, shells assembled on polished
…ass hoops, 32 cm diameter × 45 cm deep
…esigned by Verner Panton for J. Luber & Co
…*Germany*

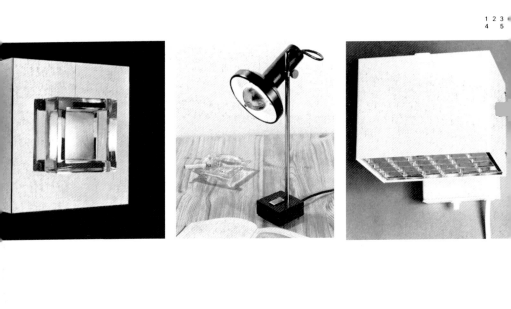

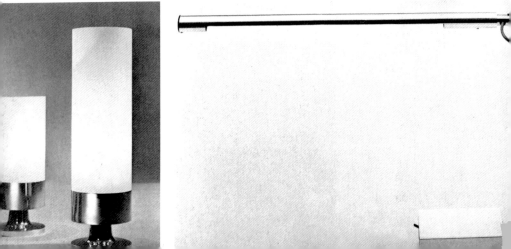

Wall light, polished chrome with crystal glass
lens' 28 × 28 cm; 16 cm deep
Designed and made by BAG Bronzewarenfabrik
AG Switzerland

Atlas Top Spot for desk, wall or ceiling
mounting, using domestic-type lamp
Designed and made by British Lighting
Industries Limited England

560 Bed lamp, iron, stove enamelled white or
brown with chromed screen of ABS plastic;
light may be adjusted and/or directed up or
down
Designed by Per Sundstedt for Lampan
Armatur Ab Sweden

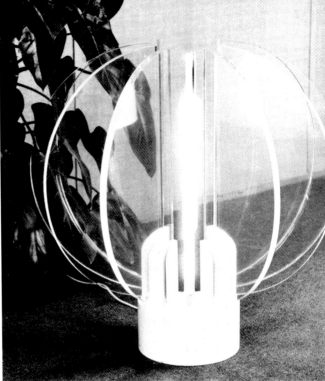

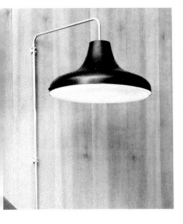

4
Consul table lamps, opal cylinders on weighted
polished aluminium bases, 10·1 diameter × 20·2
or 30·3 cm high
Designed by John Brown for Plus Lighting Ltd
England

5
Cantilever 41555 Mark II fluorescent desk
lamp, self-colour anodized aluminium with
black finished steel base: reflector rotates
and pivots about the stem which can be further
angled: overall 70·21 wide × 48 cm high
Designed by Gerald Abramovitz for Best &
Lloyd Limited England

6
LBSW swinging wall light, black or white
polystyrene shade over white louvres; 40·4 cm
diameter: anodized aluminium mounting
projects 55·19 cm
Designed by Ronald Homes for Conelight
Limited England

7
Floor lamp in metacrilato on aluminium base
lacquered white or orange
Designed by Gae Aulenti for Kartell s.r.l. Italy

8
The Ball weatherproof garden light, stainless
steel lacquered red and grey, 50 cm diameter
Designed by Max Ingrand for S. A. Max Ingrand
France

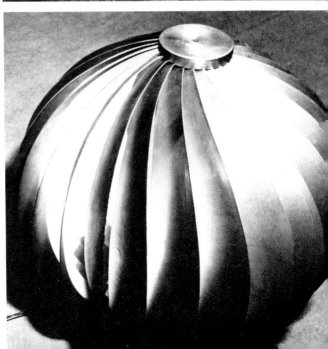

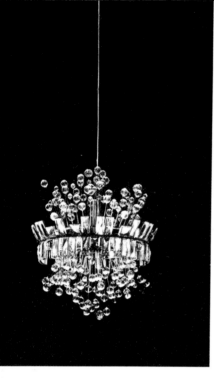

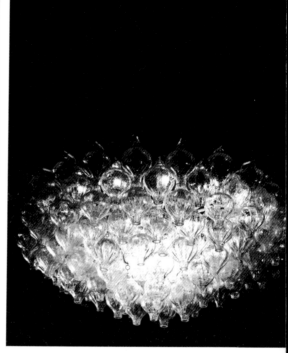

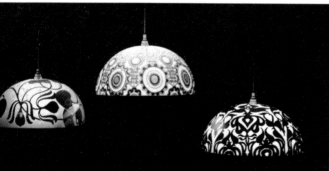

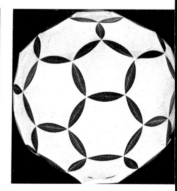

Chandelier, cut crystal and jewelry crystal
with polished brass mounting: 43 cm diameter
Designed by Ceno Kosak for J. & L. Lobmeyr
Austria

Tiffany pendants
Waterlily green and turquoise on blue 37 cm diameter
Designed by David Wren
Daisy purple/orange on white 40·4 cm diameter
Designed by Pauline Butler
Nouveau Beardsley black/white 40·4 cm diameter
Designed by Ian Logan
All for X-Ion Products Limited *England*

Tulipan chandelier blown clear glass petals'
from 20 cm to 1 m overall diameter
Designed and made by J. T. Kalmar *Austria*

Shade composed of demountable elements,
pentagons and hexagons of opalescent PVC,
40·4 cm diameter
Designed by Ch. M. Dethier for Ove *Belgium*

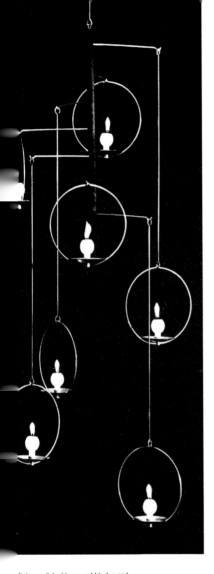

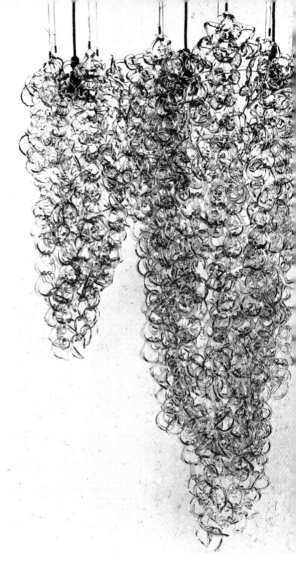

fitting, polished brass and black wood
...ed by Raija Aarikka, the candles by
...arpaneva: for Aarikka *Finland*

...:e-blue, violet, ruby, tea or clear
...ooks assembled here as a chandelier:
...ments may be freely arranged e.g. as
...* with an independent light source or
...ndirectly-lit curtain
...ed by Angelo Mangiarotti for Vistosi

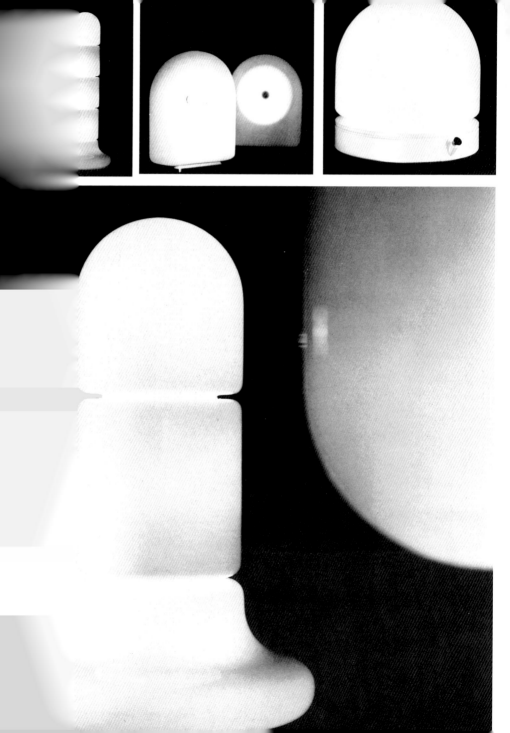

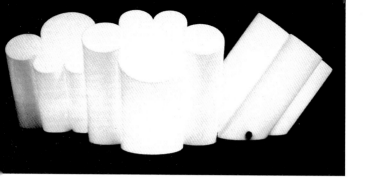

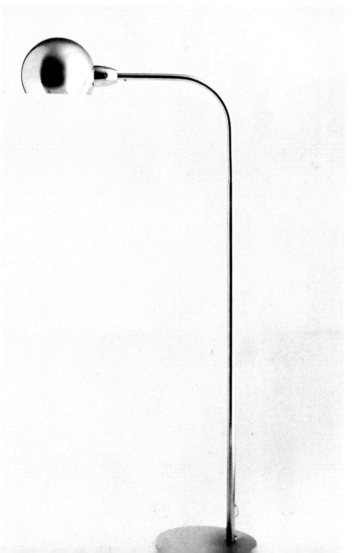

1 2 3 5
  4   6

1, 4
Table lamps composed of a base, a head and
one, two or three intermediate elements,
white glass : cm 52 diameter base × 74 high
2
Flattened globe table lamp, mould made white
glass with aluminium base : cm 44 high
All designed by Claudio Salocchi for Lumenform
Italy
3
Table lamp, Murano glass diffuser on lacquered
aluminium base with pushbutton control,
smoked rose glass/pearl white base or white
diffuser/dark maroon base : cm 45 high
Designed by Danilo and Corrado Aroldi for
Stilnovo s.p.a. *Italy*
5
Passiflora table light, yellow and white
Perspex : cm 38.5 high
Designed by Superstudio for Poltronova s.r.l.
Italy
6
Venticinque lamp with revolving head and
reflector, chromed metal : cm 110 high
Designed by Sergio Asti for Candle *Italy*

1

Cubelight, satin etched opal sphere with
amber or twilight Perspex cube
Designed and made by British Lighting
Industries Limited, *England*

2

Group of 'illuminated sticks' free arrangemer
cm 11.8, 19.6 and 27.4 deep
Designed and made by Staff & Schwarz Gm
W. Germany

3

Cirkel pendant fitting, inside opal glass, oute
havana brown or heliotrope transparent
glass cm 30.5 deep
Designed by Jo Hammerborg for
Fog & Mørup A/S, *Denmark*

4

Periscopio table lamps, metal fitting lacquere
amaranth,gloss black, pearl or ochre : cm 47 h
Designed by Danilo and Corrado Aroldi for
Stilnovo spa, *Italy*

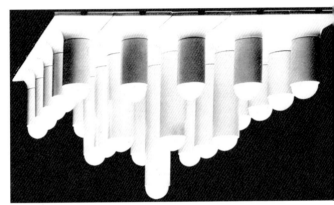

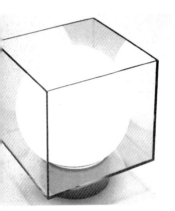

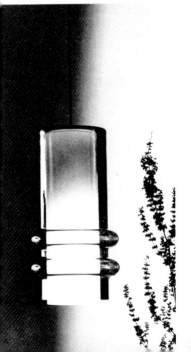

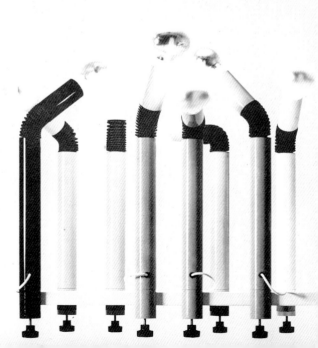

5
Self-assembly shades in heat-resistant
cardboard, plain white, green/yellow,
pink/orange, violet/turquoise or green/blue :
cm 25.4 cube
Designed and made by Staples and Gray,
England
6
Petal light in heat resistant card, white,
pink, orange or green : cm 46 diameter
Designed by Staples and Gray for Cosmo
Designs Limited, *England*
7
QD4/12/C4 fitting, extruded aluminium tubes,
anodised silver or straw-gold on steel ceiling
plate stove-enamelled black : cm 30 × 30 overall
Designed by Noel Villeneuve for Allom Heffer &
Company Limited, *England*
8
Cynthia pendant, metal structure : cm 55 square
Designed by Mario Marenco for Studio
Artemide, *Italy*

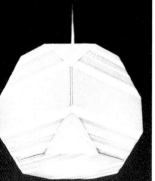

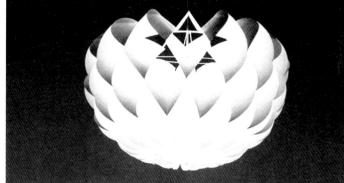

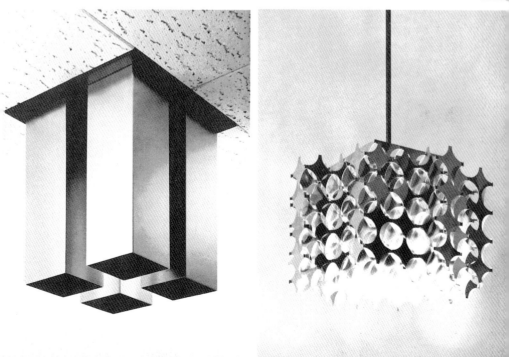

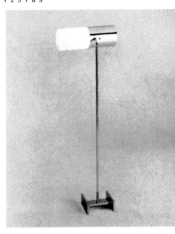

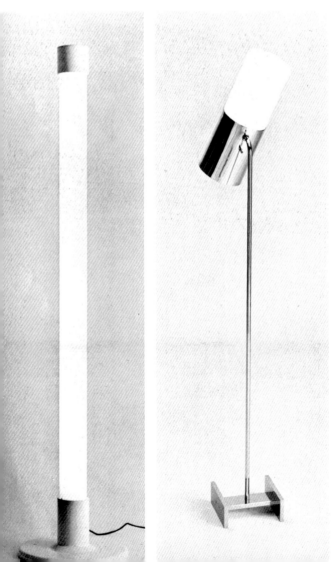

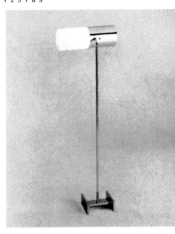

4 5 6
1 2 3 7 8 9

1
Tube standard, opaque white metacrilato with
iron lacquered white, green or black cm 142 high.
Designed by Nanda Vigo for Kartell s.r.l., *Italy*
2, 3, 7
Two standards, the shades of aluminium,
stems and stand chrome-plated brass:
2, 3 with acrylic diffuser: 7 with glass shelves.
Both designed by Paul Mayen for Habitat, Inc,
U.S.A.
4
Large floor lamp, opaque white glass and
chromed brass, seven light levels: cm 80 high
Designed by Gianni Celada for Fontana Arte,
Italy
5
Polaris table lamp, chromed metal armature
on marble base with white opal spheres:
Excelsior, the floor standard, has all-metal stand.
Designed by A. Natalini for Poltronova s.r.l.,
Italy
6
Bino lamp, metacrilato and metal:
cm 55 high with adjustable head
Designed by V. Gregotti, L. Meneghetti and
G. Stoppino for Candle, *Italy*

8
Vertical fluorescent tube light, aluminium
anodized or lacquered black, base steel and
rubber: cm 172 and 142 high
Designed by Claudio Salocchi for Lumenform,
Italy
9
Chimera standard, white Plexiglas: cm 180 high
Designed by Vico Magistretti for Studio
Artemide, *Italy*

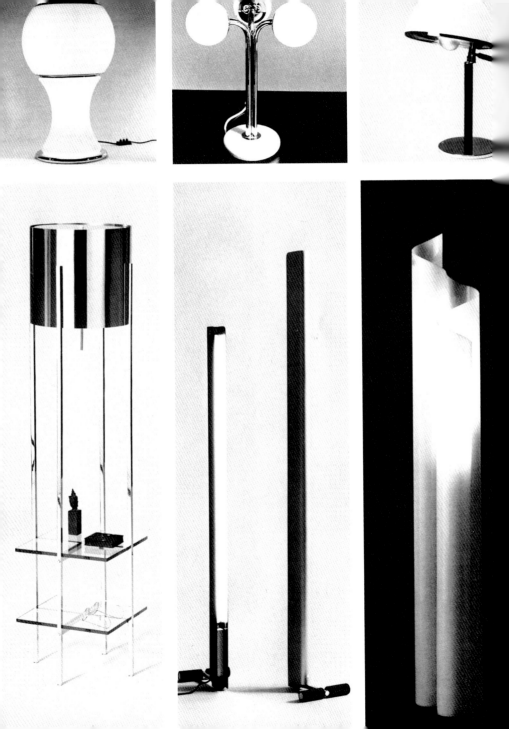

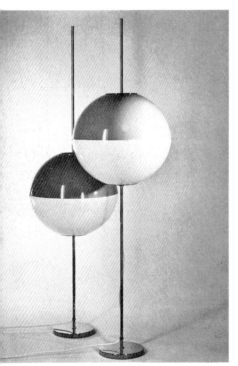

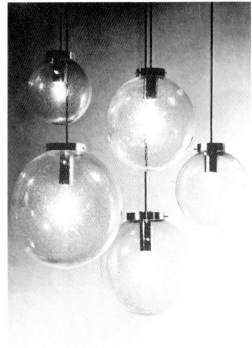

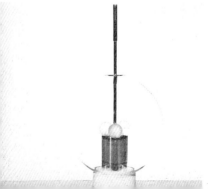

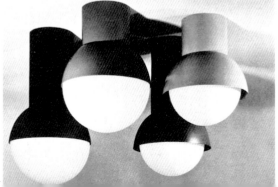

5, 6
Standard and pendant lamps, white lacquered
metal with split pine shades, natural colour:
cm 140 high × 44 diameter.
Pendant cm 60 diameter
Both designed by Hans-Agne Jakobsson for
Ellysett Ab, *Sweden*

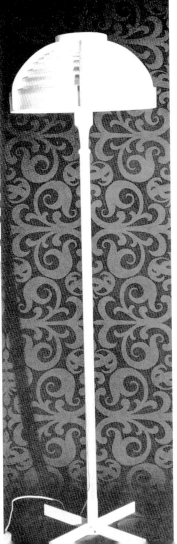

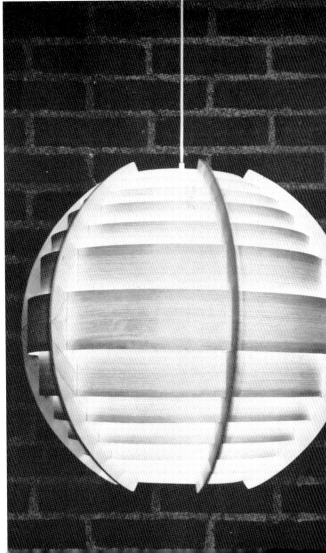

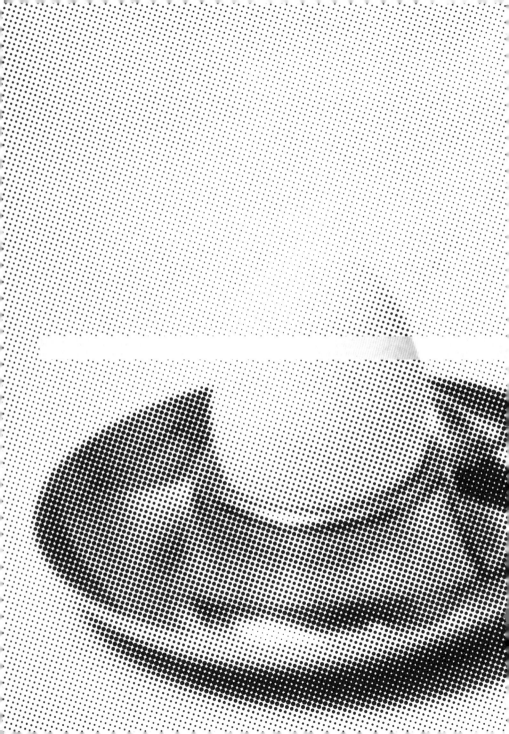

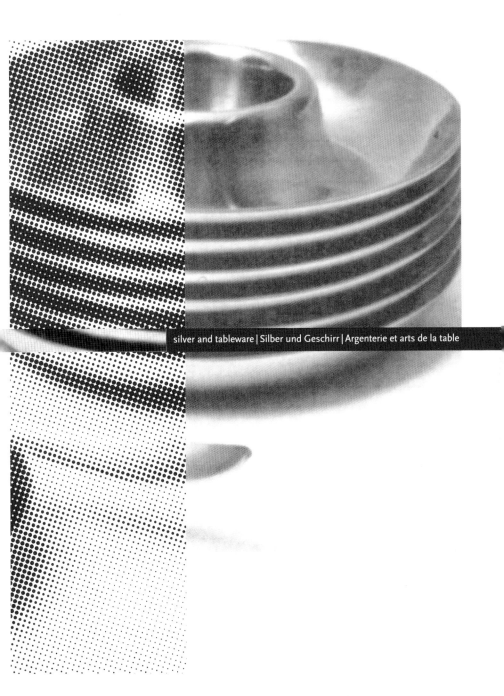

silver and tableware | Silber und Geschirr | Argenterie et arts de la table

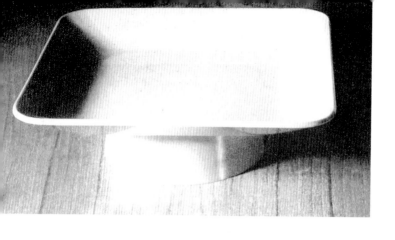

◀ Fruit dish in plastic, gre
vermilion, or black.
Designed by Shogoro Terashin
for the Tohyoh Plastic Co. L
JAPAN

Tray in Bangkok teak, 21¼ inch
long, from a series designed b
Th. Skjøde Knudsen for Skjø
Skjern DENMARK ▼

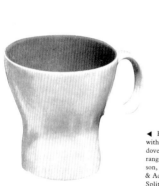

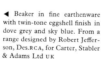

◀ Beaker in fine earthenware
with twin-tone eggshell finish in
dove grey and sky blue. From a
range designed by Robert Jeffer-
son, Des.RCA, for Carter, Stabler
& Adams Ltd UK

Split cane basket and tray, 15
inches diameter, natural and
two-tone finish, designed and
handwoven by Władysław Woł-
kowski POLAND

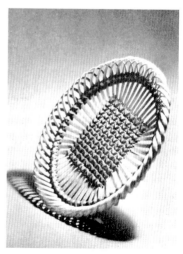

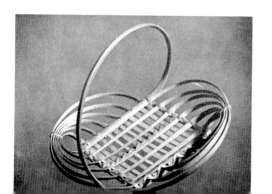

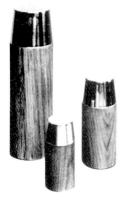

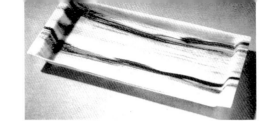

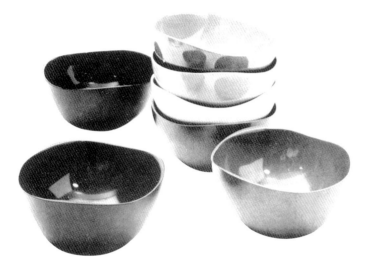

▲ Salt, pepper and sugar dredgers in teak and 18/8 stainless steel.
Designed by Heinz Decker for C. G. Hallbergs Guldsmeds AB, SWEDEN

Marbled light-grey and black opaque acrylic tray 20½ inches long, one of several opaque and transparent designs made in a wide range of colours by X-Lon Products UK

Soup bowls in Melamine, high-gloss finish, available in several colours including black, lime-yellow, forest green, cardinal red, gunmetal. Designed by Ronald E. Brookes, FSIA, for Brookes & Adams Ltd UK

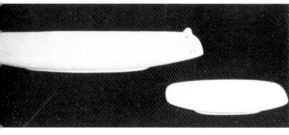

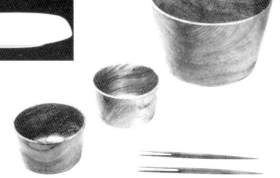

Sandwich plates in porcelain, white glaze, with handles in rattan. Designed by Tadashi Matsumoto for Sango Toki KK, JAPAN *Courtesy Japan Pottery Design Center*
Salad bowls in teak with servers in palissander.
Designed by Alfred Klitgaard for 'Alfi Teak' DENMARK

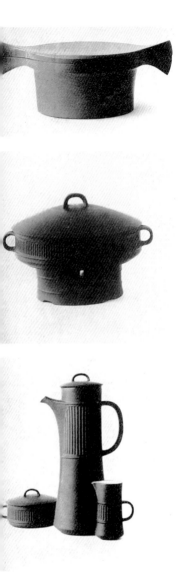

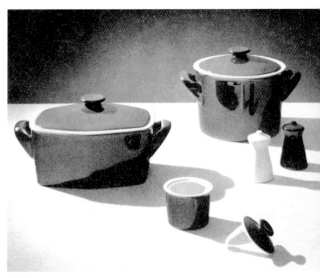

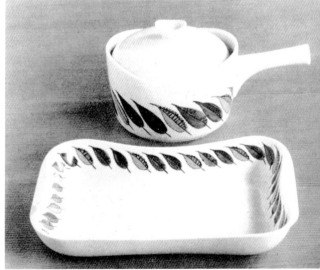

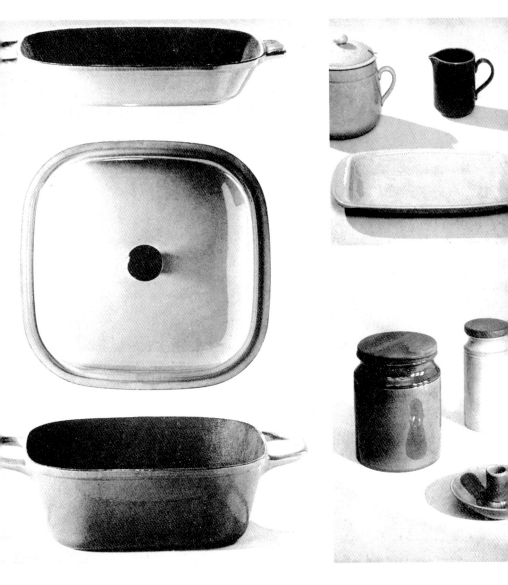

Square casserole and roasting dish in cast-iron red
vitreous enamelled ware; the lid is shaped to fit
either. From a range designed by Sigurd Persson
for Kockums SWEDEN

RIGHT: *Old Häganös* hand-thrown oven- and tableware: hard-fired earthenware with olive green,
mustard yellow, manganese brown, navy blue and
red glazes. Designed by John Andersson for
Andersson & Johansson AB, SWEDEN

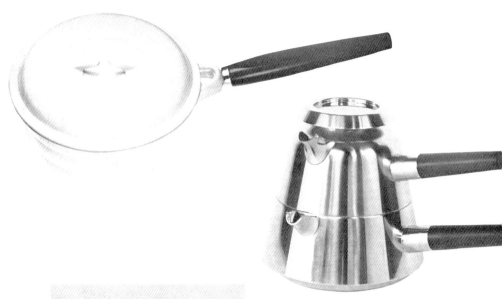

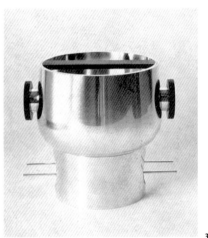

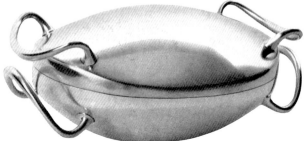

3

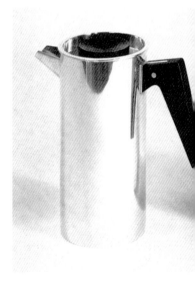

1 *Colorcast* vitreous-enamelled cast iron saucepa
blue ribbon, red pepper, or lemon rind (inside wi
A stackable design with machined base and
handle, made in three sizes by the Waterford
founders Ltd EIRE
2 Tea urn in stainless steel, designed by M
Stephensen; 3 sterling silver dish on spirit
base, designed by Søren Georg Jensen; 5 ova
with cover, sterling silver, designed by He
Koppel. All made by Georg Jensen Sølvsmed
DENMARK
4 Coffee pot in sterling silver with ebony handl
knob. Designed by Robert Welch, Des.RCA,
for J. & J. Wiggin Ltd UK

6 *Judge* stainless steel saucepan with black plastic fittings, with handle shaped to prevent the saucepan twisting in the hand. Designed by Misha Black, OBE, RDI, and Ronald Armstrong, of Design Research Unit, for Ernest Stevens Ltd UK

7 Pie blade and three-purpose picnic knife with serrated edge stainless steel blades and Whanghee cane or walnut handles. Made by Mills Moore & Co. Ltd UK

8 Iron frying pan or skillet with oven-proof black plastic hand grip, designed by Tomitaro Nachi for the Hakamada Co. JAPAN

9 *Dinette* ladles in Durfine stainless steel with spur non-slip handles in black nylon. Range awarded the Belgian 'Signe d'Or', designed by G. Beran for NV Gerritsen & Van Kempen HOLLAND

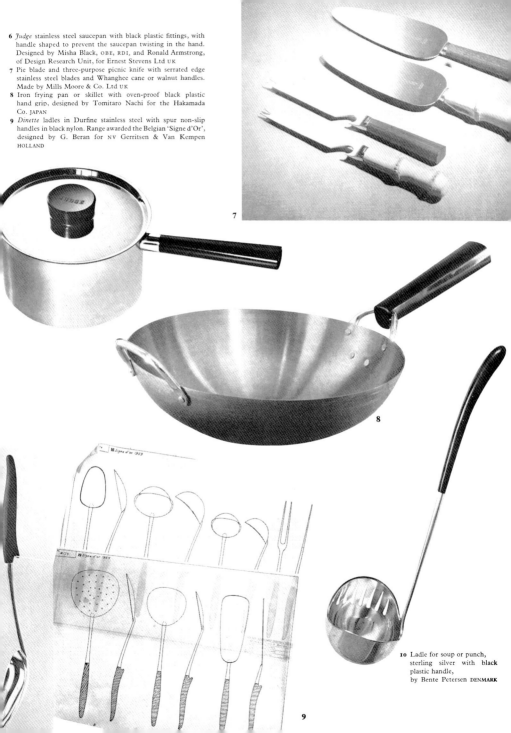

7

8

9

10 Ladle for soup or punch, sterling silver with black plastic handle, by Bente Petersen DENMARK

3

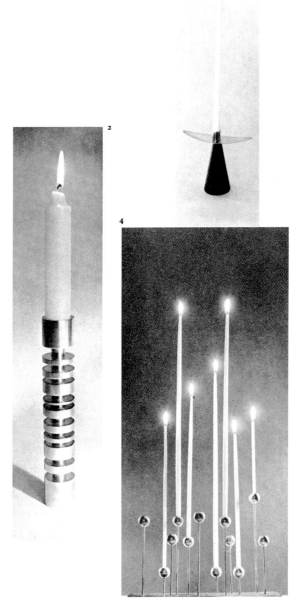

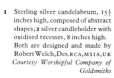

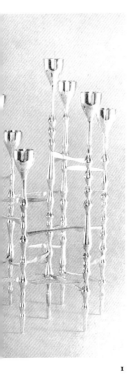

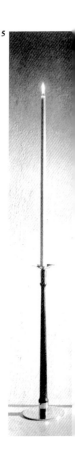

5

2

4

1

1 Sterling silver candelabrum, 15½
inches high, composed of abstract
shapes; 2 silver candleholder with
oxidised recesses, 8 inches high.
Both are designed and made by
Robert Welch, Des. RCA, MSIA, UK
Courtesy Worshipful Company of
Goldsmiths

3 Candleholder in ebonised wood
and polished brass designed by
Kenneth Clark and Paul Gell UK

4 Grouped candleholders in brass
on teak base. Unique piece
by Tapio Wirkkala for O/Y
Kultakeskus FINLAND

5 Hardwood candlestick, stained
and polished jacaranda, with
base and ring in polished brass.
Designed and made by Hans-
Agne Jakobsson AB, SWEDEN

6 Coffee set in sterling silver with
base and finials of coloured nylon.
Designed and made by Stuart
Devlin: Royal College of Art UK
Courtesy Worshipful Company of
Goldsmiths

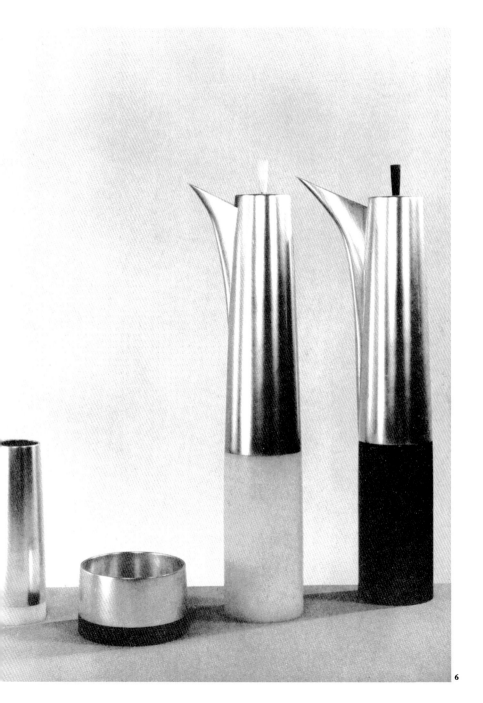

6

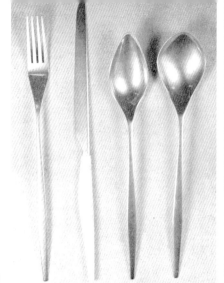

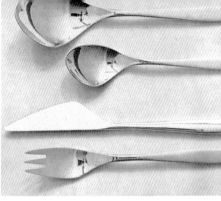

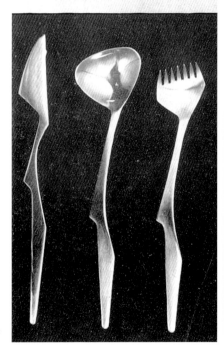

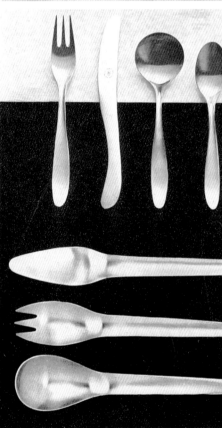

1

2

Flatware in sterling silver
1 Designed and made by Stuart
  Devlin: Royal College of Art UK
  Courtesy
  The Worshipful Company of
  Goldsmiths
2 Designed and made by Robert
  Welch, Des.RCA, MSIA, UK

Flatware in quality stainless steel
3 Designed and made by Sigurd
  Persson SWEDEN
4 Service No. 2721 designed by
  Don Wallance USA for C. Hugo
  Pott GERMANY
5 Three-piece child's set in 'Gero
  Zilduro' designed by D.W. Simonis
  for NV Gerofabriek HOLLAND

6 *Spring* service designed by David R. Mellor and Robert W
  Des.RCA, MSIA, for Walker & Hall Ltd UK
7 Service with nylon inlaid handles designed by Falle Ulda
  C. Thaysen & Co. DENMARK
8 *Opus* service designed by Tias Eckhoff for Dansk Kniv
  A/S, DENMARK
9 *Festi* service in 'Gero Zilduro' designed by D. W. Simon
  NV Gerofabriek HOLLAND

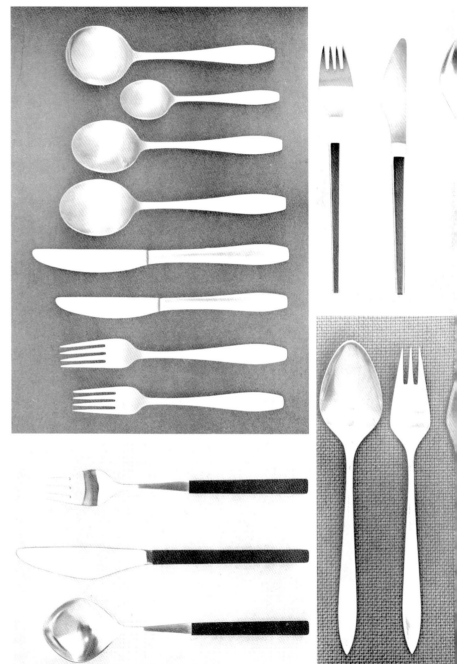

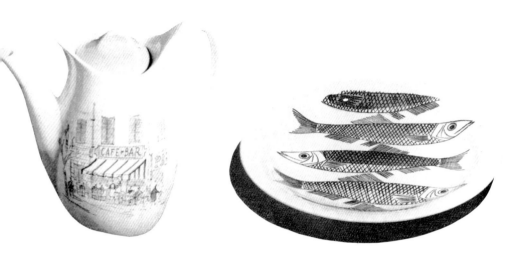

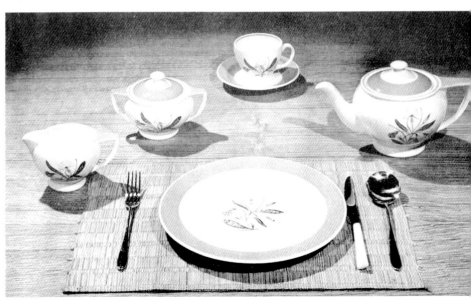

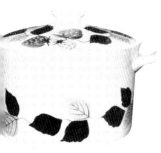

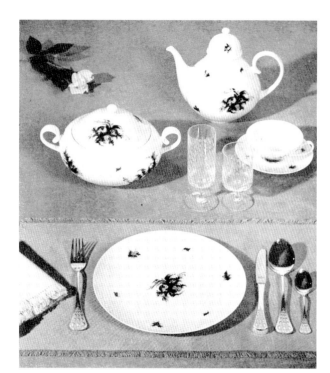

TOP ROW: Coffee pot in semi-porcelain white Staffordshire china from the *Riviera* range on 'Stylecraft Fashion' shape designed by Sir Hugh Casson, RDI, for W. R. Midwinter UK
Dinner plate from the service *My Garden* in ovenproof earthenware, white glaze with multicolour decoration.
Designed by Marianne Westman for AB Rorstrands Porslinsfabriker SWEDEN
Oven King casserole, ovenproof earthenware: high white with underglaze decoration in pink and green.
Designed by Fernando Farulli for Mancioli Natale S.C. ITALY

TOP RIGHT: *Romance* white porcelain tableware, cobalt blue underglaze decoration on relief-patterned body with complementary matching crystal glasses and silver. Designed by Bjørn Wiinblad DENMARK
Made by Rosenthal Porzellan AG, Rosenthal Glassworks, Rosenthal Domus GmbH GERMANY

◀ *Pink Campion* tea/dinner ware in fine earthenware with underglaze painted pink and grey decoration, grey-blue border.
Designed by Susie Cooper, RDI, for Susie Cooper Pottery Ltd UK

Danette service in faience, deep red exterior glaze with blue border decoration under greyish white glaze.
Designed by Nils Thorsson for The Royal Copenhagen Porcelain Manufactory A/S, DENMARK ▶

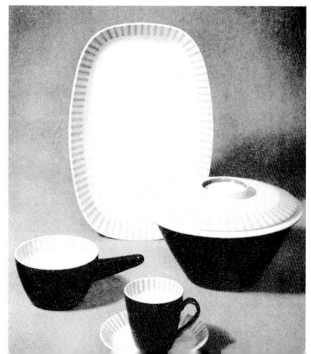

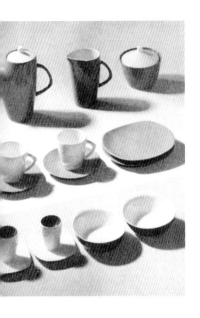

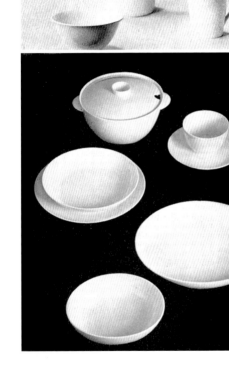

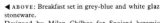

◀ ABOVE: Breakfast set in grey-blue and white glaze
stoneware.
Designed by Milan Chílbec for Spojené keramic
závody n.p. CZECHOSLOVAKIA
◀ White porcelain coffee service with overglaze 'st
decoration designed by Bele Bachem on *Berlin* sha
designed by Hans Theo Baumann; each cup bearing
different sign of the Zodiac.
Made by Rosenthal Porzellan AG, GERMANY
TOP: *Apollo* fine bone china Spode ware designed
Neil French and David White for W. T. Copeland
Sons Ltd UK
ABOVE: All purpose service No. 3510 in white porcela
made by Porzellanfabrik Langenthal AG, SWITZERLA

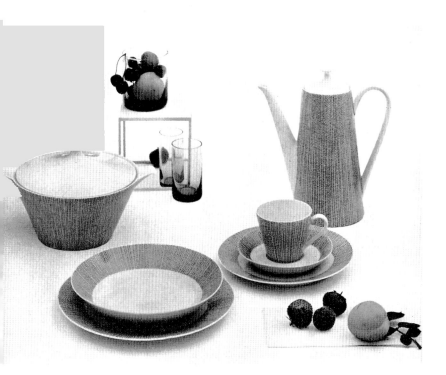

▲ White porcelain service with black linear decoration designed by H. Mayer on shape No. 311 designed by Heinrich Löffelhardt for Porzellanfabrik Schönwald GERMANY
Earthenware teapot, white glaze, with decoration in green, yellow, brown, black.
Designed by Pirkko Torvinen for Kupittaan Saviosakeyhtio FINLAND ▶
▼ Copper casserole with porcelain insert and detachable handle in teak (as shown): brass fittings.
Designed by Jens H. Quistgaard for Dansk Designs DENMARK

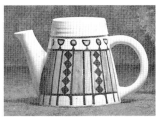

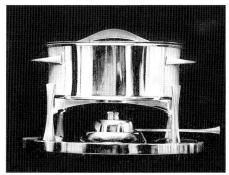

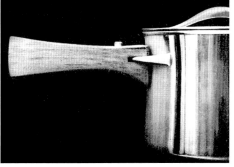

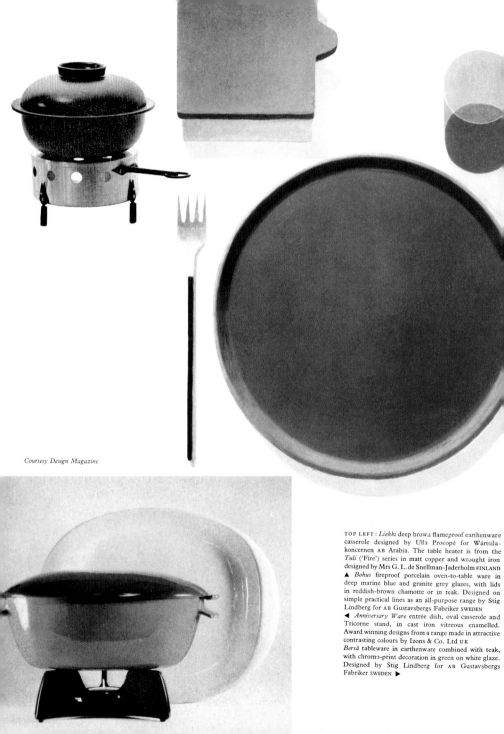

Courtesy Design Magazine

TOP LEFT: *Liekki* deep brown flameproof earthenware casserole designed by Ulla Procopé for Wärtsila-koncernen AB Arabia. The table heater is from the *Tuli* ('Fire') series in matt copper and wrought iron designed by Mrs G. L. de Snellman-Jaderholm FINLAND

▲ *Bohus* fireproof porcelain oven-to-table ware in deep marine blue and granite grey glazes, with lids in reddish-brown chamotte or in teak. Designed on simple practical lines as an all-purpose range by Stig Lindberg for AB Gustavsbergs Fabriker SWEDEN

◀ *Anniversary Ware* entrée dish, oval casserole and Tricorne stand, in cast iron vitreous enamelled. Award winning designs from a range made in attractive contrasting colours by Izons & Co. Ltd UK

Berså tableware in earthenware combined with teak, with chromo-print decoration in green on white glaze. Designed by Stig Lindberg for AB Gustavsbergs Fabriker SWEDEN ▶

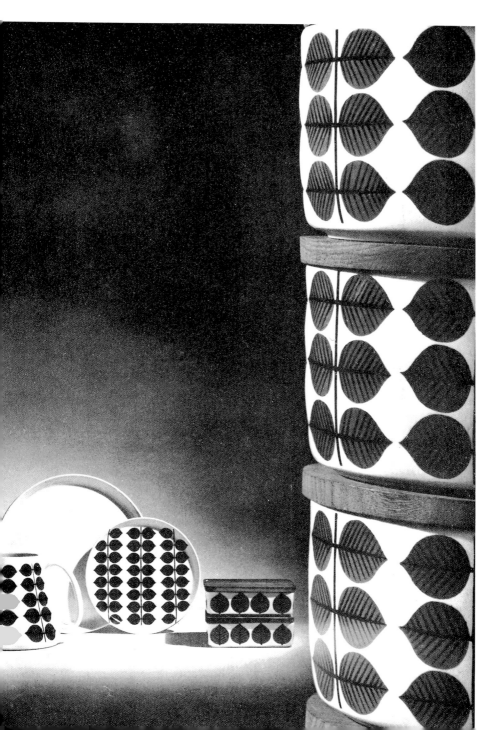

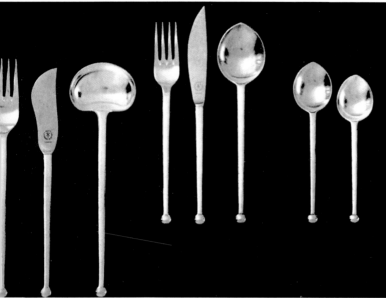

1

1 Range No. 86 in sterling silver designed by Dr. Josef Hoffmann for C. Hugo Pott GERMANY
3 Table set in sterling silver designed by Arne Jacobsen, m.a.a. for A. Michelsen DENMARK
6 Serving spoon and fork in silver with enamel inlay.
Designed by Agnar Skrede for David-Andersen NORWAY

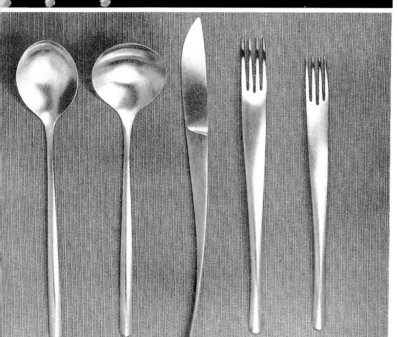

4 Table set with concave hollow ground fork bowl and serrated edge to knife blade, designed by Carl Pott.
Made in range No. 87 in sterling silver or No. 787 silver plated, by C. Hugo Pott GERMANY
7 Buffet servers from the Tjørn range in sterling silver.
Designed by Jens H. Quistgaard for Dansk Designs DENMARK

2 Prototype set in stainless steel.
Designed by Brian R. Marshall, Royal College of Art UK
5 *Spectra* table set in 18/8 stainless steel. Designed by Pierre Forssell for AB Gense SWEDEN
8 Nut crackers in stainless steel. Designed by Robert Welch, Des. RCA, MSIA, for J. & J. Wiggin Ltd UK

2

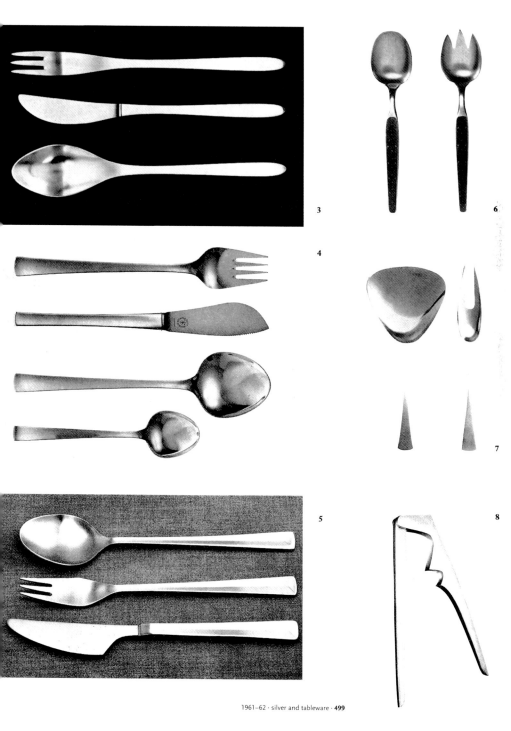

3

4

5

6

7

8

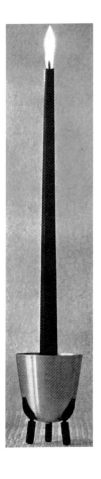

Candleholder from the *Tuli*
('Fire') series in copper, matt
finish, with wrought-iron feet.
Designed by Mrs G. L. de Snellman-
Jaderholm FINLAND

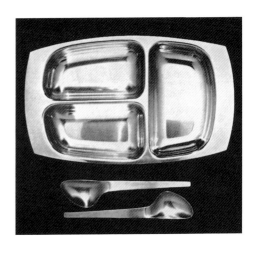

Three-portion vegetable dish
and servers in stainless steel
designed by Robert Welch,
Des.RCA, MSIA.
Dish made by J. & J. Wiggin Ltd,
servers by Mappin & Webb Ltd UK

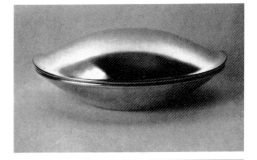

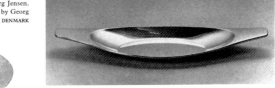

Vegetable dish designed by
Henning Koppel; tray designed
by Magnus Stephensen;
BELOW enamel-lined butter dishes
and ashtrays designed by
Søren Georg Jensen.
All made in sterling silver by Georg
Jensen Sølvsmedie A/S, DENMARK

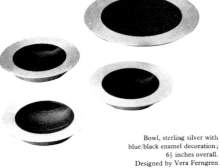

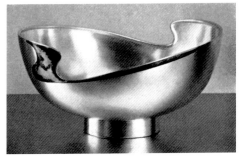

Bowl, sterling silver with
blue/black enamel decoration;
6½ inches overall.
Designed by Vera Ferngren
for C. G. Hallbergs Guldsmed AB, SWEDEN

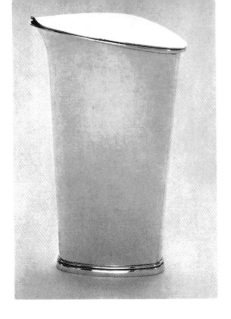

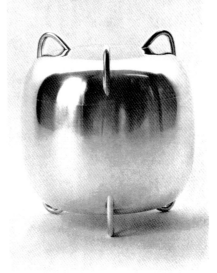

▲ Cocktail shaker in silver.
Designed by Åke Strömdahl for Hugo Strömdahl AB, SWEDEN
▶ Deep dish with fitted cover designed by Magnus Stephensen; tricorne bowl designed by Henning Koppel.
Both made in sterling silver by Georg Jensen Sølvsmedie A/S, DENMARK
▼ Enamels on copper in rich colourings, line or sgraffito decoration; large vase 18 inches deep.
Unique pieces by Edward Winter USA
Enamel on steel plate, copper-green figure on blue ground.
Unique piece by Bob Oldrich CANADA

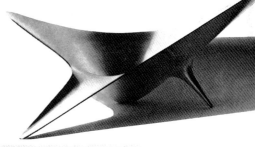

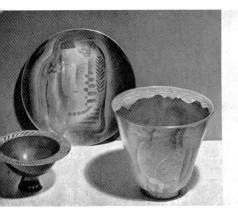

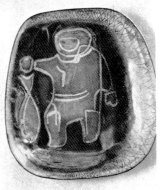

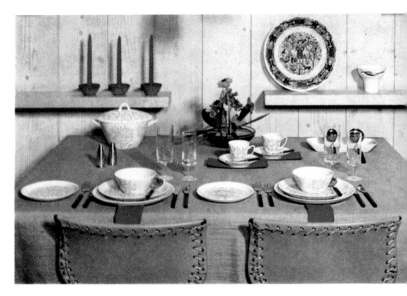

Table set with *Blue Berry* dinner and coffee service in porcelain, designed by Eystein Sandnes for Porsgrunds Porselænsfabrik; *Grenader* crystal by Axel Mörch for Magnor Glassverk; *Opus* stainless steel cutlery by Tias Eckhoff for Dansk Knivfabrik A/S. In the background teak candleholders by Frank V. Hansen, DENMARK, and ceramics designed by Anne Marie Ødegaard for Porsgrund NORWAY
Courtesy Designs of Scandinavia, London

Stoneware teapot from a series in matt and glossy brown glazes. Designed by Ulla Procopé for Wärtsilä-Arabia FINLAND

Teak condiment set designed by Mrs. G. L. de Snellman-Jaderholm FINLAND

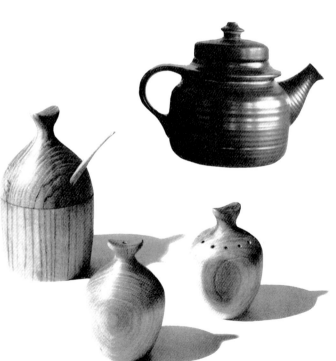

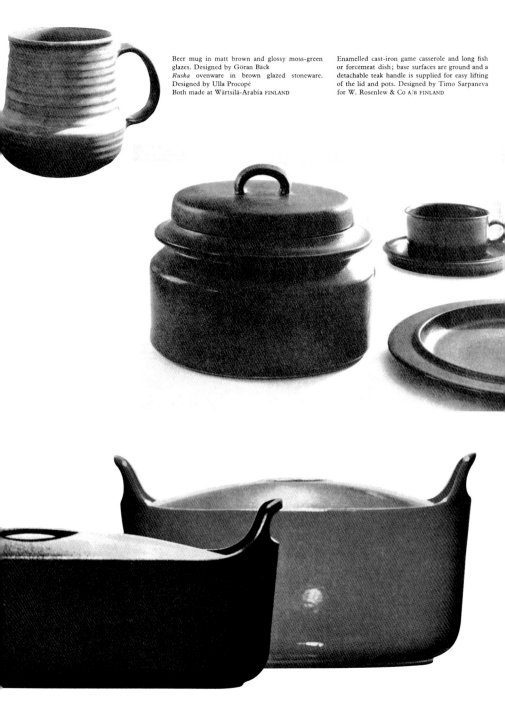

Beer mug in matt brown and glossy moss-green glazes. Designed by Göran Bäck
Ruska ovenware in brown glazed stoneware. Designed by Ulla Procopé
Both made at Wärtsilä-Arabia FINLAND

Enamelled cast-iron game casserole and long fish or forcemeat dish; base surfaces are ground and a detachable teak handle is supplied for easy lifting of the lid and pots. Designed by Timo Sarpaneva for W. Rosenlew & Co A/B FINLAND

inless steel flatware in 18/8 chrome-
kel-steel with black nylon handles;
  knife blades are of special high-
  de steel
signed by Bertel Gardberg for O/Y
kars AB FINLAND

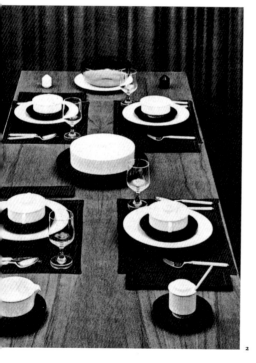

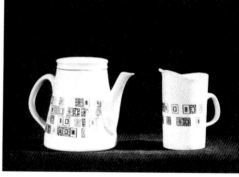

1

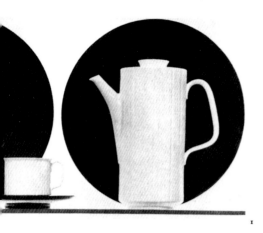

3
Teapot and jug in white china with litho decoration in two tones of yellow. Teapot 12·5 cm high
Designed by Georgia Turner, Royal College of Art UK

2

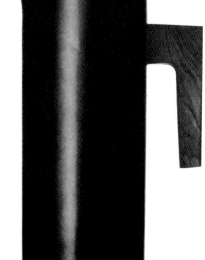

, 2
Variation dinner service in black and white with impressed design. Matching glasses with similar design on the bases. *Accord* porcelain-handled cutlery
all designed by Tapio Wirkkala, Finland, for Rosenthal Domus GmbH GERMANY

4
Thermos jug of aluminium, lacquered in black, red or olive, and with a teak handle; 26 cm high
Designed by Torben Lind for Torben Ørskov & Co DENMARK

PHOTO: JØRN FREDDIE

4

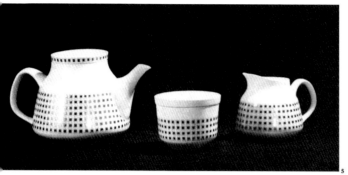

5, 6
Tea-sets in white china. Teapots
12·5 cm high. Shapes by Julia Chandler and Rosemonde M. Nuriac. **5**,
litho and applied gold decoration by
Rosemonde M. Nuriac. **6**, litho
decoration in pastel and gold by Julia
Chandler **7**,
Condiment set in white china with
impressed decoration and copper lids.
Tallest 12·5 cm high
Designed by John Dodson. All at the
Royal College of Art UK
8
Oval casserole, marmite and entrée
dish from the *Evesham* oven-to-table
range in fireproof porcelain. Made by
the Royal Worcester China Co Ltd UK

5

6

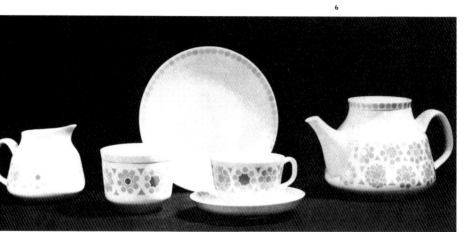

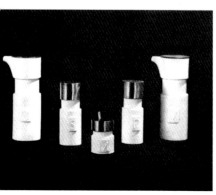

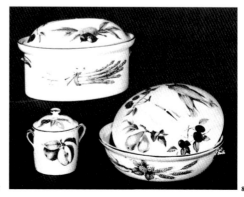

7

8

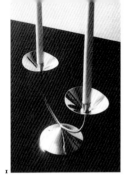

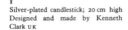

1
Silver-plated candlestick; 20 cm high
Designed and made by Kenneth
Clark UK

2
Vase and bowl of sterling silver
Designed and made by Heinz Decker
SWEDEN

3
Covered bucket-dish in sterling silver;
20 cm high
Designed by Erling Børup Kristensen
for Frantz Hingelberg DENMARK

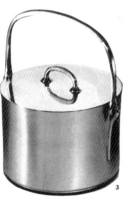

3

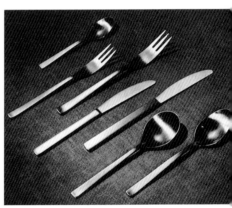

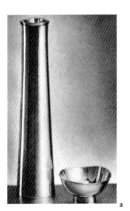

2

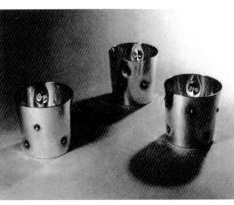

4

4
Sterling silver goblets
Designed by Barbro Littmarck
W. A. Bolin Hovjuvelerare SWEDE

5
Flatware in 18/8 chrome/nickel st
less steel, the knives of special stee
Designed by Bertel Gardberg
O/Y Fiskars AB FINLAND

6
Nocturne stainless steel flatware
Designed by Eric Clements
Mappin & Webb Ltd UK

7
Vase in sterling silver
Designed and made by Hugo Str
dahl AB SWEDEN

8
Goblets and tray in 18/8 chro
nickel steel, sterling silver and Alp
silver plate
Designed and made by C. Hugo
GERMANY

9
Rowena flatware in EPNS with st
less steel knife blade
Designed by Eric Clements
Heeley Rolling Mills UK

PHOTO 5: STUDIO WENDT
PHOTOS 6, 9: LEWIS
PHOTO 7: GRANATH

10

Small dish in 18/8 stainless steel with transparent porcelain enamels in olive, blue, burgundy and turquoise
Designed by Grete and Arne Korsmo for A/S Cathrineholm NORWAY

10

Small dish in 18/8 stainless steel with transparent porcelain enamels in olive, blue, burgundy and turquoise
Designed by Grete and Arne Korsmo for A/S Cathrineholm NORWAY

11

Candlestick in sterling silver; 23 cm high
Designed and made by John Grenville
Copyright the Worshipful Company of Goldsmiths UK

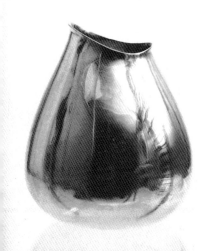

7

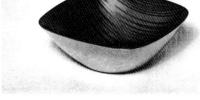

10

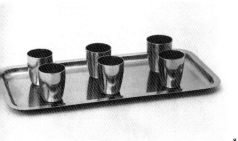

8

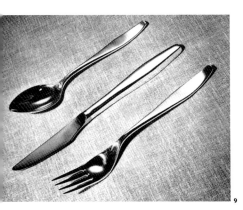

9

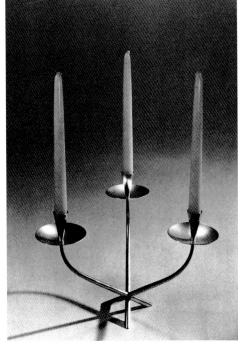

11

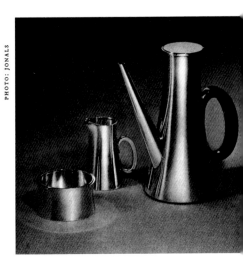

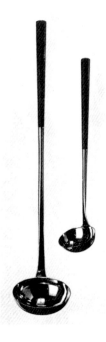

1
Soup ladles in stainless steel with teak
handles
Designed and made by Heinz Decker
SWEDEN

2
Coffee service in sterling silver, the pot
with ebonite handle; 23 cm high
Designed by Erling Børup Kristensen
for Frantz Hingelberg DENMARK

3
Coffee service in EPNS with lids
and handles in teak: coffee-pot 20 cm
high

4
'Instant-coffee' service in EPNS with
clip-on spoons; lids and tray in teak.
The cream pot seals hermetically and
can be put into the refrigerator com-
plete with contents
Both designed by Karl Dittert for
Gebrüder Kühn GERMANY

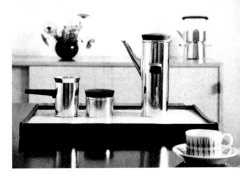

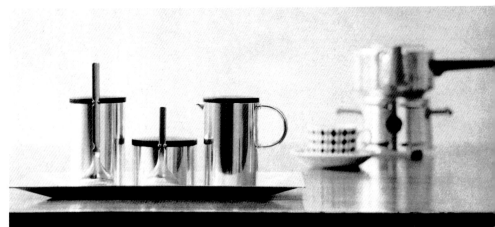

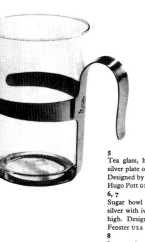

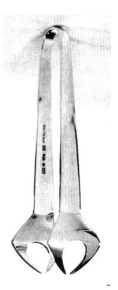

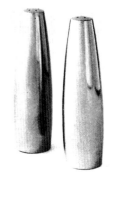

5
Tea glass, handle in sterling silver, silver plate or stainless steel
Designed by Wolfgang Tümpel for C. Hugo Pott GERMANY
6, 7
Sugar bowl and creamer in sterling silver with ivory handles; each 10 cm high. Designed and made by Fred Fenster USA
8
Ice tongs in sterling silver
Designed and handmade by Hugo Strömdahl AB SWEDEN
9
Salt and pepper shakers in stainless steel
Designed by Jens H. Quistgaard for Dansk Designs DENMARK

9

10
Condiment set in sterling silver
Designed by Tony Laws
Made by Laws & Stevens UK
PHOTO: RICHARD EINZIG

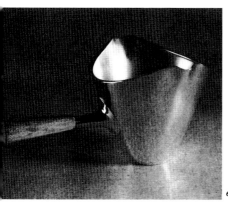

6

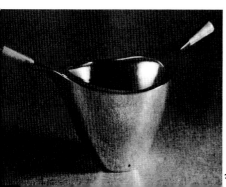

7

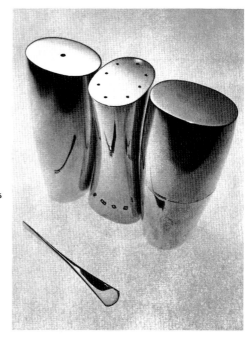

10

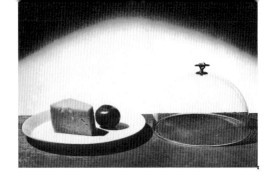

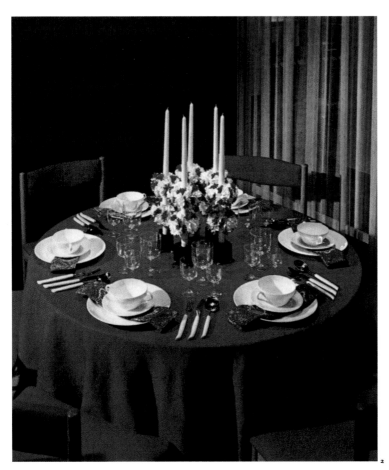

1
Domed cheese or food cover,
acrylic with gilt brass knob; 23 ?
cm diameter
Designed by Noel Lefebvre for X?
Products UK

2
Festive setting arranged with *S?*
fine white bone china, made by J?
Wedgwood & Sons Ltd and *Con?*
seur full lead crystal glasses des?
by S. Fogelberg for Thomas We?
Sons Ltd
The cutlery *Victor* is in stainless
with Xylonite handles
Designed by Eric Cork for Thoma?
Cork & Sons Ltd
All on a cloth of textured linen ma?
thirty-one colours; 122 cm wide
Fidelis Furnishing Fabrics Ltd u?
Setting designed by Elgin Ande?
for the *Daily Telegraph*

3
Green *Charade*, a 122 cm woven r?
by Nicholas Sekers for the West C?
berland Silk Mills, is the backgr?
to Spode *Elizabethan* white-and?
fine bone china tableware, Royal
lege shape. Designed by Neal Fr?
for W. T. Copeland & Sons Ltd
Wayside goblets are lead crystal
hand-engraving, designed and ?
by Harold Gordon; the fruit b?
Whitefriars M114 are designed
W. J. Wilson for James Powell & ?
(Whitefriars) Ltd
Chairs, suitable for outdoor as w?
indoor use, upholstered in *Nauga?*
on polished aluminium frames,
designed by Charles Eames for S. ?
& Co Ltd; *Pride* EPNS or sterling s?
cutlery and flatware, with stai?
steel knives, the handles of Ivor?
ivory, designed by David Mello?
Walker & Hall Ltd UK
Backcloth, a wool-texture acryl ?
fabric; 152 cm wide, in the *Mid?*
Sun Swedish range from Co?
Fabrics Ltd UK
Setting arranged by Mary Green ?
Sunday Telegraph

The two settings photographed
courtesy of the Council of Indus?
Design, by SPICE PHOTOS

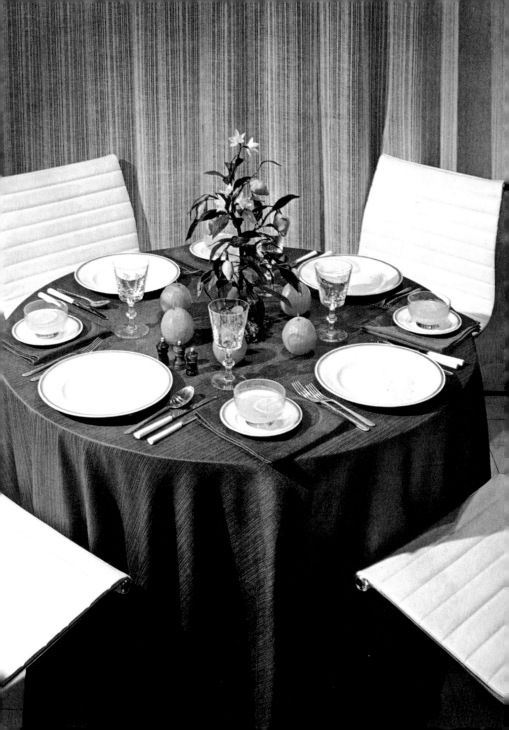

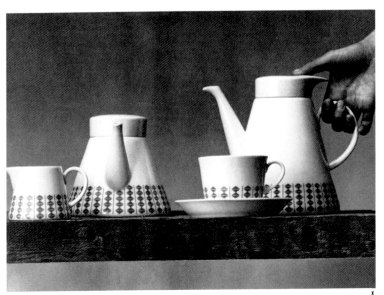

1

Good Morning breakfast set in fla
resistant hard-fired porcelain, d
rated or plain white; the lids to tea
coffee pots are unusually deep
tongued for thumb-control
Designed by Nanny Still for La
celaine de Baudour BELGIUM

2

Contrast oven-to-table fine eart
ware range with matt black/soft w
glaze
Designed by David Queensbury
W. R. Midwinter Ltd UK

1

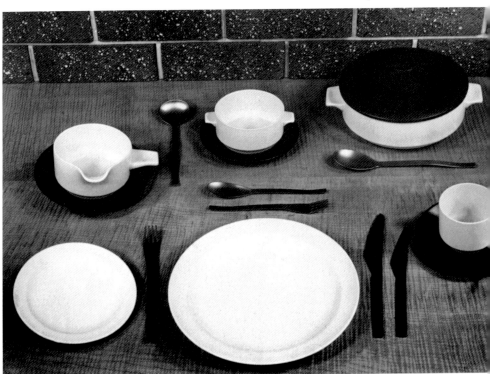

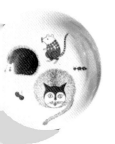
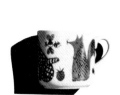
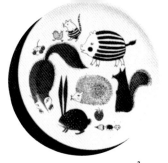

3

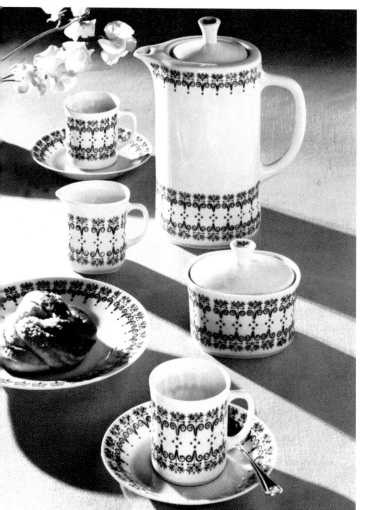

3
Noah's Ark children's ware in fine white earthenware with underglaze multicolour decoration
Designed by Gunvor Olin for Wärtsilä-koncernen A/B FINLAND
4
Aurora white feldspar china coffee set with silkscreen print decoration in blue
Shape designed by Sven Erik Skawonius, decoration by Alf Jarnestad. Made at Upsala-Ekeby AB SWEDEN

PHOTO 1 ROGER ASSELBERGHS
PHOTO 3 PIETINEN
PHOTO 4 ESSELTE

4

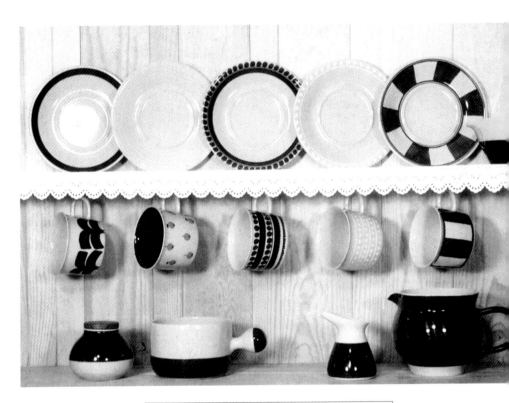

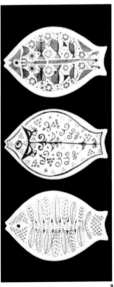

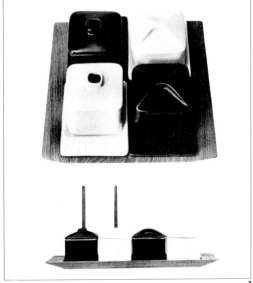

1
Cups and saucers, jugs and
variously decorated, from a stu
produced range in stoneware
Designed by Marianne West
for AB Rörstrands Porslinsfab
SWEDEN

2
Fish sideplates, Series 2359,
glaze white feldspar porcelain d
rated in blue; 20 cm long
Designed by Arne Lindaas for F
grunds Porselænsfabrik NORWAY

3
Small square jars with two types c
and square plates in midnight b
white or black/white *Domino* porc
ware; a series designed for flexibl
and arrangement on a square or m
angular wood base
Designed by Nanny Still for La
celaine de Baudour BELGIUM

4
Composition range of tableware
cutlery with stemmed cups and b
and a surface band which ca
either a motif or a flat band of cc
Designed by Tapio Wirkkala
LAND
Table glass *Composition G* is desi
by Claus Josef Riedel and Ric
Latham USA
All for Rosenthal AG W. GERMA

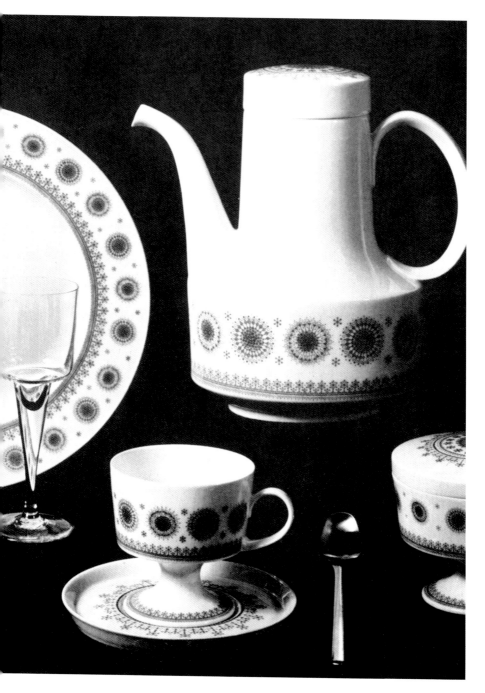

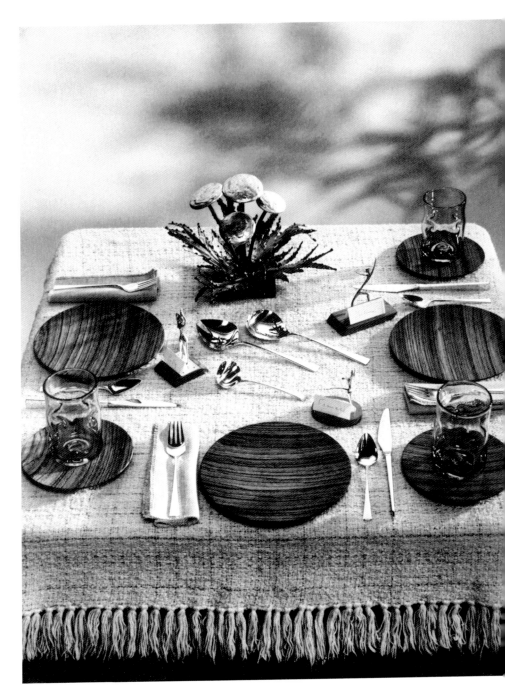

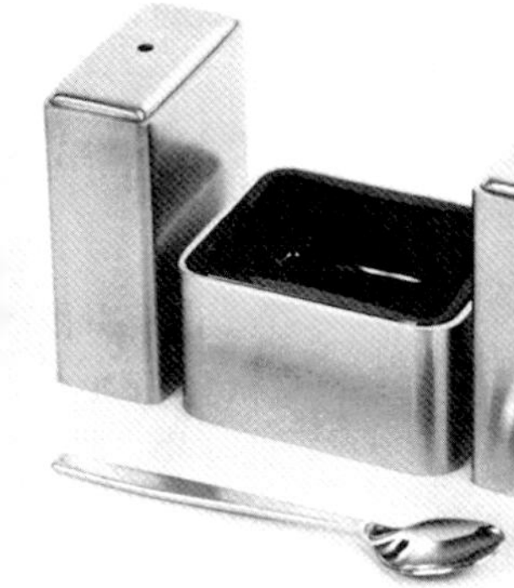

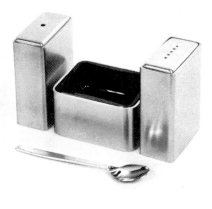

2

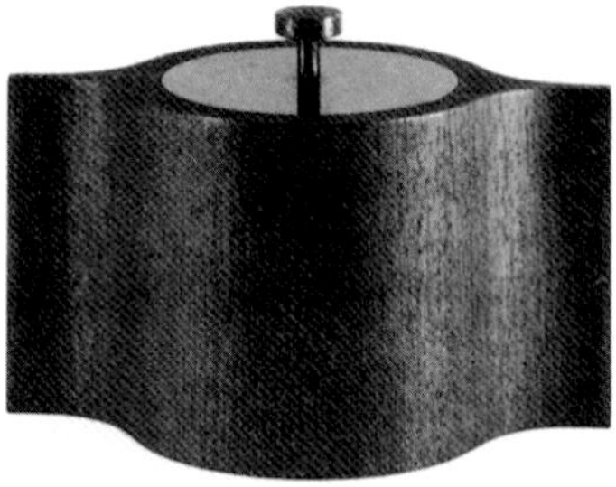

4

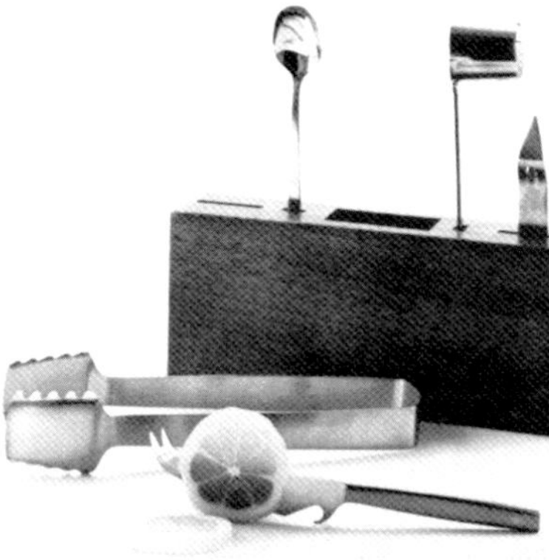

3

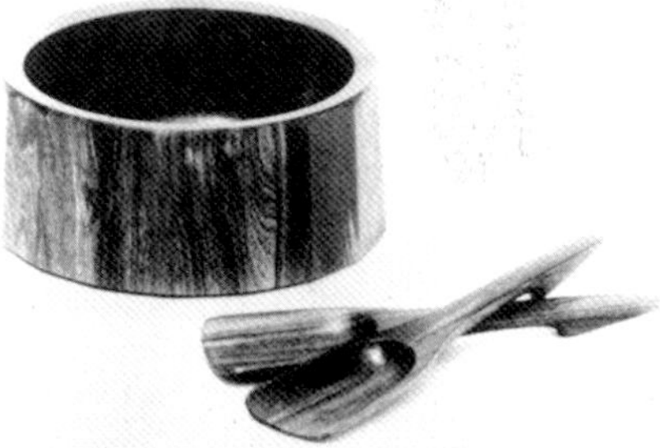

5

mal luncheon table set with
ıg silver, copper and wood on
ol texture fringed cloth hand-
ı by Catherine Welsh
a' wood dishes are by Gordon
r—the smaller size used as
rs under hand-blown dimpled
o amber glass tumblers; Sterling
flatware *Dimension* was designed
hn Pripp for Reed & Barton
figurine place-card-holders are
Gerald Foley, and the *Golden*
elion centrepiece of brazed and
d metals; 23 cm high, is by John
k
ıg arranged by Betty Alswang at
ica House, New York USA

ea brick shape three-piece con-
nt set and bar set in satin-finish
less steel; the slotted mahogany
all has a stain-resistant finish
liment set designed by Gerald
ey; bar set designed by Bedard
son USA for Viners Ltd UK

4
Ice bucket moulded in wengé, insulated, and with frosted acrylic lid
Designed by Th. Skjøde Knudsen for Skjode DENMARK

5
Salad bowl and servers in palissander, Series 1683/87; 28 cm diameter
Designed by Jens H. Quistgaard for Dansk Designs DENMARK

6
Antipasto tray Series 357 in green or amethyst demi-cristal, acid etched; wood server
Designed by Sergio Dello Strologo for Il Sestante ITALY

PHOTO 1 HANS VAN NES
PHOTOS 2, 3 WARD HART
PHOTO 4 HAMMERSCHMIDT
PHOTO 6 CASALI

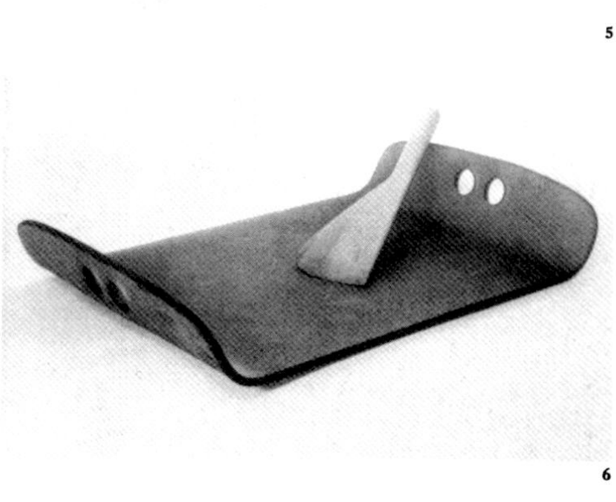

6

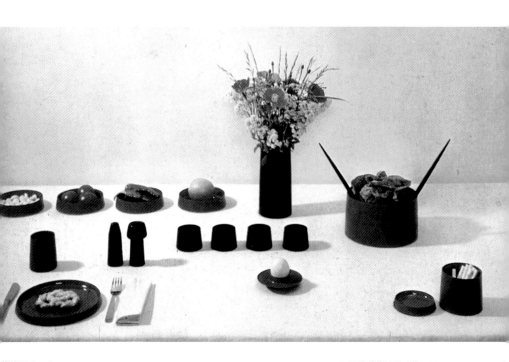

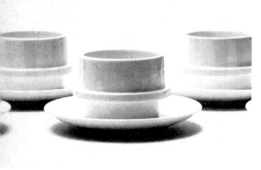

2

1
Table set with Melamine ware series 636/9, also available in dark grey and brown
Designed by Kristian Vedel for Torben Ørskov & Co DENMARK

2, 3
Handleless coffee cups in white glazed hard faience
Designed by Göran Bäck
Teapot, plate and covered dish in ovenproof stoneware with hand-painted underglaze decoration blue *Anemone* or brown *Rosmarin*
Designed by Ulla Procopé

All for Wärtsilä-koncernen AB Arabia FINLAND

4–6
Table set with white china dinner service *Galaxie*, and *Black Basalt* fine stoneware coffee set, bowls and plates
Designed by Robert Minkin for Josiah Wedgwood & Sons Ltd
White opaque glass tumblers
Designed by Timo Sarpaneva for Karhula-Iittala FINLAND
Odin stainless steel servers and cutlery
Designed by Jens H. Quistgaard for Dansk Designs DENMARK
All on chequered table mats and

matching plain napkins made of Thai silk from Liberty & Co UK
Setting arranged by Babette Hayes at Josiah Wedgwood & Sons Ltd UK

PHOTO 2 ARKO HALLAKORPI
PHOTO 3 PIETINEN
PHOTO 4 AD PHOTOGRAPHY

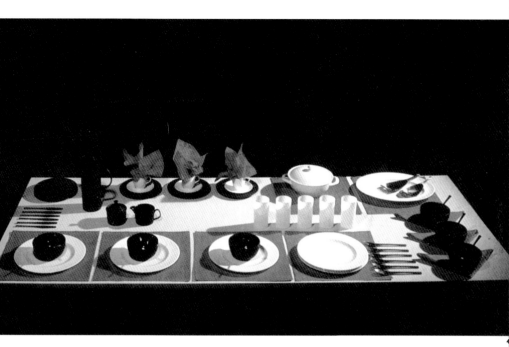

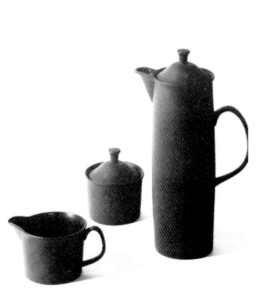

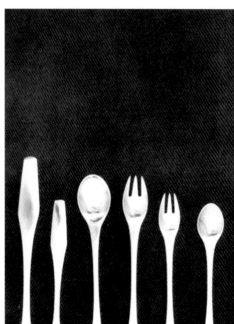

1
Enamelled-steel bowl with glass-hard surface; available in white, red, blue or olive
Designed by Kaj Franck for Wärtsilä-koncernen A/B Arabia FINLAND
2
Ash and cigarette boxes, each made from the same tube steel and black anodised aluminium, with cork base. The ash box is fitted with a removable

disc which isolates the ash and its odour: the cigarette box with a lid of smoke grey Perspex and transparent interior fitting designed and made by Christophe Gevers BELGIUM
3
Candelabra of knotless redwood, natural finish.
Designed by Hans-Agne Jakobsson for Bertil Johansson SWEDEN

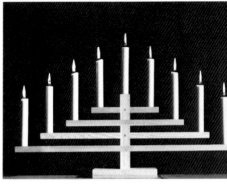

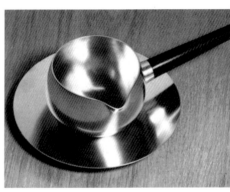

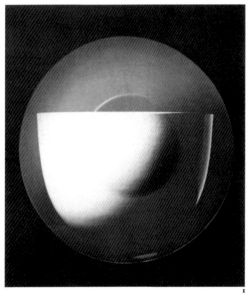

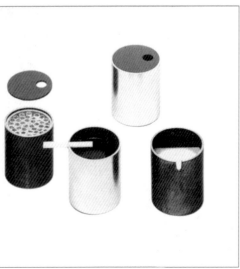

4, 5
Silver bowl and butter pipkin with ebony handle; 7 and 16 cm diameters
Silver bell on ebony stand; 13 cm high
Designed by Henning Koppel for Georg Jensen Sølvsmedie A/S DENMARK
6
Table ash box; a 6 or 8 cm cube of opaque melamine, black, red or grey, with extractible ash receptacle in aluminium anodised light grey
7
Floor ash box Series 2001A of square section anodised aluminium, with extractible inner ash receptacle and stabilized base: available in grey, natural, black or chestnut finish; 42 or 56 cm high
8
Sweet dishes in alpacca metal, cut, folded and welded from a single sheet; satin finish interior with a high polish outside
All designed by Bruno Munari for Danese ITALY
9
Cast iron fruit stand, vitreous enamelled matt black. 15 cm high, 25 cm diameter. Designed and made by Robert Welch UK

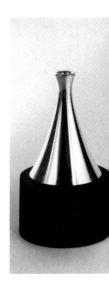

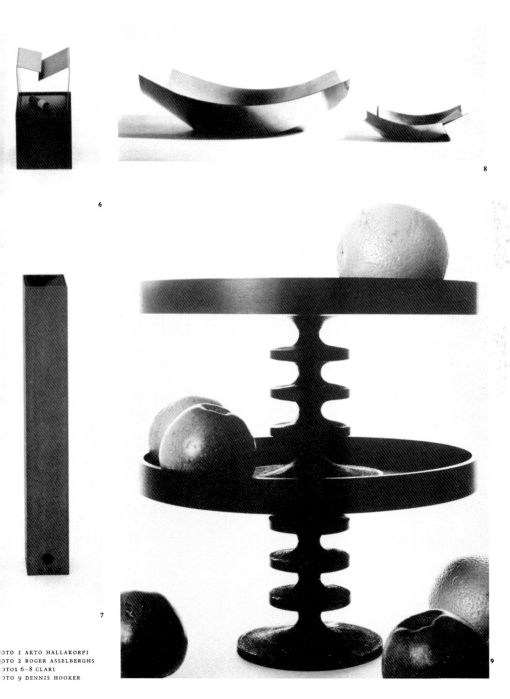

6

8

7

9

OTO 1 AKTO HALLAKORPI
OTO 2 ROGER ASSELBERGHS
OTOS 6–8 CLARI
OTO 9 DENNIS HOOKER

Embassy flatware in hand-forged
sterling silver, stainless steel blades
satin finish
Designed and made by David
Mellor UK

Cutlery in stainless steel with
satin-finished handles
Designed by Industrial Arts
Institute and made by Kobayashi
Kogyo KK JAPAN

Cheese knife in stainless steel
Designed by Ilmari Tapiovaara for
Hackman & Co FINLAND

Cutlery 1300 in stainless steel
Designed by Marianne Denzel for
Vereinigte Metallwerke Ranshofen-
Berndorf AG AUSTRIA

Stainless steel flatware
Designed by Henning Koppel for
George Jensen Sølvsmedie A/S
DENMARK

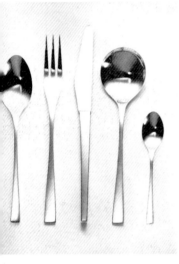

courtesy C.O.I.D.

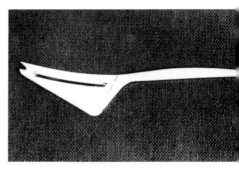

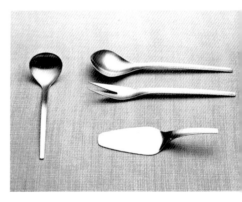

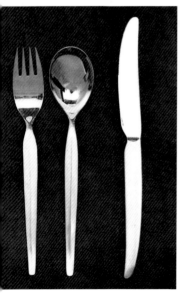

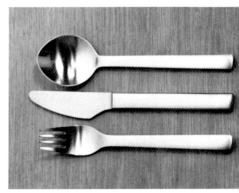

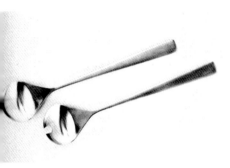

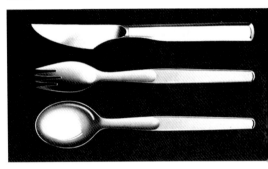

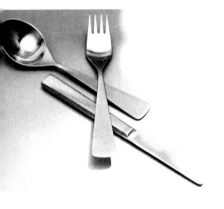

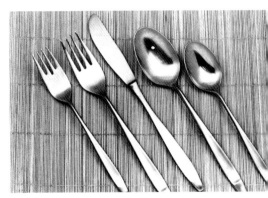

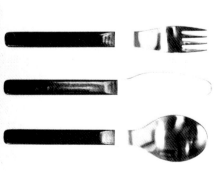

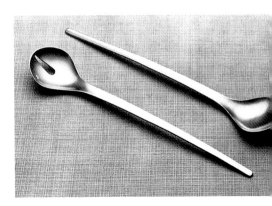

Combined egg cup and saucer 599/16
'Modular' trays and entrée dishes
the smallest 140 × 85 mm
Candle-holder for five candles.
Flatware series 2725, the knives
of special steel.
All in 18/8 chrome/nickel steel, the
trays available also in sterling silver
or alpaca silver plate
Designed by Carl Pott for C. Hugo
Pott Besteck W. GERMANY

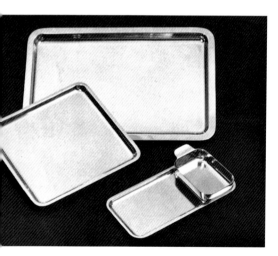

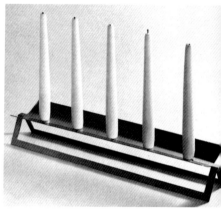

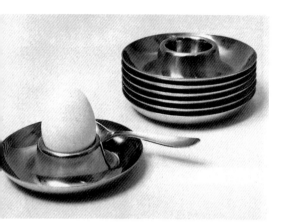

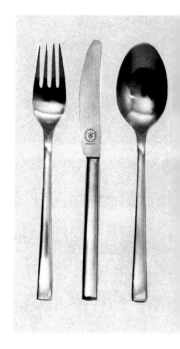

e jug with stackable cream
nd sugar bowl in stainless steel
palisander handles,
e-pot, 16 cm high
gned by Ib Bluitgen for
rsen & Burchardt A/S DENMARK

e- and tea-pots in silver and
ood, the coffee-pot 23 cm high
e by Robert Welch UK

Combined tea-pot and hot water jug,
copper with brass handles and
spouts, 37 cm high
Designed by Ib Bluitgen for
H. A. Gruberts Sonner DENMARK

New Wave cutlery in 12/12 stainless
steel
Designed by C. Melville Cass for
John Sanderson & Son Ltd UK

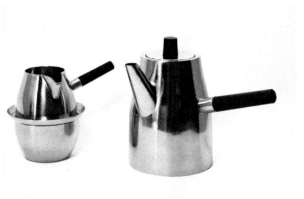

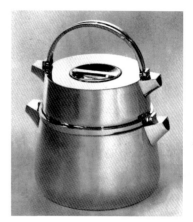

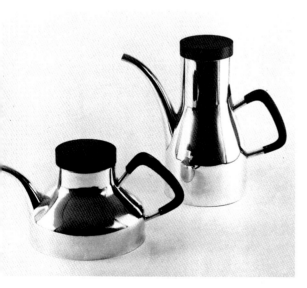

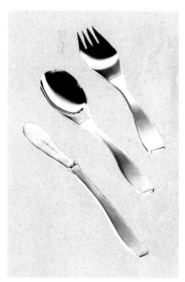

Coffee set 5140 in Gero Zilmeta
stainless steel with wine-red nylon
handles and lids
Designed by Dick Simonis for NV
Gerofabriek HOLLAND

Candle-holders of square-section
chromiated brass, single holder L88:
4-flame L87, tallest 37 cm high
Designed by Hans-Agne Jacobsson
for Hans-Agne Jacobsson AB SWEDEN

Bonbonniere, silver with knob
cut from Swedish granite
Designed by Heinz Decker for
Heinz Decker Silversmide SWEDEN

Oil and vinegar set, 20 cm high
Designed by Marianne Denzel for
Vereinigte Metallwerke Ranshofen-
Berndorf AG AUSTRIA

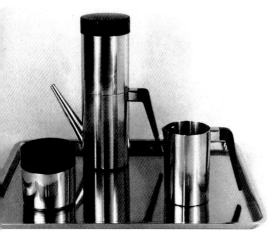

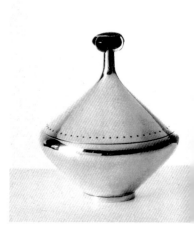

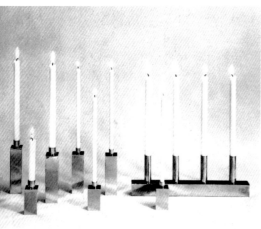

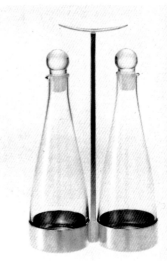

...llesticks in matt black, vitreous
...nelled cast-iron, 14 cm high
...gned and made by Robert
...ch UK

...rette box in oiled-teak with
... cane woven top, 13 cm high
...gned by Industrial Arts Institute
...e by Marumiya Shoten for
...on Sangyo Kogei KK JAPAN

Lemon-chopping board in endwood
staved teak, about 13 cm diameter
Designed by Jens H. Quistgaard for
Dansk Designs DENMARK

Candle-holders in walnut, red,
yellow, green or blue, 10 cm high
Designed by Carl Auböck for
Werkstatte Carl Auböck AUSTRIA

Condiment set in stainless steel
Designed by Eric Clements for
J. R. Bramah & Co Ltd UK

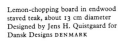

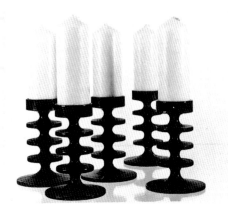

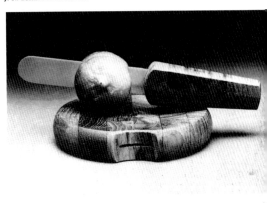

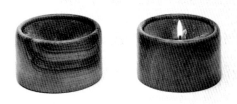

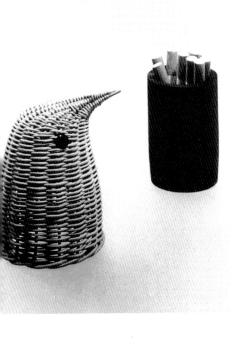

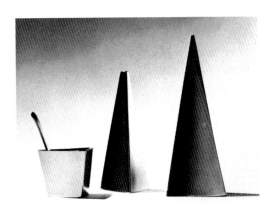

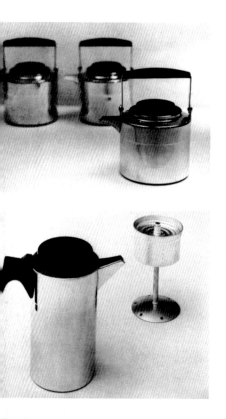

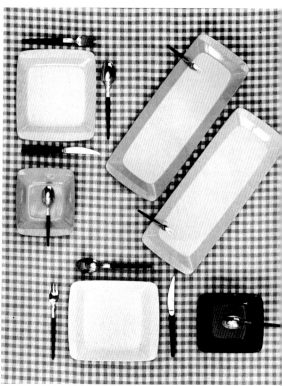

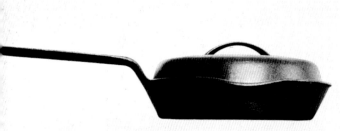

photograph Tuomi

Virva coffee-pots, *Tytti* percolator
aluminium and plastic, the pots
1·5 litre, the percolator 0·75 litre
capacity
Designed by Eero Rislakki for
Ammus-Sytytin O/y FINLAND

Covered pan, cast-iron enamelled
scarlet or matt black, lined white
23 cm diameter
Designed by Timo Sarpaneva for
W. Rosenlew & Co FINLAND

Table set of moulded Melamine,
white, yellow, orange, dark brown
Designed by Olof Bäckström for
Fiskars O/y AB FINLAND

Faience cutting board with hand-
painted cobalt underglaze
decoration
Designed and made by
Wärtsilä-koncernen AB FINLAND

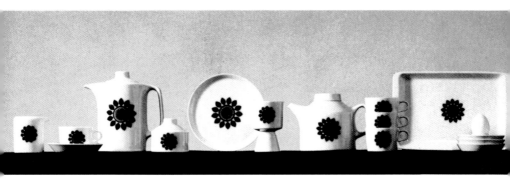

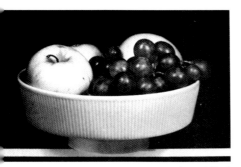

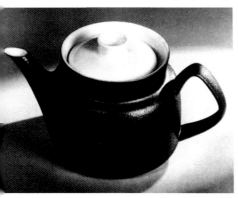

photograph Moegle

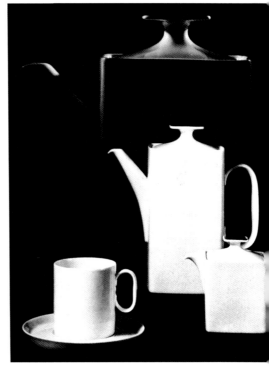

photograph Jindrich Brok

hite porcelain fruit bowl:
 cm high
esigned by Heinrich Löffelhardt
r Porzellanfabrik Arzberg
. GERMANY

ot from a tea-service in white
orcelain with brown ferric glaze
esigned by Jaroslav Pycha for
arlovarsky porcelán n p
ZECHOSLOVAKIA

top
Blue Sun tableware: porcelain with
cobalt blue decoration
Designed by Heinz H. Engler for
Porzellanfabrik Lorenz
Hutschenreuther AG W. GERMANY

Coffee and tea-service in feldspathic
china with glass inset on lids; white
and with patterns
Designed by Siguard Bernadotte and
Richard Scharrer for Rosenthal
Porzellan AG W. GERMANY

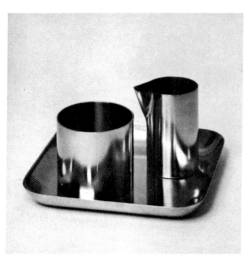

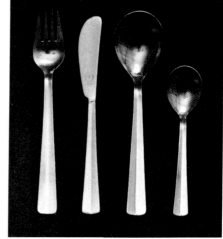

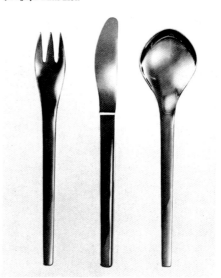

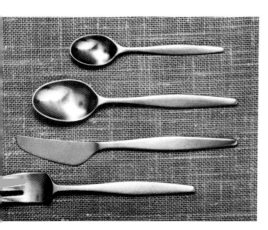

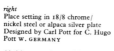

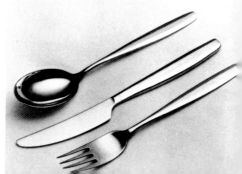

Cream set, 18/8 chrome/nickel
steel seamless
Designed by Carl Pott for C. Hugo
Pott W. GERMANY

Aztec satin-finished 18/8 chrome-
nickel steel
Made by Norsk Stalpress AS
NORWAY

right
Place setting in 18/8 chrome/
nickel steel or alpaca silver plate
Designed by Carl Pott for C. Hugo
Pott W. GERMANY

Model 1300 cutlery: stainless steel
Designed by Marianne Denzel for
Vereinigte Metallwerke
Ranshofen-Berndorf AG AUSTRIA

Cutlery in stainless steel
Designed by Bertel Gardberg for
Hackman & Co FINLAND

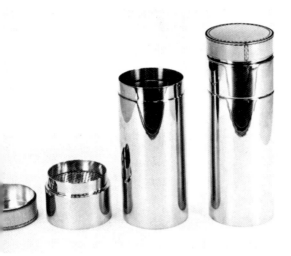

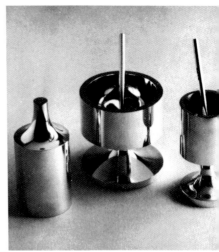

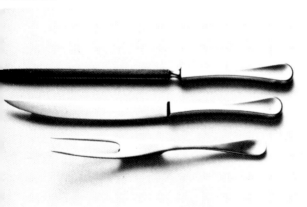

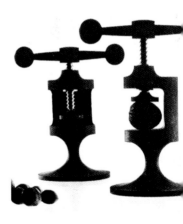

...otograph Hooker

...haker, nickel plated brass, lid of
...olished leather
...esigned and made by Carl
...uböck AUSTRIA

...lveston stainless steel carving set
...esigned by Robert Welch
...or Old Hall Tableware Ltd UK

Silver condiment set
Unique pieces designed by Robert
Welch and made by Old Hall
Tableware Ltd UK

CD 60 nutcracker in cast-iron,
vitreous enamelled matt black
Designed and made by Robert
Welch UK

2200/3604 tableware with *Stockholm,* a
new under-glaze decoration blue on white
Designed by Johann Klöcker

2075/3652 porcelain ware white with
solid red lids, and/or rims
All made by Porcellanfabrik Arzberg
W. Germany

Teapots, white stoneware with bamboo
handles, overall 20 cm high
Designed by Mosuke Yoshitake for
Tokyo Craft Co *Japan*

New pieces in the *Berså* series
white earthenware with green
transfer decoration
Designed by Stig Lindberg for
AB Gustavsbergs Fabriker *Sweden*

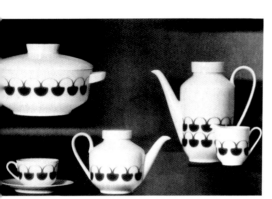

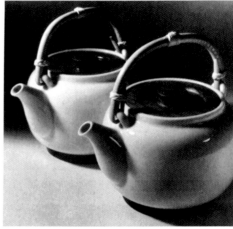

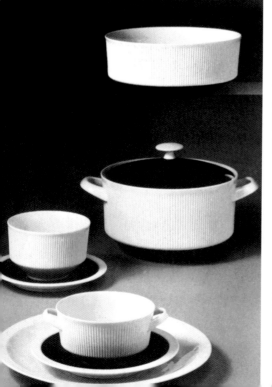

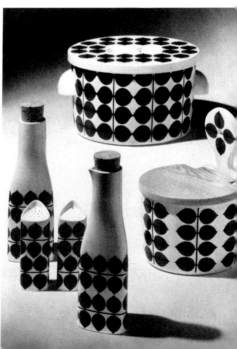

Handmade stoneware casserole, white-
speckled yellow ochre, 22 cm diameter
and two other sizes
Designed and made by Emmanuel
Cooper *England*

Handmade ceramic tea-pot, grey-brown
27 cm high
Designed and made by Christel
Godenhjelm-Nyman *Finland*

Ice pail, thin beige matt glazed porcelain
with oxidized steel spots
Designed by the Industrial Arts Institute
and made by Umeno Seitosho *Japan*

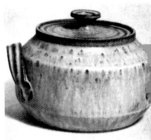

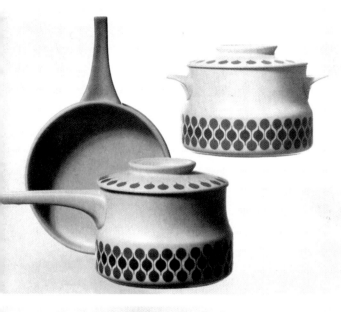

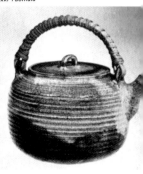

Erkki Tuomala

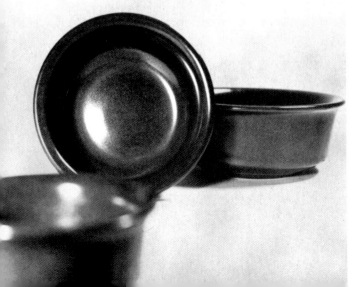

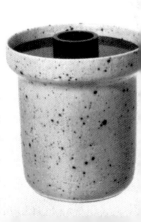

Fruit bowl, black plastic 45 cm diameter
Designed by Enzo Mari for B. Danese
Italy

Partridge in a Pear Tree fine earthenware
beaker, white glaze with blue, brown or
green resist decoration

Heirloom earthenware with black print
on brown, blue or green glaze
All designed and made by Hornsea
Pottery Co Ltd *England*

Heater of anodized aluminium and
chromed steel 15 or 30 × 15 × 7·5 cm
Designed by Bruno Munari for B. Danese
Italy

3123 spice jars, white feldspathic
porcelain with gold/grey decoration, teak
lids. 8 or 10·5 cm high.
Designed and made by Porzellanfabrik
Langenthal AG *Switzerland*

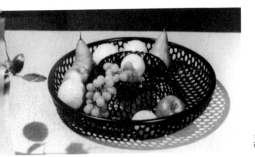

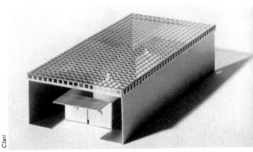

Clari

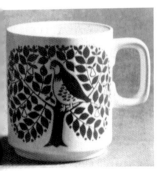

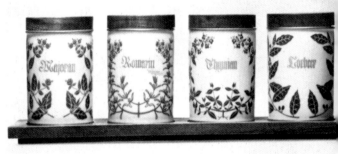

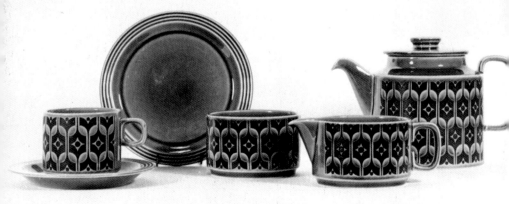

.../y mug, faience illustrated with sauna
...periences
...cor by Gunvor Olin-Grönquist for
Wärtsilä AB *Finland*

...46 stackable nursery set, shock-
...istant white porcelain with coloured
...coration, round-dance or spots
...signed and made by Porzellanfabrik
...genthal AG *Switzerland*

Beer mug, milk-white porcelain with
decoration in one of several colours
Designed by Industrial Arts Institute
and made by Narumi Seito *Japan*

Sinilintu (bluebird) coffee cup and saucer
handpainted cobalt blue, 46 cl capacity
Shape/decor by Göran Bäck/Raija
Vosikkinen for Oy Wärtsilä AB *Finland*

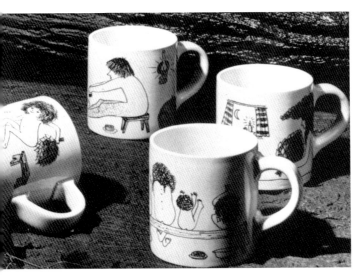

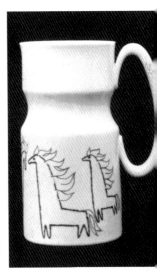

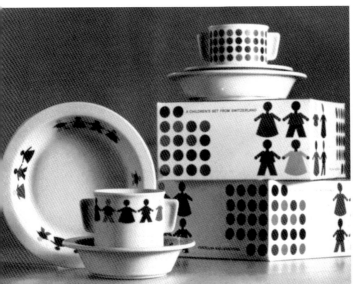

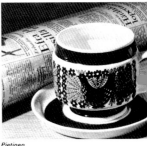

Pietinen

Salt/pepper shakers: the lid controls
the outlet of each condiment, silver
Designed by Sergio Asti for de Vecchi
Italy

Benney condiment set, 18/8 stainless
steel 9 cm high
Designed by Gerald Benney and made
by Viners of Sheffield *England*

Fine white bone china coffee set with
Black Basalt handleless coffee cups
Designed by Peter Wall for Josiah
Wedgwood & Sons Ltd *England*

Fondu pot with hot plate, stainless
steel and palisander
15 cm diameter
Designed by Ib Bluitgen and made by
Andersen & Burchardt *Denmark*

Handmade teapot, silver and moor oak
Designed and made by Sigurd Persson
Sweden

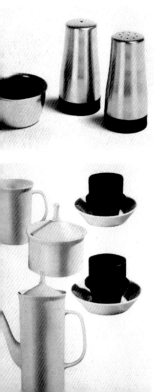

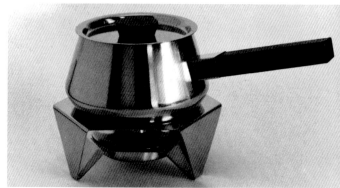

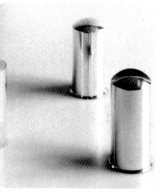

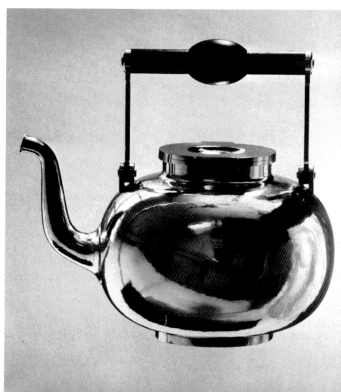

e coolers, spun aluminium and
nated teak, brown, silver or
t blue 21 cm high 24 cm diameter
igned by Industrial Arts Institute
made by Hokusei Aluminium KK
an

 Amie new coffee-pot, feldspar
elain with cobalt blue underglaze
oration
gned by Marianne Westman for
Rorstrands Porslinsfabriker
den

Cooker-to-table saucepan, the lid
doubling as serving dish, stainless
steel 170 cl capacity
Designed and made by Olsen Design
Ltd *England*

Teapot, creamer and sugar pot,
bottom, with hot water jug,
sterling silver and teak, the pot
10 cm high (a taller coffee-pot
is available)
Designed by Søren Georg Jensen and
made by Georg Jensen *Denmark*

Reeve

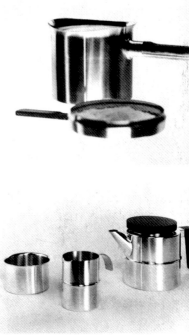

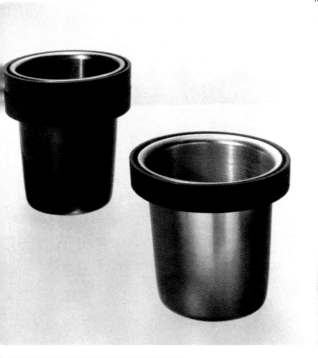

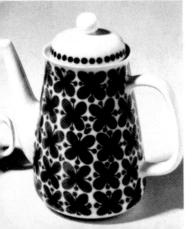

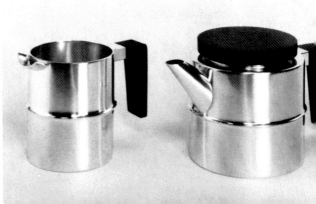

Escargot place set in 18/8 chromed steel or silver-plated Alpaka: a larger dish holding 12 snails is available

Cocktail snack dish in sterling silver or silver-plated Alpaka
All designed by Carl Pott for C Hugo Pott
W. Germany

Honey-spoon with Jena glass *Okesto* 3202, solid silver, silver-plated Alpaka or 18/8 chromed steel
Designed by Carl Pott for C Hugo Pott
W. Germany

Bistro place set in stainless steel and rosewood
Designed by Robert Welch and made by Old Hall Tableware Ltd *England*

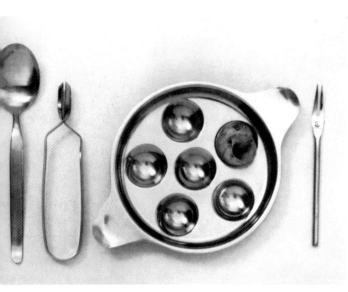

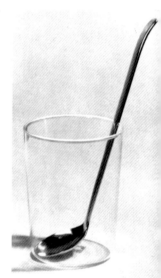

Hooker

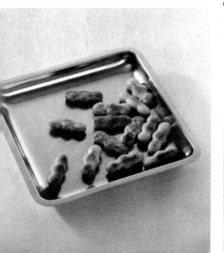

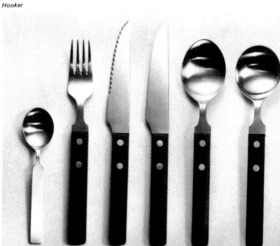

...are in satin finish stainless steel
...gned by Ilmari Tapiovaari for
...ackman AB *Finland*

...n cutlery in stainless steel
...gned by David Mellor for Walker &
...Ltd *England*

Teaglass with nickelled holder 15 cl
capacity
Designed by Timo Sarpaneva and made
by Iittala Glassworks *Finland*

Jette stainless steel cutlery
Designed by Jens H Quistgaard for
Dansk Designs *Denmark*

...o Wendt

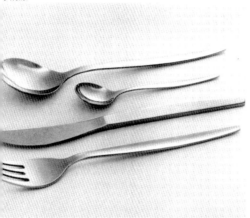

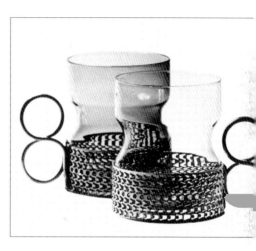

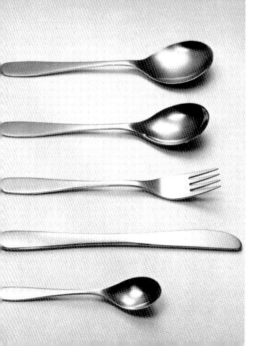

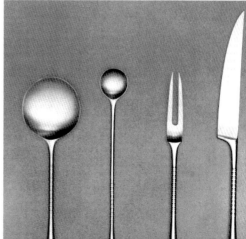

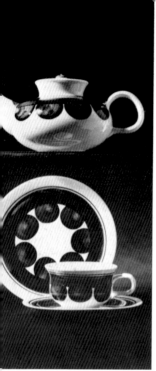

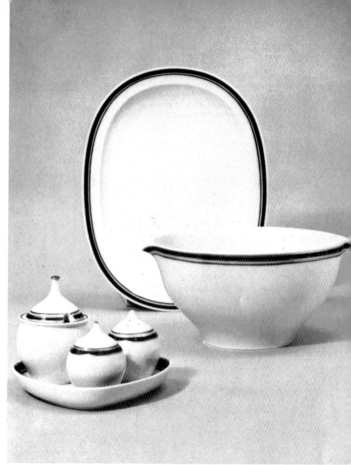

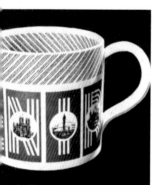

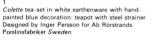

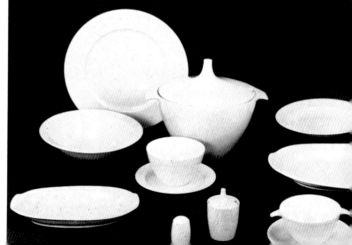

1
Colette tea-set in white earthenware with hand-painted blue decoration: teapot with steel strainer
Designed by Inger Persson for Ab Rörstrands Porslinsfabriker *Sweden*

2
London mug, alternate panels of blue and red
Designed by Richard & Elizabeth Guyatt for Josiah Wedgwood & Sons Limited *England*

3
Sheba coffee, tea and dinner service, white porcelain with cobalt-blue underglaze and gold line decoration
Designed by Johannes Hedegaard for The Royal Copenhagen Porcelain Manufactory Ltd *Denmark*

4
Halka tea and dinner service in white porcelain
Designed by Werner Winkler for VEB Porzellanwerk 'Graf von Henneberg' *E. Germany*

5
Faience storage boxes: white, blue or mahogany
with black decoration and melamine lids
Designed by Richard Lindh with decoration by
Esteri Tomula for Oy Wärtsilä Ab Arabia *Finland*

6
Channel Isle mugs and canister, gold, blue
or grey-green with incised spots and bands
Designed by Judith Onions for T. G. Green Ltd
England

7
Canisters, white, green or brown glazed
porcelain with wooden lids 9 cm diameter
Designed by Masahiro Mori for Hakusan
Porcelain Co Ltd *Japan*

5
6 7

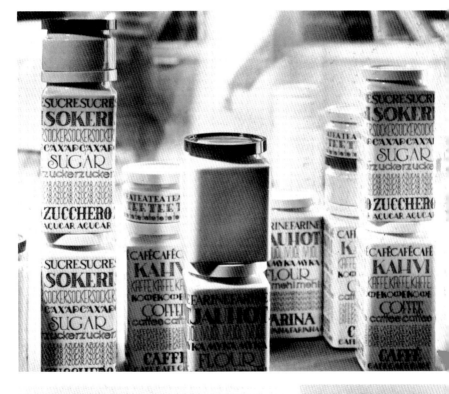

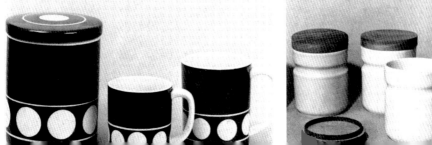

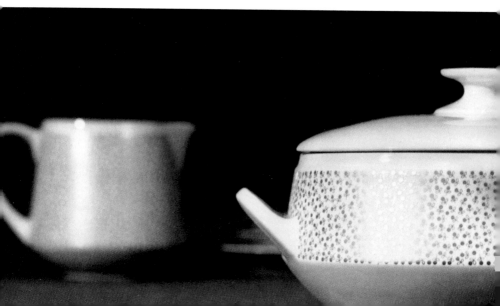

C range of tableware, faience with *Kimmel* m
gold decor
Shape by Esteri Tomula, decoration by
Richard Lindh for Oy Wärtsilä Ab Arabia *Finl*

Peppermill and casserole with matching table
heater, cast iron vitreous-enamelled matt
black, the pepper mill with rosewood knob:
casserole also available with red or blue gloss
finish, 23 cm diameter
Designed by Robert Welch for Campden
Designs Limited *England*

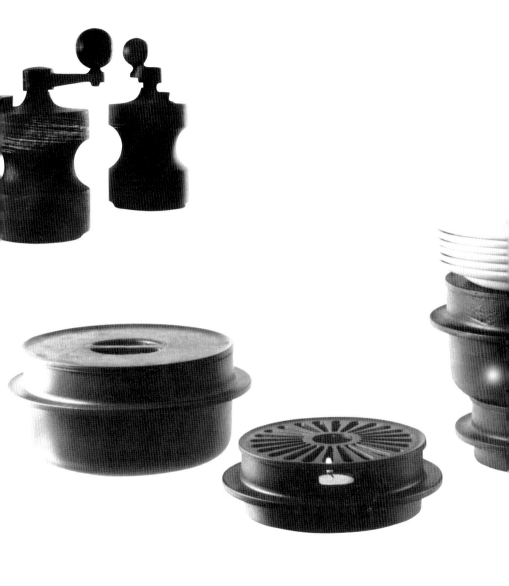

1
Candlestand, stainless steel
Designed by Peter Karpf for Herluf Poulsen
Denmark

2
Covered plate, sterling silver 25 cm wide
Designed by Henning Koppel for Georg Jensen
Sølvsmedie *Denmark*

3
Tea or coffee pot, sterling silver with buffalo-
horn handle
Designed by Karl Gustav Hansen for Hans
Hansen Sølvsmedie *Denmark*

4
Baking/serving dish, cast iron with white or
red vitreous enamel finish inside 20 × 38·5 cm
Designed by Timo Sarpaneva for W. Rosenlew
& Co *Finland*

5
Sauce warmer with double spout, cast iron with
orange, blue, yellow or white vitreous enamel
finish 35 cm diameter
Designed by Michael Lax for Copco, Inc *USA*

6, 7
Two containers from a series in pvc, black with
transparent covers, the ice-box 7, lined white,
18·6 cm diameter
Designed by Enzo Mari for Danese *Italy*

8
Brandy flasks, sterling silver with hand-
embossed decoration 38 cm high
Designed and made by Heinz Decker
Silversmide *Sweden*

1 3 5 6 7
2 4   8

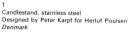

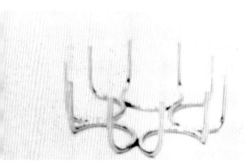

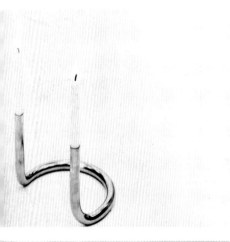

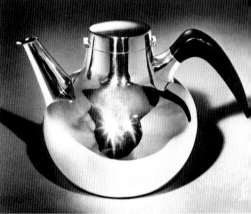

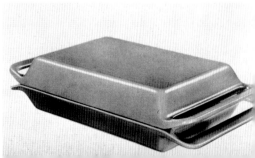

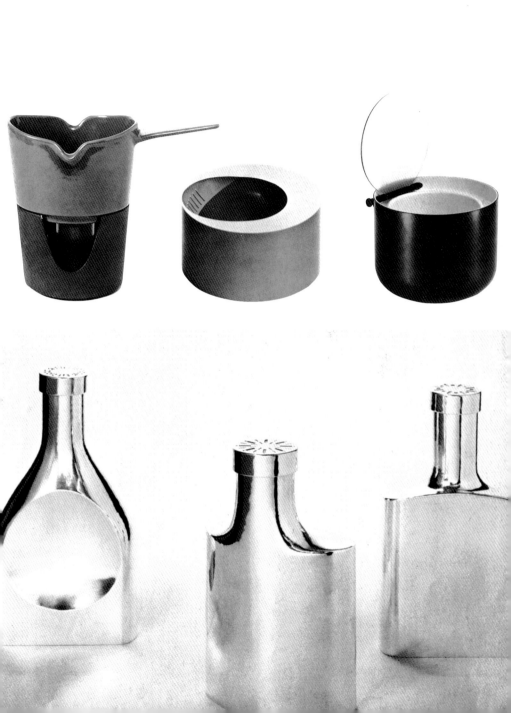

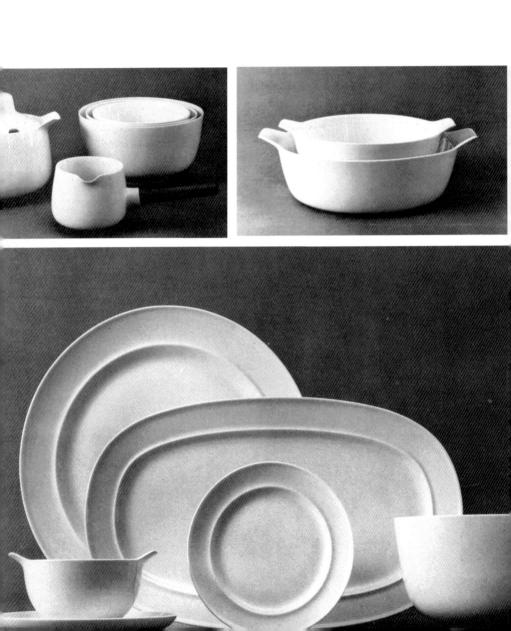

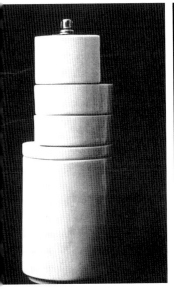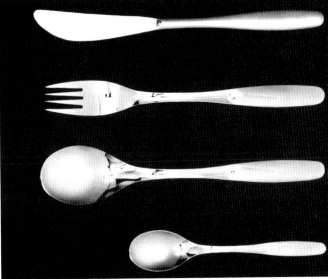

1-3
Form 678 dinnerware, all-white porcelain:
includes cruet, ovenproof bowls, soup cups,
tureen with lid, set of salad bowls and water
jug with afromosia handle
Designed by Henning Koppel for Bing &
Grøndahl, *Denmark*
4
Smoking set of lighter, two or three ashtrays
and cigarette box, porcelain glazed black or
white : cm 25 high
Designed and made by Kurt Spurey *Austria*
5
Savonia flatware, stainless steel four-piece
setting
Designed and made by Hackman & Co
Finland

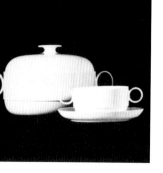
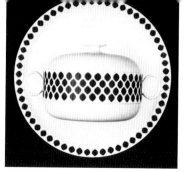
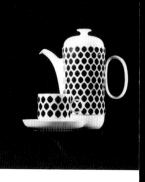
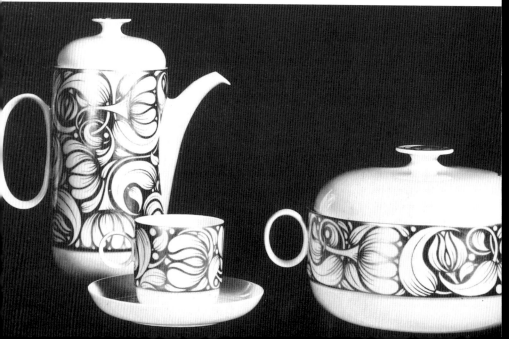

1-3
Duo tableware in white porcelain and with
Elliptic Cobalt decor
4
On the same shape, gold blossom decor
designed by Bjorn Winblad
Shape designed by Ambrogio Pozzi *Italy* for
Rosenthal Porzellan GmbH *W. Germany*
5
Bas and *Diskant* red and white Ornaminware:
four shapes are a dinner-set: plus two 'boxes'
Designed by Stig Lindberg for Ab Gustavsbergs
Fabriker *Sweden*

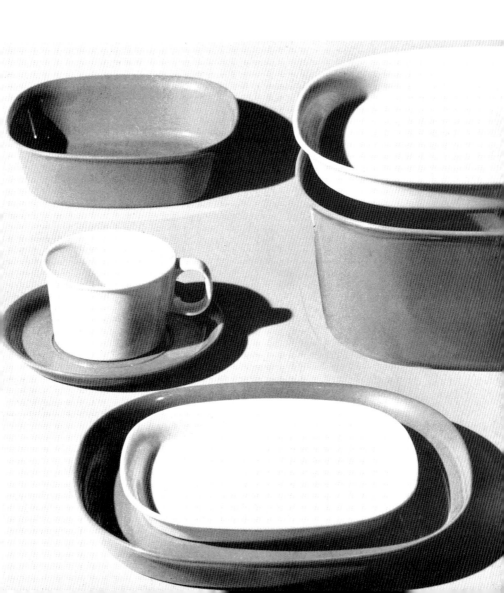

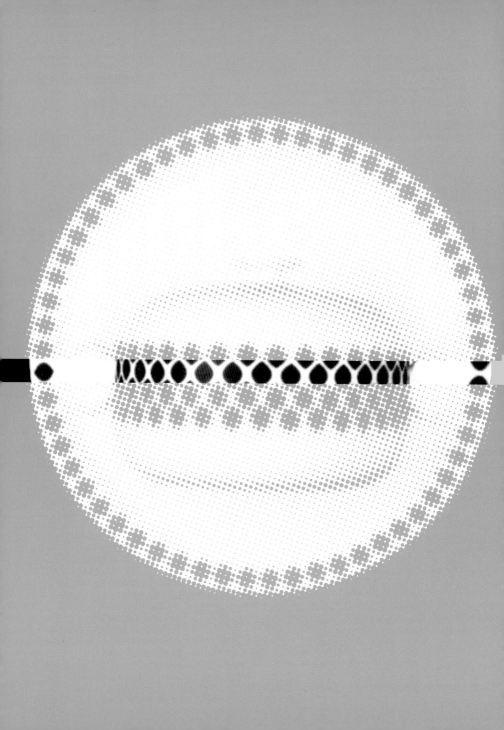

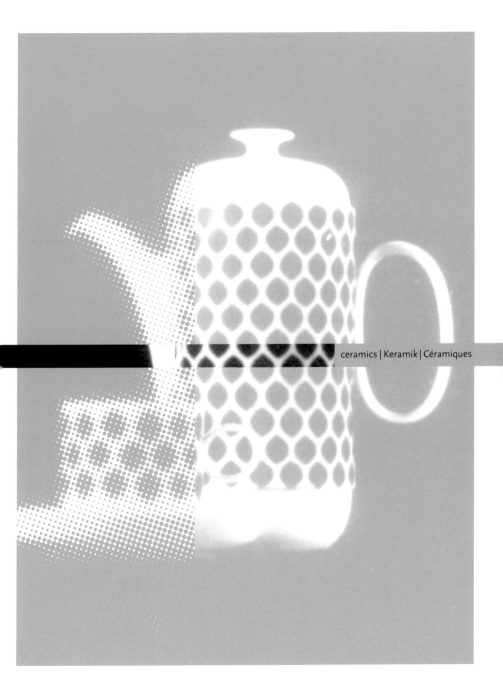

ceramics | Keramik | Céramiques

Stoneware vase and bowl, one-of-a-kind, in light brown and in dark brown glazes; height of vase 9¾ inches. By Berndt Friberg

Imprinted stoneware vase, 17½ inches high, and miniature jar in green copper glazes. Unique pieces by Stig Lindberg. All made at AB Gustavsbergs Fabriker SWEDEN ▼

Stoneware vase with upward-springing shoots, rutile glaze; 15½ inches high. By Axel Salto: The Royal Copenhagen Porcelain Manufactory A/S, DENMARK ▼

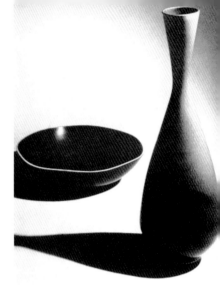

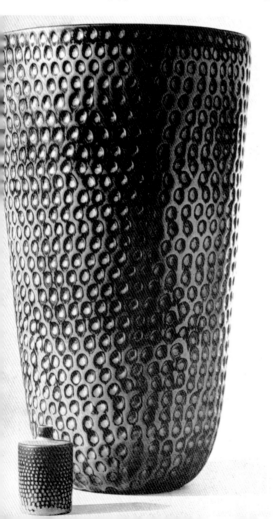

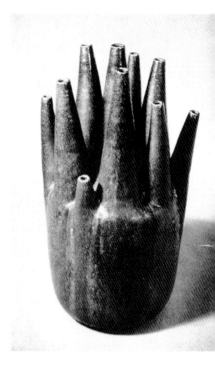

Handbuilt unique stoneware figure, yellow-brown partial glaze; 8 inches high. By Lisa Larson: AB Gustavsbergs Fabriker SWEDEN ▶

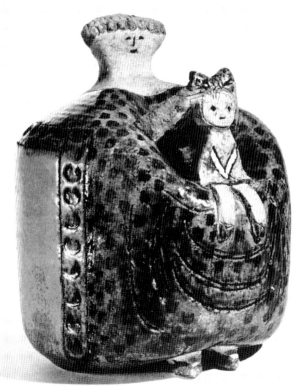

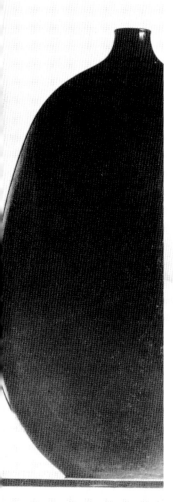

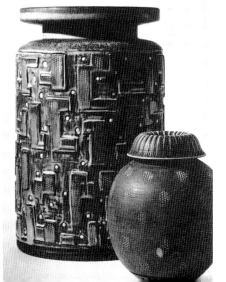

▲ Stoneware vase, dark blue glaze; 13½ inches high. By Stig Lindberg.

Unglazed *Terra-Farsta* red-brown jars with imprinted decoration; larger jar 15½ inches high. By Wilhelm Kåge.   ▶
All made at AB Gustavsbergs Fabriker SWEDEN

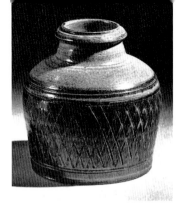

OPPOSITE: Stoneware vase, white ro
glaze, brown mottled, with fluted decc
tion; 15 inches high.
BELOW, LEFT TO RIGHT: Porcelain v
brown sgraffito decoration, 5½ inches h
and stoneware group, green, white, off-wl
and grey glazes, mottled; 5, 7, 8 inches h
All unique pieces by Lucie Rie UK
photographs Jane (

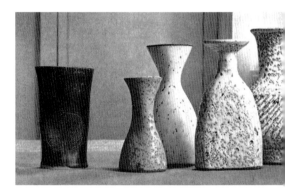

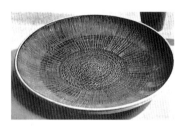

TOP: Stoneware jar, grey salt-glaze, dark slip decoration; 8½ inches high. Designed by Nils J. Kähler for A/S Herman A. Kähler DENMARK
Earthenware dish with thin semi-covering glaze, decorated sgraffito; 15 inches diameter. By Ingrid Atterberg for Upsala-Ekeby AB, Ekebybruk SWEDEN

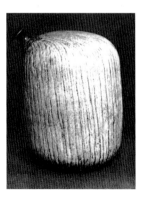

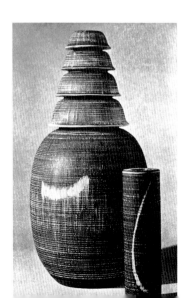

▲ *Forme* vase, enamel on silver, engraved decoration.
Unique piece by Studio Del Campo ITALY
◀ Stoneware vases, red-rust glaze, brush-work decoration; background vase 19 inches high.
Unique pieces designed by Wilhelm Kåge for AB Gustavsbergs Fabriker SWEDEN
Stoneware vase, iron glaze with incised decoration; 17 inches high.
By Erik Plöen NORWAY ▶

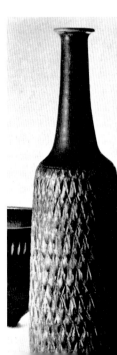

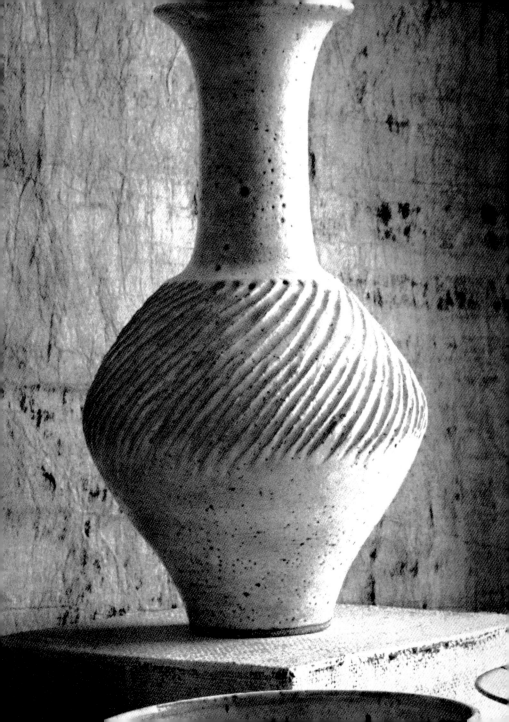

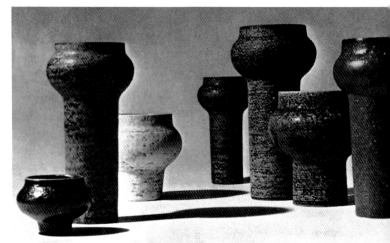

High-fired stoneware vases in brown and black clay glazes; 2 to 8 inches high. Unique pieces by Britt-Louise Sundell for AB Gustavsbergs Fabriker SWEDEN

Stoneware plant pot with inner holder, heavily textured rust and yellow wood ash glaze with pale celadon inside and on foot; 14 inches high. By Dan Arbeid: The Abbey Art Centre UK

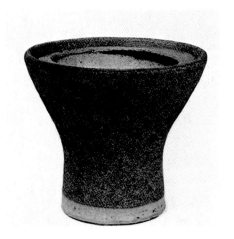

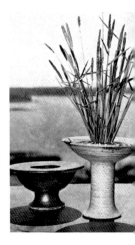

One-of-a-kind stoneware vases:
▲ in brown and sand clay glazes; 7 11 inches high. By Francesca Mascitti-Li.

◀ in dark brown, brownish red/sand, iron rust glazes; centre vase 25 inches h By Kyllikki Salmenhaara. All made Wärtsilä-koncernen A/B Arabia FINLAND

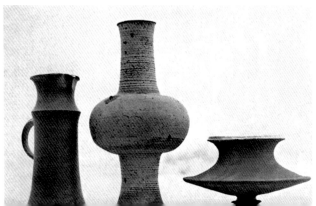

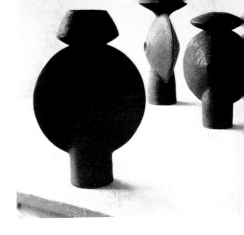

Unglazed stoneware pots, 10 inches high, and below 6, 8 and 12 inches high.
All unique pieces by Hans Coper UK

photographs Jane Gate

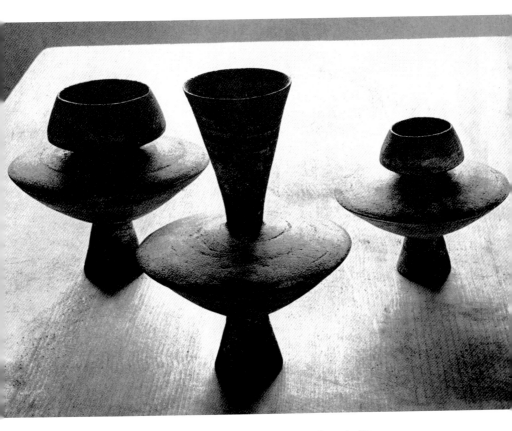

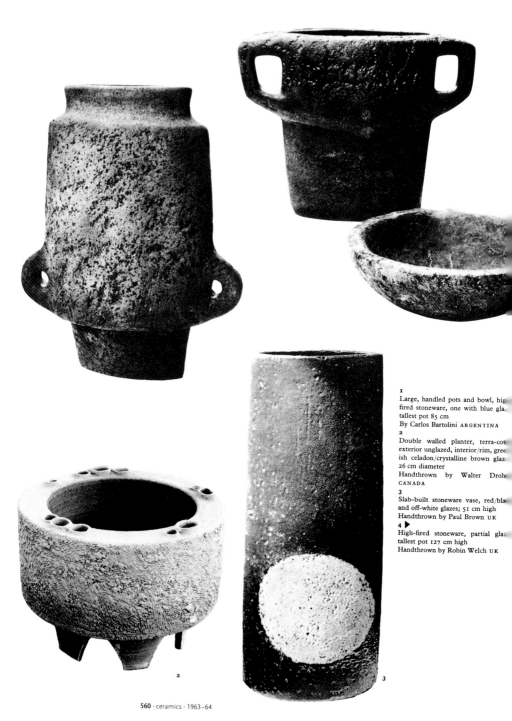

1
Large, handled pots and bowl, high
fired stoneware, one with blue gla.
tallest pot 85 cm
By Carlos Bartolini ARGENTINA
2
Double walled planter, terra-cot
exterior unglazed, interior/rim, gree
ish celadon/crystalline brown glaz
26 cm diameter
Handthrown by Walter Droh
CANADA
3
Slab-built stoneware vase, red/bla
and off-white glazes; 51 cm high
Handthrown by Paul Brown UK
4 ▶
High-fired stoneware, partial gla:
tallest pot 127 cm high
Handthrown by Robin Welch UK

2

3

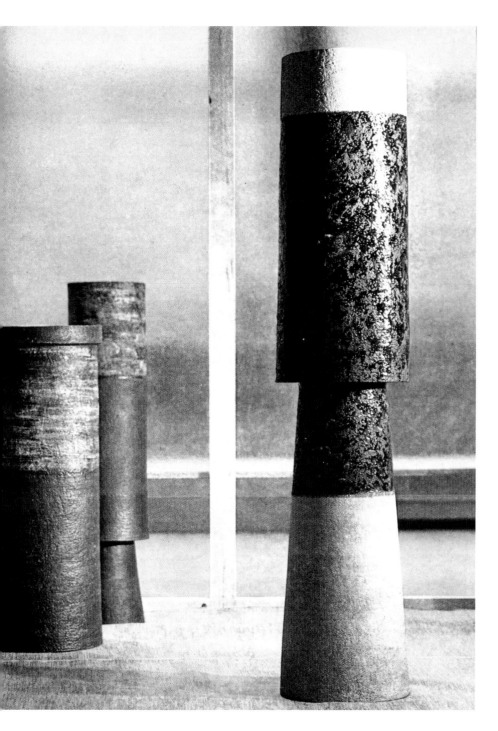

Cream and black vase in coiled
stoneware, 41 cm high
Designed by Delan Cookson UK

Slab-built stoneware pot with white
glaze and impressed stamp, 15 cm
high
Designed by Ian Auld UK

Earthenware vase with thick green
or red glazes, 22 cm high
Designed by Vaclav Dolejs UBOK
CZECHOSLOVAKIA

Earthenware jam pot with majolica
glaze in blue, turquoise, green or
honey-coloured, approximately
10 cm high
Made by the Guernsey Pottery Ltd UK

Hand-built stoneware pot in
heavily grogged red clay, glazed
inside only, 45·5 cm high
Designed by Eileen Lewenstein

Three-tiered stoneware vase
in grogged orange clay, with matt
white glaze and black lines, 76 cm
two-tiered vase with matt white
glaze, copper-green pigment, 51
high
Designed by Robin Welch AUSTR

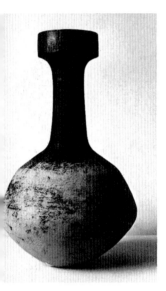

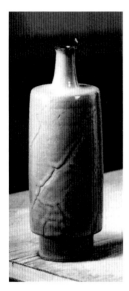

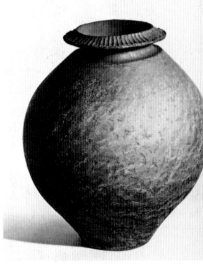

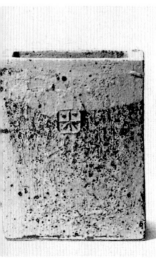

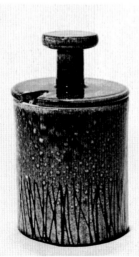

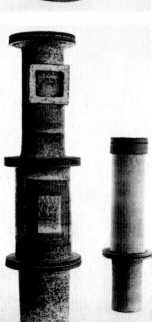

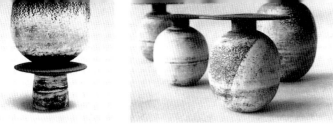

Stoneware vase with stem, 15 cm high
Wide-lipped vases, 15 and 20 cm high
Tall fungi-shaped vases, 30 cm high
All designed by Hans Coper UK

photos JANE GATE

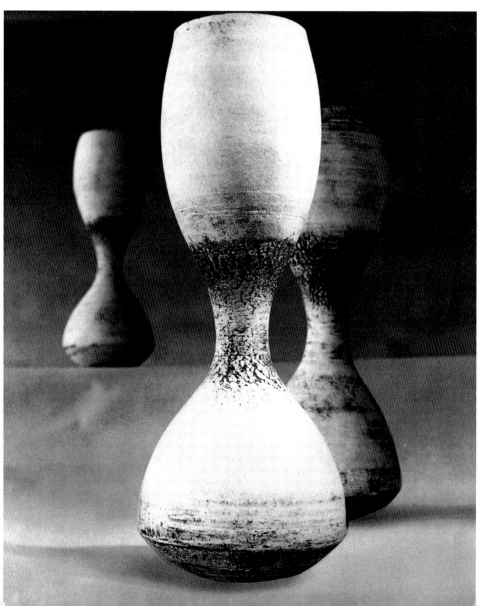

Rectangular stoneware vases in
silver, blue and amaranth-purple
6·5 to 25·5 cm high
Designed by Ettare Sottsass for
Il Sestante ITALY

Brilliant white double-pleated flower
vases, 24 cm high
Tall-necked off-centre vases in
various heights from 13·5 to 26 cm
Triple-pleated vase in brilliant white,
blue, matt white or black
25·5 cm high
All designed by Angelo Mangiarotti
for B. Danese ITALY

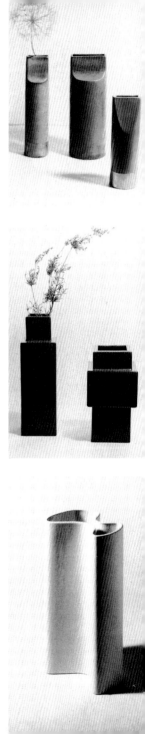

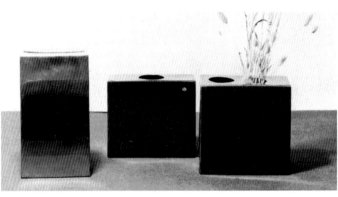

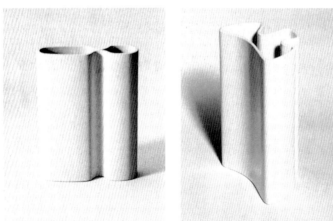

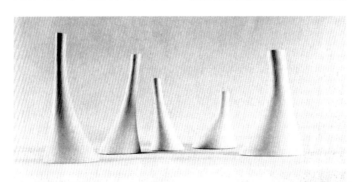

mouthed cylindrical vases,
ware in olive/gold, turquoise/
, green or amaranth-purple
d 25 cm high
s in graded cubes, green
amaranth-purple, 31 and 23 cm

gned by Ettare Sottsass for
stante ITALY

Large hand-thrown bowls, chamotte
with salt and copper glazes
20 cm diameter
Designed by Francesca Lindh

'Tree' table decorations in faience
approximately 17 cm high, shades of
putty, grey-blues and black
Designed and sculpted
by Birger Kaipiainen
All for Wärtsilä-koncernen AB
FINLAND

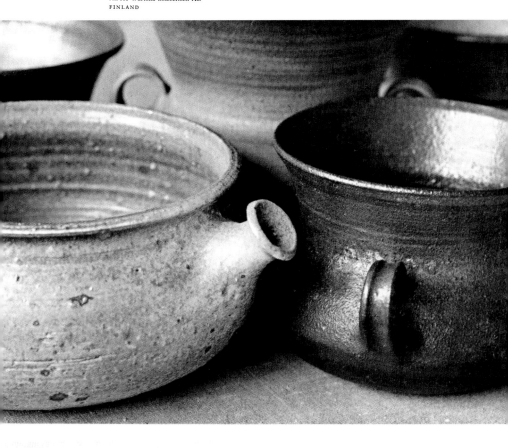

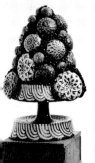 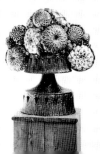

photos PIETINEN

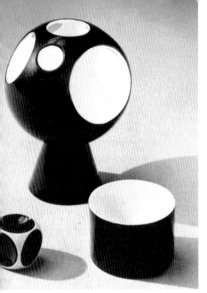

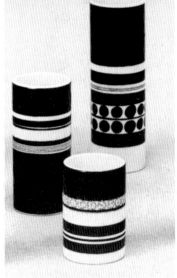

1
Lighthouse and other shapes, earthenw.
with black and white underglazes: light|
23 cm high
Designed by Mogens Andersen

2
Tenera new pieces in the series, handpa|
blue underglaze decoration, 10–20 cm h
All made by the Royal Copenhagen
Porcelain Manufactory *Denmark*

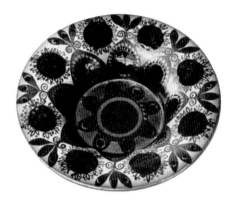

3
Faience plate decorated with blue and
lustre colours 34 cm diameter
Unique piece designed by Hilkka-Liisa

4
Mould-made garden vase: faience
44 cm high
Designed by Olli Vasa

5
Mould-made hand-built figure black ar
white, 42 cm high
Unique piece designed by Heljätuulia l|
Sundström
All made for Oy Wärtsilä Ab Arabia *Fin|*

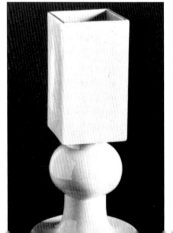

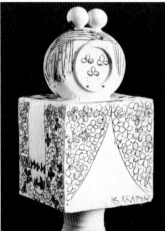

◢ *Sun* wall plate, unique piece, hand built
◣ orange, green and brown glazed and
◣lazed stoneware units: approximately
◢ 70 cm
◢igned by Rut Bryk for Oy Wärtsilä Ab Arabia *Finland*

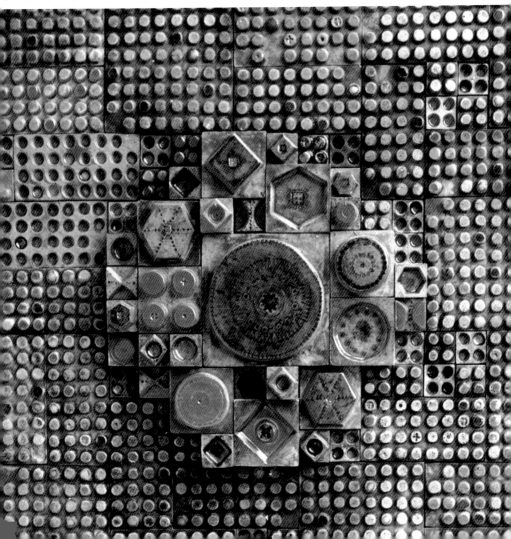

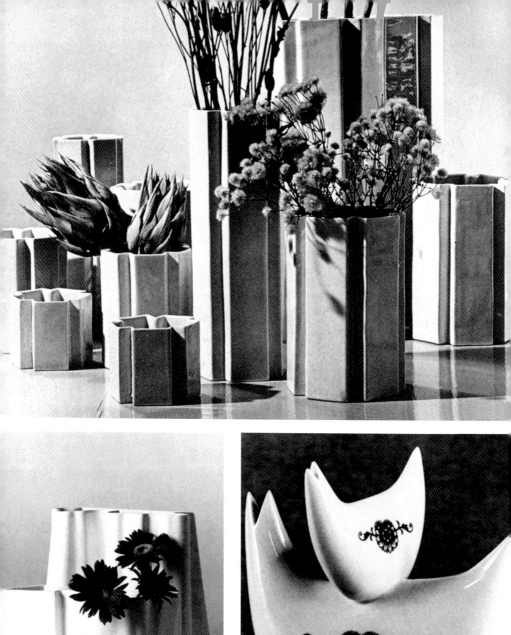
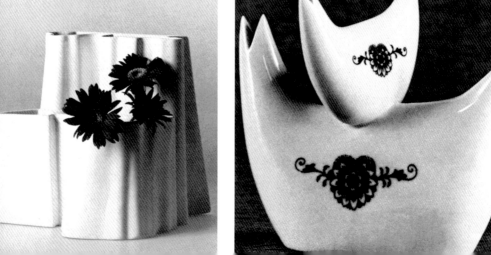

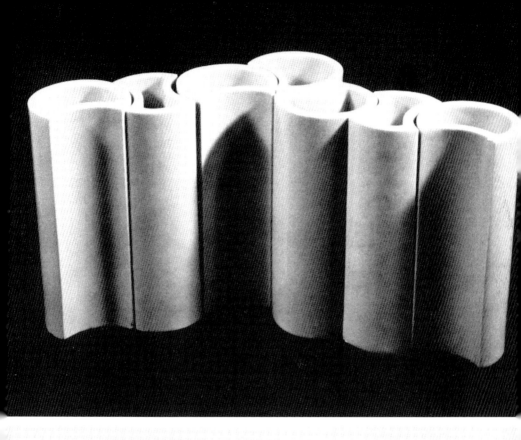

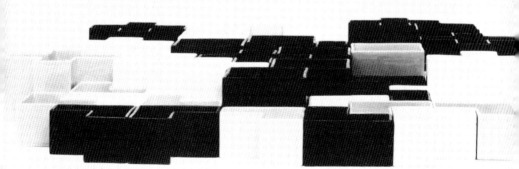

1
Octagon series vases: fine earthenware
glazed white: cm 6-30 high
Designed by Karin Bjorquist for Ab Gustavsbergs
Fabriker, *Sweden*

2, 5
Fluted vases and squared modular elements
for flowers or fruit: white, black, yellow, deep
green and red

1 4
2 3 5   Both designed by Sergio Asti for Gabbianelli *Italy*

3
Sculpture in white porcelain with cobalt
under-glaze die stamped decoration:
cm 19.5 high
Designed by Vladimir David UBOK for
Karlovarsky Porcelan, n.p. *Czechoslovakia*

4
Composition vases in moulded porcelain
cm 25 high
Designed and made by Kurt Spurey, *Austria*

INDEX
Designers and architects
Designer und Architekten
Designers et architectes

Credits
Bildnachweis
Crédits

Artemide, Milan: 8, 10 right, 25 right
Bonham's, London: 25 left
Christie's Images, London: 11, 17, 18, 20–21, 23 right
Fiell International Ltd. – (photos: Paul Chave)
3 (Ross & Miska Lovegrove Collection), 4–5, 10 left,
12, 14, 16, 19, 24 (Ross & Miska Lovegrove Collection)
Louis Poulsen, Copenhagen: 15
Sotheby's, London: 9